# THE BARDIC SOURCE BOOK

*To Martyn and Jessica Ruby Simpson*
*who keep the bardic mysteries alive*

# THE BARDIC SOURCE BOOK

## INSPIRATIONAL LEGACY AND TEACHINGS OF THE ANCIENT CELTS

### EDITED AND SELECTED BY JOHN MATTHEWS

Foreword by Robin Williamson

BLANDFORD

**A BLANDFORD BOOK**

First published in paperback in the United Kingdom in 1999 by Blandford
A Cassell Imprint

Wellington House
125 Strand
London WC2R 0BB

Previously published in hardback 1998

Distributed in the United States by Sterling Publishing Co., Inc.
387 Park Avenue South, New York, NY 10016–8810

A Cataloguing-in-Publication Data entry for this title is available from the
British Library

ISBN 0 7137 2785 3

Designed by Chris Bell

Printed and bound in Great Britain by Mackays of Chatham

# CONTENTS

# FOREWORD

# BARDIC
# DREAMING

A bard out of Ireland, with 'Banachadee'.
Said: 'Gluntow guk dynydrach, hala mischy doch –
Rax her a rug of the roast, or sho shall rhyme thee.
Mich macmory ach mach mountir moch loch –
Set her doun, give her a drink, what deil ails thee?
O dermyn, O Donall, O Dochardy droch.
Thir are the Ireland kingis of the Irishery:–
O Kewlyn, O Connochar, O Gregor MacGrane.
   The Shennachy, the Clarsach,
The Ben shene, the Ballach,
The Crekery, the Corach,
   Sho kennis them ilkane.[1]

FROM JUST A FEW LINES of this strange poem of mockery from the aristocratic Scots poet with the English name, Sir Richard Holland (fl.1450), a great deal may be learned about bards. The bard is out of Ireland, a Celtic phenomenon, not part of the English tradition. His first remark, 'Banachadee', is to call down the blessings of God on the house. He is a strange, unofficial priest in outlandish garb. He demands the best of meat and drink, threatening satire if he is not treated according to his expectations. Among the various bits of gibberish in the poem are some words of comprehensible Gaelic: 'hala mischy doch' ('she can take drink' – he refers to himself as 'she' in the Gaelic idiom, where self is feminine). He brags of his genealogical prowess. He declares himself a master of the 'Shennachy' (story-telling), the 'Clasarch' (harp repertoire) and the 'Ben shene', the 'Ballach' and so on (all kinds of merry, sorrowful and healing music).

Fourteen hundred years after the Romans are supposed to have wiped out the druids, here is a bard, a kind of druid, familiar enough to mock with the same sort of leeriness with which cynics today might mock gypsy soothsayers.

Is it just that, poor as they were, on the fringe of the western ocean and lacking jewels, the Gaels of Scotland and Ireland and the Brittonic Celts of Wales have treasured poetry and honoured the seeker of insight? Most nations have wisdom-venerating traditions of some kind, but is there something in the

Celtic languages or is there in the land itself, some predisposition to foster those who will utter a word of power? The bards have a peculiarly atavistic place in our ancestry: sacred poets (more wizards than poets, really), singers of praise and satire for the support or discomfiture of rulers, and masters of the secret heart of music.

The three worlds interlace. Here we are, blinking in the day of time. Our ancestors had a notion for the other world, what was before, what is to be, and they have left us a lore of gateways, a preoccupation with inspiration, directions from the heart of the Great Reality and a deep sense of quest in life. This source book provides a comprehensive view of the sheer breadth of the bardic legacy. In its pages you may read some of what is known of the ancient training of bards and how the power of inspiration was acquired by memorizing the tales and verses, by initiation, by imitation and by inner and outer journeys.

My own life, in a way, unwittingly followed aspects of this bardic path before I knew it was a path or where it might lead. I spent fifty-three years becoming a singer, harper, story-teller, learning the old tales and seeking to acquire my own voice – basically seeking, I suppose, simply to become a better human being. I used to read Jack Kerouac at school, and I wanted to write as he did, spontaneously. In my search for Kerouac's antecedent masters, I found, via Walt Whitman, William Blake and, via Blake, Iolo Morgannwg and thus the Celtic mysteries.

I grew up in Edinburgh of Scots-Irish family at a time when, to many, the Irishman was a Paddy living in the peat bogs, the Scot was a joke about 'Donald where's your troosers?' and Taffy the Welshman was a nursery-rhyme thief. About this time I began to realize that the country-dance music I heard Jimmy Shand play on the radio, the marching piper on the castle ramparts and the Robert Burns songs my grannies loved were actually 'folk music'. Now, after all these years of the folksong revival, the ballads, the jigs and reels and, more recently, the story-telling revival, the once moribund Celtic heritage shows every sign of life and enjoys a rekindled respectability. There is a renewed sense of self-esteem, and I am happy to have been part of it.

In addition to these signs, however, in the last twenty years there has been throughout the English-speaking world a revival of interest in Celtic philosophy and religion. A book such as this one, devoted to bardic sources, would have been unavailable twenty years ago, the texts contained here regarded as arcane or inaccessible. The writings of John and Caitlín Matthews, R.J. Stewart and many others have been instrumental in the spreading of this learning. I find that these friends and I have reached many similar insights, although my area has been primarily the performance of the material and, through that performance, the re-establishment of Celtic art.

> There is no shortage of mysteries. What would happen if you were to
> understand one of them?
>
> *Rumi*

Readers of this book will probably know something of these mysteries already. We would probably agree that only real understanding stands between us and a pillaged world, a barren normalcy of fact and concrete. We desperately need people who are passionately alive in an enchanted reality, co-inhabited by the spirits, the ancestors and the gods. The bards of old inhabited a magic reality of their own making, and they made of their lives a fairy tale. They could not be caged by possibilities, nor could they be bought. Their story is not over, however. Poetic insight is more important in our lives than ever in this computerized, industrialized age. Although we are force-fed by the media and by the music industry, we can still see that singers with their own voices are needed now more than ever.

Moments of clarity occur to everyone. It might be at the snapping of a twig or the catching of a falling leaf; it might be at times of choice, a woman between two men, a man between two women; it might be when, as we watch the night sky, we see the small star beside the young moon. Many of us feel a bond to that ancestral wisdom, though it may be dimly lit and tenuous. This sense of linkage is not felt only by those connected by a blood line; there is an inner kinship, felt throughout the world. To such as these there comes in youth a vision, a dream of yearning, and their feet mount the steps of ancient stairways, stepping stones of the heart, ladders of moonlight.

The gods were, are and will be. They speak for themselves.

I spit into the salt in my own palm.[1]

*y gwir yn erbyn y byd* – Truth against the world

And as the bard of Ireland was saying in the opening poem:

*bennacht De dilis le anaman na marbh* – the sweet blessing of God on the souls of the dead

*Robin Williamson*
*1997*

---

**Note**

1    From *The Book of Howlett* by Sir Richard Holland, quoted from *The Penguin Book of Scottish Verse* (ed. Tom Scott).

*Illustration to William Gray's Poem 'The Bard', 1761.*

# INTRODUCTION
# THE STORY OF THE BARDS

T THE BEGINNING of one of the most important texts in this anthology, 'The Proceedings of the Great Bardic Institution' (see Chapter 15), a master poet named Dallan, who was later responsible for composing a great praise song to the Christian Saint Columba (see Chapter 12), makes a poem praising a king named Hugh (or Aedh) the Dark.

> A hero of fortune art thou O Hugh
> Thou daring, determined foe,
> Thy goodness as the great ocean;
> Thou canst not be subdued,
> Thou canst not be impeded,
> O Hugh, son of Druach the Dark.
> Good and great is his substance,
> Without censure, and without reproach,
> Thou sun after leaving its stars
> Which is aweful to me,
> Thou white chess-board
> We will return, O hero.

Later in the same text, when King Hugh displeases Dallan, the bard composes another poem (see page 12), which reverses the praise and turns it into an insult. However, there is an even deeper and more complex meaning in the original poem.

On the face of it, this praises the bravery and generosity of the poet's patron – enough to win a golden torque or an arm band as well as a place near the fire and a cut of the tenderest meat. However, according to the modern scholar of Druidry, John Minahane, if we look at it again, this time acknowledging the secret poetic language with which the bards were able to communicate messages that only they could understand, we find a very different story. As Minahane ably demonstrates in his book *The Christian Druids*, with a slight re-arrangement of a few syllables in the Irish, a very different meaning can be made from the same words!

Thus, if one can read the hidden meaning of the poem just quoted, what Dallan is really saying is:

Aedh mic Duach duibh,
you career no one celebrates,
you house of tiny winecups,
you giver of a soon eaten lunch,
You frightened pale sheep
that ploughmen will dine with,
you famine, grey as grease
from a cracked-legged brass candlestick,
you hoste of cold feasts
provider of crumbs,
you entertainer of the black beetle,
you disgrace, you yeaaeh!
                    *(translated by J. Minahane)*

This is an example of what is sometimes referred to as 'The Dark Speech', meaning the speech of initiates. For such indeed the bards were. One has only to listen to some of the names and titles they have borne to realize this: the Cauldron-Born, the Carpenters of Song, Ceridwen's Children, the Bright Lords of Wisdom.

When we hear these names we see at once that the bards are more than simply poets – at least as we understand that term today and not that there is anything simple about being a poet. They are also seers, visionaries and shamans, who know the true power of words and how to make bridges between the worlds with them, who can open magical doors with a poem or, like the great Welsh bard Taliesin, make chains fall off the wrists and ankles of a prisoner by the uttering of a single phrase. They are magicians, then, as well as singers who could charm their noble patrons into giving them rich golden torques or arm bands by singing of their deeds and lives – though not always, as we saw just now, as flatteringly as was at first apparent.

As with much of the information concerning the Celtic peoples and their traditions, we derive most of our knowledge of the bardic mysteries from two sources – the early writings of Classical authors, who frequently came in contact with the Celts, and the insular writings that have survived, mostly in late versions, and that were composed by native bards and story-tellers.

Chief among the first of these sources is Caesar, whose accounts of his own encounter with the people of Britain and Gaul are among the most valuable, if somewhat biased, records we possess. Thus, in his celebrated *De Bello Gallico*, we find the following: 'report says that in the schools . . . the druids . . . learn by heart a great number of verses, and therefore some persons remain 20 years under training'.

For 'druids' in this extract, read 'bards', for the two roles were at various times virtually interchangeable. In fact it was more like twelve years that the bards spent learning their skills. In *Manners and Customs of the Ancient Irish*, the great Irish scholar Eugene O'Curry gives the following breakdown of what would have been a typical curriculum of bardic training, based on a document relating to the middle and late period of bardic activity.

Year 1: 50 Ogams or alphabets. Elementary Grammar. Twenty Tales.
Year 2: 50 Ogams. Six easy lessons in Philosophy. Some Specified Poems. Thirty Tales.
Year 3: 50 Ogams. Six minor lessons of Philosophy. Certain Specified Poems. Grammar. Forty Poems.
Year 4: *The Bretha Nemed* or Law of Privileges. Twenty Poems of the Species called *Eman*. (Births). Fifty Tales.
Year 5: Grammar. Sixty Tales.
Year 6: The Secret Language of the Poets. Forty Poems of the Species Called *Nuath* (Twins). Seventy or Eighty Tales.
Year 7: *Brosnacha* (Miscellanies). The Laws of Bardism.
Year 8: Prosody. Glosses (the meaning of obscure words) *Teinm Laeghda*. (Illumination of Song) *Imbas Forosnai*. (Light of Foresight) *Dicheltal do Chennibh* (Extempore Incantation), *Dindsenchas* (Land Lore).
Year 9: A specified number of compositions of the kind called *Sennet* (?), *Luasca* (three oscillating springs over a Druid's head?), *Nena* (?), *Eochraid* (keys), *Sruith* (streams) and *Duili Feda* (Wisdom Tales). To master 175 tales in this and the next two years.
Year 10: A further number of the compositions listed above (part of the 175 tales).
Year 11: 100 of the compositions known as *Anamuin*.
Year 12: 120 Cetals (Orations). The Four Arts of Poetry. During this and the two years previous to master 175 tales, along with 175 of the tales learned by the Annruth – 350 tales in all.

Some of this is mysterious and some the terms cannot be easily translated. But what it tells us is that over a period of twelve years a bardic student was expected to learn, by heart, at least 150 ogams, 580 tales, approximately 240 poems in various metres and forms, as well as grammar, history, land lore, orations, the arts of seership, bardic law and the Law of Privileges. Not forgetting the *Secret Language of Poetry* and a few things that are not necessarily included in this list. As R.A.S. Macalister remarks in his study of the secret language, *The Secret Languages of Ireland*:

Suppose that the pupils were allowed two months annual holiday, which is probably liberal: in other words, let us for arithmetical convenience keep them at school 300 working days in the solar year. Then, if they learn no more than ten lines of poetry in a day, they will have acquired a total of 3,000 by the end of the year, and in twenty years will have mastered 60,000 lines. This is considerably more than twice the length of the two Homeric epics. Even if they learned only one line *per diem*, they would have assimilated matter roughly equal in amount to the first ten books of the 'Iliad': if they enlarged their daily task to thirty or forty lines, they would in the end possess, stored in memory, matter equal in length to the prodigious 'Mahabarata'.

13

Let us try for a moment to picture the way in which this astonishing feat of memory and skill was achieved. In the book just quoted, Macalister paints an eminently believable picture of the kind of scene one might have encountered in one of the bardic schools – any time between the earliest days of, say 200 B.C. to the end of the Middle Ages, when the schools began to die out.

> The master first repeated a line, or a quatrain, or whatever was regarded
> as the unit of verse. The students repeated it after him till they were perfect
> in pronunciation and intonation. The master then answered it, explaining
> its grammatical structure word by word, and setting forth its meaning and
> the truth . . . which it was intended to convey. When he was satisfied that
> the pupil had assimilated his teaching, he proceeded to the next section of
> the composition. In this slow, laborious way we may suppose the sacred
> cannon to have passed from generation to generation.

This, of course is only the tip of the iceberg. Below the water line lies a great deal more than the learning of words. Indeed, the skills of a poet are only beginning when they have learned the verses of lore and wisdom. Compositions of their own must be created to add to the store of tradition. What is missing from the list of ogams, tales and laws is the initiatory element present in all bardic tradition. It is hinted at in the fact that the bard is expected, in Year 8, to learn the three prime methods of divination: *Teinm Laida, Dichetl Do Chenaib* and *Imbas Forosna*, all of which had both a magical and incantatory element.

In the great Irish epic poem, *The Tain*, which is the ultimate object of search in the satirical account of the bards quoted above, we see Queen Medb encountering the seeress Fedelm, who has 'come from learning verse and vision in Alba' (Scotland, the White Island). At once Medb asks her, 'Have you the Imbas Forosna, the Light of Foresight?', making it clear that she is aware of the importance of vision in the work of the bards. It is these two poles, verse and vision, that define the bardic mysteries. Indeed, the two are inseparable, since verse without vision is dead, and vision is itself best expressed in verse. In fact, the poets are also shamans of a kind, entering the Otherworld through trance and returning with the fruits of their vision.

There are so many examples of this in Celtic tradition that it is hard to pick out just one or two to quote. If we turn to three of the most famous shaman-poets whose work has survived – two of whom are represented in this collection – we will begin to get the flavour of the kind of work they were producing. (We must remember, however, that these were often not written down until long after their authors were dead, so that what we hear is rather like the versions of the Homeric epics, which probably bear little relation to the words actually composed by the blind bard of the Greeks.)

Let us begin with a short piece attributed to the hero-poet Fionn mac Cumhail. His story is full of magic, shamanism and transformation, and he imbibes his wisdom through the eating of a sacred salmon that swam in the waters of the Otherworld but was caught in the river Shannon. When Fionn ate of its flesh he imbibed poetic wisdom, and at once composed the following poem:

**Fionn's Poem to May Day**

May: fair aspected, perfect season:
blackbirds sing where the sun glows.

The hardy cuckoo calls
a welcome to noble summer:
ends the bitter storms
that strip the trees of the wood.

Summer cuts the streams;
swift horses seek water;
the heather grows tall;
fair foliage flourishes.

The hawthorn sprouts;
smooth flows the ocean –
Summer causing it to sleep;
blossom covers the world.

The true man sings
gladly in the bright day,
sings loudly of May –
fair aspected season.
*(translated by John Matthews)*

These are words that come from a deep inspiration, from an identification with the natural world that is almost symbiotic. Receiving the *awen*, the poet dives deeply into the natural world, returning with words that invoke the mystery of creation itself.

The second great shaman-poet is better known to us as Merlin. In Welsh tradition he is called Myrddin, and he is also an inspired poet. There may, in fact, be no connection between the two figures, but there are sufficient points of contact to convince me they are one and the same. There are a number of poems extant that are attributed to Myrddyn – and to his sister Ganeida, who is just as important a seer and visionary. Here is part of Myrddin's poem 'Hoinau' ('Greetings'), in which he complains to his only companion in a wilderness to which is visionary abilities – seen as madness by the rest of the world – have banished him.

### Greetings

Listen, little pig,
O happy little pig!
Do not go rooting
On top of the mountain,
But stay here,
Secluded in the wood,
Hidden from the dogs
Of Rhydderch the Faithful.

I will prophecy –
It will be truth! –
From Aber Taradyr
The Cyrmy will be bound
Under one warlike leader
Of the line of Gwynedd.
Usurpers of the Prydein
He will overcome.

Listen, little pig,
We should hide
From the huntsmen of Mordei
Lest we be discovered.
If we escape –
I'll not complain of fatigue! –
I shall predict,
From the back of the ninth wave,
The truth about the White One
Who rode Dyfed to exhaustion,
Who built a church
For those who only half believed.
Until Cynan comes
Nothing will be restored.

Here poetry and prophecy are one – the stark utterances of the bard in the icy woodland as gnomic as anything in the Celtic literature. A more detailed discussion of this and other poems attributed to Myrddin, will be found in Chapter 6 of this collection.

The last of this trio – or perhaps triad would be more appropriate – is Taliesin, perhaps the greatest of those whose work has survived. In a poem called, appropriately enough, *Taliesin's Bardic Knowledge*, he sums up the vast array of his personal wisdom. It is, like many of the works ascribed to this figure, something of a miscellany, much of it gleaned no doubt from a vast body of bardic wisdom still kept in memory until at least the sixth century when the poet flourished. It consists mostly of Taliesin asking questions, which he then proceeds to answer, thus showing off his prodigious knowledge while teaching his listeners a few things along the way! Here is just a part of it:

### Taliesin's Bardic Lore

Here is a chant of a primordial kind.
Who existed before darkness or light?
Where are the roots of the world?
On what day was Adam created?

Common men do not receive knowledge.
Sorrowful is he who by evil deeds
has lost the friendship of heaven's country.

Whence comes night and day?
Why is the eagle grey?
Why is night dark?
Why is the linnet green?
Why does the sea swell?
Why is this not known?

There are three fountains
on the mountain of skill,
there is a citadel
over the ocean's wave.
Fawning praiser,
tell me the name of its porter?

Who was the confessor
Of the Mary's Mabon?
What was the best deed
Adam ever performed?

Who will measure Annwn?
Who can tell the thickness of its veil?
Who can tell the size of its maw?
Who can tell the value of its stones?

Why do the treetops bend and bow?
What is this smoke amid the trees?
Perhaps Llew and Gwydion
perform their magic there?
Do they know the ancient books
when they perform their art?

Whence comes darkness
When the day ends?
Where does it go
When the day dawns?

I am a bard,
I do not vouchsafe my secrets to slaves.
I am a guide, I am a judge.
If you sow, you labour;
       *(translated by John Matthews)*

This tells us a good deal about the kind of knowledge possessed by the bards. But it is to Taliesin's personal history, given in full in Chapter 4, that we can turn for a description of an actual bardic initiation. This story can be taken on a number of levels – as a parable of the search for wisdom, as a personal story of initiation, or as an account of a shamanic journey. It is also, I believe, an account of a bardic initiation. Although some of the links in the chain are missing, there is some evidence to suggest that in ancient Celtic tradition the bardic pupil was taken to a cave and left inside to contemplate a sign carved in stone. The initiate then took a drink of initiation – the constituents of which are hinted at in the poems of Taliesin but have otherwise vanished from our knowledge. The drink had an effect like the drugs taken by shamanic practitioners in South America and elsewhere – it put them into a trance in which they saw things with inner visionary sight.

In the story Taliesin is reborn as a poet and makes his first song at once. This, I believe, is what happened in the cave. The novice entered, drank the drink, made a journey, came out into the light and made a poem – which was as often as not a prophetic utterance relating facts received in vision.

Evidence of a similar method of seeking inspiration, or *awen* as it is termed in Welsh (the Irish is *imbas*), is to be found both in the remains of later bardic poetry, and in a text dating from 1722 (quoted on pages 28–30). In a roughly contemporary Irish poem, we find the following passage:

You're comfortable, O Fearghal Og:
You have gained gifts from the threefold;
Without the help of a teacher for your verse
You make fine art on horseback.

Without a dark bothy, without hardship,
Taking permission to achieve high verse;
A grassy bank, a mountain view,
An airy vista is all you need.

In the beds where winning poems are made,
The face of Tadhg Og O Huguinn –
Unlike your rainswept one –
Was soaked by his own drops.

Myself now, when *I* make a poem,
I prefer, guarding me from error,
A screen against the sun; to be under a roof,
A dark bed to protect me.

If I did not close my eyelids
Against the brilliant rays,
Like a veil between me and my lay,
I would loose all my skill.
             *(translated by Caitlín Matthews)*

Here the poet, Fear Flatha O Gnimh, takes his poetic brother Fergh Og Mac an Bhaird (the Bard) to task for composing out in the open. Her prefers a 'dark bed' in a 'dark bothy' where he can compose undisturbed. Fergh, who composes 'on horseck', has his face washed by the rain, rather than the tears of inspiration.

Later still, in the *Memoirs of the Marquis of Clanricarde* we find a further description of the practice of visionary poetry. It is quoted in full in the opening essay by Daniel Corkery (Chapter 1) and it speaks of the seer-poet being taken to a dark place and left alone until it is time for him to emerge with a poem. In another description, also quoted by Corkery, the eighteenth-century traveller, Martin Martin, describes a similar custom still practised in the Western Isles of Scotland (see page 30).

Taliesin, of course, possessed more than just the power of words – which are strong enough in themselves. As a result of his initiation he was able to change shape and assume the form of anything he wanted. He could be a tree, a spade, a creature, a stone – anything. He tells us some of these things in a number of gnomic poems, which are sometimes jokingly referred to as the 'I have beens', because the poet begins each line with 'I have been . . .' Here is an example:

I have been a sow, I have been a buck,
I have been a sage, I have been a snout,
I have been a horn, I have been a wild sow,
I have been a shout in battle.
I have been a gushing torrent,
I have been a wave on the long shore.
I have been a gentle rain.
I have been a speckled cat in a forked tree.
I have been a circle, I have been a head,
I have been a goat in an elder tree.
I have been a crane-bag well filled,
     – A sight to behold.
             *(translated by W.F. Skene)*

In the second part of Taliesin's own story, which will be found on pages 84–96, we see that he knew how to use words in other ways, causing the boastful bards to utter nonsense, and the chains binding the poet's own patron to fall from his wrists and ankles.

But the bardic traditions do not end with the magical tales of the sixth century. Indeed there is an extraordinary sense of continuity, extending throughout the Middle Ages, into the Renaissance and into far more recent times. Celtic poets continued to compose works in praise of their masters, comparing them to heroes of old, to generous lords who would have listened to the songs of the first singers himself, and using the same verse forms as their distant ancestors. Even in recent times, the Welsh Eisteddfod has seen heated discussion on metrical rules that were in use in the sixth century and earlier.

The whole question of the poet's position within Celtic society is complex. His role overlapped that of both the other professional classes, the Druid and the Seer, so that it is sometimes difficult to decide which role a particular character is fulfilling. An early seventeenth-century tract in English called 'Tri Chof Ynys Brydain' ('The Three Antiquities of Britain'), which will be found in Chapter 11, describes the bardic system as follows:

> The office and function of the British or Cambrian Bards was to keep and preserve *tri chof ynys Brydain*: that is the three records or memorials of Britain, or which otherwise is called the British antiquity which consists of three parts. . . The one of the said three *cof* is the History of the notable Acts of the kings and princes of this land of Britain and Cambria; and the second of the three cof is the language of the Britons for which the bards ought to give account for every word and syllable therein when they are demanded thereof and to preserve the ancient tongue and not to intermix it with any foreign tongue. . . And the third cof was, to keep the genealogies or descent of the nobility, their division of lands and their arms.

In other words the three chief concerns of the bards were recognized as being the preservation of the language, the memorial of history and the knowledge of genealogy and heraldry. The Celtic scholar Patrick K. Ford, discussing the role of the poets in an illuminating introduction to his edition and translation of the work of the ancient poet Llywarch Hen, remarks:

> The seers, endowed with extrahuman capabilities, were the custodians of all the sacred tribal wisdom. Their office required frequent recitation from this store of wisdom for purely functional purposes within the society.

Professor Ford goes on to outline the principal aspects of the poet's art within Celtic culture: to praise their rulers, satirize their enemies and recite the genealogies which preserved the unity of the tribe. He concludes: 'The corpus of institutionalized knowledge also included what may have been the cornerstone of early tribal lore, a fund of gnomic wisdom.' In fact, this body of 'gnomic wisdom' need not have been all that large. We still possess an idea of what that store of knowledge consisted, in the form of the catalogues of materials such as the Welsh and Irish *Triads*, the *Twenty-four Knights of Arthur's Court*, the *Stanzas of the Graves* or the Irish *Dindschencas* (Land Lore). And it is equally certain that the poets and seers continued to seek new ways to refine their wisdom, to find deeper and deeper levels, new ways of applying the traditions they had learned. Endless combinations of words and thoughts were possible and must have been explored time upon time, always with differing results.

That the importance of this teaching was still recognized as late as the seventeenth century is indicated both by the continued existence of the bardic schools and by the words of the poet Irish Giolla Brighde Mac ComMidhe, who stated that: 'If poetry were destroyed . . . and we [were left] without knowledge of history and old-poetry, without [knowledge] of anything but the name of every man's father, then none would have fame.'

A similar sentiment is invoked in the *Welsh Triads*, where it is said: 'Three things that give amplitude to a poet: knowledge of histories, the poetic art, and old verse.' The *Triads* are undoubtedly the last remnants of the bardic tradition. At one time the bard and story-teller would have been expected to know the entire corpus of stories recorded in the *Triads*. But since these were transmitted orally we have lost a large number of the stories in question and can only hazard guesses at what they may once have been. The number mentioned exceeds 500. But not everything was lost.

There is a suggestion that the native bardic codes were taken over and Christianized by the monks of the Celtic Church. If this is the case, it could explain the mixture of pagan and Christian elements in the earliest poems. The monks, finding an entire system of bardic law, which codified the types of poetry, subject and metre deemed fit subjects for composition, adapted them in such a way as to keep them alive but in line with their own beliefs. Thus, instead of being destroyed, the tradition was reshaped to the needs of the time, just as it has been again and again since then – though probably never so radically.

But the standing of the bard was drastically reduced during the Middle Ages, to the extent that we hear of Rhys ap Tewdyr, who held sway over south Wales in 1100, bringing stories and bardic lore from Brittany to teach to the bards of Wales! And, despite a late flowering of poetic art in the thirteenth and fourteenth centuries, there was less and less recourse to the ancient lore of the primary bards such as Taliesin, Fionn or Myrddin. In effect there evolved two distinct poetic schools, those of the bards and the (much despised) minstrels. Robert Graves, summarizing the situation in his grammar of poetic lore, *The White Goddess*, writes:

> The two poetic schools did not at first come in contact, the 'big-bellied'
> well-dressed court-bards being forbidden to compose in the minstrel style
> and penalized if they visited any but the houses of princes or nobles; the
> lean and ragged minstrels not being privileged to perform at any court, nor
> trained to use the complicated verse-forms required of the court-bards.

But the Celts were deeply wedded to their traditions, and despite the fact that under the harsh rule of their Norman masters the native princes were forbidden to maintain bards of the court or to have them compose valedictions in their own tongue, the traditions did survive – though in what fragmentary state we can only conjecture. It is possible that this led to the forgery, or adaptation, of certain ancient lore to the times, and that when freedom to practise the old bardic ways returned in the sixteenth and seventeenth centuries, as well as an outside interest among antiquarians across the border, much was hastily 'restored' that might have benefited from a more considered attention, thus giving rise to the suspect writings of antiquarians such as Iolo Morgannwg (see Part Three).

Whatever the truth of this, we still owe to the bardic tradition a profound debt of gratitude. It is the bards who, through the centuries, have helped to preserve the traditions of these islands. That they have added to them is, of course, inevitable, for these traditions are in no wise dead. The inner history of the Celts is still to be found within the bardic remains which are the subject of this collection.

In various sources we hear of poets and their associates carrying a branch, of gold, silver or bronze. The most familiar, and undoubtedly the most important of these was the Silver Branch, which, in addition to being recognized as an emblem of the poet's craft, had a deeper significance as a symbol of entry to the Otherworld. In Celtic tradition, the Silver Bough is almost always awarded to a mortal either by the queen of the Otherworld or one of her ladies. As a metaphor for the bardic mysteries it promises us that by reading and studying both the ancient and the more recent texts that have survived we can discover the ancient magic still flowing in the words of the first great poets of the Celtic race as well as in those of contemporary masters, and that then, as now, their words can be doorways onto a magical reality.

*John Matthews*
*Oxford, 1997*

# PART ONE

# THE FIRST SINGERS

THE EARLIEST CELTIC BARDS are closer to magicians and shamans than they are to poets. The words they wrote possess a severe beauty, which performs a practical function, as in the casting of spells and incantations, while at the same time being aesthetically pleasing. Thus the poems of Taliesin (see Chapter 5) are intimately linked to his magically mysterious story (see Chapter 4) and to his function as a shaman and wonder-worker – one of the last of a long line of such figures dating from prehistory – and in the poems of Myrddin (Merlin, see Chapter 6) we find a powerful prophetic burden, which is echoed in many of the works that have survived their diffusion through the ages.

The works of these early bards are not always easy to understand without an extensive knowledge of the culture of the time in which they were written and recorded, and the latter often happened long after the former, requiring a further effort of understanding. Despite any initial difficulty, however, the words do make a great deal of sense, even to our modern ears, and they are, in addition, imprinted with the heritage of Celtic myth, legend and magic. which were the stock-in-trade of the bards. Thus, for example in Chapter 8, 'The Cooking of the Great Queen' (which might be better titled 'The Cauldron and the Spit' since it deals with both these objects at some length), we are in the presence of some very ancient mythic themes. The Great Queen is really the Morrigan, a fearsome battle goddess who appears throughout the Irish myth cycles and is later metamorphosed into the 'Morgan le Fay' of Arthurian literature.

Works such as this, which deal with an important figure like the Morrigan, who naturally possessed cooking utensils of mythic proportions, constitute the kind of bardic texts that would have been recited in the chieftain's hall, perhaps to the accompaniment of a harp. In this collection you will find a number of texts of this kind, including, by turn, the heroic, the magical, the incantatory and the satirical. The satirical especially feature as an important part of the ancient bardic tradition, and in Fred Norris Robinson's illuminating article, 'Satirists and Enchanters in Early Irish Literature' (Chapter 7), we will discover the perils that lay in wait for anyone foolish enough to insult a bard, who was believed to be able literally to raise boils on the face of his traducer. Nor was it wise to underpay a bard, since this too could incur his wrath.

We begin this section with one of the best summations of what we know about the bardic schools of Britain and Ireland by Daniel Corkery, whose 1924 book *The Hidden Ireland*, from which this extract comes, remains a classic study of the poetic tradition in Ireland. This is followed by the 'Gododdin' poems, a sequence of linked elegiac poems, which describe a fateful military expedition against the Angles by the warriors of Manau Guotodin (modern-day Edinburgh) in a battle that took place at Catraeth (Catterick in Yorkshire) around A.D. 600 and that ended in the death of them all. We know nothing of the author except his name, Aneurin, and the possibility that he may have fought (and survived) the battle he describes. His work can justly be described as the first Celtic epic poem – parts of it date from the sixth century – and it remembers the heroes of Gododdin in a memorable and moving way.

Next comes 'Prolegomena to the Study of Old Welsh Poetry' by the great Celticist Edward Anwyl, who died at the tragically early age of thirty-four. In this essay he deals with the problems facing those who seek to interpret the oldest Welsh bardic sources, and he offers helpful insights into their understanding. He sets both the Gododdin poems and the works of Taliesin and Myrddin into context, thus preparing the way for the versions of 'The Mabinogi of Taliesin' (Chapter 4), in a strikingly lyrical translation by the nineteenth-century bardic poet 'Idrison'. This is followed by a series of translations of poems attributed to the semi-mythical poet by Thomas Stephens, one of the first of a number of early Celtic scholars to attempt these difficult works. I am particularly glad to be able to include these versions here, both because of their quality (which is closer to the tone of the original than many that came after) and because of their rarity (they are to be found only in an obscure nineteenth-century Welsh magazine).

John Veitch's spirited interpretation of the Merlin (Myrddin) poems follows, and the first section ends with a consideration of the role of the bard as satirist and enchanter and the myth-laden poem of the Morrigan mentioned above.

There is, of course, a vastly larger literature of the bards than these few examples. However, it is hoped that the brief selection from the best of these early works included here will encourage readers to seek out some of the many others, which have begun to appear in reliable modern translations. The Further Reading at the end of this volume should prove a rich hunting-ground for those who wish to go further than this anthology.

# 1

# THE BARDIC SCHOOLS

## DANIEL CORKERY
### from *The Hidden Ireland*

I N COMMON WITH almost every other institution of the Gael, the bardic school
as a factor in the life of the nation has not been so much misunderstood or
underestimated as entirely omitted by those who have, previous to our own
day, thought themselves fitted to write Irish history. They did not, it is only fair to
say, wilfully make such omissions: they could not, however, avoid making them
when they employed, in telling the story of Ireland, the same formulae that had
simplified their own labours, or the similar labours of others, in dealing with the
chronicles of other peoples. They saw only what they had come to see. How big
a thing they failed to notice when this system of the bardic schools escaped them,
and how untrustworthy, and indeed misleading, their story is as a consequence,
will be understood from these words:

> If we turn to Ireland . . . we find a country where for some 1,500 years, as far
> back as historic knowledge can reach, one national force has overshadowed
> and dominated all others. It has been the power of a great literary tradition.
> Political power was not centralized, and no single man was in a position to
> determine what the people should think, believe, or do. But in the learned
> tradition of the race there was a determined order. In their intellectual and
> spiritual inheritance was the very essence of national life, the substance of its
> existence, the warrant of its value, the assurance of its continuity.[1]

Who, having risen from the books of the historians – the books on which we were
all reared up – will not cry out on meeting these words for the first time: Can it
be true? Can it be true that for all their painstaking conning of haphazard memoirs and crafty State-papers, those writers of history never once happened on the
one national force that overshadowed and dominated all others? Can it be
believed that not having struck against it, they never missed it, never felt somehow

that their stories did not adhere, one to another; did not account, one for the other? One shrinks from saying that the essence of national life, consisting, as it always does, of an intellectual and spiritual inheritance, is stuff for the artist, rather than for the historian, to come upon, to handle, to purge, to shape, so that his duller co-mates may be made a little more wise – one shrinks from saying this, yet the artist's large and even loose way of discourse is in the end often less astray, one thinks, than that patient, anxious chronicling of events that has no feeling for the undercurrents that sweep them along, hurtling, clashing, or sundering.

Elsewhere in that same pamphlet Mrs Green states: 'Irish civilization was thus from the beginning marked by intellectual passion.'[2] Now, the bardic schools were the seat of that passion. In them was the flame nursed, fed, distributed – 'síolta teine' ('seeds of fire'). To realize, then, in any fitting way, that national force which overshadowed and dominated all others, one must make some study of this unique factor in Gaelic civilization: unless we do so, we shall fail not only to understand Irish history as a whole, but we shall fail in our present purpose, namely, to fathom the life of those 'pariahs' of the eighteenth century who, so unlike us, had no difficulty in apprehending the power and depth of that image with which Eibhlín Dubh brought her keening to a close.

It is not probable that we shall ever discover the origins of the bardic schools. 'At what time they were founded we don't know, for the bardic order existed in prehistoric times, and their position in society is well established in the earliest tradition.'[3] They were ancient when St Patrick came amongst us. In the pagan days poet and Druid were perhaps one; and even after those schools had become Christian some vestiges of the old cult still survived in them; but this, of course, could naturally be said of life in general, for pagan ways of thinking, pagan traditions and customs, lingered on through whole centuries. When the schools did at last become Christian, they did not become monastic; and they are not to be confused with the famous monkish schools, the ruins of which are still to be seen in so many of our valleys. The Bardic Schools were lay, officered by laymen; and existed side by side with the great schools of the clerics. Whether there was any connection between the two types of school, monastic and bardic, does not seem to have been given the study it deserves. Did such great establishments as Bangor, Clonfert and Clonmacnoise lay claim, at any time, to include the local bardic schools within their orbits, or did they dominate them while not enclosing them? Or did the bardic schools, maintaining their ancient traditions, think of themselves as set over against the monastic schools, deeming them as only of yesterday? It is easy to say that either type had its own province, the one secular, the other religious; but when we consider that two such neighbouring schools would share in the same patronage, that the professors of both would meet in this patron's assemblies, in his council chamber, for instance, where bishops and chief poets helped him, and that the courses of both schools would freely overlap, it is not so easy to think of them as quite disparate entities, each working within a sphere of its own. Did one type dominate the other?

The mere existence of those schools, whether or not the Church schools tutored them, shows how different was the life of Ireland from that of Europe; it gives point, too, to the assertion that a literary tradition dominated the other national forces, for that literary tradition would have been in the keeping of those schools. This being so, rivalry, if such there was, between the two types of school, monastic and bardic, must have had its effects, direct or indirect, on the life of the nation. The question is vast, difficult, and fascinating; and one trusts that someone fitted to do so will take it in hand.

Whatever may have been the relative positions of the monkish schools and those of the bards, the latter, all authorities agree, were the university system of the nation – granting degrees, or what corresponded to such, and bestowing privileges on both professors and students simply because they were professors and students.[4]

In Europe of the Dark and Middle Ages the universities were frankly Church institutions, with Churchmen ruling in their professoriates; whatever influence those universities wielded in European life and thought was, therefore, a Church influence, which means practically that whatever influence the higher learning exerted in Continental thought was a Church influence, for except in those universities where else was there any repository of that learning? In Ireland, on the other hand, the bardic schools, which obviously exerted great influence in the nation's life, were a repository of learning, and were, at the same time, frankly a lay institution. The great monastic schools had, too, of course, much of the university spirit in them, and did also exert great influence on the life of the country; this influence, however, one may roughly equate with that wielded by the Church universities of the Continent. But one searches Europe in vain for the equivalent of our bardic school system. In this regard, then, European civilization was less varied than Irish civilization. That factor, which Europe lacked, a secular, intellectual centre, who shall fathom its various promptings and achievements on its native soil? What part, great or little, exciting or assuaging, did it play in the local wrestlings of Church and State, if there were such? And in how much is it responsible for that non-European tang which one feels everywhere both in Irish life and in Irish letters in all the centuries down to the nineteenth?

Professor Bergin tells us that he has never come on a description of a bardic school in Irish – naturally, for, of course, the institution was too familiar to all to need any; especially was it familiar to those for whom the poets and chroniclers wrote, the patrician class. Of references to the schools, there is, however, and just as naturally, no end. In English there is an account in the *Memoirs of the Marquis of Clanricarde* (published 1722), which Professor Bergin believes to be trustworthy:

> Concerning the poetical Seminary or School, from which I was carried
> away to clear other things that fell in my way, it was open only to such as
> were descended of Poets and reputed within their Tribes. And so was it
> with all the Schools of that kind in the Nation, being equal to the Number
> of Families that followed the said calling. But some more or less frequented
> for the difference of Professors, Conveniency, with other Reasons, and
> seldom any come but from remote parts, to be at a distance from Relations
> and other Acquaintances that might interrupt his Study. The Qualifications
> first requir'd were reading well, writing the Mother-tongue, and a strong

Memory. It was likewise necessary the Place should be in the solitary Recess of a Garden or within a Sept or Enclosure far out of the reach of any Noise, which an Intercourse of People might otherwise occasion. The Structure was a snug, low Hut, and beds in it at convenient Distances, each within a small Apartment without much Furniture of any kind, save only a Table, some Seats, and a Conveniency for Cloaths to hang upon. No Windows to let in the Day, nor any Light at all us'd but that of Candles, and these brought in at a proper Season only. The Students upon thorough Examination being first divided into Classes, wherein a regard was had to every one's Age, Genius, and the Schooling had before, if any at all, or otherwise. The Professors (one or more as there was occasion) gave a Subject suitable to the Capacity of each class, determining the number of Rhimes, and clearing what was to be chiefly observed therein as to Syllables, Quartans, Concord, Correspondence, Termination and Union, each of which were restrain'd by peculiar Rules. The said Subject (either one or more as aforesaid) having been given over Night, they work'd it apart each by himself upon his own Bed, the whole next day in the Dark, till at a certain Hour in the Night, Lights being brought in, they committed it to writing. Being afterwards dress'd and come together into a large Room, where the Masters waited, each Scholar gave in his Performance, which being corrected or approv'd of (according as it requir'd) either the same or fresh subjects were given against the next day. This Part being over, the Students went to their Meal, Which was then serv'd up; and so, after some time spent in Conversation and other Diversions, each retired to his Rest, to be ready for the Business of the next Morning. Every *Saturday* and on the Eves of Festival Days they broke up and dispers'd themselves among the Gentlemen and rich Farmers of the Country, by whom they were very well entertain'd and much made of, till they thought fit to take their leaves, in order to re-assume their Study. Nor was the People satisfied with affording this Hospitality alone; they sent in by turns every Week from far and near Liquors and all manner of Provision towards the Subsistence of the Academy, so that the chief Poet was at little or no Charges, but, on the contrary, got very well by it, besides the Presents made him by the Students upon their first coming, which was always at Michaelmas, and from thence till the 25th of March, during the cold season of the Year only, did that close Study last. At that time the Scholars broke up and repair'd each to his own Country, with an Attestation of his Behaviour and Capacity from the chief Professor to those that had sent him.

The reason of laying the Study aforesaid in the Dark was doubtless to avoid the Distraction which Light and the variety of Objects represented thereby commonly occasions. This being prevented, the Faculties of the Soul occupied themselves solely upon the Subject in hand, and the Theme given; so that it was soon brought to some Perfection according to the Notions or Capacities of the Students. Yet the course was long and tedious, as we find, and it was six or seven Years before a Mastery or the last Degree was conferred, which you'll the less admire upon considering the great Difficulty of the Art, the many kinds of their Poems, the Exactness and Nicety to be observ'd in each, which was necessary to render their Numbers soft, and the Harmony agreeable and pleasing to the Ear.

As every Professor, or chief Poet, depended on some Prince or great Lord, that had endowed his Tribe, he was under strict ties to him and Family, as to record in good Metre his Marriages, Births, Deaths, Acquisitions made in war and Peace, Exploits, and other remarkable things relating to the Same. He was likewise bound to offer an Elegy on the Decease of the said Lord, his consort, or any of their children, and a Marriage Song when there should be Occasion. But as to any Epick, or Heroick Verse to be made for any other Lord or Stranger, it was requir'd that at least a Paroemion or Metre therein, should be upon the Patron, or the Name in general . . .

The last Part to be done, which was the *Action* and *Pronunciation* of the Poem in Presence of the Maecenas, or the Principal Person it related to, was perform'd with a great deal of Ceremony in a Consort of Vocal and Instrumental Musick. The poet himself said nothing, but directed and took care that everybody else did his Part right. The Bards having first had the Composition from him, got it well by Heart, and now pronounc'd it orderly, keeping even pace with a Harp, touch'd upon that Occasion; no other musical Instrument being allowed for the said Purpose than this alone, as being Masculin, much sweeter and fuller than any other.

In Gaelic Scotland those schools continued to exist into the eighteenth century; and Professor Bergin quotes from Martin's *Description of the Western Islands of Scotland*:

I must not omit to relate their way of Study, which is very singular. They shut their Doors and Windows for a Day's time, and lie on their backs with a Stone upon their Belly, and Plads about their Heads, and their Eyes being cover'd they pump their Brains for Rhetorical Encomium or Panegyrick; and indeed they furnish such a Stile from this Dark Cell as is understood by very few; and if they purchase a couple of Horses as the reward of their Meditation, they think they have done a great Matter. The Poet or Bard had a Title to the Bridegroom's upper Garb – that is, the Plad and Bonnet – but now he is satisfy'd with what the Bridegroom pleases to give him on such occasions.

Both these descriptions are from without. In Ireland the schools had died before they were written, and in Scotland were dying. Presently we shall find how one who had himself lain in those 'beds of booths', in those dark cells, could rise up in spirit to bless them; and Tadhg Óg Ó Huiginn gives us to understand that in his brother's school the students were sorry to hear the cuckoo's first song, for the break-up of the session was then near.

O ye who were in his house and sought art and residence, well might it be hateful to you to hear the utterance of the cuckoo.[5]

The composing in the dark, Professor Bergin thinks, was a survival of some rite or ceremony of pagan origin. No doubt he is correct, yet when we consider the severity of the mental discipline practised in those schools, the care taken to choose a solitary recess, the custom of separating students from their own kindred, we do not find the shutting out of the garish daylight contrary to the spirit of the whole system.

The building was only an ordinary house or hut – the central figure, the chief *file,* the head *ollamh,* was indeed the school: where he went, the school went, sometimes on circuit from king to king. *Filí* and not *bards* it was that both conducted and used those schools, the bards, as compared with the *filí,* being a lower order, *untrained* poets – singers of songs, reciters of verse, strolling jongleurs. The word *bard,* however, in modern times, has come to include all varieties of poets, and it will, therefore, serve our turn now.

The bards never have had any representative in England.

They correspond in a way to the University men, but their fixed place in society was higher than any that his attainments alone have ever been able to secure for the University man in England. They were, indeed, until the fall of the old Irish order, an intellectual aristocracy, with all the privileges and, no doubt, many of the prejudices of a caste. They held their position by virtue of their birth and the practice of their art.[6]

But other writers find the closest analogy to them and their profession in the bar.[7] The bar is not, however, a hereditary craft; the bardic profession was; yet since new names are found frequently coming in among the familiar ones – the O'Huiginns and the O'Dalys – in the literary annals, the profession, it is evident, had some means of recruiting its strength with fresh blood. Brilliance in the schools may have had the power of winning to a coveted position, or royal prerogatives may have exerted themselves: it is certain, anyway, that an open door there was somewhere, but whether a back or a front door, and what magic phrase opened it, we do not at present know.

The training in the schools was long and arduous; and having gone through it, the student had little else of his craft to learn.

He was, in fact, a professor of literature and a man of letters, highly trained in the use of a polished literary medium, belonging to a hereditary caste in an aristocratic society, holding an official position therein by virtue of his training, his learning, his knowledge of the history and tradition of his country and his clan. He discharged, as O'Donovan pointed out years ago, the functions of the modern journalist.[8] He was not a song writer. He was often a public official, a chronicler, a political essayist, a keen and satirical observer of his fellow-countrymen. . . . He might be a poet, too, if in addition to his training he was gifted with the indefinable power, the true magic, of poetry. But whether he was a poet in this higher sense or not, he always composed in verse.[9]

Only those who have read some of the works of those poets, and tried to place them in the national polity, will adequately appreciate the careful wording of this passage. It clarifies our conception of them; it corrects our equating of them with the poets of other times and countries – strayed revellers, without a place in sun or moon; and, finally, it hints that we should seek out from among that literary association those who were poets, judging these on their merits, if poetry be our quest, and judging the others as we will – as chroniclers, perhaps, but not as poets. Our idea of the whole matter is still further clarified to remember that down to the middle of the seventeenth century, prose was not thought of as an art-form: a copyist would transcribe a poem word for word, but was content to record merely the matter of a piece of prose.

Those poets seized and maintained their pride of place not as individuals, but as a body. They were numerous in all centuries down to the seventeenth. Before the Danes came into Ireland they had become so powerful that 'They were three times banished by the kings of Ireland; but the province of Ulster defended them against the vengeance of the other Irish.'[10]

St Colmcille, as we have all read, pleaded for them at Drumceat; and though at this crisis, and time and again in the following centuries, laws were framed to regulate them, what between their numbers, their wealth, their power of satire, their indispensability as chroniclers, and, it is hinted, their use of the hunger-strike, they seemed to have lived always a little on the thither side of the law. Why they were so numerous is not difficult to understand. 'The island was divided up into the domains of a large number of feudal lords, each of whom – at any rate, in the North, West and South – would have his family bard.'[11] And Dr Hyde, translating his own Irish, says:

> There was neither prince nor great noble in Ireland who had not visits
> from poets bringing poems or abhráns in their praise, for which they used
> to receive a large price. Theobald Butler, Lord of Cahir, and his wife, Mary
> Cusack, had the full of a book of poems in their praise. This Butler died in
> 1596. In the same way the O'Byrnes had the full of a book of poems
> written upon them, which is called 'The Book of the O'Byrnes.' O'Conor
> Donn has a volume in praise of the clann Samhradhain, or MacGoverns,
> and there is a book in Copenhagen, in Denmark, written in praise of the
> Maguires, and it is pretty certain that there was no great family in Ireland
> but possessed a book of the same kind.[12]

They stood strongly upon their rights.

> O'Hosey, or O'Hussey, poet of the Maguires, on being appointed ollave, or
> poet-in-chief, reminded his patron in his laureate ode that the ollave
> ranked in all ways as an equal with a king and a bishop. 'To him is due
> the warmth of loving-kindness, the primest of all largesse, the initiative in
> counsel; the seat closest to the prince and a share of his bed, with
> payment, whether "in wood" or "in sanctuary".'[13]

And with this we may compare: 'On his father's death in 1432, Eoghan O'Neill, says the annalist, "went to Tulach Óg, and was there inaugurated king on the stone of the kings by the will of God and men, of bishops and chief poets".'[14] And another bard, John O'Cluan, apologizing for having struck his lord, Aed O'Connor, writes thus:

Thine 'tis in payment of my blow to lop the right hand from me, O gentle noble countenance; thy due 'tis to have a lay of its value, or else the very hand, O Gairide's griffin. Not kine, not horses, not artificers' gold are promised thee, O ruddy one benign of face! Neither hand shalt thou have, no, nor foot; but a poem in lieu of that which I have done.[15]

Such voices out of the far centuries prompt us to think that in Ireland, if nowhere else, the homely, slighted shepherd's trade held its head rather high! They throve, as one might expect: 'It has been computed that in the petty princedom of Tyrconnell or Donegal, the real estate allocated to the maintenance of the *literati* amounted in value to £2,000 a year of our present currency; and we find Daire Mac Brodin, poet to the Fourth Earl of Thomond (about 1570–1650), residing still on his own patrimonial estate in the Castle of Dunogan, Barony of Ibrican, in the west of County Clare.'[16]

Neither record will surprise us if we recollect that sometimes a poet received as much as a hundred marks (£600) for a poem or abhrán; and Tadhg Óg Ó Huiginn, who lived in the fifteenth century, says that he never received less than twenty cows for a poem from Tadhg Mac Cathal O'Connor-Sligo.[17]

The studies of the students in the bardic schools were chiefly: history, law, language, literature. The history was that of Ireland, the law was that of Ireland, namely, the Brehon Law system; the language was that of Ireland, the literature that of Ireland – and through the medium of the native language were all subjects taught. These schools, then, considered as a university, differed widely from the European type, where the main study was given over on the one hand to a law system – the Roman Law – that was the relic of a dead empire, and on the other, to the literatures of languages that were no longer living. To the same degree as the Continental university cultivated the dead and the alien, the Irish university cultivated the living and the native; and if both lagged far behind the ideal type of university, there is as much to be said for the Irish conception as for the foreign. In the Irish schools, the present-day tendency to use the home-language as the medium of instruction was anticipated by more than a thousand years. National literatures on the Continent had to struggle against the university; whereas there Dante might easily never have written his poems in his mother-tongue, nor indeed Villon his, the Irish language was the very apple of their eye to the bardic schools. That language they took, and ruling out dialect and the passing turn of speech, refined it and set it apart as a special dialect, a language for literature, which became known from end to end of Ireland. It was known also in Scotland. It remained unchanged for centuries. With all that it came to contain of law, prayer, history and literature, it served at the one time as seed-bed and harvest of the mind of the Gaelic nation.

It was, as stated, the foundation-stone of all the studies in those schools: it was not, however, from very early times, the only language studied in them. Zimmer's theory that there was, as a result of the barbarian invasions, a flight of Gallic scholars to Ireland in the fifth century, is now fairly well understood, if not agreed upon: Professor Kuno Meyer appeared to accept it, while Professor MacNeill rather discredits it;[18] yet, recollecting the studies in those bardic schools, one at least wishes it to be true. To think of these scholars – Christians for the most part – as introducing a new strain into the scholarship of our fathers; to conceive of them as preparing in those schools a path for St Patrick and his disciples, so explaining the bloodless conversion; to see them as opening up these schools to the riches of the Greek and Latin tongues, so establishing the tradition out of which fourteen hundred years later the peasant Donnchadh Ruadh was to write in Latin his memorable epitaph on Tadhg Gaedhlach, another peasant – to derive from that hurried descent on our shores of exiled scholarship certain of the most salient characteristics of those schools in the after centuries – to think thus, is, it must be feared, only that rounding off of a beautiful tale for which the creative instinct in us craves. But when one remembers the traffic of Irish missionaries with Europe in the early centuries, such a theory is not needed to explain the interest of the bardic schools in Greek and Latin – the languages of European scholarship, as their own was of Irish scholarship. Wherever the impulse came from, their professors soon became acquainted with them, and the tradition lived on from century to century, with memorable results, as will afterwards be noted. All down the centuries the chiefs were educated in those schools, and, said Stanihurst, 'The Irish speak Latin like a vulgar language, learned in their common schools of leechcraft and law.'[19] While, turning to a later writer, we find:

> The more one studies the works of these bards, the more one is impressed with the range of their attainments. They were not in holy orders, and yet they must have been better versed in Latin than most of the clergy. . . In any case, it was no mean achievement on the part of men like Tadhg Ó Huiginn to show such acquaintance with the voluminous Latin religious literature of the day in addition to the huge store of native learning exemplified in their other works.[20]

Protected by law as well as custom, the academic spirit naturally made its home in these schools. If one pick up at random any set of verses produced in them, one has to hand an example on which to argue either for or against that spirit. Too plainly, almost, that chance set of verses will show the inbreeding from which these poets' flock of ideas came to suffer, a disease most incident to academies. Everywhere in their poems one finds a refinement which, while it never becomes lackadaisical or effeminate, does certainly only too clearly make us aware of their contempt for the crudeness that so often accompanies the note of the daring and novel. That rigid turn of mind which kept their literary medium in a strait-jacket for whole centuries, afraid not so much of growth as the dangers that go with it, kept the doors of the inventive faculties severely sentried, and for the self-same reason. The movement of their minds is swift, precise, and often piercing, but one wishes for livelier contrasts, for richer colour, for readier emotions. There was, however, gain as well as loss.

> From their study of good models and their association with the best teachers, the poets derived one characteristic which is common to the whole bardic order, and that is a sustained dignity of style. Their respect

for their position, their hereditary pride, and their excessive devotion
to traditional precedents, gave them at least a rooted dislike of
vulgarity.

To which it is hardly necessary to add what the same authority writes elsewhere:

There are several poems in praise of the harp, but the literary classes
appear to have looked down upon the singer, whom they classed with the
geócach, or buffoon. Tom Moore's picture of the bard singing and playing
in the intervals of draining bumpers would have shocked the real bard as
something very vulgar indeed.[21]

The great bulk of the work left us by them consists of encomiastic verse – panegyrics of their patrons. Of all they wrote, this species of verse was, of course, most likely to be preserved, for each great house had its *duanaire,* or collection of poems, written in its honour. Into these panegyrics the poets wove a great amount of genealogical matter, which to us nowadays is wearisome: our standards are different, our whole world is different; yet one never knows when a beautiful stanza may not suddenly be come upon. From the view of history, the value of such verse, and the amount of it remaining to us is vast, is at present inestimable. Their religious poetry is more attractive than this encomiastic verse: here are freshness and genuine inspiration; qualities that also are found in the stray non-official poems and snatches of poems that the dreadful centuries have spared to us.

It is likely that these poets were more academic than those of any other country ever were – not excepting even the Pléiade of French literature. 'Sons of learning' they really were, and as such they were never weary of speaking of the science of verse. It was their dearest study: their metres became more and more intricate, and their verse, what between this intricacy and the special dialect they used, more and more a study rather for the schools themselves than an outlet for a people's emotion. A profession that was hereditary, a rich, strongly organized caste, an over-elaborated catechism of art – one reckons up such characteristics and finds it hard to equate these darlings of the nation with our idea of poets in general: in art who does not fear privilege and organization? – yet, after all, some very notable works of art were produced in little Italian cities at a time when many of the self-same characteristics adhered to the artists who swarmed in them. If our colleges of bards, like those associations of artists, only occasionally threw up a man of genius – what else could have been expected? But while we come upon the work of the unique Flemish or Italian stone-carver, with all manner of preparations made properly to apprehend his genius, we happen upon the Gaelic poet, not only heavy with ignorance, but ill-bestead, it is likely, by whatever alien standards we lean upon. What remains to be done is first to publish all the verse we have inherited from these bards, such as it is; and secondly, to make more readily accessible the work of those of them who were poets as well as men of letters. Even when this is done, it will still be difficult, not to appraise the work before our eyes, but to appraise the whole endeavour; for we can never be sure that the best work of these schools has not perished. That portion of it which remains has not been preserved to us through the ordinary sifting-process that a national literature undergoes; Opinion – that of the mass of men, that of the critics, that of the 'passionate few', who, more than all others, keep the good things of Art before men's eyes – Opinion, blended of these three voices, has had practically nothing to say to what has survived of the poetry of the bards: nothing else than the self-same chance that brings a soldier alive from the battlefield where thousands have fallen, has decided what was to survive of those academicians' work. Much, therefore, has yet to be accomplished before we can dare to speak of them as we do of the schools of poetry that elsewhere arose and disappeared.

Those poems, because of their close-knit structure, their subtle music, are the despair of translators – 'The lyrics of Aonghus Ó Dálaigh and his fellows are as untranslatable as those of Horace':[22] in choosing, then, some specimens of bardic poetry, it may be well to find a few clustering about a common subject, a subject that will have an interest of its own for us as helping on our study: The theme we choose as fulfilling this condition is, besides, one that the old poets themselves would have rejoiced for, namely, the schools themselves. Here is a little poem that one never forgets. We do not know when it was written, probably in the seventeenth century, nor by whom. It has but one quality to recommend it; that, however, the most difficult of all, the most elusive, the least frequently compassed – we call it 'charm':

### An Scoláire

Pleasant the scholar's life
When his books surround him;
'Tis clear to ye, O people,
No better is in Ireland.

O'er him the strongest lord
Rules not as prince or king;
For him no Church's dues,
Nor fines nor early rising.

Early rising, shepherding,
These he never yields,
And just as little worries him
Tillage or watching in the night.

Great the harvest of his plough
Coming in the front of Spring;
And the yoke of his plough-team,
A handful of pens!

At backgammon, at the harp
So sweet, he'd love a spell;
Or a spell in joyous company,
With his friends around him.

But the Irish mode of student life was almost at an end when this nameless one chose so to praise it. Here is a poem, written by Mathghamhain Ó hIfearnáin, or Mahon O'Heffernan – early in the seventeenth century, a time of confiscations and plantations, which more clearly mirrors the troubled state of things:

**Ceist! cia do cheinneóchadh dán?**[23]

Question! who will buy a poem? Its meaning is genuine learning of scholars. Will any take, or does any lack, a noble poem that shall make him immortal?

Though this is a poem with close-knit science, I have walked all Munster with it, every market from cross to cross – nothing gained from last year to this time.

Though a groat were a small earnest, not one man or woman offered it: no man mentioned the reason; neither Gael nor Gall gave heed to me.

Such an art as this is no profit to me, though it is a misfortune that it should fall to the ground: it were more honourable to become a maker of combs – what use is it to anyone to profess poetry?

Corc of Cashel lives not, nor Cian, who never spared their cattle, nor the price of them, open-handed men at paying the bardic companies – alas! it is good-bye to the race of Eibhear.

They never lost the palm for generosity, until Cobhthach and Tál died: many a host I leave untold, for whom I might have continued to make poetry.

I am a merchant ship that has lost its cargo, after the Fitzgeralds who deserved renown. I hear no answer – a case that has tormented me.
'Tis an idle business about which I put a question.

Surely a beautiful lyric. Even in the prose translation, does not one feel the accent of true poetry? Is not one subtly aware that the theme is heightened – how, when, one hardly knows – to that level where the words take on a new garb, a new life, in short, to the lyric plane? And as we read are we not gently conscious of some effort towards an answering reserve and dignity stirring within ourselves? As for its subject, there cannot have been many poets of that time who did not treat some variation of it: it was in all their thoughts: the patrician houses, that had sheltered them from time immemorial, were broken and deserted or in the keeping of aliens; and in consequence the poets, for the first time dispossessed, found themselves forlorn wanderers – 'mar ubhall ó thuinn go tuinn' ('as an apple from wave to wave, I am tossed from neighbour to neighbour'), sings Fearfeasa ón Cáinte, in a poem to the famous Florence MacCarthy – himself a prisoner in the Tower. All these poems are gathered up, one may say, in O'Gnive's funeral lamentation of the bardic schools, as it has been called. In this, as on a tombstone, are enumerated the more famous of the poet families whose world was now in ruins – the O'Higginses, the O'Dalys, the MacMelaughlins, the Keoghs, the MacGraths, the O'Coffeys, the Mac-an-wards, the MacConmees.[24]

It may, however, be more profitable for us here to transcribe the verses of some unknown poet – in Irish literature, significant fact, the name of the unknown poets is legion – who, writing about the same time, gives us poignantly to understand how deep and warm remained the recollection of these bardic schools in the hearts of those who had in the young years of their manhood lain in their 'beds of booths':

### Aonar Dhamhsa Eidir Dhaoinibh[25]

I am alone among men; tonight I am joyless: left desolate after the others, finding no food of gladness.

I do not understand these speakers who speak our mother-tongue:
I can find none that I know, for I see no one like myself.

Every full encampment is to me the same as a desert after my comrades, yet it would be crowded to me if there were but one poet within.

The three forges wherein I was wont to find mental delight, that I cannot visit these forges wears away the armoury of my mind.

The house of memorizing of our gentle lads – it was a trysting-place of youthful companies – embers red and shining, that was our forge at the first.

The house of reclining for such as we, the university of art, poetic cell that kept us from beguilement, this was the great forge of our trained ánruith.

The house of the critic of each fine work of art was the third house of our three forges, which multiplied the clinging tendrils of knowledge, wherein the very forge of science was wont to be.

Three sanctuaries wherein we took rank, three forges that sustained the loving companies of artists, houses that bound comrades together.

A blessing on them for their nobility, men to whom hard poems were no perplexity: that gathering worthy of love, dark verse was to them no darkness.

In their midst a spring day or a winter's night was brief: lacking them those who have escaped make a month now of a single day.

Hard is their toil when men of learning find not the bright-threaded artistry of illustrious scholars, to whom belonged the mystic import of words.

Woe to the quarter whence came their slackness in meeting together!
The cause of the dispersion of the school is that the Gaels of Macha are
in bondage.

A noble poem, rising up mightily to verses 9 and 10 – one that must surely have
brought tears in the disastrous aftertime to the eyes of those who had studied in
these schools or come intimately to know of them. Even today, in our very different world, after giving them even such shallow study as we here have done, one
does not listen to this nameless voice unmoved. Or do I deceive myself? Do I also
deceive myself in thinking that such a poem illuminates our subject, that
Clanricarde's description, even when helped out by such other particulars as we
have added, needs just such an enkindling light as this to heighten our curiosity to
that warmth of feeling through which alone we may see into the life of things?. . .
One other poem we will give. In a different mood, another poet, Eochaidh Ó
Heóghusa, brings us to feel with him and his fellows on finding their occupation
gone: I take the liberty of transcribing Professor Bergin's version, translation and
notes, except such as are purely linguistic:

### On a Change in Literary Fashions

The following poem was written in 1603. Its date is fixed by the reference
to the visit to England of Rudhraighe Ó Domhnaill, when he got the title
of Earl of Tyrconnell.

    The author was the celebrated Eochaidh Ó Heóghusa, sometime poet
to the Maguires of Fermanagh. He deals in a good-humoured manner with
the effect upon men of letters of the convulsions of society. The downfall
of the Gaelic aristocracy had deprived men like him of the educated
audience they had been trained to please. Henceforth they might win a
precarious living by competing with strolling singers. It was as if a poet
laureate had to seek engagements at a music-hall. A contemporary poet
treats the same theme with bitter sarcasm: 'A vulgar doggerel – "soft"
vocables with which it is all-sufficing that they but barely be of even
length – concoct such plainly, without excess of involution, and from that
[poor literary] form shall thy promotion be the greater.' – (O'Grady, Cat.,
page 393.) Though Ó Heóghusa defies anyone to fail to understand him,
now that he appeals to the groundlings, I confess that two or three lines
of this poem are obscure to me.

    The text is from MS. 6131–3 in the Bibliothèque Royale, Brussels.
Osborn Bergin.[26]

A change for the better is to be commended: I have found at this time
an exchange poor but fortunate, which has turned out profitable for
me.

I have abandoned the delicate series of keen and earnest admonitions for a
common sort of easy art which brings me more praise.

By the obscurity of carven ornament I used to earn disgust: many protested
that my verse was unworthy of favour.

Henceforth, though great is the luck, I renounce a single groat of the profit thereof, if one stanza of my poetry passes the understanding of anyone in the world.

Free and easy verse on the open road! – since that is what is asked of me, I will discharge the debts, by the leave of the Earl of Tyrconnell.

The dunces of the world would not beat me in softness and artlessness: I have gone out in the rain like the rest – a wise course.

I have abandoned – what greater luck? – my hard mysterious ways: if he hear some of my verse it will make the Earl laugh.

Lest I be put out of the protection of those from whom splendour was won (?), I refuse to let Tyrconnell's prince go upon a jury to try me.

Through bad verse many a one is full of love for me this year: I would earn more affection but for my fear of the Earl.

Aodh's son, the sober-minded, a man who found my hard (verse) very soft, it is easy for me to be brave now that he is away in England.

Every poem I composed hitherto used almost to break my heart: this new fashion that has come to us is a great cause of health.

If the chief of Bearnas find fault with any quatrain that is made by me, there will be many opposed to him: a change for the better is to be commended.

These four poems are all from the one period: they breathe of an old and deep-rooted culture, of long ages of slowly maturing thought and patiently mellowing art. One might deduce from them that not alone were the bardic schools academic, taking pride in their aloofness, but that over against them was somewhere a rebellious spirit. Everything about the schools – their cult of secrecy, of tradition; their power to assuage, to excite, to wound; their security, the rivalry between them – all were of a nature to induce satire, either bitter or humorous. One could hardly credit the whole tale, if such a rebellious spirit, native to man, had not left us its testimony. That fine old story, 'Imtheacht na Tromdháimhe', is part of that testimony. In it we find the bards, their poems, their literary language, their pride, their whims, all mocked and brought to nothing in loud laughter. One wonders if the Gael ever made any other story so racy of himself. It is more Gaelic than 'Deirdre', for that story, in common with the tale of Troy, and indeed every other great tragedy ever written, has for its chapters – Beauty, Desire, Love, Death – moves, that is to say, in the vast yet simple regions of man's heart, and not amid the ramifications of his institutions: with these comedy nurtures itself, later to exhibit itself most surprisingly and most takingly when, with malicious relish, with a smacking of the lips, it has swallowed down and digested these same institutions. Comic satire coming fully home only to those who are acquainted with the mode of life (and letters) that is laughed at, we savour the rich marrow of this witty tale of Guaire the Generous only inasmuch as we have made our own of the institutions of the Gael. Here are Kings and petty Kings. Here are Hermits and Saints. Here is the College of Bards, or rather one College of Bards, processioning from Court to Court, breaking those they feed upon. Here are Harpers, Timpanists, Story-tellers, and the obligations of *geasa*. And above all, here is the Gael's dread of satire – that trait which is over all our literature and history. The comic spirit had gulped them all down, had smacked its lips over them, before this tale emerged from its brain, so cruel yet so wise. The story, then, is of the nature of that literature that does not arise among a people until that people has institutionalized its manners and customs. It is a comedy of manners; it is, with the vast difference that constantly surprises us when we try to equate the Gaelic world with the European, it is our *'Les Précieuses Ridicules'*, it is our *'Les Femmes Savantes'*. Lustier, as befits an early tale, than these, its action moving across whole countrysides instead of within ladies' chambers, rougher even, it is for all that essentially the same in theme – satire not on culture, not on poetry, but on pedantry, on the mechanics of culture, inasmuch as these threaten to kill culture's real self. 'It is a satire upon the satirists, and is severe enough to have produced the traditional "three blisters of reproach" on the faces of the entire Bardic Assembly.'[27] There must have been many such tales; every age must have fashioned its own variation, and every countryside must have had its own favourite among them; and one is glad of it all; for because of it we may know how alive those bardic schools were, how deep their foundations, how beloved of the people, for, as Turgenev, who was never wrong in his reading of the heart, pointed out, we laugh at those we love.

To make an end: The bardic school, snug in a quiet glen, was clustered about a poet, who was bard to a provincial King or to a King of one of the hundred States into which the land was divided. To the school students gathered in the autumn, coming from far distances. They brought their local dialect with them, to be weaned from it, in time, and made adept in the literary language that all the scholarship of Ireland was preserved in. The head teacher often accompanied his patron on his visits to the Kings of the other States, and on such journeys the flock of students followed him, meeting other Colleges of Bards in debate and in rivalry. Everywhere they went they found the self-same literary language awaiting them, and they knew that the treasures of that language, the sagas, the later romances, the Ossianic poems, the mass of bardic poems, the genealogies, the official history, would be as familiar to the other students they fell in with as they were to themselves. And since the learned classes sat at the same table as the Kings and nobles, and since those Kings and nobles had themselves, in all probability, gone through the schools, the discussions on literature, on poetry, on history, were not, we may be sure, confined alone to the students and professors. The number of such schools was large, the number of professors large, great their pride of place, ample their privileges, honourably esteemed their work, lavishly rewarded. And the endeavour, undestroyed, hardly interrupted by the wars or the forays, went on and on for

41

hundreds and hundreds of years. If a great literary tradition did not result, so widespread that in course of time it must have touched every active, every unclouded mind in the community – if this did not result, then the whole endeavour was but an expense of spirit in a waste of shame – a thought that is unthinkable.

## Notes

1. Alice Stopford Green, *Irish National Tradition*.
2. 'At this period [9th century], whatever may have been their literary attainments, they were more remarkable for a bold independence of mind, a curiosity, activity, and vigour of thought, which contrasted strongly with the genius of Bede and Raban.' Newman, *The Benedictine Centuries*. (It did not strike him to ask how these Irishmen had come by this intellectual dexterity.)
3. Professor Bergin, 'Bardic Poetry' in *Ivernian Journal*, April–June, 1913, v, 19.
4. However that may be, there grew up in several of these cities schools for the study of law. That at Bologna was made famous by the greatest of these early teachers, Irnerius (1067–1138), in the same manner that Abelard raised Paris to distinction, and large numbers of students collected here. Thus Bologna became a centre for study, and as these students and teachers were given privileges, it became the first organized university. Monroe, *A Text Book in the History of Education.*
5. *The Bardic Poems of Tadhg Dall Ó Huiginn*, I, edited by E. Knott, Irish Texts Society. (In *Studies*, March 1924, Professor Bergin gives a fine translation of the whole of this moving and beautiful poem.)
6. See the introduction by Professor Robin Flower to Professor T.F. O'Rahilly's 'Dánta Grádha'.
7. Cf. *Bardic Poems of Tadhg Dall Ó Huiginn*, I.
8. O'Donovan's words are: 'They discharged the functions and wielded the influence of the modern newspaper and periodical press.'
9. Bergin, 'Bardic Poetry', *op. cit.*
10. Douglas Hyde, *Irish Poetry.*
11. E.C. Quiggin, *Prolegomena to the Study of the Later Irish Bards.*
12. Douglas Hyde, *Irish Poetry.*
13. Eleanor Hull, *A Text Book of Irish Literature.*
14. Eoin MacNeill, *Phases of Irish History.*
15. E.C. Quiggin, *ibid.*
16. Eleanor Hull, *ibid.*
17. Eleanor Hull, *ibid.*
18. Eoin MacNeill, *op. cit.*
19. 'Description of Ireland' (1587), quoted by Professor Curtis in *Studies*, June, 1919.
20. E.C. Quiggin, *op. cit.*
21. Bergin, 'Bardic Poetry', *op. cit.*
22. Preface by Professor Bergin to *Aonghus Ó Dálaigh*, by Fr MacKenna.
23. Edited and translated by Bergin, *Irish Review*, April 1913.
24. Douglas Hyde, *op. cit.*
25. Edited and translated by Bergin, *Irish Review*, January, 1913.
26. Cf. *Studies*, December, 1918.
27. See *Guaire*, the modernized version of the Tale.

# 2

# THE GODODDIN POEMS

## ANEURIN
### from *The Four Ancient Books of Wales*
### by William F. Skene

This is the 'Gododdin'. Aneurin composed it.

### I

Of manly disposition was the youth,
Valour had he in the tumult;
Fleet thick-maned chargers
Were under the thigh of the illustrious youth;
A shield, light and broad,
Was on the slender swift flank,
A sword, blue and bright,
Golden spurs, and ermine.
It is not by me
That hatred shall be shown to thee;
I will do better towards thee,
To celebrate thee in poetic eulogy.
Sooner hadst thou gone to the bloody bier
Than to the nuptial feast;
Sooner hadst thou gone to be food for ravens
Than to the conflict of spears;
Thou beloved friend of Owain!
Wrong it is that he should be under ravens.
It is evident in what region
The only son of Marro was killed.

### II

Caeawg, the leader, wherever he came,
Breathless in the presence of a maid would he distribute the mead;

The front of his shield was pierced, when he heard
The shout of battle, he would give no quarter wherever he pursued;
He would not retreat from the combat, until he caused
Blood to stream; like rushes would he hew down the men who would
    not yield.
The Gododdin does not relate, in the land of Mordai,
Before the tents of Madawg, when he returned,
Of but one man in a hundred that came back.

### III

Caeawg, the combatant, the stay of his country,
Whose attack is like the rush of the eagle into the sea, when allured by
    his prey;
He formed a compact, his signal was observed;
Better was his resolution performed: he retreated not
Before the host of Gododdin, at the close of day.
With confidence he pressed upon the conflict of Manawyd;
And regarded neither spear nor shield.
There is not to be found a habitation that abounded in dainties,
That has been kept from the attack of the warriors.

### IV

Caeawg, the leader, the wolf of the strand,
Amber wreaths encircled his brow;
Precious was the amber, worth wine from the horn.
He repelled the violence of ignoble men, and blood trickled down;
For Gwynedd and the North would have come to his share,
By the advice of the son of Ysgyrran,
Who wore the broken shield.

### V

Caeawg, the leader, armed was he in the noisy conflict;
His was the foremost part of the advanced division, in front of the hosts.
Before his blades fell five battalions.
Of the men of Deivyr and Brenneich, uttering groans:
Twenty hundred perished in one hour.
Sooner did his flesh go to the wolf, than he to the nuptial feast;
He sooner became food for the raven, than approached the altar;
Before he entered the conflict of spears, his blood streamed to the
    ground.
It was the price of mead in the hall, amidst the throng.
Hyveidd Hir shall be celebrated as long as there will be a minstrel.

### VI

The men went to Gododdin with laughter and sprightliness,
Bitter were they in the battle, displaying their blades;
A short year they remained in peace.

The son of Bodgad, by the energy of his hand, caused a throbbing.
Though they went to churches to do penance,
The old, and the young, and the bold-handed,
The inevitable strife of death was to pierce them.

## VII

The men went to Gododdin, laughing as they moved:
A gloomy disaster befell their army;
Thou slayest them with blades, without much noise:
Thou, powerful pillar of living right, causest stillness.

## VIII

The men went to Catraeth, loquacious was their host;
Fresh mead was their feast, and also their poison.
Three hundred were contending with weapons;
And after sportive mirth, stillness ensued!
Though they went to churches to do penance,
The inevitable strife of death was to pierce them.

## IX

The men went to Catraeth, fed with mead, and drunk.
Firm and vigorous; it were wrong if I neglected to praise them.
Around the red, mighty, and murky blades
Obstinately and fiercely fought the dogs of war.
If I had judged you to be on the side of the tribe of Brenneich,
Not the phantom of a man would I have left alive.
A friend I have lost, myself being unhurt;
He openly opposed the terrible chief –
The magnanimous hero did not seek the dowry of his father-in-law;
The son of Cian of Maen Gwyngwn.

## X

The men went to Catraeth with the dawn;
They dealt peaceably with those who feared them.
A hundred thousand and three hundred engaged in mutual overthrow.
Drenched in gore they served as butts for lances;
Their post they most manfully defended
Before the retinue of Mynyddawg Mwynvawr.

## XI

The men went to Catraeth with the dawn;
Regretted are their absence and their disposition;
Mead they drank, yellow, sweet, ensnaring.
In that year many a minstrel fell.
Redder were their swords than their plumes.
Their blades were white as lime, their helmets split into four parts,
Before the retinue of Mynyddawg Mwynvawr.

## XII

The men went to Catraeth with the day:
Have not the best of battles their disgrace?
They made biers a matter of necessity.
With blades full of vigour in defence of Baptism.
This is best before the alliance of kindred.
Exceedingly great was the bloodshed and death, of which they were the
    cause,
Before the army of Gododdin, when the day occurred.
Is not a double quantity of discretion the best strengthener of a hero?

## XIII

The man went to Catraeth with the day:
Truly he quaffed the foaming mead on serene nights;
He was unlucky, though proverbially fortunate:
His mission, through ambition, was that of a destroyer.
There hastened not to Catraeth
A chief so magnificent
As to his design on the standard.
Never was there such a host
From the fort of Eiddyn,
That would scatter abroad the mounted ravagers.
Tudvwlch Hir, near his land and towns,
Slaughtered the Saxons for seven days.
His valour remained until he was overpowered;
And his memory will remain among his fair associates.
When Tudvwlch, the supporter of the land, arrived,
The station of the son of Cilydd became a plain of blood.

## XIV

The man went to Catraeth with the dawn;
To them were their shields a protection.
Blood they sought, the gleamers assembled:
Simultaneously, like thunder, arose the din of shields.
The man of envy, the deserter, and the base,
He would tear and pierce with pikes.
From an elevated position, he slew, with a blade,
In iron affliction, a steel-clad commander;
He subdued in Mordai those that owed him homage;
Before Erthgi armies groaned.

## XV

Of the battle of Catraeth, when it shall be related,
The people will utter sighs; long has been their sorrow.
There will be a dominion without a sovereign, and a murky land.
The sons of Godebawg, an upright clan,
Bore, streaming, long biers.

Sad was the fate, just the necessity,
Decreed to Tudvwlch and Cyvwlch Hir.
Together they drank the clear mead
By the light of the rushes,
Though pleasant to the taste, its banefulness lasted long.

## XVI

Before Echeching, the splendid Caer, he shouted:
Young and forward men followed him;
Before, on the Bludwe the horn was poured out
In the joyful Mordai;
Before, his drink would be bragget;
Before, gold and rich purple he would display;
Before, high-fed horses would bear him safe away;
Gwrthlev and he, when he poured out the liquor,
Before, he would raise the shout, and there would be a profitable diminution;
He was a bear in his march, always unwilling to skulk.

## XVII

And now the early leader,
The sun is ascending,
The sovereign from which emanates universal light.
In the heaven of the Isle of Prydain.
Direful was the flight before the shaking
Of the shield in the direction of the victor;
Bright was the horn
In the hall of Eiddyn;
With pomp was he invited
To the feast of the intoxicating mead;
He drank the beverage of wine
At the meeting of the reapers;
He drank transparent wine,
With a daring purpose.
The reapers sing of war,
War with the shining wing;
The minstrels sang of war,
Of harnessed war,
Of winged war.
No shield was unexpanded
In the conflict of spears;
Of equal eye they fell
In the struggle of battle.
Unshaken in the tumult,
Without dishonour did he retaliate;
His will had to be conciliated
Ere became a green sward
The grave of Gwrvelling the great.

## XVIII

Qualities they will honour.
Three forward (chiefs or bands) of Novant,
A battalion of five hundred;
Three chiefs and three hundred;
There are three Knights of battle.
From Eiddyn, arrayed in golden armour,
Three loricated hosts.
Three Kings wearing the golden torques;
Three bold Knights.
Three equal battles;
Three of the same order, mutually jealous.
Bitterly would they chase the foe;
Three dreadful in the conflict;
Lions, that would kill dead as lead.
There was in the war a collection of gold;
Three sovereigns of the people.
Came from the Brython,
Cynri and Cenon
And Cynrain from Aeron,
To greet with ashen lances.
The Deivyr distillers.
Came there from the Brython,
A better man than Cynon,
A serpent to his sullen foes?

## XIX

I drank mead and wine in Mordai,
Great was the quantity of spears
In the assembly of the warriors.
He prepared food for the eagle.
When Cydywal sallied forth, he raised
The shout with the green dawn, and dealt out tribulation;
Splintered shields about the ground he left,
With darts of awful tearing did he hew down;
In the battle, the foremost in the van
The son of Syvno wounded; the astronomer knew it.
He who sold his life,
In the face of warning,
With sharpened blades committed slaughter;
But he himself was slain by crosses and spears.
According to the compact, he meditated an attack,
And admired a pile of carcases
Of gallant men of toil,
Whom in the upper part of Gwynedd he pierced.

## XX

I drank wine and mead in Mordai,
And because I drank, I fell by the side of the rampart; the fate of
    allurement.
Colwedd the brave was not without ambition.
When all fell, thou didst also fall.
Thus, when the issue comes, it were well if thou hadst not sinned.
Present, it was related, was a person of a daring arm.

## XXI

The men went to Catraeth; they were renowned;
Wine and mead from golden cups was their beverage;
That year was to them of exalted solemnity;
Three warriors and three score and three hundred, wearing the golden
    torques.
Of those who hurried forth after the excess of revelling,
But three escaped by the prowess of the gashing sword,
The two war-dogs of Aeron, and Cenon the dauntless,
And myself from the spilling of my blood, the reward of my sacred
    song.

## XXII

My friend in real distress, we should have been by none disturbed,
Had not the white Commander led forth (his army):
We should not have been separated in the hall from the banquet of
    mead,
Had he not laid waste our convenient position.
He who is base in the field, is base on the hearth.
Truly the Gododdin relates that after the gashing assault,
There was none more ardent than Llivieu.

## XXIII

Scattered, broken, of motionless form, is the weapon,
To which it was highly congenial to prostrate the horde of the Lloegrians.
Shields were strewn in the entrance, shields in the battle of lances;
He reduced men to ashes,
And made women widows,
Before his death.
Graid, the son of Hoewgi,
With spears,
He caused the effusion of blood.

## XXIV

Adan was the hero of the two shields
Whose front was variegated, and motion like that of a war-steed.
There was tumult in the mount of slaughter, there was fire,
Impetuous were the lances, there was sunshine,

There was food for ravens, for the raven there was profit.
And before he would let them go free,
With the morning dew, like the eagle in his pleasant course,
He scattered them on either side as they advanced forward.
The Bards of the world will pronounce an opinion on men of valour.
No ransom would avail those whom his standard pursued.
The spears in the hands of the warriors were causing devastation.
And ere was interred under his horses,
One who had been energetic in his commands,
His blood had thoroughly washed his armour:
Buddvan, the son of Bleiddvan the Bold.

## XXV

It were wrong to leave him without a memorial, a great wrong.
He would not leave an open gap through cowardice;
The benefit of the minstrels of Prydain never quitted his court.
On the calends of January, according to his design.
His land was not ploughed, since it lay waste.
He was a mighty dragon of indignant disposition,
A commander in the bloody field after the banquet of wine; –
Gwenabwy, the son of Gwen, of the strife of Catraeth.

## XXVI

True it was, as songs relate,
No one's steed overtook Marchleu.
The lances of the commander
From his prancing horse, strewed a thick path.
As he was reared to bring slaughter and support.
Furious was the stroke of his protecting sword;
Ashen shafts were scattered from the grasp of his hand.
From the stony pile;
He delighted to spread destruction.
He would slaughter with a variegated sword from a furze-bush;
As when a company of reapers comes in the interval of fine weather,
Would Marchleu cause the blood to flow.

## XXVII

Issac was sent from the southern region;
His conduct resembled the flowing sea;
He was full of modesty and gentleness,
When he delightfully drank the mead.
But along the rampart of Offer to the point of Maddeu,
He was not fierce without heroism, nor did he attempt scattering without
    effecting it,
His sword resounded in the mouths of mothers;
He was an ardent spirit, praise be to him, the son of Gwyddneu.

## XXVIII

Ceredig, lovely is his fame;
He would gain distinction, and preserve it;
Gentle, lowly, calm, before the day arrived
In which he learned the achievements of the brave:
May it be the lot of the friend of songs to arrive
In the country of heaven, and recognize his home!

## XXIX

Ceredig, amiable leader,
A wrestler in the impetuous fight;
His gold-bespangled shield was conspicuous on the battle-field,
His lances were broken, and shattered into splinters,
The stroke of his sword was fierce and penetrating;
Like a man would he maintain his post.
Before he received the affliction of earth, before the fatal blow.
He had fulfilled his in guarding his station.
May he find a complete reception
With the Trinity in perfect unity.

## XXX

When Caradawg rushed to battle,
Like the woodland boar was the gash of the hewer;
He was the bull of battle in the conflicting fight;
He allured wild dogs with his hand.
My witnesses are Owain the son of Eulad,
And Gwryen, and Gwyn, and Gwryad.
From Catraeth, from the conflict,
From Bryn Hydwn, before it was taken,
After having clear mead in his hand,
Gwrien did not see his father.

## XXXI

The men marched with speed, together they bounded onward;
Short-lived were they – having become drunk over the clarified mead.
The retinue of Mynyddawg, renowned in a trial,
Their life was the price of their banquet of mead; –
Caradawg and Madawg, Pyll and Ieuan,
Gwgawn and Gwiawn, Gwyn and Cynvan,
Peredur with steel arms, Gwawrddur and Aeddan.
A defence were they in the tumult, though with shattered shields,
When they were slain, they also slaughtered;
Not one to his native home returned.

## XXXII

The men marched with speed, together were they regaled
That year over mead; great was their design:

How sad to mention them! how grievous the longing for them!
Their retreat was poison; no mother's son nurses them.
How long the vexation and how long the regret for them –
For the brave men of the wine-fed region!
Gwlyged of Gododdin, having partaken of the inciting
Banquet of Mynyddawg, performed illustrious deeds,
And dear was the price he gave for the purchase of the conflict of
    Catraeth.

### XXXIII

The men went to Catraeth in battle-array and with shout of war,
With the strength of steeds, and with dark-brown harness, and with
    shields,
With uplifted javelins, and sharp lances,
With glittering mail, and with swords.
He excelled, he penetrated through the host,
Five battalions fell before his blade;
Ruvawn Hir, – he gave gold to the altar,
And gifts and precious stones to the minstrel.

### XXXIV

No hall was ever made so loquacious, –
So great, so magnificent for the slaughter.
Morien procured and spread the fire,
He would not say that Cenon would not make a corpse
Of one harnessed, armed with a pike, and of wide-spread fame.
His sword resounded on the top of the rampart.
No more than a huge stone can be removed from its fixed place
Will Gwid, the son of Peithan, be moved.

### XXXV

No hall was ever so full of delegates:
Had not Moryen been like Caradawg,
With difficulty could he have escaped towards Mynawg.
Fierce, he was fiercer than the son of Fferawg;
Stout was his hand, he set flames to the retreating horsemen.
Terrible in the city was the cry of the multitude;
The van of the army of Gododdin was scattered;
In the day of wrath he was nimble – and was he not destructive in
    retaliating?
The dependants of Mynyddawg deserved their horns of mead.

### XXXVI

No hall was ever made so immovable
As that of Cynon of the gentle breast, sovereign of valuable treasures.
He sat no longer at the upper end of the high seat.
Those whom he pierced were not pierced again;

Sharp was the point of his lance;
With his enamelled armour he penetrated through the troops;
Swift in the van were the horses, in the van they tore along.
In the day of wrath, destruction attended his blade,
When Cynon rushed forward with the green dawn.

### XXXVII

A grievous descent was made on his native place;
He repelled aggression, he fixed a boundary;
His spear forcibly pushed the laughing chiefs of war:
Even as far as Effyd reached his valour, which was like that of Elphin;
Eithinyn the renowned, an ardent spirit, the bull of conflict.

### XXXVIII

A grievous descent was made on his native place,
The price of mead in the hall, and the feast of wine;
His blades were scattered about between two armies,
Illustrious was the knight in front of Gododdin.
Eithinyn the renowned, an ardent spirit, the bull of conflict.

### XXXIX

A grievous descent was made in front of the extended riches;
The army dispersed with trailing shields. –
A shivered shield before the herd of the roaring Beli.
A dwarf from the bloody field hastened to the fence;
On our part there came a hoary-headed man to take counsel.
On a prancing steed, bearing a message from the golden-torqued leader.
Twrch proposed a compact in front of the destructive course:
Worthy was the shout of refusal;
We cried, 'Let heaven be our protection;
Let his compact be that he should be prostrated by the spear in battle.'
The warriors of the far-famed Aclud
Would not contend without prostrating his host to the ground.

### XL

For the piercing of the skilful and most learned man,
For the fair corpse which fell prostrate on the ground,
For the falling of the hair from off his head,
From the grandson of the eagle of Gwydien,
Did not Gwyddwg defend with his spear,
Resembling and honouring his master?
Morieu of the sacred song defended
The wall, and deposed the head
Of the chief in the ground, both our support and our sovereign
Equal to three men, to please the maid, was Bradwen,
Equal to twelve was Gwenabwy the son of Gwen.

## XLI

For the piercing of the skilful and most learned man,
He bore a shield in the action;
With energy did the stroke of his sword fall on the head.
In Lloegyr he caused gashings before three hundred chieftains.
He who takes hold of a wolf's mane without a club
In his hand, must naturally have a brave disposition under his cloak.
In the engagement of wrath and carnage
Bradwen perished – he did not escape.

## XLII

A man moved rapidly on the wall of the Caer,
He was of a warlike disposition; neither a house nor a city was actively
    engaged in battle.
One weak man, with his shouts,
Endeavoured to keep off the birds of battle.
Surely Syll of Mirein relates that there were more
That had chanced to come from Llwy,
From around the inlet of the flood;
Surely he relates that there were more
At an early hour,
Equal to Cynhaval in merit.

## XLIII

When thou, famous conqueror!
Wast protecting the ear of corn in the uplands
Deservedly were we said to run like men of mark.
The entrance to Din Drei was not guarded.
Such as was fond of treasure took it;
There was a city for the army that should venture to enter.
Gwynwyd was not called, where he was not.

## XLIV

Since there are a hundred men in one house,
I know the cares of distress.
The chief of the men must pay the contribution.

## XLV

I am not headstrong and petulant.
I will not avenge myself on him who drives me.
I will not laugh in derision.
Under foot for a while,
My knee is stretched,
My hands are bound,
In the earthen house,
With an iron chain
Around my two knees.

Yet of the mead from the horn,
And of the men of Catraeth,
I, Aneurin, will compose,
As Taliesin knows,
An elaborate song,
Or a strain to Gododdin,
Before the dawn of the brightest day.

## XLVI

The chief exploit of the North did the hero accomplish;
Of a generous breast was he, liberal is his progeny;
There does not walk upon the earth, mother has not borne.
Such an illustrious, powerful, iron-clad warrior.
By the force of the gleaming sword he protected me,
From the dismal earthen prison he brought me out,
From the place of death, from a hostile region: –
Ceneu, the son of Llywarch, energetic, bold.

## XLVII

He would not bear the reproach of a congress,
Senyllt, with his vessels full of mead;
He enriched his sword with deeds of violence;
He enriched those who rushed to war;
And with his arm made pools (of blood).
In front of the armies of Gododdin and Brennych.
Fleet horses were customary in his hall.
There was streaming gore, and dark-brown harness.
A long stream of light there was from his hand.
And like a hunter shooting with the bow
Was Gwen; and the attacking parties mutually repulsed each other,
Friend and foe by turns;
The men did not cut their way to flee,
But they were the general defenders of every region.

## XLVIII

Llech Lleutu and Tud Lleudvre,
The course of Gododdin,
The course of Ragno, close at hand,
The hand that was director of the splendour of battle,
With the branch of Caerwys.
Before it was shattered
By the season of the storm, by the storm of the season,
To form a rank in front of myriads of men,
Coming from Dindywydd,
Excited with rage,
Deeply did they design,
Sharply did they pierce,

Wholly did the host chant,
Battered was their shield;
Before the bull of conflict
Their van was broken.

## XLIX

His languid foes trembled greatly,
Since the battle of most active tumult,
At the border of Banceirw,
Around the border of Bancarw;
The fingers of Brych will break the bar,
For Pwyll, for Disteir, for Distar,
For Pwyll, for Roddig, for Rychwardd,
A strong bow was spent by Rys in Riwdrech.
They that were not bold did not attain their purpose;
None escaped that was once overtaken and pierced.

## L

It was no good deed that his shield should be pierced.
On the side of his horse;
Not meetly did he place his thigh
On the long-legged, slender, gray charger.
Dark was his shaft, dark,
Darker was his saddle.
Thy man is in his cell,
Gnawing the shoulder of a buck;
May he have the benefit of his hand!
Far be he!

## LI

It was well that Adonwy came to Gwen;
Gwen was left without Bradwen.
Thou didst fight, kill, and burn,
Thou didst not do worse than Moryen;
Thou didst not regard the rear or the van.
Of the towering figure without a helmet.
Thou didst not observe the great swelling sea of knights.
That would hew down, and grant no quarter to the Saxons.

## LII

Gododdin, in respect of thee will I demand
The dales beyond the ridges of Drum Essyd.
The slave to the love of money is without self-control.
By the counsel of thy son let thy valour shine forth.
It was not a degrading advice.
In front of Tan Veithin,
From twilight to twilight, the edge gleamed.

Glittering exterior had the purple of the pilgrim.
Gwaws, the defenceless, the delight of the bulwark of battle, was
     slain.
His scream was inseparable from Aneurin.

### LIII

Together arise the associated warriors,
To Catraeth the loquacious multitude eagerly march;
The effect of mead in the hall, and the beverage of wine.
Blades were scattered between the two armies.
Illustrious was the knight in front of Gododdin: –
Eithinyn the renowned, an ardent spirit, the bull of conflict.

### LIV

Together arise the associated warriors,
Strangers to the country, their deeds shall be heard of.
The bright wave murmured along on its pilgrimage,
While the young deer were in full melody.
Among the spears of Brych thou couldst see no rods.
Merit does not accord with the rear.
Moryal in pursuit will not countenance evil deeds,
With his steel blade ready for the effusion of blood.

### LV

Together arise the associated warriors.
Strangers to the country, their deeds shall be heard of.
There was slaughtering with axes and blades,
And there was raising large cairns over the men of toil.

### LVI

Together arise the warriors, together met,
And all with one accord sallied forth;
Short were their lives, long is the grief of those who loved them.
Seven times their number of Lloegrians they had slain;
After the conflict women raised a lamentation;
Many a mother has the tear on her eyelash.

### LVII

No hall was ever made so faultless
Nor a hero so generous, with the aspect of a lion of the greatest
     course,
As Cynon of the gentle breast, the most comely lord.
The city, its fame extends to the remotest parts;
It was the staying shelter of the army, the benefit of flowing melody.
In the world, engaged in arms, the battle-cry,
And war, the most heroic was he;
He slew the mounted ravagers with the sharpest blade;

Like rushes did they fall before his hand.
Son of Clydno, of lasting fame! I will sing
To thee a song of praise without limit, without end.

## LVIII

From the banquet of wine and mead
They deplored the death
Of the mother of Hwrreith.
The energetic Eidiol.
Honoured her in front of the hill,
And before Buddugre,
The hovering ravens
Ascend in the sky.
The foremost spearmen fall
Like a virgin-swarm around him
Without the semblance of a retreat
Warriors in wonder shook their javelins,
With pallid lips,
Caused by the keenness of the destructive sword.
Wakeful was the carousal at the beginning of the banquet;
To-day sleepless is
The mother of Reiddun, the leader of the tumult.

## LIX

From the banquet of wine and mead
They went to the strife
Of mail-clad warriors: I know no tale of slaughter which accords
So complete a destruction as has happened.
Before Catraeth, loquacious was the host.
Of the retinue of Mynyddawg, the unfortunate hero,
Out of three hundred but one man returned.

## LX

From the banquet of wine and mead they hastened,
Men renowned in difficulty, careless of their lives;
In bright array around the viands they feasted together;
Wine and mead and meal they enjoyed.
From the retinue of Mynyddawg I am being ruined;
And I have lost a leader from among my true friends.
Of the body of three hundred men that hastened to
Catraeth, alas! none have returned but one alone.

## LXI

Pressent, in the combat of spears, was impetuous as a ball,
And on his horse would he be, when not at home;
Yet illusive was his aid against Gododdin.
Of wine and mead he was lavish;

He perished on the course;
And under red-stained warriors
Are the steeds of the knight, who in the morning had been bold.

## LXII

Angor, thou who scatterest the brave,
Like a serpent thou piercest the sullen ones,
Thou tramplest upon those that are clad in strong mail
In front of the army:
Like an enraged bear, guarding and assaulting,
Thou tramplest upon spears.
In the day of conflicts
In the swampy entrenchment:
Like Neddig Nar,
Who in his fury prepared
A feast for the birds,
In the tumultuous fight.
Upright thou art called from thy righteous deed,
Before the director and bulwark of the course of war,
Merin, and Madyen, it is fortunate that thou wert born.

## LXIII

It is incumbent to sing of the complete acquisition
Of the warriors, who around Catraeth made a tumultuous rout.
With confusion and blood, treading and trampling.
The strength of the drinking horn was trodden down, because it had
    held mead;
And as to the carnage of the interposers
Cibno does not relate, after the commencement of the action.
Since thou hast received the communion thou shalt be interred.

## LXIV

It is incumbent to sing of so much renown,
The loud noise of fire, and of thunder, and of tempest,
The noble manliness of the knight of conflict.
The ruddy reapers of war are thy desire,
Thou man of might! but the worthless wilt thou behead,
In battle the extent of the land shall hear of thee.
With thy shield upon thy shoulder thou dost incessantly cleave
With thy blade (until blood flows) like refined wine from glass vessels.
As money for drink, thou art entitled to gold.
Wine-nourished was Gwaednerth, the son of Llywri.

## LXV

It is incumbent to sing of the illustrious retine,
That, after the fatal impulse, filled Aeron.
Their hands satisfied the mouths of the brown eagles,

And prepared food for the beasts of prey.
Of those who went to Catraeth, wearing the golden torques,
Upon the message of Mynyddawg, sovereign of the people,
There came not without reproach on behalf of the Brython,
To Gododdin, a man from afar better than Cynon.

## LXVI

It is incumbent to sing of so skilful a man;
Joyous was he in the hall; his life was not without ambition;
Bold, all around the world would Eidol seek for melody;
For gold, and fine horses, and intoxicating mead.
Only one man of those who loved the world returned, –
Cynddilig of Aeron, the grandson of Enovant.

## LXVII

It is incumbent to sing of the illustrious retinue
That went on the message of Mynyddawg, sovereign of the people,
And the daughter of Eudav Hir, the scourge of Gwananhon,
Who was appareled in purple robes, certain to cause manglings.

## LXVIII

The warriors celebrated the praise of Nyved,
When in their presence fire was lighted.
On Tuesday, they put on their dark-brown garments;
On Wednesday, they polished their enamelled armour;
On Thursday, their destruction was certain;
On Friday, was brought carnage all around:
On Saturday, their joint labour did no execution;
On Sunday, their blades assumed a ruddy hue;
On Monday, was seen a pool knee-deep of blood.
Truly, the Gododdin relates that, after the toil,
Before the tents of Madawg, when he returned,
Only one man in a hundred came back.

## LXIX

Early rising in the morn
There was a conflict at the Aber in front of the course,
The pass and the knoll were in conflagration.
Like a boar didst thou lead to the mount,
There was treasure for him that was fond of it; there was room;
And there was the blood of dark-brown hawks.

## LXX

Early rising in an instant of time,
After kindling a fire at the Aber in front of the fence,
After leading his men in close array,
In front of a hundred he pierced the foremost.

It was sad that you should have caused a gushing of blood,
Like the drinking of mead in the midst of laughter.
It was brave of you to stay the little man
With the fierce and impetuous stroke of the sword.
How irresistible was he when he would kill
The foe! would that his equal could be found!

## LXXI

He fell headlong down the precipice;
Song did not support his noble head:
It was a violation of privilege to kill him when bearing the branch,
It was the usage that Owain should ascend upon the course,
And extend, before the onset, the best branch,
And that he should pursue the study of meet and learned strains.
An excellent man was he, the assuager of tumult and battle,
His grasp dreaded a sword;
In his hand he bore an empty corselet.
O sovereign, dispense rewards
Out of his precious shrine.
Eidol, with frigid blood and pallid countenance,
Spreading carnage, his judgment was just and supreme,
Owner of horses
And strong trappings,
And ice-like shields;
Instantaneously he makes an onset, ascending and descending.

## LXXII

The leader of war with eagerness conducts the battle,
A mighty country loves mighty reapers.
Blood is a heavy return for new mead.
His cheeks are covered with armour all around,
There is a trampling of accoutrements – accoutrements are trampled.
He calls for death and brings desolation.
In the first onset his lances penetrate the targets,
And for light on the course, shrubs blaze on the spears.

## LXXIII

A conflict on all sides destroyed thy cell;
And a hall there was to thee, where used to be poured out
Mead, sweet and ensnaring.
Gwrys make the battle clash with the dawn;
The fair gift of the tribes of the Lloegrians;
Punishment he inflicted until a reverse came.
May the dependants of Gwynedd hear of his renown.
Gwananhon will be his grave.
The lance of the conflict of Gwynedd,
The bull of the host, the oppressor of sovereigns,

Before earth pressed upon him, before he lay down;
Be the extreme boundary of Gododdin his grave!

## LXXIV

An army is accustomed to be in hardships.
Mynawg, the bitter-handed leader of the forces,
He was wise, ardent, and stately:
At the social banquet he was not at all harsh.
They removed the valuable treasures that were in his possession:
And not the image of anything for the benefit of the region was left.
We are called! Like the sea is the tumult in the conflict;
Spears are mutually darting – spears all equally destructive;
Impelled are sharp weapons of iron, gashing even the ground,
And with a clang the sock falls on the pate.
A successful warrior was Fflamddur against the enemy.

## LXXV

He supported war-horses and war-harness.
Drenched with gore on red-stained Catraeth
Is the shaft of the army of Dinus,
The angry dog of war upon the towering hill.
We are called to the honourable post of assault;
Most conspicuous is the iron-clad Heiddyn.

## LXXVI

Mynawg of the impregnable strand of Gododdin,
Mynawg, for him our cheeks are sad:
Before the raging flame of Eiddyn he turned not aside.
He stationed men of firmness at the entrance,
He placed a thick covering in the van,
Vigorously he descended upon the furious foe;
He caused devastation and sustained great weight.
Of the retinue of Mynyddawg there escaped none
Except one frail weapon, tottering every way.

## LXXVII

Since the loss of Moryed there was no shield-bearer,
To support the strand, or to set the ground on fire;
Firmly did he grasp in his hand a blue blade,
A shaft ponderous as a chief priest's crozier;
He rode a gray stately-headed courser,
And behind his blade there was a dreadful fall of slaughter;
When overpowered, he did not run away from the battle.
He poured out to us sparkling mead, sweet and ensnaring.

## LXXVIII

I beheld the array from the high land of Adoyn;

They descended with the sacrifice for the conflagration;
I saw what was usual, a continual running to the town,
And the men of Nwythyon entirely lost;
I saw men in complete order approaching with a shout;
And the heads of Dyvynwal and Breych, ravens devoured them.

## LXXIX

Blessed conqueror, of temper mild, the bone of the people,
With his blue streamer displayed, while the foes range the sea.
Brave is he on the waters, most numerous his host;
With a bold breast and loud shout they pierced him.
It was his custom to make a descent before nine armaments,
In the face of blood, of the country, and of the tribes.
I love the victor's throne which was for harmonious strains,
Cynddilig of Aeron, the lion's whelp!

## LXXX

I could wish to have been the first to fall in Catraeth,
As the price of mead in the hall, and the beverage of wine;
I could wish to have been pierced by the blade,
Ere he was slain on the green plain of Uffin.
I loved the son of renown, who caused blood to flow,
And made his sword descend upon the violent.
Can a tale of valour before Gododdin be related,
In which the son of Ceidiaw has not his fame as a man of war?

## LXXXI

It is sad for me, after our toil,
To suffer the pang of death through indiscretion;
And doubly grievous and sad for me to see
Our men falling from head to foot,
With a long sigh and with reproaches.
After the strenuous warriors of our native land and country,
Ruvawn and Gwgawn, Gwiawn and Gwlyged,
Men most gallant at their posts, valiant in difficulties,
May their souls, now after the conflict,
Be received into the country of heaven, the abode of tranquillity.

## LXXXII

He repelled the chain through a pool of blood,
He slaughtered like a hero such as asked no quarter.
With a sling and a spear; he flung off his glass goblet
Of mead; in the presence of sovereigns he overthrew an army.
His counsel prevailed wherever he spoke.
A multitude that had no pity would not be allowed
Before the onset of his battle-axes and sword;
Sharpened they were; and his sounding blade was carefully watched.

## LXXXIII

A supply of an army,
A supply of lances,
And a host in the vanguard,
With a menacing front:
In the day of strenuous exertion,
In the eager conflict,
They displayed their valour.
After intoxication,
And the drinking of mead,
There was no deliverance.
They watched us
For a while;
When it shall be related how the attack
Of horses and men was repelled, it will be pronounced the decree of fate.

## LXXXIV

Why should so much anxiety come to me?
I am anxious about the maid –
The maid that is in Arddeg.
There is a precipitate running,
And lamentation along the course.
Affectionately have I deplored,
Deeply have I loved,
The illustrious dweller of the wood!
And the men of Argoed.
Woe to those who are accustomed
To be marshalled for battle!
He pressed hard upon the hostile force, for the benefit of chieftains,
Through rough woods,
And dammed-up waters,
To the festivities,
At which they caroused together: he conducted us to a bright fire,
And to a white and fresh hide.
Gereint from the south raised a shout;
A brilliant gleam reflected on the pierced shield.
Of the lord of the spear, a gentle lord;
Attached to the glory of the sea.
Posterity will accomplish
What Gereint would have done.
Generous and resolute wert thou!

## LXXXV

Instantaneously his fame is wafted on high,
Irresistible was Angor in the conflict,
Unflinching eagle of the forward heroes;
He bore the toil, brilliant was his zeal;

He outstripped fleetest horses in war;
But he was mild when the wine from the goblet flowed.
Before the new mead, and his cheek became pale,
He was a man of the banquet over delicious mead from the bowl.

## LXXXVI

With slaughter was every region filled;
His courage was like a fetter:
The front of his shield was pierced.
Disagreeable is the delay of the wrathful
To defend Rywoniawg.
The second time they raised the shout, and were crushed
By the war-horses with gory trappings.
An immovable army will his warlike nobles form,
And the field was reddened when he was greatly enraged.
Severe in the conflict, with a blade he slaughtered;
Sad news from the battle he brought;
And a New-year's song he composed.
Adan, the son of Ervai, there was pierced,
Adan! the haughty boar, was pierced,
One damsel, a maid, and a hero.
And when he was only a youth he had the rights of a king.
Being lord of Gwyndyd, of the blood of Glyd Gwaredawg.
Ere the turf was laid on the gentle face
Of the generous dead, now undisturbed,
He was celebrated for fame and generosity.
This is the grave of Garthwys Hir from the land of Rywoniawg.

## LXXXVII

The coat of Dinogad was of various colours,
And made of the speckled skins of young wolves.
'Whistle! whistle!' the juggling sound!
I fain would dispraise it; it is dispraised by eight slaves.
When thy father went out to hunt,
With his pole on his shoulder, and his provisions in his hand,
He would call to his dogs of equal size, –
'Catch it! catch it! seize it! seize it!'
He would kill a fish in his coracle,
As a noble lion kills (his prey).
When thy father went up to the mountain
He would bring back the head of a roebuck, the head of a wild boar, the
    head of a stag,
The head of a spotted moor-hen from the mountain,
The head of a fish from the falls of Derwennyd.
As many as thy father could reach with his flesh-hook,
Of wild boars, lions, and foxes.
None would escape except those that were too nimble.

## LXXXVIII

If distress were to happen to me through extortion,
There would not come, there would not be to me anything more
    calamitous.
No man has been nursed in a hall who could be braver
Than he, or steadier in battle.
And on the ford of Penclwyd his horses were the best;
Far-spread was his fame, compact his armour;
And before the long grass covered him beneath the sod,
He, the only son of Ffervarch, poured out the horns of mead.

## LXXXIX

I saw the array from the headland of Adoyn,
Carrying the sacrifice to the conflagration;
I saw the two who from their station quickly fell;
By the commands of Nwython greatly were they afflicted.
I saw the men, who made a great breach, with the dawn at Adoyn;
And the head of Dyvynwal Vrych, ravens devoured it.

## XC

Gododdin, in respect of thee will I demand
In the presence of a hundred that are named with deeds of valour.
And of Gwarchan, the son of Dwywei of gallant bravery,
Let it be forcibly seized in one region.
Since the stabbing of the delight of the bulwark of battle,
Since earth has gone upon Aneurin,
My cry has not been separated from Gododdin.

## XCI

Echo speaks of the formidable and dragon-like weapons,
And of the fair game which was played in front of the unclaimed course of
    Gododdin.
He brought a supply of wine into the tents of the natives,
In the season of the storm, when there were vessels on the sea,
When there was a host on the sea, a well-nourished host.
A splendid troop of warriors, successful against a myriad of men,
Is coming from Dindywydd n Dyvnwydd.
Before Doleu in battle, worn out were their shields, and battered their
    helmets.

## XCII

With slaughter was every region filled.
His courage was like a fetter;
The front of his shield was pierced.
Disagreeable is the delay of the brave
To defend Rywyniawg.
The second time they reposed, and were crushed

By the war-horses with gory trappings.
An immovable army will his warlike and brave nobles form,
When they are greatly affronted.
Severe in the conflict with blades he slaughtered;
Sad news from the battle he brought;
And an hundred New-years' songs he composed.
Adan, the son of Urvai, was pierced;
Adan, the haughty boar, was pierced;
One damsel, a maid, and a hero.
And when he was only a youth he had the rights of a king,
Lord of Gwyndyd, of the blood of Cilydd Gwaredawg
Ere the turf was laid on the face of the generous dead,
Wisely collected were his treasure, praise, and high-sounding fame.
The grave of Gorthyn Hir from the highlands of Rywynawg.

## XCIII

For the piercing of the skilful and most learned man,
For the fair corpse which fell prostrate on the ground,
Thrice six persons judged the atrocious deed early in the morning;
And Morien lifted up his ancient lance,
And, shouting, unbent his tight-drawn bow
Towards the Gwyr, and the Gwyddyl, and Prydein.
Towards the lovely, slender, bloodstained body
The sigh of Gwenabwy, the son of Gwen.

## XCIV

For the afflicting of the skilful and most learned man,
There was grief and sorrow, when he fell prostrate on the ground;
His banner showed his rank, and was borne by a man at his side.
A tumultuous scene was beheld in Eiddyn, and on the battle-field.
The grasp of his hand prevailed
Over the Gynt, and the Gwyddyl, and Pryden,
He who meddles with the mane of a wolf without a club in his hand,
He must naturally have a brave disposition under his cloak.
The sigh of Gwenabwy, the son of Gwen.

# 3

# Prolegomena to the Study of Old Welsh Poetry

## EDWARD ANWYL
### from *Transactions of the Honourable Society of Cymmrodorian*

IT WILL PROBABLY be readily admitted by those acquainted with Celtic studies that the most difficult subject in the sphere of Welsh literature is the critical interpretation and translation of the oldest Welsh poetry, and this is a problem of interest not only to Welshmen, but to a wider circle, as part of the larger question of the origins of the vernacular literature of Western Europe. The difficulty referred to is due in no small degree to the obsolete character of the vocabulary, but it is also due to the difficulty of correcting the text on the one hand, and that of classifying and interpreting the allusions to persons and places on the other. Much work has been done by students of Celtic in these various directions, but, in the absence of some short introductory treatment, the novice often fails to appreciate the problems for solution, and the significance of the various scattered pieces of research that are intended as answers to them. Further, the progress of these studies has been hampered in the past by an inadequate study of the historical grammar of the Welsh language, and of the peculiarities of the earlier syntactical constructions as distinguished from those of later times. The great work of Zeuss, though of abiding value, needs supplementing, especially on the poetical side of old Welsh grammar.

The present writer has given a preliminary statistical account of several of the older verbal forms in an Appendix to *Welshmen,* by the Rev. T. Stephens, but it would be well if all the grammatical forms could be similarly tabulated. Another important line of research which is indispensable to the elucidation of the older poetry, is a close study of the older prose remains of Welsh in order to determine, if possible, their structure, literary affinities, and topographical relations. The present writer has also contributed a preliminary discussion of some of these points, especially in relation to the 'Four Branches of the Mabinogi', to the *Zeitschrift für Celtische Philologie.* The present paper is a development of the same study, and is the outcome of a consideration of the inter-relations of the oldest prose and poetic writings of the Welsh people.

In dealing with these subjects, again, it has to be borne in mind that, whatever may be the origins of these forms of literature, they come to us in what may be termed a mediaeval dress. Just as the 'Four Branches of the Mabinogi' in their present form reflect the ideas of the Feudal System, so, too, many of the poems attributed to Taliesin and others reflect the monastic studies of the Middle Ages. Hence, in order to elucidate them, it is not necessary merely to guess at the underlying fragments of ancient mythology and legend, but also to study the medium through which these are presented. It is necessary, also, to form some idea of that conception of poetry and of the poet which made them possible. Celtic studies are here in special need of correlation on the literary side with researchers into the origins and early developments of the other literatures of Western Europe.

Again, apart from the comparison of Irish and Welsh literature, it is important that, as far as possible, the various stories commonly called 'Mabinogion', the older body of poetry, Gildas, the chronicle called 'Nennius' in its various recensions, the lives of the Welsh saints, and Geoffrey of Monmouth's *History of the Kings of Britain,* should be studied together. Along with these should also be closely investigated the oldest genealogies. These investigations may give us a clue to the families from whose spheres of influence portions of the older literature emanated, the districts where they were originally evolved, or to which they were transferred, and the probable literary centres of the ancient Welsh. Already very valuable and suggestive work in this direction has been done by Professor Zimmer in his *Nennius Vindicatus,* whereby he has brought into view the probable existence of old British or Welsh centres of literary activity in the North at Dumbarton or Carlisle, in Gwynedd, and in the Builth district.

In dealing with the old stories and old poems of Wales it is important to discover, wherever possible, the motives that appear to have led to their formation and development. It is from this point of view that the genealogies deserve careful study, in order to see what compositions may conceivably owe their origin to family or ecclesiastical pride. In the elucidation of the old genealogies a great debt of gratitude is due especially to Mr Egerton Phillimore and Mr Anscombe. A single name may at times prove an invaluable clue in these intricate and delicate researches.

The body of Welsh poetry here dealt with is commonly known as that of 'The Four Ancient Books of Wales', being *The Black Book of Carmarthen, The Book of Aneurin, The Book of Taliesin,* and *The Red Book of Hergest.* The interrelations of most of the poems contained in Skene's edition are sufficiently clear to reveal the fact that they represent in many respects a common tradition; nor does it require much research to show that, within the collection as a whole, there are various strata, which may often be distinguished with respect to their place of origin and their time of composition. The historical allusions, for example, of the 'Hoianau' poem (contained in the *Black Book of Carmarthen*) make it clear that it belongs to the twelfth century; while the orthography of 'Gorchan Maelderw' in the *Book of Aneurin* makes it quite clear that that poem, together with the analogous parts of the 'Gododdin', is earlier, at any rate, than the *Book of Llandav.* Again, the occasional lapses into an older mode of spelling, as in Poem xxiii of the *Book of Taliesin,* called 'Trawsganu Kynan Garwyn m. Brochwel Ysgythrog', where we have trefbret for trefret, pympönt for pymhönt, dymet for dyuet, suggest that the poem was copied from a manuscript in which the spelling was uniformly of an older type. Again, the reference in l. 885 of the 'Gododdin' to the death of Dyvynwal Vrych (Donald Brec), who died in 642, shows that the line, at any rate in the form there found, is subsequent to that date. Similarly, in l. 934 of the same poem, the reference to Gynt (= gentes, i.e. the Scandinavians) shows that, at least in that form, the line is subsequent to the Scandinavian incursions. We know, too, from the existence of a verse of the same series in an eleventh century MS. of St Augustine's 'De Trinitate', which is in the Library of Corpus Christi College, Cambridge, that verses of this same series of stanzas were known at that time. We have another instance in the *Book of Taliesin*. Even if we had no other reasons for forming that opinion, the existence of a reference to Bede in poem xvi, l. 38, would be a proof that the poem containing the reference was later than his time, that is, unless the line or the reference was interpolated. Again reverting to the 'Gododdin', the references to Elfin (l. 376) and to Beli (in l. 385) make it suspicious that they refer by an anachronism to Elfin, King of Alclud (Dumbarton), who died in 722 A.D., and to Beli his son. If this be so, then the other verses in praise of Eithinyn, such as those beginning 'Kywyrein ketwyr kywrennin' and those of corresponding characteristics, must have been written, at least, during the lifetime of Beli, the son. Moreover, it is obvious from the rhyme alone that all the old poems were composed after the old declensional and conjugational endings had been entirely lost.

If, again, we consider topographical allusions, we note that the numerous references to places in Powys and the neighbouring parts of England in the so-called 'Llywarch Hen' poems, make it highly probable that we have here a body of poetry which, in its nucleus and its imitators, flourished in the literary centres of Powys. A few allusions, such as those to Llyn Geirionydd, Nant Ffrancon, and Dyganhwy, in some of the Taliesin poems, create a presumption that the poet who wrote them was not unconnected either with the court of Gwynedd or with some Carnarvonshire or Anglesey monastery. We are tempted also to suspect that the body of old poetry, which forms the nucleus of the *Book of Taliesin* and the similar poetry of the *Book of Aneurin*, was either itself preserved in Dyganhwy, Bangor Deiniol, Bangor Seiriol, or Clynnog, or was based on some annals, containing references to events in the North, which we do not now fully possess. The reference in the Welsh Laws to the preservation of 'Breiniau Gwyr Arfon' by Bangor Deiniol and Bangor Beuno makes it not improbable that, in these and kindred monasteries, there were preserved brief annals and records, which afforded material to the bards and monks. There is extant in the Welsh Laws an interesting specimen of such a record, giving an account of the relations between the men of Arfon and the men of Strathclyde in the time of Rhun, son of Maelgwn Gwynedd. These brief annals were probably in close relation to the genealogies of the ruling families, and these families in the Cunedda districts, as well as those of other 'men of the North', may in some cases, owing to intermarriage, have comprised the names of some of the earlier inhabitants.

Professor Zimmer has suggested in his *Nennius Vindicatus* that in the original work of Nennius and in the North Wales recension, older annals from the North have played a part, notably in the account of the struggles between the Britons of the North and the men of Deira and Bernicia; it is highly probable, too, that chronicles of similar type have supplied the personal and local names which have been incorporated in the poems of the *Four Ancient Books*. As we shall see presently, these poems are not merely historical in character: they are an attempt at artistic treatment of historical themes which would be of special interest to certain Welsh families.

It is probably in brief annals such as these, too, combined with oral narrative, that we are to look for the materials which have been combined into the form of triads. These triads have obvious points of contact with the old poetry on the one hand, and with the prose narratives on the other. These chronicles need not by any means have belonged in all cases to the North; some of them may equally well have been evolved in the courts or in the leading monasteries of Gwynedd, Powys, Gwent and Dyfed, or even in the smaller territories of local dynasties. It is not improbable, too, that the pedigrees and the chronicles associated with them were the channels through which the names of ancient gods and goddesses, from whom certain families claimed descent, passed into later legend in association with historical names, as we find them for example in the 'Four Branches of the Mabinogi'.

The identification of the Northern localities of the old poetry has been ably prosecuted by Mr Skene, Mr Egerton Phillimore and others, but many names are still unidentified. Nor do Mr Skene's identifications in all cases carry conviction. In spite of his valuable service in bringing into prominence the Northern local background of many of the poems, he has often been too hasty in identifying place-names owing to a superficial similarity of sound. The great merit of his work consists in the fact that it enables us to realize dimly how long the descendants of 'Gwyr y Gogledd' regarded themselves, while in Wales and of Wales, as belonging to a larger Wales and to Britain as a whole, regarded not in mere isolation but as a part of the civilized world of the Roman Empire. It was probably this underlying and unsuppressed imperial instinct that made them dwell with evident delight on such imperial figures as Macsen, Helen and Arthur. The Welsh narratives scarcely ever confine the scenes of the exploits of their secular or ecclesiastical heroes to Wales, and the Welsh ruling families long regarded themselves as the survivors of Roman civilization. The after-glow of the Roman Empire long lingered in Britain. Evidence of the impression which Rome and the Latin tongue had made on Wales is afforded, not only by the number and quality of Latin words in Welsh, by the frequency of Latin names, but also by the attempts of Welshmen in remote corners of Wales to write the inscriptions of tomb-stones in Latin, in spite of their manifest ignorance of Latin spelling and grammar. There were probably men in Wales over a thousand years ago who expected a speedy end to the Welsh language.

In dealing with the early literature of Wales it is well to remember that ecclesiastical documents such as the Lives of the Welsh Saints, and more secular documents such as the *Mabinogion*, should be studied together. The ruling families of the monasteries and the ruling families of the courts were most closely related, and it is difficult, if not impossible, to separate the ecclesiastical literary centres of early times from the secular. In both these types of centres there was an equal pride in the exploits of the ancient families to which the saints and the ruling dynasties belonged, and the perpetuation in song of the exploits of the 'Men of the North' and others would be as natural for a monastic as for a courtly bard.

No one who studies early Welsh history and literature can fail to remark the prominence of families and traditions from the North in post-Roman times. It is not improbable that when Cunedda came into Wales from Manaw Gododdin, he came by the express invitation of the Brythons, who found themselves in need of experienced military support against the incursions of Irishmen from the West and the recrudescence of activity on the part of the mixed Goidelic and pre-Celtic population. After the withdrawal of the Roman fleets from the British seas, Britain was exposed to inroads of Irish pirates from the West as well as of Teutonic pirates from the East, alike eager for the plunder of one of the finest provinces of the Roman Empire. Except in the North, Britain at the time of the departure of the Romans was, from all indications, in a state of profound peace and quiet civilization. Hence the Brythons of Wales, in the face of invasion from the West, naturally turned for aid to the experienced military Brythons of the North, and gratefully accepted their continuance at the head of affairs in Wales. Though the Elegy on Cunedda Wledig in the *Book of Taliesin* (poem xlvi) is undoubtedly much later than his time, as is shown, for example, in the rhymes Cunedaf and gŏynaf, yet it may possibly be modelled on some older composition, or may be based on some annalistic document. In dealing with the early vernacular literature of Wales we have always to bear in mind its aristocratic character, and its relation to the ideas and traditions of the ruling families, who long preserved their interest in the district from which their fathers had come.

Behind the heroic traditions of the Northern families, however, we are driven, by the parallel study of the old poems and the *Mabinogion,* to consider whether some of the traditions of still older families may not have survived, linked it may be with their genealogies. Through intermarriage with the older strata of the population the men of the North would enter into the inheritance of these legends, which would in course of time be incorporated with theirs, though still regarded as belonging to an older epoch. It is possibly this distinction that is perpetuated in the apparently scrupulous care taken in the 'Four Branches of the Mabinogi' and, indeed, throughout the *Mabinogion,* to draw clear lines of demarcation between the various legendary periods, in accordance with a tendency discernible in Nennius and even in Geoffrey, in spite of his anachronisms. It looks as if there was a kind of traditional framework, into which the narrative of early British events was supposed to fit. The literary men of the courts and of the monasteries were doubtless equally assiduous in filling in this framework with all kinds of local stories, now attributed to this hero, now to that, largely derived from the never-failing staple of aetiological myth. Nor must we forget the possibility that even the men of the North may have brought with them some such tales as, for example, stories of Manawyd or Manawyddan, the eponymous hero of Manaw Gododdin, or that places in Wales, according to the wont of settlers, may have been renamed after places in the North or after the heroes of the Northern legends. The difficulty of tracing the topographical relations of these legends is increased when we remember that the geography of legends tends to expand with the expansion of men's ideas and territorial interests, a tendency of which we have a conspicuous example in the Arthurian geography of Geoffrey of Monmouth. It is not improbable that this phenomenon is an important feature even of the 'Four Branches of the Mabinogi' as we have them in their present form.

Another point which should always be borne in mind in dealing with Welsh as well as other legends is, that to historical names non-historical stories may become attached, and that the stories so attached may be far more ancient than the names. In dealing with the old stories of Wales, whether in prose or poetry, it would be well to reduce them to their simplest terms, thus bringing to view their typical plots. If this were systematically done with the stories of the other branches of the Celtic family, and, indeed, over a wider area, it would be easy to institute a kind of synoptic comparison of these plots. The writer is well aware how much admirable work has already been done in this direction by distinguished students of Celtic, such as Principal Rhŷs, and other students of folklore, but it would nevertheless be a great convenience if the various types of stories could be succinctly tabulated for the purpose of comparison, according to their characteristic plots, expressed in the briefest possible terms. Such a concise treatment would be of great value in comparing the ancient stories of Wales with those, for instance, of Ireland.

If we now turn to the older poetry of Wales, we see that much of it reflects the period of heroic struggle against the English. This is the case in the *Book of Aneurin*, in a few poems of the *Book of Taliesin*, in one or two poems (notably that in praise of Geraint) in the *Black Book of Carmarthen*, and in some of the Llywarch Hen poems of the *Red Book of Hergest*. While the *Book of Aneurin* and the poems of the *Book of Taliesin* mainly commemorate the Northern struggles against the men of Deira and Bernicia, those of the *Red Book of Hergest* and the corresponding portions of the *Black Book of Carmarthen* commemorate the struggle in the Severn Valley and the adjacent districts. Some of the heroes of the conflict in both cases belong to the same cycle, and, whatever may be the age of the actual compositions as we have them, they are probably based on older annals and lists of famous battles, but they are unfortunately much too vague to supply us with definite historical information. It must be remembered, too, that a critical analysis of the 'Gododdin' shews it not to be one poem, but to be composed of portions of several poems. An analysis of the 'Gododdin' (which itself contains repetitions) side by side with 'Gorchan Maelderw' shews clearly that these two poems consist of more or less identical portions of one and the same series of poems. In the greater part of the 'Gododdin' and the Gorchanau of the *Book of Aneurin* ('Gorchan Tutvwlch', 'Gorchan Adebon', 'Gorchan Cynvelyn' and 'Gorchan Maelderw') the copyist changed the orthography of the MS. from which he was copying into that of the early part of the thirteenth century, but, fortunately, he has, here and there, been careless in the performance of this task, and, in a large part of 'Gorchan Maelderw' he has left the spelling of the MS. before him practically unaltered, thus revealing a part of the poem in its pre-Norman dress, and even in a form which comes very near to that of the glosses of the eighth and ninth centuries. It is evident, too, that what was here copied was merely a string of fragments, so that the original poems from which they are taken, and which were the originals also of the larger fragments that are now in the 'Gododdin', were older still, though how much older it would be difficult to say. It is interesting to note that 'Gorchan Maelderw' is attributed in the MS. to Taliesin, whereas the very same portions in the 'Gododdin' are attributed in the same manuscript to Aneurin. It should also be observed that in 'Gorchan

Maelderw' and in certain portions of the latter half of the 'Gododdin', the account of the battle of Catraeth, with which the poem deals, differs somewhat from that of the earlier portion. In 'Gorchan Maelderw' and its cognate portions of the 'Gododdin', all the Britons are represented as being killed, except one, and he appears to be Cynon ab Clydno Eiddin. In the earlier portion of the 'Gododdin' those who are represented as escaping out of the general slaughter are said to be Cynon, together with 'deu gatki aeron' (Kyndilic and Kynan) and Aneurin, into whose mouth the narrative of the battle and the praises of the warriors (living and dead) who fought at the battle, are put. Moreover, Aneurin, where he is represented as escaping, is so represented in two ways: one way is that after being wounded ('om gwaetffreu') he escapes through the power of his song; the other, where he is represented as being freed from an underground dungeon by Ceneu son of Llywarch. It is clear from both the 'Gododdin' and 'Gorchan Maelderw' that the leading theme of these two poems is the praise of Cynon ab Clydno Eiddin, probably a much more important personage in early Welsh history and legend than his present fame might lead us to suspect. Of his early fame it may be noted that there is some reflection in Owain and Luned. Some indication, too, of this earlier prominence is given by the number of Englynion on him in 'Englynion y Beddau'. We should probably not be far wrong in regarding this group of poems as being one section of the poetry composed in honour of the Coel family (Coeling) and especially the 'Cynverching' (family of Cynvarch) branch of that stock, the branch to which Urien Rheged belonged. It should be borne in mind that it was the duty of a family bard not merely to glorify the living, but also to preserve and to enhance the fame of the dead ancestors of his living patrons, and this he could hardly do better than by amplifying and embellishing in verse the chronicles of the battles in which they showed their prowess. Owing to the close relationship, too, between the families of the Welsh saints and those of the princes, the above-mentioned motive would operate even among the monastic bards. The importance of the Coel family is well illustrated in a statement made in 'Bonedd Gwyr y Gogledd' (*Hengwrt* MS. 536). 'Trychan cledyf kynuerchyn a ttrychan ysgŏyt kynnŏdyon a ttrychan wayŏ coeling pa neges bynhac yd elynt iddi yn duun. Nyt amethei (hon) honno.'

As the 'Gododdin' is now given in the *Book of Aneurin*, the verses have, in several cases, been transposed from their original order, so that what we now have are *disjecta membra*; and in some places there appear to be irrelevant interpolations. The earlier part of the 'Gododdin' appears to have affinities with 'Gorchan Tutvwleh'; for, in both, Tutvwlch and Kyfwlch are jointly commemorated along with Cynon. 'Gorchan Cynfelyn', which mentions Eithinyn, a 'Gododdin' hero, differs from 'Gorchan Maelderw' in referring to the escape of three men from Catraeth, one of whom is Cynon, and the other two Cadreith and Catleu o gatnant, together with Aneurin, who, after being wounded, is ransomed, by the sons of Coel (reading meib) for pure gold, steel and silver. The Cynfelyn here commemorated is probably Cynfelyn Drwsgl, the brother of Cynon ab Clydno Eiddin. Possibly the chief centres from which these poems emanated were Dyganhwy, Bangor Seiriol (in Anglesey, the land of Caw's descendants), Bangor Deiniol, Bangor Beuno (not far from which was a Cefn Clutno) and Llanbadarn. The latter centre is here mentioned because one of the 'Englynion y Beddau' represents

Cynon ab Clydno Eiddin as having been buried there. Cor Seiriol in Penmon and Cor Beuno in Clynnog both appear to have acquired a high reputation for their learning. Elaeth Frenin ab Meyrig (the supposed author of 'Kygogion Elaeth' in the *Black Book of Carmarthen*) was a monk at Bangor Seiriol, and Nidan ab Gwrfyw ab Pasgen ab Urien Rheged is said to have been some time an abbot there. It may well be that it is to the old monastic schools, even more than to the courts of the princes, that we are to look in the early period for the development of Welsh literature, and it is not impossible, were more known of these schools, that they were the direct successors of still earlier teachers. In dealing with the earlier poetry it should not be forgotten that even the 'Gododdin' contains numerous religious allusions.

The poem of the *Book of Aneurin* called 'Gorchan Maelderw' is of great interest, because, in one of the portions of it written in an archaic orthography, the name of Arthur unmistakably occurs in the words 'bei ef Arthur' (even if he were Arthur). These words suggest that even then, within the cycle of the Catraeth poems, Arthur's praise and fame were great. Indeed, from every point of view the indications (as in the *Black Book* poems) point to the conclusion that, within the circle of traditions connected with the struggle against the English, Arthur, though rarely mentioned, was throughout a commanding figure.

Let us now turn for a moment to poems of another series. The early poetry of Powys, which is attributed to Llywarch Hen, bases its chief claim to antiquity on the undoubted fact that several of the poems are similar in form to some 'englynion' of the ninth century, which are found in the *Juvencus Codex* of the Cambridge University Library. Some of these poems, such as those in praise of Geraint ab Erbin, are also found in the *Black Book of Carmarthen*. Hence, it may be concluded that the nucleus of this poetry formed part of that heroic tradition which commemorated the leaders of the struggle against the English in parts of the Severn Valley, being, in fact, the East Wales analogue of the tradition of the struggle in the North found in the 'Gododdin' and kindred poems. It is of interest to observe that in the poems of both series Arthur appears as a prominent figure. The poems of the Powys and Severn struggles appear to have as their prose counterpart a chronicle such as that which Professor Zimmer in his *Nennius Vindicatus* has shewn to underlie the Builth recension of Nennius, while the poems of the 'Gododdin' series appear to have closer affinities with the chronicles which underlie the Venedotian recension. From one courtly or monastic literary centre to another the story of Arthur and his associated companions, such as Cai, Bedwyr, Owain ab Urien, Caradog Vreichvras, Cynon ab Clydno Eiddin, seems to have spread through the Wye and Severn Valleys, and notably the Usk Valley (until Caerleon on Usk became a great Arthurian locality) and even much further afield. Nennius already speaks of Arthur, at Carn Cabal near Builth, hunting the 'Porcus Troyt', and of the grave of Arthur's son in Erging. We know, too, from Giraldus Cambrensis, that the highest point of the Breconshire Beacons was known in his time as Kadeir Arthur, the throne of Arthur.

The bulk of the Llywarch Hen poetry, as we have it in the *Red Book of Hergest*, is marked by a meditative pathos, and it is to this pathos that it owes much of its charm. These poems appear to have been written by someone acquainted with the traditional story of Llywarch Hen and with the narrative of the struggle of the Welsh against the English around Pengwern. The poet's favourite vein of reflection is over the departure of the brilliance and joy of the past. In this vein he represents Llywarch Hen as mourning over the loss of youth with its joy and vigour, over the death of his children, over the loss of his former lords, Urien and Cynddylan, and also over the former glories of the ancient palaces of Pengwern and the neighbourhood. As compared with the spirit of the 'Gododdin' and kindred poetry, it may be said that the Llywarch Hen compositions appeal to the sense of pathos and of contrast in a broader and more catholic way. In both types there is a strong appeal to the sense of contrast, but in the 'Gododdin' the contrast depicted is between the confident gaiety and exuberant hilarity which preceded the battle of Catraeth, and the disastrous event of the contest, between the host that went to battle and the fragment of it that returned. In the Llywarch Hen poetry the contrast is between the glory of the past and the ruin of the present. Neither group of poems is the bare unreflecting primitive poetry of narrative: it is a poetry which seeks to appeal to minds thoroughly alive to the pathos and tragedy of life as exemplified in the events and the results of the great struggle of the Britons.[1] It is the 'lacrimae rerum' in this body of poetry that give it an abiding interest. What influence (if any) the study of Vergil, the universal school book of the Roman Empire and of the Middle Ages, may have had in giving this direction of pathos to Welsh poetry it is now impossible to say.

The poetry with which we have hitherto dealt, though not without religious allusions, is in the main of a humanistic character, but in addition to these poems the body of poetry now under consideration comprises a number of poems that are primarily religious, and others which contain a strong tincture of mediaeval theology combined with other elements. The most curious poetry of the latter type is that mainly, though not exclusively, found in the *Book of Taliesin*, where theology, mediaeval natural history and various legends are presented together through a medium which reveals a very curious conception of the poetic art. In this body of poetry, some of which contains materials derived from the Northern traditional stock, the poet is depicted not as mourning over the disastrous battles of the past or lamenting the departed greatness of his race, so much as rising supernaturally above human limitations of time and place, and reviewing the famous events of the heroic and legendary past, in which he himself is represented as having been present. This idea is partly the result of the thought that the materials of the body had been in existence from time immemorial, partly a development from the favourite mediaeval idea of metamorphosis, the latter idea being part and parcel of the universal magical conceptions of the time. The composer of the poems, in recounting his supposed past experiences, seems to have quarried in some ancient chronicles containing lists of the battles of Urien Rheged and others, and of the localities in which they were fought. Nor is it unlikely that some older lines were bodily adopted and incorporated from ancient heroic poems and elegies. These old traditions appear to have had a special charm for some of the poets of the *Book of Taliesin*, and they would seem to have been particularly fond of traditions and legends which flourished in Anglesey and Carnarvonshire. The references to Geirionydd and Nant Ffrancon appear to indicate the neighbourhood of the Conwy valley and Dyganhwy as one of the poets' gathering-ground of legend. To this district we may perhaps link the Hiraethog district and the valley of the Dyfrdwy beyond. From the

Carnarvonshire side the poet probably obtained a stock of Don and Beli legends, from Dyganhwy and the neighbourhood the local legends of Taliesin, while from the Hiraethog and the Dee district came the legends of Bran and Branwen, with the topographical associations of which I have dealt in my articles on the 'Four Branches of the Mabinogi' in the *Zeitschrift für Celtische Philologie*. The Branwen legend was also associated with Merionethshire and Anglesey, and the legend of Pryderi with Merionethshire. In the 'Four Branches of the Mabinogi' it may be noted that the topographical associations of the Don family are mainly with the West side of Carnarvonshire. The district of the Conwy valley and the nearest parts of Anglesey and Carnarvonshire probably felt a certain local interest in Seithennin, the father of St Tudno, in Urien Rheged (the ancestor of Grwst of Llanrwst and of Nidan, at one time head of the monastery of Penmon), in Lleenawg, from whose name Castell Lleiniog on the Anglesey side of the Menai Straits seems to be called, in Dona of Llanddona, a descendant of Brochwel Ysgythrog, in Maelgwn Gwynedd, whose court was at Dyganhwy and possibly in Arthur, if the name Bwrdd Arthur is ancient. The composer of many of these Taliesin poems is not content, however, to build merely on a basis of traditional and local legend, but interweaves his fantastic imaginings into a tissue of mediaeval natural philosophy, largely derived from the stock manuals of the dark ages, the works of Isidore of Seville and Bede, who were the chief successors of the encyclopaedists Martianus Capella and Cassiodorus. The poet expresses his respect for Bede in the line

Nyt ðy dyðeit geu llyfreu beda.

i.e., The books of Bede do not speak falsehood.

The conception of a poet revealed in many of these poems seems very strange to us at the present day, but it bears a very strong resemblance to the mediaeval conception of Vergil (known in mediaeval Welsh as 'Fferyll', and mentioned under that name in one of the Taliesin poems). The magical connotation of the name 'Fferyll' may be seen from the fact that it is the origin of the Welsh 'fferyllydd', chemist. According to the mediaeval conception of Vergil, as we see from Professor Comparetti's account of Vergil in the Middle Ages, he was not only a man of supreme learning, but was also endowed with super-human powers. Fortunately, owing to the general atmosphere of these poems, the bent of the composers towards natural history has preserved for us some interesting old Welsh terms, such as 'adfant', the upper world; 'difant' (whence 'difancoll'), the lower world; 'elfydd', the earth; 'annwfn', the under world, 'anghar', 'affwys' and 'affan', apparently of the same meaning. The latter may, however, be borrowed through Latin from Greek αφανές from Latin are certainly derived the terms 'aches', the flood tide; and 'reges', the ebb tide, from 'accessus' and 'recessus' respectively. How greatly interested the Britons were in the tides we see from several passages in the *Book of Taliesin* and the *Black Book of Carmarthen*, from the *De Mirabilibus Britanniae*, and from a treatise *De Mirabilibus*, formerly attributed to St Augustine, and now believed to be the work of a Briton. The term 'llafanad', formed by means of a Welsh ending -ad from 'llafan' (a parallel form of 'llafn', like mediaeval 'gauar' and 'gafyr'), which comes from Latin 'lamina', may be roughly translated 'element', but it probably reflected originally a conception of existence, whereby its various substances tended to form 'laminations' or layers. It may be noted, too, that the familiar terms of 'Macrocosm' and 'Microcosm' appear in these poems as 'Y Byt Mawr' and 'Y Byt Bychan'. The use of these and other terms suggests affinities between the medium of ideas through which the traditions and legends are presented, and an obscure type of philosophical doctrine which lived on as a kind of undergrowth in the Roman Empire and the Dark Ages, a body of doctrine believed by some to have had a share in the formation of the Jewish Kabbala. One of its best known representatives is the Poemander of Hermes Trismegistus.

It should be noted that in an interesting dialogue between the soul and the body found in the *Black Book of Carmarthen*, the Taliesin doctrine of 'Y saith llafanad' is put into the mouth of the body. In this account the body is formed by the meeting together of the seven 'laminations', of which fire, earth, wind, mist, flowers, are named, but the other two, water and air (see the *Book of Taliesin*, poem lv) are omitted, around the pure substance ('pur').

This super-human conception of the poet shows itself, as we have seen in his attitude towards the past, but it is no less visible in his attitude towards the future. The prophetic powers of the poet come here especially into view. Here again we have an interesting point of contact with the mediaeval conception of Vergil as a prophet. In Wales, the role of the prophetic bard is that of prophesying to the remnants of the Britons ultimate victory over their enemies, under the leadership of some of the leaders of the past, notably, Cynan and Cadwaladr. These vaticinations were put sometimes into the mouth of Taliesin, sometimes into the mouth of Myrddin Wyllt. The earliest 'Myrddin' prophecy is that put into the mouth of Merlinus Ambrosius in Nennius, in a narrative which has evident affinities with that of 'Lludd and Llevelys'. This prophecy was afterwards developed by Geoffrey of Monmouth, and became extremely popular. In 1180 a commentary was written upon it by Alanus de Insulis, and in 1208 a translation of the prophecies was made into Icelandic. A version appeared also in French and became very popular. In 1379 an Italian translation was made which also attained popularity. In 1478 a German version was published, and in 1498 a version appeared in Spanish. It should be noted that the favourite Myrddin of Welsh poetry is Myrddin Wyllt, who is not associated with the Nennius story at all, but with Rhydderch Hael and Gwenddoleu, as we see in the 'Hoianau' and 'Afallenau'.

As already stated, the framework of the Welsh Myrddin poems is the story of Myrddin Wyllt, as may be seen in the twelfth-century poems of the 'Afallenau' and 'Hoianau' of the *Black Book of Carmarthen*. In his madness after the Battle of Arderydd, Myrddin utters his prognostications as to the future of the Welsh people. His companion in his wanderings is a little pig, and we catch sight also of a lady who appears to stand in much the same relation to Myrddin as the Sibyl to Virgil in the legend of the Middle Ages. Her name is Chwimleian or Chwipleia, and she appears to be the same as Viviane of the Breton stories. In the *Book of Taliesin*, poem vi, called 'Arymes Prydein', is a Myrddin vaticination, as well as poem xlvii, which begins with the line

Dygogan awen dygobryssyn,

and poems i and liii. In the *Red Book of Hergest* (as given in Skene) the type in question is represented by poems xviii, xix, xx, xxi, as well as poems i and ii, 'Kyvoessi Myrdin a Gwendyd' and 'Gwasgargert Myrtin' respectively. Poems of a prophetic type long continued popular in England and in Wales. When we turn to distinctively religious poems and hymns there are many points of contact, as might have been expected, with the general trend of mediaeval thought, as seen, for example, in a collection like Mone's Latin Hymns of the Middle Ages. In the *Black Book of Carmarthen* we have in the first place a 'Dialogue between the Soul and the Body' (Skene, vol. ii, poems v, vi and vii). This poem ends with a description of the Day of Judgment on Mount Olivet, a favourite subject of mediaeval hymnology. Poem ix of the same manuscript is meant to be a warning to the wicked of his fate. In poems x, xi and xii, there are reflections of mediaeval theology. In poem xi, it is interesting to note the Divine names Eloy and Adonay, probably taken from a list given by Isidore of Seville. In this poem, too, we have the names 'Paul ac Anhun' (Antony), which suggest the monastic atmosphere of the writer. Poem xiii gives some interesting non-scriptural stories about Job, Eve and the infant Christ. In poems xx and xxi we have compositions attributed to 'Elaeth' or 'Elaeth Frenin', who is said to have become a monk. Poem xxv is of similar type, while in xxvii there are references to Sanffreid (St Bridget), Gwosprid (St Osbert) and St Peter. The whole of this poem is a curious combination, in the style of the Llywarch Hen poetry, of a hymn with an account of the preparations for a journey. In poem xxix we have one of those Welsh mediaeval poems where religious emotion is blended with an enquiring interest in natural phenomena.

The *Book of Taliesin* also affords several specimens of religious poems of the above type, side by side with others which have a curious admixture of legend, natural history or magical imagination. In poem i (as printed in the Book of Taliesin) from l. 21 to the end there are clear indications of the religious milieu in which this type of poetry arose. Poem ii (162 lines) is called 'Marwnat Y Vil Veib', and reflects in its heavenly and earthly hierarchy the Pseudo-Dionysian theology which dominated the church of that time. The poem contains some curious scraps of Latin and of geography. Poem v (173 lines) is a description of the Day of Judgment and of the punishment of Christ's crucifiers. In poem xxii we have a meditation on the 'Plagues of Egypt' (*Plaeu yr Eifft*), while poem xxiv is an account of Moses' Rod (*Llath Moesen*). There is another poem (No. li) of the same cycle on the twelve tribes of Israel (*Deudec tref yr Israel*). Poem xxvi is a short poem on the Trinity, and xxix is of interest not only on account of its scriptural allusions, but also on account of its reference to Alexander the Great, a feature which indicates its affinity with poems xxvi and xxviii, and with the mediaeval Alexander literature generally. This literature was especially popular in France and Ireland. Poem xli appears to refer to the cruelty of Erof (for Erodd = Herod); while poems lv and lvi, to which reference has already been made, are called 'Kanu y Byt Mawr' (the Macrocosm) and 'Kanu y Byt Bychan' (the Microcosm). These two latter poems are clearly based on the writings of Isidore of Seville, Bede and similar authors. Further researches into the books read in the monasteries in the early Middle Ages, such as may be seen for example in the Catalogues of the Ancient Libraries of Canterbury and Dover, will undoubtedly throw much light on the religious and other poems of the *Four Ancient Books*. Before these poems can

be safely used for the purpose of comparative mythology it is necessary to elucidate the mediaeval medium through which they are presented, just as in the study
of the 'Four Branches of the Mabinogi', and other old stories, it is important to
bear in mind the re-casting which they have undergone to suit mediaeval ideas. In
the mediaeval matrix of many of these poems, however, there are embedded many
highly interesting portions of early legend, whose topographical affinities have
now been ascertained with some measure of success. An important problem
which remains is that of classifying these legends according to their various inter-
relations and affinities. In this work some help may be given by 'Englynion y
Beddau' and other poems.

In dealing with the old poetry of Wales and its kindred literature it is well to
keep apart the framework of persons, incidents and localities in which the stories
are placed, and the essential features of the stories themselves. Stories far older
than the framework may here as elsewhere have become attached in course of time
to the historical names of Northern or Welsh native families. Even in dealing with
the topographical connections of the legends we have to proceed with great
caution, inasmuch as certain places may have been called after characters in the
stories. Families, too, in their emigrations, in accordance with the methods of
emigrants everywhere, may have renamed certain places after places in their old
homes, and legends themselves with their associated names often travel far afield.

The existence of the poems with which we are now dealing in their present
form shows that they have a literary history behind them: they have recognized
metres, a recognized poetic vocabulary and a sense of taste and style, and the more
they are understood the more vividly do they reflect the ideals and interests which
guided the minds of the Welsh people when Europe was emerging from the night
of barbarism.

## Note

1    The verses called 'Englynion y Beddau', which have affinities with the traditions and
     legends of several districts, also belong to the poetry of reflective meditation over the past.
     They are probably a development from a smaller nucleus. In the topographical elucidation
     of the old legends they are of real service.

# 4

# THE MABINOGI OF TALIESIN

## 'IDRISON'
### from *The Cambrian and Caledonian Quarterly*

THERE WAS A NOBLEMAN in former times, of Penllyn, who was called Tegid the Bald, and his patrimony was in the middle of the lake of Tegid; and his married wife was called Keridwen, and of that wife a son was born named Morvran ab Tegid, and a daughter named Creirvyw, who was the fairest damsel in the world, and a brother of theirs was the ugliest person among men, and this was Avagddu.

Then Keridwen, the mother of Avagddu, considered it as not likely that he should have reception among the nobility, from his being so ugly, unless he were endowed with some pre-eminent gifts or sciences; for this was at the commencement of the era of Arthur and the round table.

And thereupon, by having recourse to books of chemistry, she prepared to concoct a cauldron of genius and sciences for her son, so that his reception might be more honourable, on account of his sciences, and his knowledge in respect to the future state of the world.

So she began to boil the cauldron, the which, after it should be made to boil, could not be suffered to leave off boiling until the end of a year and a day, so that three blessed drops should be obtained through the grace of the spirit. And little Gwion, the son of a yeoman of Llanvair Caereinion, in Powys, was placed by her to attend the cauldron, and a blind man named Morda to keep up the fire under it, with a command not to suffer the boil to break until a year and a day should elapse: and she also, through the books of the astronomers, and by the hours of the planets, being daily collecting of such various herbs as had some peculiar virtue.

And on a certain day, as Keridwen was collecting herbs, and the end of the year drawing near, these drops of the pure water flew out of the cauldron, and lighted upon the finger of little Gwion; and, from its being so hot, at the instant he put those three precious drops into his mouth, and no sooner had he done so, than he obtained a knowledge of every thing that might occur in future; and he was thus forewarned that his principal care must be to avoid the wiles of Keridwen, for her inventive powers were great, and out of extreme fear he fled towards his own country; and the cauldron was broken in two, because the whole of the steel was of a deleterious nature, except those three precious drops, and thus the steeds of Gwyddno Long-shank were poisoned by drinking of the water from the brook into which the cauldron ran, and therefore the brook thenceforth was called the poison of Gwyddno's horses. And thereupon Keridwen was observed returning home, and seeing her labour for a twelvemonth lost, she snatched up a billet, and struck the blind Morda upon his head, so that one of his eyes fell down his cheek; whereupon he then said, 'badly hast thou disfigured me, and I being innocent! thou hast suffered no loss on my account.' 'Thou hast spoken the truth,' said Keridwen, 'it was little Gwion that robbed me;' and so she followed him upon a run. And thereupon he observed her, and so he changed himself into the form of a hare, and ran off; and then she also appeared as a hound bitch, doubled him, and turned him towards a river; and then he appeared as a fish, and she also in the form of an otter bitch, and pursued him under the water; so that he was compelled to appear as a bird in the air, and she as a hawk to pursue him, and so gave him no quiet in the air; and as she was overtaking him, and he having the fear of death upon him, he observed a heap of winnowed wheat on a barn floor, and so alighted into the wheat, and appeared in the form of one of the grains, and thereupon she also appeared as a black crested hen, and into the wheat she went, which, scratching with her feet, she recognized him, and swallowed him; and, as said in the narrative, she was nine months pregnant of him; and, after her delivery, she could not in her heart kill him, so beautiful he seemed, but she wrapped him in a leathern bag, and cast him to the will of man into the sea, on the 29th of April.

And at that time Gwyddno had a wear on the sand between Dyvi and Aberystwyth, near to his own castle; and in that wear there was obtained to the value of a hundred pounds at every May eve. At that time, Gwyddno had one son, who was called Elphin, being one of the most untoward of youths, and suffering the greatest privation, which was a cause of grief to his father, fearing that he was born in an evil hour: and through the advice of his counsellors, his father gave him the drought of the wear for that year, to see if ever any luck befel him, and to make a beginning of employment for him.

The following morning, as Elphin was examining the wear, and finding there was nothing in it, was going away, he discovered a leathern bag suspended from a pole of the wear; then one of the wear men said to Elphin, 'Thou hast never been unfortunate before this night, for thou hast broken the virtues of the wear, wherein there used to be obtained the value of a hundred pounds on every May eve.'

'Now,' said Elphin, 'what if there might be an equivalent to the hundred pounds in this?'

The skin was untied, and the opener of it saw the forehead of a boy, and he exclaimed, 'See, here is a fair front!'

'Fair Front let his name be,' said Elphin, raising him up between his hands, bewailing his misfortune, and pensively placed him in a pannier on one of his horses, and at the instant he made the horse canter that only trotted before, thus conducting him so softly as if he were sitting in the easiest chair that possibly could be, and thus carrying the boy, composed the verses called 'The Consolation of Elphin,' with an eulogy, and a prophecy of honourable advancement to him; and the Consolation was the first song made by Taliesin, and which was to console Elphin on the way home as he sorrowed at the loss of the drought of the wear; and above all he was concerned that the fault and misfortune were attributed to him. The Consolation was to this effect:

Fair Elphin cease to lament!
Let no one be dissatisfied with his own,
To despair will bring no advantage.
No man sees what supports him;
The prayer of Cynllo will not be in vain;
God will not violate his promise.
Never in Gwyddno's wear
Was there such good luck as this night.

Fair Elphin, dry thy cheeks!
Although thou thinkest thou hast to gain,
Too much grief will bring thee no good;
Nor doubt the miracles of the Almighty:
Although I am but little, I am highly gifted.
From seas, and from mountains,
And from the depths of rivers,
God brings wealth to the fortunate man.

Elphin of lively qualities,
Thy resolution is unmanly;
Thou must not be over sorrowful:
Better to trust in God than to forbode ill.
Weak and small as I am,
On the foaming beach of the ocean,
In the day of trouble, I shall be
Of more service to thee than 300 salmon.

Elphin of notable qualities,
Be not displeased at thy misfortune;
Although reclined thus weak in my bag,
There lies a virtue in my tongue.
While I continue thy protector
Thou hast not much to fear:
Remembering the names of the Trinity,
None shall be able to harm thee.

The foregoing, with various other verses were sung by Taliesin for the comfort of Elphin, during his journey, who, on arriving at home, presented the contents of the pannier to his wife, who nursed the child dearly and tenderly.

From that time forward the wealth of Elphin increased more and more day after day, and he obtained the favour and love of the king; who, some short time afterwards, kept open court in Christmas time at the castle of Dyganwy, surrounded by his lords, both spiritual and temporal, with a great number of knights and esquires.

In this assembly the following conversation took place: 'Is there in the whole world a king so powerful as Maelgwn, and so endowed by heaven with spiritual gifts? In the first place, comliness of person, and urbanity, and strength, besides all the energies of the soul; and along with these gifts, they say, the Father has bestowed upon him one eminent gift that is superior to the others altogether, which is, happiness in having a queen whose form and demeanour, and wisdom, and chastity, are qualities possessed by her in a higher degree than by all the noble ladies in the kingdom.'

Besides this subject, they threw out questions amongst themselves, as to who was the bravest of his men; who had the finest and swiftest horses and grey-hounds; who had better informed and wiser bards than Maelgwn. These were at the time in great esteem amongst the dignitaries of the kingdom; and at that time none were advanced to the office at present called a herald, except such as were learned men; and not only were they employed in the service of kings and princes, but were required to be well versed in genealogies, armorial bearings and the deeds of kings and princes, as well in respect to foreign kingdoms as to the olders of these kingdoms; and particularly as to the history of the principal nobility. It was necessary also, for all of them to be most ready with their answers in the several languages of Latin, French, Welsh, and English; and, in addition to this, to be great historians, and to be of good memory, and accomplished in poetry, so as readily to compose metrical verses in each of those languages.

And of these there were at the court of Maelgwn, during that festival, as many as four and twenty; and chief over them was one who was called Heinin the Bard.

Thus, after all had extolled the king, and enumerated his virtues, it happened that Elphin should express himself in this manner:

'Truly, no one is able to compete with a king but a king; however, let that be granted, and indeed if he were not a king, I might say that I have a wife equal in respect to personal chastity to any lady that can be found in the kingdom. And besides, I have one bard who is better informed than all the bards of the king. In a little time the king was informed of all the boasting of Elphin by some of his companions, for which the king commanded him to be confined in a strong prison, until he should be enabled to obtain true information in respect to the chastity of his wife, and also in respect to the talents of his bard.'

Then, after Elphin had been placed in a tower of the castle, with heavy fetters on his legs, which fetters were said to be of silver, on account of his being of royal blood, the account shows that the king employed Rhun, his son, to prove the chastity of the wife of Elphin, which Rhun was one of the most lascivious characters that ever lived; for neither wife nor maiden escaped free from imputation, with whom he obtained but a short space for discourse.

And as Rhun was coming in great haste towards the mansion of Elphin, with fall intention to debauch his wife, Taliesin told his mistress what he had long observed, from the conduct of the king in confining his master, and the way that Rhun had come with the design of assailing her chastity; and therefore he advised his mistress to dress one of the maids of the kitchen in her clothes. This the lady gladly complied with unsparingly, by ornamenting her hands with a profusion of the choicest rings in the possession of herself and her husband. In this manner Taliesin directed his mistress to place the maid to sit at the table in her stead to supper, and Taliesin contrived to make her appear like her mistress, and the mistress to be like the maid.

Thus as they were seated in the most sumptuous style at supper, as has been described, Rhun suddenly appeared at the hall of Elphin, and was joyfully ushered in, for all the attendants knew him well; and they quickly introduced him into the room to their mistress, in whose resemblance the maid got up from the supper, and politely welcomed him; and afterwards she again sat to supper, Rhun being seated along with her; and presently he began to joke with obscene expressions with the maid, who studied to preserve the semblance of her mistress: and indeed, the narrative shows that the maid became so inebriated as to begin to fall asleep; and it is also stated that Rhun infused some powders in her drink, which caused her to sleep so soundly, as not at all to feel his cutting her little finger off her hand, on which was a ring with the signet of Elphin, which he had sent as a token of his wife a little while before. In this manner he did whatever he thought proper to the girl; and then he took the finger with the ring round it, as a token for the king of his having succeeded, by showing the manner how he had cut off her finger on leaving her, without her being awaked out of her sleep.

From these reports the king was greatly delighted; and in consequence he sent for his council, to whom he explained the whole of the matter, from beginning to end: also commanding Elphin to be brought from the prison, that he might be reprimanded for his boasting; and thereupon he addressed Elphin in this manner:

'Elphin, be it known to thee, and doubt thou not, that it is but folly for any man in the world to believe a woman in respect to her personal chastity, farther than he may be able to observe her; and that thou mayest ascertain how thy wife broke her marriage vow the very night last past, behold, here is her finger as a proof for thee, with thy signet ring round it, which was cut from her hand in her sleep, by the person that slept with her; so that, as thou mayest not have to boast by saying she had not transgressed in respect to her chastity.'

To these words Elphin replied in the following manner: 'By thy permission, honourable king, permit me to say, that I am by no means able to deny my ring, for there are many people who can identify it; but, in truth, I solemnly assert that the finger round which it is was never joined to the hand of my wife; for, in certain truth, it has upon it three particular things, not any one of which was ever upon either of the fingers of the hands of my wife, and the first of the three is conclusive, by the leave of your grace, wheresoever my wife may at present be, whether sitting, or standing, or lying down, this ring will not stick even upon her thumb; and you may plainly observe, it must be difficult to force this ring over the joint of the smallest finger of the hand from which this finger was taken; and the second thing is, that my wife has not been on any Saturday, since I have known her, without having her nails pared before going to bed; and, indeed, you can plainly see that the nail of this finger has not been cut for a month; and the third thing is this, that the hand from which this finger has been cut has kneeded some dough of rye within the three days prior to this finger being cut off it; and I will confirm it as true to your goodness, that my wife has not kneeded rye dough since she has been a wife to me.'

Then the king became extremely angry with Elphin for standing out so stoutly against him on behalf of the chastity of his wife; and on that account the king commanded him the second time to prison, saying that he should not be liberated from thence, until he proved his boasting to be true, as well in respect to the talent of his bard as to the purity of his wife: these were during the time in the palace of Elphin, making merry; and, in the meanwhile, Taliesin informed his mistress how Elphin was in prison on their account; but he desired her to appear cheerful, and explained to her the manner he would go to the court of Maelgwn to liberate his master. Thereupon she inquired by what means he would free his master; and then he replied in this manner:

A journey will I perform,
And to the gate I will come;
The hall I will enter,
And my song I will sing;
My speech I will pronounce
To silence royal bards.
In presence of their chief,
I will greet to deride,
Upon them I will break,
And Elphin I will free.
Should contention arise,
In presence of the prince,
With summons to the bards
For the sweet-flowing song,
And wizards' posing lore
And wisdom of Druids.

In the court of the sons of the
    distributor
Some are who did appear
Intent on wily schemes,
By craft and tricking means,
In pangs of affliction
To wrong the innocent.
Let the fools be silent,
As erst in Badon's fight, –

With Arthur of liberal ones
The head, with long red
    blades;
Through feats of testy men,
And a chief with his foes.
Woe be to them, the fools,
When revenge comes on them.

I, Taliesin, chief of bards,
With sapient druids' words,
Will set kind Elphin free
From haughty tyrant's bonds.
To their fell and chilling cry,
By the act of a surprising steed,
From the far distant North,
There soon shall be an end.
Let neither grace nor health
Be to Maelgwn Gwynedd,
For this force and this wrong;
And be extremes of ills
And an avenged end
To Rhun and all his race:
Short be his course of life,
Be all his lands laid waste;
And long exile be assigned
To Maelgwn Gwynedd!

Having spoken thus, Taliesin took leave of his mistress; and at length he arrived at the court of Maelgwn, who, in royal state, was about entering the hall to dinner, in the manner usual with kings and princes, on every high festival in that age. And just as Taliesin had come into the hall, he observed there was room for him in an unfrequented place near where the bards and minstrels were wont to repair to perform their service and devotion to the king, as is still customary in proclaiming largess upon high festivals. So the time was now arrived for the bards or the heralds to proclaim the largess and liberality of the king; and these came towards the place where Taliesin was squatting in a corner, who stretched out his lip after them, and on it he played 'blab blab' with his finger; they took not much notice of him in passing, but walked on till they came before the king, to whom they made their obeysance with their bodies, as it was proper for them to do, without uttering a single word, but extending out their lips and mouthing at the king, playing 'blab blab' with their fingers and lips, as they had seen the boy doing before, which sight filled the king with wonder and amazement, supposing them to be drunk, owing to a profusion of liquors; therefore he desired one of the lords that ministered at his table to go to them, to request that they would call to mind where they were standing, and how they ought to conduct themselves. This he did with pleasure; but they were not prevailed upon to desist from their folly. On that account, he sent the second and the third time, and ordered them to leave the hall. At length the king desired one of the 'squires to give a blow to the chief of them, who was called Heinin the Bard; then the 'squire took a broom and struck him on his head so that he fell back on his breech, whence he got up on his knees, and then he besought the king's grace for permission to show him that such inadvertence did not arise from neglect, nor from want of thought, nor from ebriety, but from the power of some spirit that was within the hall; and in addition to this Heinin spoke as follows:

'Illustrious king, be it known to your grace, it is not from the effect of a profusion of liquors that we are dumb, and seem as drunken men, but through the impulse of a spirit sitting in yonder corner in the form of a child.'

From that spot the king commanded a 'squire to fetch him, and who went into the corner where Taliesin was sitting, and thence brought him into the presence of the king, who asked him what he was, and from whence he came. Then Taliesin answered him satirically, as is seen here:

### Notices of the Powers of the Bard

In water there is a quality endowed with a blessing; on God it is most just to meditate aright; to God it is proper to supplicate with seriousness, since no obstacle can there be to obtain a reward from him.

Three times have I been born, I know by meditation; it were miserable for a person not to come and obtain all the sciences of the world, collected together in my breast, for I know what has been, what in future will occur.

I will supplicate my Lord that I get a refuge in him, a regard I may obtain in his grace; the Son of Mary is my trust, great in him is my delight, for in him is the world continually upholden.

God has been to instruct me and to raise my expectation, the true Creator of heaven, who affords me protection; it is rightly intended that the saints should daily pray, for God, the renovator, will bring them to him.

## A Challenge to the Bards of Maelgon

Is it not natural to be excited
by the allurement of praise;
by the belief in a narrative,
as to what the world has been?
as to who is accomplished to sing
before the throne of Jesus,
in the presence of the three
    hosts,
when He shall be judging?
what minstrel will sing
when Cynan shall be called
to a summoned chair,
in the presence of Cadwalader,
when there shall be a natural
    end
to Cynan son of Bran?

If you be primary bards
to the master of sciences,
declare ye mysteries
that relate to the inhabitants of
    the world:
there is a noxious creature,
from the rampart of Satanas,
which has overcome all
between the deep and the shallow;
equally wide are his jaws
as the mountains of the Alps;
him death will not subdue,
nor hand or blades;
there is the load of nine hundred
    waggons
in the hair of his two paws;
there is in his head an eye
green as the limpid sheet of icicle;
three springs arise
in the nape of his neck;
sea-roughs thereon
swim through it;

there was the dissolution of the
    oxen
of Deivrdonwy the water-gifted.
The names of the three springs
from the midst of the ocean;
one generating brine
which is from the Corini,
to replenish the flood,
over seas disappearing;
the second without injury
it will fall on us,
when there is rain abroad,
through the whelming sky;
the third will appear
through the mountain veins,
like a flinty banquet,
the work of the King of kings.

A most strange creature will
    come
from the sea marsh of Rhianedd,
as a punishment of iniquity
on Maelgwn Gwynedd;
his hair, his teeth,
and his eyes being as gold;
and this will bring destruction
upon Maelgwn Gwynedd.

It is I who am a diviner
and a leading bard,
who know every passage
of the cave of silence;
I shall liberate Elphin
from the belly of the stony
    tower;
I am Taliesin,
chief of the bards of the west,
who will loosen Elphin
out of the golden fetter.

## Again to the Bards of Maelgwn

Thou retained bard above,
thou retained bard below,
there is not a spot that is known
under the sun and in its round;
neither is it known to you
what is told by tongues;
nor what is stated as certain
between your truth and falsehood;
you who are puny bards, country
    crows,
you hardly escape flying away.
The bard who cannot silence me,
may he not experience silence
until he goes to be covered
by earth and gravel.
He who listens to me,
may he be loved by the Son of God.

Elphin the son of Gwyddno
is in the land of Arthro,
under thirteen locks,
for praising his teacher.
It is I who am Taliesin,
chief of the bards of the west,
who knows every outlet
of the cave of silence,
who will loosen Elphin
from his golden fetter.

## The Casualites of the Bard

First, I have been formed a comely person,
in the court of Ceridwen I have done penance;
though little I was seen, placidly received,
I was great on the floor of the place to where I was led;
I have been a prized defence, the sweet muse the cause,
and by law without speech I have been liberated
by a smiling black old hag, when irritated
dreadful her claim when pursued:
I have fled with vigour,
I have fled as a frog,
I have fled in the semblance of a crow, scarcely finding rest;
I have fled vehemently,
I have fled as a chain,
I have fled as a roe into an entangled thicket;
I have fled as a wolf cub,
I have fled as a wolf in a wilderness,
I have fled as a thrush of portending language;
I have fled as a fox, used to concurrent bounds of quirks;
I have fled as a martin, which did not avail:
I have fled as a squirrel, that vainly hides,
I have fled as a stag's antler, of ruddy course,
I have fled as iron in a glowing fire,
I have fled as a spear-head, of woe to such as has a wish for it;
I have fled as a fierce bull bitterly fighting,
I have fled as a bristly boar seen in a ravine,
I have fled as a white grain of pure wheat,
on the skirt of a hempen sheet entangled,

that seemed of the size of a mare's foal,
that is filling like a ship on the waters;
into a dark leathern bag I was thrown,
and on a boundless sea I was sent adrift;
which was to me an omen of being tenderly nursed, and the Lord of
    heaven then set me at liberty.

### The Bard Declares his History

Primary chief bard
am I to Elphin,
and my original country
is the region of the summerstars;
Joannes the diviner
called me Merddin,
at length every king
will call me Taliesin.

I was with my Lord
in the highest sphere,
on the fall of Lucifer
into the depth of hell;
I have borne a banner
before Alexander;
I know the names of the stars
of the north and the south.
I have been on the galaxy
at the throne of the Distributor;
I was in Canaan
when Absalom was slain;
I conveyed the divine Spirit
to the level of the vale of Hebron;
I was in the court of Don[1]
before the birth of Gwdion.
I was instructor
to Eli and Enoc;
I was at the place of the crucifixion
of the merciful Son of God;
I have been loquacious
prior to being gifted with speech;
I have been winged by the
genius of the splendid crosier;
I have been for three periods
in the court of Arianrod;[2]
I have been the chief director
of the work of the tower of Nimrod;
I am a wonder whose origin is not
    known.

I have been in the ark,
with Noah and Alpha;
I have seen the destruction of
Sodom and Gomorra;
I was in Africa
before the foundation of Rome;
I am now come here
to the remains of Troia.

I have been with my Lord
in the manger of the ass;
I strengthened Moses
through the water of Jordan;
I have been in the firmament
with Mary Magdalene;
I have suffered hunger
for the Son of the Virgin.
I have obtained the muse
from the cauldron of Ceridwen;
I have been bard of the harp
to Lleon of Lochlin.
I have been on the White Hill,
in the court of Cynvelyn,
in stocks and fetters
for a day and a year.
I have been a teacher
to the whole universe;
I shall be until the day of doom
on the face of the earth;
my body it will not be known
whether flesh or fish.
I have been in an easy chair
above the ecliptic,
and this revolves
between three elements;
then I was for nine months
in the womb of the hag Ceridwen;
I was originally little Gwion,
and at length I am Taliesin.

When this composition was made known to the king and his nobles, they became greatly surprised; for they heard not from the mouth of a boy so little any thing that could be compared to this song. And when his majesty knew that its author was the bard of Elphin, he ordered Heinin, his chief and wisest bard, to bring an answer to Taliesin, and to contend with him. But he, on coming forward, could only play blab blab with his lip; and, when the four and twenty other bards were sent for, they did the same thing, and they could not do otherwise. Thereupon Maelgwn asked Taliesin what might be his errand there; and so the other answered in verse in this manner:

>Puny bards, I am trying
>to secure the prize, if I can;
>by a gentle prophetic strain
>I am endeavouring to retrieve
>the loss I may have suffered;
>complete the attempt, I hope,
>since Elphin endures trouble
>in the fortress of Teganwy.[3]
>His confinement may not be over
>    much,
>strengthened by my muse I am
>    powerful;
>mighty on my part is what I seek;
>for, three hundred songs and more,
>are combined in the spell I sing
>There ought not to stand where
>    I am
>neither stone and neither ring;
>that there ought not to be about me
>not any bard who may not know
>that Elphin son of Gwyddno
>is in the land of Artro,[4]
>secured by thirteen locks,
>for praising his instructor:
>and then I Taliesin,
>chief of the bards of the west,
>shall loosen Elphin
>out of a golden fetter.

As Taliesin was thus reciting his composition at the gate, there arose such a storm of wind, that the king and all his nobles thought the castle would fall on their heads; and thereupon the king ordered Elphin to be hastily brought out of prison, and that he might be placed before Taliesin; and immediately it is said that Taliesin sang a song, so that the fetters opened from about the legs of Elphin.

After this he sang a prelude, that is called the master-piece of the bards, as it follows here:

>What was the first man
>made by the God of heaven;
>what the fairest flattering speech
>that was prepared by Jenav;
>what meat, what drink,
>what roof his shelter;
>what the first impression
>of his primary thinking;
>what became his clothing;
>who carried on a disguise,
>owing to the wiles of the country,
>in the beginning?
>Wherefore should a stone be hard,
>why should a thorn be sharp-pointed;
>who is hard like a flint,
>who is salt like brine;
>who sweet like honey;
>who rides on the gale;
>why ridged should be the nose;
>why should a wheel be round;
>why should the tongue be gifted
>    with speech
>rather than another member?
>if thy bards, Heinin, be competent,
>let them reply to me, Taliesin.

After that he sang this prelude, which is called the Castigation of the Bards.

If thou art a bard completely
    imbued
with genius not to be controlled,
be thou not untractable
within the court of thy king;
until thy rigmarole shall be known,
be thou silent Heinin
as to the name of thy verse,
and the name of thy vaunting;
and as to the name of thy grandsire
prior to his being baptized.
Avaunt, ye bards above,
avaunt, ye bards below!
My beloved is below,
in the fetter of Arianrod.
It is certain you know not
how to understand the song I utter,
nor clearly how to discriminate
between the truth and what is
    false;
puny bards, crows of the district,
why do you not take to flight?
A bard that will not silence me,
silence may he not obtain,
till he goes to be covered
under gravel and pebbles:
such as shall listen to me,
may heaven listen to him!

In addition to this, Taliesin sang the prelude inserted here, that is called the Gall
of the Bards, in the presence of the bards of Maelgwn collected together.

Minstrels persevere in their false custom,
immoral ditties are their delight;
vain and tasteless praise they recite;
falsehood at all times do they utter;
innocent persons they ridicule;
married women, by their flattery,
through mischievous intent they deceive;
the pure white virgins of Mary they corrupt;
those who believe them they bring to shame;
they cause uneasiness to moral men,
as they pass their lives away in vanity;
at night they get drunk, they sleep the day;
in idleness without work they feed themselves;
at courts they inquire after feasts;
every senseless word they bring forward;
every deadly sin they praise;
every vile course of life they lead;
concerning the days of death they think not;
neither lodging nor charity do they give;
and from no sensuality do they refrain,
indulging in victuals to excess.
The birds do fly, the fish do swim,
the bees collect honey, worms do crawl,
every thing travails to obtain its food,
except minstrels and useless idlers.
I deride nor learning, nor minstrelsy;
for they are given by heaven to lighten thought.
Be silent, then, ye unlucky rhyming bards,
for you cannot judge between truth and falsehood.
If you be primary bards formed by heaven,
tell your king what his fate will be.

After Taliesin had delivered his lord out of prison, and asserted the chastity of his mistress, and silenced the bards, so that not any one of them dared to utter a single word, he requested of Elphin, that he would make a wager with the king of his possessing a horse swifter than all the horses of his majesty; and this was done by Elphin; and the day, the time, and the place were fixed upon; and the spot is to this day called Morva Rhianedd, or sea-marsh of the Maidens.[5] So the king and his retinue came there, with twenty-four horses, the swiftest that were in his possession. And on the spot, after a long examination, the course was marked out, and the horses were appointed to run. To that place likewise came Taliesin, bringing with him twenty-four holly rods, made black by charring, and which he ordered the boy who rode the horse of his master to put in his girdle, with giving him directions to let all the horses of the king go before him; and as he could overtake them, each one after the other, he was to take one of the rods, and to give a stroke across the crupper of the horse; and after that he was to take another rod; and thus he did in like manner to all the horses, as he could overtake them, giving a strict command to the rider to watch carefully on what spot the horse might fall, and so put his cap down in that spot. All this was accomplished by the boy,

*The Contention of the Bards from an eighth-century stone cross.*

93

as well in giving a stroke to each one of the king's horses, and of putting his cap down on the spot where the horse fell; and to the place Taliesin brought his master, after his horse had won the race, and he ordered Elphin to put men at work to dig a pit. In this spot, after they had dug out the earth to a considerable depth, they found a large cauldron, which was full of gold, and at the time Taliesin said, 'Elphin, this is as payment and reward for bringing me out of the wear, and for nursing me from that time to this day.'

On the spot where what is spoken of above was performed there is a pool of water, which is called to this day, the pool cauldron.

After that the king ordered Taliesin to be brought before him: and of him he asked for information concerning the beginning of the human race; and thereupon Taliesin composed the prelude, which at this day is called one of the four canons of song, and it begins thus:

> The Almighty made,
> down the Hebron vale,
> with his plastic hands,
> 　　Adam's fair form;
>
> And five hundred years,
> void of any help,
> there remained and lay
> 　　without a soul.
>
> He again did form,
> in calm paradise,
> from a left-side rib,
> 　　bliss-throbbing Eve.
>
> Seven hours they were
> the orchard keeping,
> till Satan brought strife,
> 　　With wiles from hell.
>
> Thence they were driven,
> cold and shivering,
> to gain their living,
> 　　into this world.
>
> To bring forth with pain
> their sons and daughters,
> to have possession
> 　　of Asia's land.
>
> To Adam and his mate
> was given a spade,
> to break up the soil,
> thus to get bread,

> An angelic hand,
> from the High Father,
> brought seed for growing
> 　　That Eve might sow;
>
> The wheat pure and white,
> summer tilth to sow,
> every man to feed,
> 　　till great yule feast.
>
> But she then did hide
> of the gift a tenth,
> and all did not sow
> 　　of what was dug.
>
> In the place thus sown
> filched was the seed,
> as Daniel the seer
> 　　doth prophesy.
>
> Black rye then was found,
> and not pure wheat grain,
> to show the mischief
> 　　thus of thieving
>
> The wheat rich in grain
> and red flowing wine
> Christ's pure body make,
> 　　Son of Alpha.
>
> The wafer is flesh,
> the wine is spilt blood,
> the Trinity's words,
> 　　sanctify them.

The concealed books
from Emmanuel's hand
were brought by Raphael
    as Adam's gift,

When in his old age,
to his chin immersed
in Jordan's water,
    keeping a fast.

Twice five, ten and eight,
she was self-bearing,
the mixed burden
    of man-woman.

And once, not hidden,
she brought forth Abel,
and Cain the forlorn,
    the homicide.

Twelve spotless virgins,
and of angels four,
did Eleison send
    To Eve's abode.

To show aid should come
against all trouble,
when no safety came
    to them by strife.

Extreme were the cares
which affected men,
before they had signs
    that mercies came.

Lest dire ills came on,
Moses did obtain
the aid of the three
    most special rods.

Salmon did obtain,
in Babel's tower,
all the sciences
    of Asia land.

So did I obtain,
in my bardic books,
all the sciences
    in Europe known.

Oh! what misery,
through extreme of woe,
prophecy will show
    on Troia's race!

Their course, their bearing,
their permitted way,
and their fate I know,
    unto the end.

A coiling serpent,
proud and merciless,
on her golden wings,
    from Germany.

She will overrun
England and Scotland,
from the Llyçlyn shore
    to the Severn.

Then will the Brython
be as prisoners,
by strangers swayed,
    from Saxony.

Their Lord they will praise,
their speech they will keep,
their land they will lose,
    but wild Walia.

Till some change shall come,
after long penance,
when equally rife
    the two crimes come.

Britons then shall have
their land and their crown,
and the stranger swarm
    shall disappear.

All the angel's words,
as to peace and war,
will be fulfilled
    to Troia's race.

Taliesin afterwards recited various predictions, in verse, to the king, as to the future events in the world, which are given in the collection entitled the Primitive Bards.[6]

As the 'various predictions' alluded to above contain no particulars of the history of Taliesin himself, his Mabinogi may properly terminate here.

It may be an useful illustration to point out where the principal scenes of this Mabinogi were acted; and this we are enabled to do from their names being still preserved by tradition, in the localities where they occurred.

There is a lake called *Llyn Pair*, or pool of the cauldron, about three miles from Towyn, on the old Maçynllaith road through the mountains; the outlet of this lake is among large rocks, and the stream falls into a black pool below, and thence runs into the sea by Bottalog; and where it runs through the low ground, it abounds with the water hemlock. In the Mabinogi the name of the river is *Gwenwyn meirç Gwyddno*, 'the poison of Gwyddno's horses', though its present name is *Avon Llyn y Pair*. About a mile from this lake there is a farm retaining the name of *Gwydd Gwion*, or Gwion wood, from a personage so called in the tale. Three or four miles in the sea, between the outlets of the rivers *Ystwyth* and *Teivi*, are the remains of the fort of Gwyddno, the father of Elphin, and is well known to the people on the neighbouring coast. In the summer of 1770, I sailed over the ruins, in a very calm day, and thus for about three minutes, I had a clear view of them, appearing about twelve feet below the surface of the water; and many of the stones seemed to be large slabs, and lying in confusion on the heap.

## Notes

1   *Llys Don* is the bardic appellation of the constellation Cassiopeia; and so *Caer Gwdion* is the galaxy.
2   The constellation called the northern crown, literally the *court of the silver circle*.
3   The ruins of the fort of *Teganwy*: there are still some remains of it on the northern side of the estuary of the Conwy river.
4   A small estuary, two miles south of Harleç, in Meirion.
5   This is about three miles from Conwy, on the coast towards Abergeleu.
6   Out of the book of Iolo Morganwg, being the collection of Hopkin T. Phylip of Glamorgan; made about A.D. 1370.

# 5

# THE POEMS OF TALIESIN

## THOMAS STEPHENS
### from *Archaeologica Cambrensis*

APPENING IN TRANSLATING the works of the earlier bards to alight upon the poem which follows, I thought the identification of one of the historical characters, and the illustration it affords of the close relationship subsisting up to the beginning of the seventh century between the people of Wales and of Cornwall and Devon, would prove interesting to some of your readers. I have accordingly forwarded it to you. In addition to the historical value above indicated, the poem possesses much interest, from the probability of its affording a date, if not dates, to form contributions towards an authentic life of Taliesin. On reference to the 'Literature of the Kymry' . . . it will be seen that I have ranked this poem among those wrongly attributed to Taliesin; but having recently gone over the ground again, and roughly translated all that appears to me to be the produce of the sixth and seventh centuries, I have seen reason to believe in the antiquity of this little poem, whoever may have been its author.

I have also altered my views with respect to one or two others: 'Canu y Gwynt', I am inclined to think, refers to Owen ab Urien Rheged, not to Owen Gwynedd, and appears to throw light upon the relation of Urien to South, or rather South-West, Wales; 'Marwnad Aeddon o Von' (the 'Aeddan ab Ervai of Aneurin'), is, I think, ancient, though about one half of it wears the marks either of corruption, or of an ecclesiastic author. I incline to the latter view, and should attribute it to Cuhelyn (550 to 600). Four of the six poems marked 'doubtful' I now consider to be ancient: 'Kerdd Daronwy' is referred to the subsequent centuries: 'Marwnad Cunedda' is still involved in difficulties; the poem appears to be ancient; but can Taliesin be its author? No modern man could embrace a personal knowledge of Cunedda and Urien Rheged in one life: 'Anrhec Urien' also stands the test of criticism, and is retained among the genuine poems of Taliesin. And now that I have made this confession of critical faith, we will return to the admiral of the Southern Seas – Corroy the son of Dairy, or Dairn.

The text of the original is in a very bad state, and the translation must only be accepted as an approximation to the meaning of the original.

### Elegy on Corroy the Son of Dairy [i.e. Curoi mac Daira – Ed.]
*by Taliesin*

#### I

From a broad fountain the stream is filled;
There will come a dispensing with the worth of the reckless:
I have been agitated by the death of Corroy.
If there came a man of harsh passions
More mischievous than he, – not much is spoken of him:
The son of Dairy held command on the South Sea;
Before his burial, celebrated was his praise.

#### II

From a broad fountain the brook is filled:
Saddling in haste will be dispensed with;
I have been agitated by the death of Corroy.

#### III

From a broad fountain the deep is filled:
The arrow traverses the strand pensive and angerless;
The hero was a subjugator, – great was his front rank.
Towns followed after the leader;
They went fresh to the quarrel of brands.
While the demon of war heaped carnage in the mornings,
Tales were known from heaven to earth.
In the contention of Corroy and Cocholyn,
Many were the conflicts on the boundaries:
The chief of the encampment sprang from a gentle race.
A city there is kindling love; it will not fall nor tremble;
Blessed is the fortune of the soul by whom it is deserved!

In translating, or rather in attempting to translate, this poem, the name of Corroy's opponent piqued my curiosity; I forthwith went in search of his history to the Anglo-Saxon annals; and, much to my delight, the personage whom I sought appeared in good company, being Cuichelm, one of the West Saxon kings. There were two West Saxon kings of this name, one of whom, the brother of Ceawlin, perished in 593, in battle, probably against the Britons; but as that is the only notice of him that we have, the probability is that Cocholyn was another person of the same name. His history is comprised in a few notices which we shall extract from the *Anglo-Saxon Chronicle*:

A.D. 611. – This year Cynegils succeeded to the kingdom of the West Saxons.

614. – Cynegils admitted his son Quichelm to a share in the kingdom, and both fought a great battle against the Britons (of Damnonia, probably) and slew two thousand and sixty-five Welshmen, at a place called Bampton.

But whether it be Bampton in Oxfordshire, or Bampton in Cornwall is undecided. Dr Giles adopts the former alternative.

623. – At this time, after the brothers Sexred and Siward, there reigned over the East Saxons Sigebert, surnamed the Little, son of Siward, who with his brother Sebert (Sexred) was, by the righteous judgment of God, slain by Kinegils, king of the West Saxons, and Quichelm his son; for, on the death of their father, they returned to the worship of idols, and expelled Mellitus, bishop of London, and not one of their army escaped to tell the tale. – *Wendover.*

626. – Cuichelm, for some reason, sent one Eumer to assassinate Edwin king of Northumbria. Eumer failed in his object; and Edwin, in revenge, made war upon the West Saxons, slaying five petty kings, and a great number of the people. Roger of Wendover states that Edwin slew Quichelm, at a place called in consequence 'Quichelmeslaune;' but that account differs from all the other chronicles, and appears to be erroneous.

628. – Cynegils and Cuichelm fought against Penda king of the Mercians, at Cirencester, and then made a treaty, both parties being exhausted.

636. – This year King Cuichelm was baptized at Dorchester, and the same year he died.

The name is variously written Cuichelm, Quichelm, and Kichelm.

Of Corroy the son of Dairy, or Dairn, I am unable to give any satisfactory account; and the determination of his whereabouts must depend upon an inference. In 614 was fought the battle of Bampton; and as Corroy would probably be engaged in that, it becomes of importance to have the place of that battle ascertained. Dr Giles states that 'Bampton in Devonshire is by far too remote to admit the supposition that the battle in question was fought there;' and he therefore concludes that Bampton in Oxfordshire is more likely to be the place. But I am compelled to differ from that opinion. The West Saxons, under Ceaulin, had conquered Gloucester, Cirencester and Bath, in 577; Ceolric succeeded Ceaulin in 592, and was followed in 597 by Coelwulf, who 'fought and contended incessantly against either the Angles or the Welsh, (of Devon, Somerset and Dorset?) or the Picts or the Scots;' and in 636 we find Cuichelm in possession of Dorchester,[1] in the western part of Dorset, not very far from the Devon boundary. From these facts, and from the fact that the West Saxons had been in possession of Oxfordshire long before 614, I am led to conclude that the Bampton of the *Chronicle* is the town of Bampton on the eastern boundary of Devon. If so, we may from thence deduce the conclusion, that the boundaries which Corroy defended were the boundaries of Devon, and that he was a chief of the Damnonian people.

One other question remains to be decided, and that is, who is the author of this poem? Judging from the structure of the poem, its difference from the other poems of the chief of bards in style, and decided inferiority as an artistic composition, I should incline to the belief that Taliesin cannot be its author. Its antiquity admits of no doubt; it is, in the *Myvyrian Archaiology*, positively stated to have been the production of that bard; and, however internal evidence may lead us to doubt this paternity, it is by no means impossible that Taliesin may have written the poem; – that is, there are no insuperable chronological difficulties in the way of that supposition. Taliesin appears to have retired to North Wales after the death of Urien, in 584; the poem on 'Gwaith Dyffryn Gwarant' seems to have been addressed to Ynyr Gwent (who is usually placed earlier) after that period; and this bard is said to have written an elegy on Iago ab Beli, king of Gwynedd; that monarch died, or was slain, about 603; and, accordingly, it is quite possible that the bard who wrote his elegy might have written a poem dating soon after the year 614. Anrheg Urien seems to have been written in North Wales, 'ar lan Llyn Geirionydd', Caernarvonshire, where Taliesin, when an old man, appears to have made the acquaintance of his young contemporary Aneurin. This elegy to Iago ab Beli is mentioned by Llwyd (*Arch.*, 256,) among the contents of a Hengwrt MS. called 'Hanesyn Hên.' What has become of the poem? It is not in the *Myvyrian Archaiology.*

We here assume that the poem was composed during the lifetime of Quichelm; but it is questionable whether we can confine its production within those limits. The manner in which the contest between Corroy and Cocholyn is spoken of, implies that it had ceased, and that Corroy, who appears to have died a natural death, had survived his opponent; if so, the poem cannot have been written before 640; and, in that case, Taliesin could scarcely have been its author. Criticism and chronology appear, therefore, to coincide in referring the poem to some subsequent and inferior bard; for, though it is improbable, it is not impossible, that Taliesin may have been living in 640. He was evidently living when Aneurin made known to him his intention of devoting his talents to celebrate the battle of Cattraeth; and some of the events commemorated in the poems of the bard of Gododdin, occurred at various periods from A.D. 576 to 642; but to this point we shall again have occasion to recur. In this conflict of probabilities, all that can be safely asserted is the antiquity of the poem; and its authorship had better be left an open question.

I propose to furnish a series of short Papers on the Bardic Poems of the Sixth Century to the *Archaeologia Cambrensis*, and shall from time to time take the liberty of calling the attention of your readers to such portions of our literary history as may promise interest and instruction. Lovers of early literature will also be glad to hear, that M. de Villemarque has recently published a translation of the *Poémes des Bardes Bretons du VI. Siécle.*

'Anrec Urien', the poem which forms the subject of the present notice, is printed from the *Llyfr Coch, The Red Book of Hergest*, at page 50 of the first volume of the *Myvyrian Archaiology*, and in the original appears as follows. Judging from the orthography, the copy under consideration would appear to have been written between 1200 and 1500, that being the period assigned to the prevalence of the letter *k* in Welsh MSS. by an excellent authority, Edward Lhuyd, whose critical rule is thus stated:

> The letter *k* never occurs in our oldest British manuscripts, but being
> afterwards introduced by the Normans, (who made frequent use of it in

their old French), I find that about the year 1200, *k* was constantly used in the initial syllables, and *c* in the termination; and it continued afterwards, though not so very much used, till about the year 1500. Since which time most writers omitted it, using *c* constantly in its stead, in imitation of the ancients, which is yet not so convenient, because 'tis in other languages subject to a double pronunciation.'

*Arch. Britt.*, page 228

## Anrec Urien
*Llyfr Coch*

Gogyfercheis
Gogyvarchaf
   Gogyverchyd
Urien Reget
Duallovyet
   Y Leuenyd
Eur ac Aryant
Mor eu divant
   Eu dihenyd
Kyn noc y dau
Rug y duylau
   Y guesceryd
Ieuaf a unaeth
Coll ac alaeth
   Am feirch peunyd
Keneu y vraut
Kynnin daervaut
   Ni by geluyd
Urien a wnaeth
Dialynyaeth
   Y gewilyd
Kynnin vynnu
Kyvarchuelu
   Eu dihenyd
Deutu Aerven
Diffuys dilen
   Dydau lwyd
Seleu delyit
Enynnyessit
   Or a dybyd
Dybi y vaeth
A ryd alhaeth
   Oc eu herwyd
Cochliu lavneu
Truy valch eiryeu
   Am ffruyth eu guyd

Wy Kynnhalyant
Lle peduar cant
   Y peduar guyr
[Dufyr dyvnav (dyvnvas)
Bendigwyf clav
   Ac oe herwyd
Yr ae Kaffo
Kynvinaul vo
   Yn dragyuyd
Dydeu collet
Or ymdiret
   Yr ardelyd
A llau heb vaut
A llavyn ar gnaut
   A thlaut lûyd
Oes feibionein
Nyt ymgyghein
   Ymmerueryd
Nyt ymganret
Nyt ymdiret
   Neb oe gylyd
Dreic o Wyned
Diffwys dired
   Dirion drefyd
Lloegrwys yd a
A lletaut yna
   Harchollyd
Torrit meinueith
Yn anoleith
   Ar gyfhergyd
Muy a gollir
Noc a geffir
   O Wyndodyd
O gyt gyghor
Kyvrung esgor
   Mor a Mynyd

Gotrissit Brythyon
Yn at poryon
   Ar antyrron gyueithyd
Ef a dau byt
Ny byt Kerdglyt
   Ni byd Kelvyd
Alaf gar maer
Arthauc vyd chuaer
   Wrth y gilyd
Llad a bodi
O Eleri
   Hyt chuil fynyd
Un gorvydyauc
Antrugarauc
   Ef a orvyd
Bychan y lu
Yn ymchuelu
   Or Mercherdyd

Arth or deau
Kyvyt ynteu
   Dychyfervyd
Lloegruys lledi
Afrivedi
   O Bowysyd
Guaith cors Vochno
O diango
   Bydaud deduyd
Deudeng guraged
Ac nyt ryved
   Am un gur vyd
Oes Ieuonctid
Aghyvyrdelit
   Y vaeth dybyd
Beru ymdivant
Barnauc or cant
   Nys ryvelyd]

Uryen o Reget hael ef syd ac a vyd
Ac a vu yr Adaf letaf y gled
Balch yghynted or tri Theyrn ar dec or gogled
A un eu enu Aneuryn guautryd Auenyd
A minneu Dalyesin o lann llyn geirionnydd
Ni dalywyf yn hen
Ym dygyn aghen
Oni Moluyf Uryen.  Amen.

*Tal. ae Dyuaut*

This poem presents considerable facilities for translation, in the easy flow of the metre, and the simplicity of the diction; and the following will probably be found a tolerably correct version.

Postponing for the moment all considerations as to the antiquity of the poem, and assuming its genuineness, we are here presented with several interesting biographical and historical facts. We here meet with a brother of Urien, named Keneu, of whom there is no other notice, and learn the personal characters of the two brothers; and we have also the novel information that Urien was the youngest son of Cynvarch, whose children ought therefore to be placed in the following order:

Llew, married to Anna, sister of Arthur;[2]
Arawn;
Keneu;
Eurddyl, wife of Elifer Gosgorddvawr;
Urien, married to Modron, daughter of Avallach.

Another fact worthy of note is, the subject of contest – the fruit of trees – apple-trees, most probably:

Blades were reddened
Through proud words
    For the fruit of their trees.

We have here also a vivid portraiture of the effects of hostile contests, in hands without thumbs, swords on the flesh, small gatherings, the losses of the valleys, the misery of youth, the destruction of fortresses, the scarcity of warriors, public distrust and general insecurity. Allusion is made to one, and, if Aerven (Aeron, or Arvon?) and Cors Vochno do not refer to the same event, to two battles; and, if there were two battles, one of them, i.e. the first, would possibly be that in which Urien is said to have done such signal service to his country, in expelling the Gwyddelians from the principality. If the sons of Cunedda co-operated with him on this occasion, Professor Rees must have placed Cunedda much too early; but perhaps this point had better be reserved until we come to treat of the poem called 'Marwnad Cunedda.' We have another fact worthy of note in the declaration that Urien was one of the 'thirteen kings of North Britain;' and the residence of the bard, with the asserted intimacy between him and Aneurin, should be carefully borne in mind.

The metre in which the poem is composed is called Huppynt, and is also designated Llostodyn, or Colofn Vraith, or Awdl Losgyrniog;[3] and it is said to have been invented, with other metres, by the bard Taliesin.[4] It is accounted a good metre, and admits of many variations without losing its leading feature; but perhaps the best way to render its form intelligible to the English reader would be to quote an illustration from Wordsworth's verses to the Daisy:

In youth from rock to rock I went,
From hill to hill, in discontent
Of pleasure high and turbulent,
    Most pleas'd when most uneasy;
But now my own delights I make,
My thirst at every rill can slake,
And gladly Nature's love partake
    Of thee, sweet Daisy!

This metre, in which the first and second sets of three lines form triplets, and in which the fourth line rhymes with the eighth, corresponds exactly to a variation of the Huppynt; but in Taliesin's poem it is presented in a simpler form. The first and second sets of lines are couplets, and the third and sixth rhyme together, as in the following example from Lord Byron:

My dear Mr Murray,
You're in a great hurry,
    To set up this ultimate canto;
But (if they don't rob us)
You'll see Mr Hobhouse
    Will bring it safe in his portmanteau.

These lines are also well adapted to illustrate the elastic movement of the Cambrian poem, which may be rendered in the following words:

## Translation

I have freely greeted,
I will freely greet
    The familiar greeter;
Urien of Rheged.
Comprehended
    Be his joyfulness.
Gold and silver
The sea was their consumer
    And destroyer,[5]
Before they came
Between the hands
    Of the scatterer.
(Though) youngest, he caused
Loss, and sorrow
    For horses daily;
Keneu his brother
An eagerhanded brawler
    Did not prove false;
Urien did make
Retaliation
    For the shame (or the discredit);
The brawler obtained
Reproach
    For his end.
On the two sides of (or about)
    Aerven,[6]
An uncovered precipice,
    There came success;
Spies were captured,
And (fire) was kindled,
    Wherever he came;
The coming of the fosterer
Did cause sorrow;
    And because of him (or them)
Blades were reddened,
Through proud words
    For the fruit of (his or their)
        trees;
The four warriors
Maintained the place
    Of four hundred.[7]
[With the deepest water,[8]
I will bless the wounded;
    And on account thereof,
Whoever obtains it,
Blessed will be
    To all eternity.

There will befall a loss
From the enterprise
    To the districts;
And hands without thumbs,
And blades on the flesh,
    And a poor muster.
The life of young sons
Will not be harmonious
    In the distraction.
There will be no fellowship,
Nor reliance
    Of one upon another.
A dragon from Gwynedd
Of precipitous lands
    And gentle towns,
To the Lloegrians will go,
And the inflictor
    Will there scatter them about.
Masonry will be broken,
And exterminated,
    In the concussion;
And more men will be slain
Than the Gwyndodians.
    Will be in number.
From mutual counselling
Between enemies
    On mountain and sea,
The Britons will be oppressed
And become refuse,
    And the co-operators will be
        ungentle.
There will come a time
When minstrels will not be clad
    Nor men be skilful,
When Mayors will love wealth
And sisters be bearish (gruff)
    To one another;
Killing and drowning,
From Eleri
    As far as Chwilfynydd[9]
A conquering and
Unmerciful one
    Will triumph;
Small will be his army
In returning
    From Wednesday's fight.
A bear from the South,

He shall arise,
  And shall meet
Lloegrians scattering
Vast numbers
  Of Powysians.[10]
Whoever escapes
From the battle of Cors Vochno,
  Will be fortunate;
There will be twelve women,

And no wonder,
  For one man:
The period of youth,
Ungentle
  Will be its nursing;
Spears will cause bereavement,
And of a hundred men, it is
  thought
There will be no warrior.]

Urien of Rheged, generous he is, and will be,
And has been. Proud in the hall; Since Adam, his is the widest-
    spreading sword
Among the thirteen kings of the North.
And one is named, or, ⎫
Do I know his name? ⎭ Aneurin the flowing song'd minstrel,[11]
And I Taliesin from the borders of Geirionnydd Lake.[12]
And when I am old,
May I be in greatest need,
If I praise not Urien.

We now come to the most difficult part of our subject. Is this poem, with its sudden transitions, its mixture of prediction and retrospection, its allegorical allusions, and its jumble of facts and fiction, the genuine production of the bard Taliesin? My first impressions were adverse; they were founded upon the fact that, of all the poems which can be attributed to Taliesin, this is the only one which assumes the predictive form; and I was strengthened in that belief, by the resemblance which exists between this and the *Hoianau* fictitiously attributed to Merddin. In both poems it is stated that 'a bear shall arise from the south;' and both speak of the battle of Cors Vochno. The *Hoianau* speak of this battle, in the order of place, after the battle of Machawy, which occurred in Radnorshire (see *Pughe's map*) in the year 1033; and as other battles mentioned in the same verse, after the battle of Machawy, were also posterior in the order of time, I inferred that this may have been so, and thence concluded that the poem could not have been ancient. Having since considered the subject more carefully, I incline to believe that objection to be still tenable; but let us first see if the facts cannot be explained without sacrificing the integrity of the poem, the first and concluding parts of which are certainly genuine, whatever may become of the middle.

We may imagine the actual events to have occurred in the following order: The dragon from Gwynedd ravaged the lands of the Lloegrians, the inhabitants of the midland counties, who at this time perhaps had not thoroughly coalesced with the Saxons; the Lloegrians retaliated, and drove the men of Powys before them towards the sea-coast, and Urien, the 'bear from the South,' coming up from Rheged,[13] intercepted and defeated them at Cors Vochno. This theory assumes Urien to have resided originally in the south, and to have afterwards gone to North Wales; it clashes with the received notions, but it is supported by the words of Taliesin, who, speaking of Urien as one of the northern kings, calls him 'Urien *from* Rheged' (Urien o Reget); and it has the additional advantage of settling the difficulty about the geography of 'Rheged,' and of simplifying the biography of Urien. However, for the present, I simply throw this out as an hypothesis.

There is however another and far more satisfactory explanation. Two-thirds of the poem has no necessary reference to Urien, and, indeed, appears to belong to an age much later than that of Taliesin; a part of it is manifestly genuine, that is the beginning and the end; but the portion placed within brackets I conceive to be an interpolation, which, from the affected predictive form, is more likely to have been wilful than accidental. The lines in the 'Hoianau' are as follows:

> I will predict a battle on the wave,
> And the battle of Machawy, and a river battle,
> And the battle of Cors Vochno, and a battle in Mon.
> *Lit. of the Kymry,* page 270

Now it is highly probable that, as we have no account of two battles of Cors Vochno, and cannot positively connect the place with one, that both poems refer to the same event; and if the *Hoianau* were composed in the twelfth century, we are warranted in assuming that it occurred at a period not far distant; for it is highly probable that it was fresh in the public mind at that time. The battle of Machawy was similarly present to the public memory; and if the order of naming them is not without significance, the battle of Cors Vochno must have taken place some ten or twenty years later than 1033. Under this impression, let us pass our eyes down the historic page, and attempt to discover the facts here related. Cors Vochno is a large marsh in the upper part of Cardiganshire, on the sea shore.

The events we seek will be found to have occurred between the years 1056 and 1061, in the reign of Griffith ab Llywelyn ab Seisyllt, king of North Wales; but in order to be ourselves accurate, and to note the minute fidelity of the bardic details, let us mark the words of the poem, which seems to be a valuable contemporaneous record:

> A dragon from Gwynedd
> Of precipitous lands
>     And gentle towns,
> Will go to the Lloegrians;
> And the inflictor
>     Will there scatter them about;
> Masonry will be broken,
> And exterminated
>     In the concussion;
> And more men will be slain,
> Than the Gwyndodians
>     Will be in number.

Now in the year 1055 we find some facts which admirably tally with this description:

> 1055. – There was a witenagemot in London, and Ælfgar the eorl, Leofric the eorl's son, was outlawed without any kind of guilt; and he went then

to Ireland, and there procured himself a fleet, which was of eighteen ships besides his own, and they went then to Wales, to King Griffin, with that force, and he received him into his protection. And then with the Irishmen, and with Welshmen, they gathered a great force; and Rawulf the eorl gathered a great force on the other hand at Herefordport. And they sought them out there; but before there was any spear thrown, the English people fled, because they were on horses; *and there great slaughter was made,* about four hundred or five; *and they made none on the other side.* And they then betook themselves to the town, *and that they burned*; and the great minster which Æthelstan the venerable bishop before caused to be built, that they plundered and bereaved of relics, and of vestments, and of all things; and slew the people, and some they led away.

*Anglo-Saxon Chronicle*

Harold, the son of Earl Godwin, was sent to punish the Welsh, and advanced as far as Snowdon, where, according to the *Gwentian Chronicle*, he was defeated by Griffith. Wendover says he ravaged the country terribly; but a better authority, the *Anglo-Saxon Chronicle*, states that the English 'went out *not far* among the Welsh, and that Harold made peace with Griffith.'

> 1056. – Griffith defeated and slew Leofgar, a warlike bishop of Hereford, who had taken the field against him.

> 1058. – Griffith again ravaged the English land, in company with a Norwegian force under Macht the son of Harald, and brought home much spoil.

In these events we clearly recognize the facts mentioned by the bard, the slaughter of large numbers of the English, the scattering of the Lloegrians about, the breaking of the fortifications of Hereford, and the all but extermination of the town and its inhabitants. The other verses reverse the picture, and these too we shall find to be counterparts of historic facts.

In the *Gwentian Chronicle*, they are related under the year 1060; and in the *A. S. Chron.*, as usual, three years later. It should here be borne in mind that the family of Iestyn ab Gwrgant, lord of Glamorgan, had been before this in possession of the throne of South Wales, that Griffith ab Llywelyn drove them out and kept them at bay, and that in consequence they were perpetually at war. In 1060, Owen, the grandson and rightful successor of Rhydderch ab Iestin, died, and his brother Caradoc, 'the bear from the south,' prosecuted the family claim.

> 1060. – Caradoc ab Rhydderch ab Iestin engaged Harold to bring an army into South Wales, and there he was joined by a large army of the men of Glamorgan and Gwent. They then went against Griffith, who came to meet them with a large army of the men of Gwynedd, Powys, and South Wales, and a great battle ensued, where Griffith was killed through the treachery of Madoc Min, bishop of Bangor, the same who had previously caused, through treachery, the death of his father, Llewelyn ab Seisyllt.'[14]

Harold on this occasion was accompanied by his brother Tosti, Harold commanding the sea forces, and Tosti those on land;[15] and it is said that they nearly depopulated the country, leaving scarcely a man alive in it.[16] In these facts we have all the essential features of the poem, the counselling among enemies, the forces on land and sea, the ungentle co-operators, and the consequent depopulation. All that remains to complete the demonstration is to identify this battle with that of Cors Vochno; this I cannot do; but there are very strong probabilities in its favour; and it would be difficult to find another spot which would answer the requirements of the case, and permit of co-operation between land and sea forces, and be at the same time near the boundaries of Powys and South Wales. The English chronicles fix no place; but the *French Chronicle* of Geoffrey Gaimar agrees with the *Gwentian Chronicle.* in placing it in the upper portion of South Wales.

This conclusion is also, to some extent, confirmed by one of Gwalchmai's odes to Owen Gwynedd, ab Gr ab Cynan, ab Iago:

> I will extol the generous descendant of Iago
> Who brightened the disgrace of Cors Fochno,
> Who ejected the Flemings, and set their vale in flames, &c.

This defeat of the Flemings took place at Aberdyfi, says one authority (*Myv.*, ii, page 423), and at Aberteivy (Cardigan), says another and better authority (*ibid.*, page 557), in the year 1136; at that time this battle was still fresh in the public memory; and we may thence infer that it had occurred not very long before. I cannot find another battle in that district of sufficient magnitude to answer the requirements of the case.

Having determined that a part only of this poem can be accounted genuine, it becomes our duty to draw the line between the true and false, between the production of the sixth, and that of the eleventh, century. This is not by any means an easy task, as the dress at present worn by the whole is that of the thirteenth; and therefore orthography, usually a valuable ally, completely fails us here. I have drawn the line at the point indicated, not without a suspicion however that the verse

> Dufyr dyvnav,
> Bendigwyf clav,
>     Ac oe herwyd
> Yr ae Kaffo,
> Kynvinaul vo
>     Yn dragyuyd

may belong to the first part. Can the Rev. J. Williams (Ab Ithel), whose researches have taken a more ecclesiastical turn than my own, inform me whether the sentiments here expressed could have been entertained in the sixth century, or do they savour of later corruptions of Christianity? From that point forward there is a remarkable similarity of sentiment, between the opening and closing verses of the supposed spurious poem; both speak in despairing terms of the miseries of a depopulated country; both lament the condition of the juvenile inhabitants; and both were probably the effusions of the same muse. Of the verse, beginning 'Dreic o Wyned,' I have no doubt; and the distrust spoken of in the verse preceding it is clearly referable to the turmoil and treachery of the period during which Griffith ab Llewelyn was betrayed and murdered. Much doubt hangs over the fate of this brave monarch; it does not seem that he was slain in battle; but, being defeated, he appears to have been deserted by his own subjects, and to have wandered a fugitive in the wildernesses of Wales, until he was betrayed by Madoc Min. The words of one chronicle make this appear very distinctly:

> One thousand and sixty years was the age of Christ, when Griffith ab Llywelyn, the head and shield and defender of the Britons, fell *by the treachery of his own men.* He who was invincible before, was now deserted among desolate glens.[17]

And a good summary of all these facts is given in one MS. of the *Anglo-Saxon Chronicle*:

> 1063. – This year Harold the earl, and his brother Tosty the earl, as well with a land force as a ship force, went into Wales, and they subdued the land; and the people delivered hostages to them, and submitted; and went afterwards [during harvest][18] and slew their King Griffin, [by reason of the war that he warred with Harold the earl,] and brought to Harold his head; and he appointed another king thereto, [and Harold brought his head to the king, and his ship's head,[19] and the rigging therewith].

Who is the author of the middle part? I cannot name any one. Griffith is said to have been a liberal patron of the bards, and to have been profuse in his presents;[20] but hitherto there has been no poem referred to that period. If our speculation be not unfounded, that is no longer the case; and if our views be sound and trust-worthy, we shall have done some little towards a proper classification of our ancient remains, added one poem to our literary store, and thrown one ray of light on one of the darkest and most barren periods in Cambrian history.

But although unable positively to refer the poem to any individual bard, there can be no great harm in a quiet bit of speculation. The intellectual movement so prominent in the twelfth century had already begun in the eleventh; and Griffith ab Llewelyn has the merit of having done much to improve both the political and intellectual condition of his subjects. We learn this from the account of his death in the various chronicles.

> And most illustrious were he and his father of all the princes that were in Wales before their time; and best for valour, and war, and for peace, and for government, and for liberality, and for justice; and through their wisdom and understanding, they brought Gwynedd, and Powys, and South Wales into union, so that the Kymry were strong against Saxons, and all enemies and strangers.
>
> *Gwentian Chronicle, Myv., ii, pages 515, 516*

> A.D. M°LXI, died Griffith ab Llewelyn, golden-torqued king of Wales, and its defender, after many spoils and victorious conflicts with his enemies, *and after many feasts, and merriment, and great gifts of gold and silver,*

*and garments of great value,* he who was a sword and a shield over the whole face of Wales.

> *Brut y Saeson, Myv.,* ii, page 516

After huge spoils, and immeasureable victories, and innumerable rich gifts of gold, and silver, and gems, and ermined vestments.

> *Llyfr Coch MSS., Myv.,* ii, page 397

Feasts afford presumptive evidence of the existence of bards; and as they were the chief parties thus rewarded, they must probably have been numerous. This monarch, in 1062, was succeeded in North Wales by his half brothers, Bleddyn and Rhiwallon ab Kynvyn, the sons of Angharad, the daughter of Meredith ab Owen, prince of South Wales, who, after the death of her first husband, Llewelyn ab Seisyllt, married Kynvyn ab Gwerystan, lord of Kibwyr; and in the South by Meredith ab Owen, a lineal descendant from Howel Dda. Bleddyn was a worthy successor, and his character is thus portrayed:

> He was the gentlest and most merciful of kings, and he injured none unless they rose against him, and when there was a rising, it was with reluctance that he avenged the insurrection. He was kind to his relations, and the defender of the orphan, the poor, and the widowed; and *the supporter of the wise,* and the honour and the ground-wall of churches, *the diverter or comforter of the countries,* and *generous to all,* fierce in war, and eager for peace and the defence of all.
>
> *Llyfr Coch MSS., Myv.,* ii, page 398

The Iolo MSS. are not unimpeachable authorities; but the preceding extracts go far to confirm the following statement:

> After that, Bleddyn the son of Kynvyn, and his brother, Rhiwallon the son of Kynvyn, after obtaining possession of Gwynedd and Powys, made an honourable feast in Conway, by proclamation and notice of a year and a day, and invited there graduates in the science of song and of stringed music, where laws and institutions and privileges were framed for them, in the time when William the Conqueror took the crown of England from the Saxons. And at that feast the bards of stringed music, under the protection of the bards who were chiefs of song, and others of poets and minstrels; and at that festival, there was appointed a system and code, genealogy and herald bards were established where they had not previously existed, possessed of official privileges, by the national arrangement of Wales; and a system was instituted for the science of armorial bearings and their appurtenances.
>
> *Iolo MSS.,* page 630

Assuming this account to be true, the said feast must have taken place about 1067; the Norman Conquest took place in 1066, and Rhiwallon was killed in 1068. Here, then, we have evidence of a flourishing order of bards; but we are acquainted with the name of only one person who could have composed the poem

in question, and who could have been at this feast. The poem, *which was proba-*
*bly composed soon after the battle of Cors Vochno, and before the death* of
Griffith ab Llywelyn, i.e. in 1060 or 1061, is written from a North Welsh standpoint, and the author was probably a Venedocian. Now both these requisites are
found in the person of Bleddyn Ddu, of whom Lhuyd gives us the following
account: –

> Bledhyn Dhy. *Poeta anno,* 1090. (His poems addressed) I Dhyn, i abad
> aber Konuy, &c., (are said to be in the *Red Book of Hergest*,) L. K. H.
> Col., 1249–84.
>
> *Arch. Britt.*, page 255

The *Cambrian Biographer* states that none of his works remain; but Williams follows the fuller statement of Lhuyd, without adding to it, and without developing
the significance of the et cetera; and, strange to say, these poems, of which Lhuyd
gives so minute an account, are not inserted in the *Myvyrian Archaiology.* Are they
not in existence? The Rev. J. Jones of Nevern (Tegid) is well acquainted with the
*Llyfr Coch*, and possibly may have a copy of it: cannot he furnish us with some
information on this point? But to return. From the fact that one of Bleddyn's
poems is addressed to one of the abbots of Aberconway, we are to some extent
warranted in believing him to have been resident in North Wales, and therefore,
so far as the standpoint is concerned, in a position to write the poem under notice.
Lhuyd does not furnish us with the data from which he asserts Bleddyn Ddu to
have been a poet of the year 1090; but, assuming the fact to be so, it is easily conceivable that he might have written a poem in the year 1061. There is another poet
of whom the same assertion might be made, but not with equal confidence.
Meilyr, who sang the elegy of Trehaearn ab Caradoc in 1080, and of Griffith ab
Cynan in 1137, is said by Lhuyd to have been a '*poeta anno* 1070.' There is a
poem by Meilyr still later than 1137, that on his own approaching death, which
cannot be referred to any period much earlier than 1150; and the editors of the
*Myv. Arch.* place him from 1120 to 1160. If we adopt either of these dates, Meilyr
could scarcely have been its author, even if he had lisped in numbers, for the poem
has the sober tone, and ripe feeling, of a man in years. The balance of probabilities is therefore in favour of Bleddyn Ddu.

The poem as it stands in the *Myvyrian* is a thing of shreds and patches, and
appears to consist of three parts, a beginning, a middle, and an end, but having no
reference to each other. The first part is genuine, and so is the conclusion; but they
do not appear to be connected; and the conclusion belongs apparently to a different poem, as it is not resolvable into the same metre as the initial verses.

The date of the genuine part of the composition, the battle of Aerven, and the
intimacy between Taliesin and Aneurin, will probably come under discussion
another time.

My last paper so far exceeded the length which I deemed reasonable for a commentary on a single poem, that several topics were left untouched. These, I will
briefly discuss before entering upon the consideration of another poem. First then

of Aerven, the scene of some of Urien's exploits. In a note I threw out a suggestion that it might have been Aeron, or Arvon; but the probability is in favour of its being an old name for the river Dee. That Aerven is the name of a river, appears quite clear from the description given in the poem:

> On *the two sides* of Aerven,
> Of uncovered precipices,
>     He placed success.

I do not know the history of the event here recorded, nor whether the Dee in any part of its course flows between rocky precipices; but, in Richards' *Dictionary,* Aerven is positively identified with that river: 'Aerfen, Dyfrdwy, s.f. the river Dee. Aerfen bengrech felen fawr.'

Here Richards adds other descriptive traits; but from which of the bards he derives the quotation he does not state. However, thus much we may assume, that some authority is better than none; and though we do not know what authority this author has for the assertion, it is not credible that he made it without being warranted in so doing.

The next topic is, where was RHEGED? Some say in South Wales; some say in Cumberland; but all confess themselves to be in doubt. This subject invites a long discussion; but I must refrain for the present, and defer the full examination until Urien Rheged comes fairly before us. In the meantime, I may as well indicate my own opinion. Let us take a map of ancient Britain, and start from Manchester; from thence two Roman roads run through Lancashire, one going to Lancaster, and ending there, and the other straight on from Manchester to Cumberland, and the south of Scotland; confining our attention to the latter, and following its course from Manchester, we come to the next Roman station at Ribchester. This is called by one authority, Coccium, and by another, Rhigodunum; and RHIGOD-dunum, I believe, was the RHEGED which we seek.

The third topic of which we promised to treat, was the intimacy between the bards Taliesin and Aneurin; the existence of which is proved by allusions in the poems of both. One of these allusions has already come under our notice:

> Urien of Rheged: since Adam,
> His has been the widest spreading sword,
> Of the thirteen kings of the North.
> Do I know the name of Aneurin the flowing-song'd minstrel,
> I being Taliesin, of the banks of Lake Geirionnydd?

The words, 'of the thirteen kings of North Britain,' may belong to either the first or the last part of these lines. If we attach them to the last, they will read thus:

> Of the thirteen kings of the North,
> Do I know the name of Aneurin?

We thus connect Aneurin with the north, and invest him with a kingly character. In any case, Aneurin is clearly placed in the north of England, while Taliesin is located on the banks of lake Geirionnydd, in Caernarvonshire. This place seems to possess some strong fascination for, and certainly derives much celebrity from, the bards; Taliesin lived upon its banks; Llywarch ab Llywelyn, my old friend, 'the poet of the pigs,' appears to have resided there; and the chair-bard of Rhuddlan has long been endeared to his countrymen by the cognomen of Ieuan Glan Geirionnydd. From all the evidence that I can collect, Taliesin was much older than Aneurin. In the lines under consideration, the descriptive term 'flowing-song'd minstrel,' indicates that the one was in the prime of mental vigour; and the allusion made to Taliesin, in the *Gododdin,* where Aneurin indicates that the plan and subject of that poem had been submitted to the other, appears to warrant the same conclusion. Besides this, their poems, in their titles and contents, tend to establish the same point. Taliesin was probably consulted upon the plan of the *Gododdin* at the beginning of the seventh century, when he certainly was an old man; but the *Gododdin* treats of some events which took place about 640, when Taliesin was dead and in his grave. So much then for the residence of Taliesin, and his intimacy with Aneurin; but we reserve a fuller biography for a more fitting occasion.

Let us now proceed to discuss another poem. The one selected for this occasion is the 'Elegy of Aeddon of Mona', which, though referring to, and illustrative of, the existence of 'the Gael in Gwynedd,' appears to have escaped the notice of the very able and acute author of that essay. The poem occurs in the *Myvyrian Archaiology,* (i, page 70) and runs thus:

### Marwnad Aeddon o Von

**I**

Echrys Ynyt[21]
Gwaut hu Ynys
   Gwrys gwobretor
Mon mad gogei
Gwrhyd Erfei
   Menai ei dor.
Lleweis wirawd
Gwin a bragawd
   Gan frawd esgor
Teyrn wofrwy
Diwedd pob rhwy
   Rhwyf rewinetor.[22]
Tristlawn ddeon
Yr Arch Aeddon
   Can rychior
Nid fu nid fi
Ynghemelrhi
   Ei gyfeissor.
Pan ddaeth Aeddon
O wlad Wydion
   Seon tewdor
Gwenwyn pur ddoeth
Pedair pennoeth.
   Meinoeth tymhor

Cwyddynt gytoed
Ni bu clyd coed
   Gwynt yngoror[23]
Math ag Eunydd
Hudwyd gelfydd
   Rydd elfinor
Ym myw[24] Gwydion
Ac Amaethon
   Atoedd cynghor
Twll tal y rodawg
Ffyrf ffodiawg
   Ffyrf diachor
Cadarn gyfedd
Ymhob gorsedd
   Gwnelid ei fodd.
Cu Cynaethwy
Hyd tra fyw fwy
   Crybwylletor
Cadarn gyngres
Ei faranrhes
   Ni bu werthfor.
[Am bwyf gan Grist
Hyd na bwyf trist
   Pan ebostol

113

Hael Arch Aeddon
Gan Engylion
   Cynwysetter.]


II

Echrys Ynys
Gwawd hwynys
   Gwrys gochwymma
Yrhag buddwas
Cymry ddinas
   Aros ara
Dragonawl ben
Priodawr perchen
   Ym Mretonia
Difa gwledig
Or bendefig
   Ae tu terra
Pedeir morwyn
Wedy eu cwyn
   Dygnawd eu tra

Erddygnawd wir
Ar for heb dir
   Hir eu trefra
Oi wironyn
Na ddigonyn
   Dim gofetra
Ceryddus wyf
Na chrybwyllwyf
   Am rywnel da
I lwrw lywy
Pwy gwaharddwy
   Pwy attrefna
I lwrw Aeddon
Pwy gyneil Mon
   Mwyn gywala
[Am bwyf gan Grist
Hyd na bwyf trist
   O ddrwg o dda
Rhan trugaredd
I wlad rhiedd
   Buchedd gyfa.]

*Taliesin*

Like 'Anrheg Urien', this poem has lost its original simplicity. The verses here placed in brackets do not occur in the Rev. Edward Davies' copy; and it is quite probable that these are monkish additions. Excepting the two concluding verses, the first part appears to be tolerably pure; but the Latin terminations of one or two verses in the second part excite my suspicion. Of themselves, these would not be sufficient to invalidate the antiquity and genuineness of the poem; but, in truth, the verses as they stand here, have evidently suffered much from copyists; and their present orthography is very modern. This is easily proved by the occurrence of the letter *dd*, the history of which is given by Lhuyd with his usual accuracy and minuteness:

> D in old manuscripts, whether Welsh or Cornish, has two pronunciations; for, besides the common reading, as in the English and other languages, it serves in the midst and termination for *dh*, or the English *th*, in *this, that*, &c. So *medal* (soft) is to be read *medhal*, &c. The *dd* was introduced to express this sound about the year 1400, and in the time of Henry VIII., &c., *d*, pointed at the top or underneath, by H. Lluyd and W. Salisbury, at home; and by Dr Gryffydh Roberts and Roger Smyth in the Welsh books they printed beyond sea. In the reign of Queen Elizabeth, Dr J. D. Rhys, Dr D. Powel, and others, used *dh*, which was afterwards rejected by Dr Davies, and *dd* restored.
>
> *Arch. Brittan.*, page 227

Another feature provocative of philological comment is the word *Lleweis*, in the third verse of the first part. Probert met with it in translating the *Gododdin*, and straightway converted a British chief into a *lioness*; many Welshmen would probably have done the same; but the meaning of the word is to *eat* or *drink*. No doubt the term is borrowed from the practices of lions and other animals. But, asks some reader, where did the Kymry become acquainted with the lion? I know not, unless the Romans brought those animals with them for their gladiatorial shows; but this is certain, the Kymry knew the animal well. Aneurin looks upon it as the lord of the forest; and our countrymen, contemplating that animal as the *beau ideal* of a feeder, applied the term 'lionize' as a metaphorical description of eating and drinking. The word is obsolete in Wales;[25] but the term is used in England for an object which is made a show of, as 'the lion of a party.' See, for instance, the character of Mrs Leo Hunter, in the *Pickwick Papers*. Another recent instance of word-forming is the name *chick-a-poppo*, given by the Ojibbeways to champagne, in consequence of the *chicking* and *popping* sound attendant upon the opening of bottles of that wine.

One other feature I must notice before laying the translation before the reader, and that is the intense love of nature which is shown in this, as well as in all the older poetry of Wales. The author in this poem, whom we may conclude to have been Taliesin, describes Mona with a devotion worthy of Wordsworth, Tennyson, or the bard who turned up the daisy, as

Mona (land of) charming cuckoos.

Our modern bards, almost to a man have left nature, with all her cuckoos, to sing their own praises. Puritanism has no affection for such simple joys; and but few Cambrian bards would now venture to say they were such lovers of nature, as to have a kind word for the cuckoo. The old bards, however, had more of the milk of human kindness; the cuckoo's note was sweet to the ears of Llywarch Hen; Gwalchmai held communion with it often, as also did Davydd ab Gwilym; and we all respect the genial bard who sang:

Pwy feddylsai cansai 'r gog
Mewn mawnog ar y mynydd?

It is true that *gogei* may mean *cooks,* and the bards were rather fond of good living; but the other reading is preferable.

The poem, rendered into English, reads somewhat as follows:

### The Elegy of Aeddon of Mona

I

Terrible island!
Boldly praised island
   Of the severe rewarder!
Mona! (land of) charming cuckoos,
Of the manliness of Ervei;
   Menai is its portal!
(There) I drank liquor,
Wine and braggett,
   With a brother – now departed.

The universal ruler,
The end of all emulation,
   The ruinator of sovereignty,
Rueful Destiny!
Demanded Aeddon,
   For the grave.
There has not been,
There will not be, his equal
   In tribulation.

When Aeddon came
From the land of Gwydion,[26]
　　The strong door of Seon;[27]
He was an acute afflictor;
In four nocturnal (attacks),
　　In the serene season,
His contemporaries fell;
The woods afforded no protect-
　　ion,
　　The wind was on their
　　　　skirts,
Math and Eunydd,[28]
Skilful with the magic wand,
　　Set the elements at large;
In the time of Gwydion[29]
And Amaethon,
　　There was counsel.
Pierced was the front of his
　　shield;
He was strong and fortunate,
　　Strong and irresistible.
He was mighty in the carouse;
In every congress
　　His will was done.
Kind forerunner,
While I am living,
　　He shall be celebrated.
The powerful combination
Of his front rank
　　Was not serviceable (to his
　　　　enemies).
[May I be with Christ (i.e. dead),
If I am not sorrowful,
　　That the generous apostle,
Demanded Aeddon,
To be contained
　　Among the angels.]

## II

Terrible island!
Boldly praised island
　　Of the ardent ruler.
In the presence of the victor youth,
The fortress of the Kymry
　　Remained tranquil.
The dragon chief,
Was a rightful owner
　　In Britannia;
Consuming dominator,
Lord of a coast
　　Facing land!
Four damsels,[30]
After their lamentation,
　　Will suffer misery.
In affliction dire,
On sea, without land,
　　Tedious will be their existence.
On account of his integrity,
There is no cessation
　　Of their sorrow.
I am blameable
That I do not mention
　　The good he did to me.
For the impetuous paragon,
Who will prohibit,
　　Who will put in order?
For the impetuous Aeddon,
What benign associate
　　Will support Mon?
[May I be with Christ,
If I am not sorrowful
　　For the evil, of the good
Share of mercy,
In the land of renown
　　And perfect life.

*Taliesin*

It now becomes our duty to give some account of our hero; but this is no easy matter, for our historians and biographers are silent upon the point. Not a scrap of his history is ready made; and therefore we must endeavour to construct it. Aeddon is certainly a Gaelic and not a Kymric name. There are but three other persons of that name known to Cambrian history, and of these, two were Irish; while the third occurs as a singular exception among Kymric names, viz., that of Aeddan ab Blegored, a Glamorgan man. Of the two others, Aeddan Voeddog, a saint, was connected with Ireland; and Aeddan Vradawg, viz., Aeddan ab Gafran, was king of the Irish-Scots of Argyleshire. Furthermore, the termination *on* is not Cambrian, and has a suspicious affinity with Don, Gwdion, Amaethon, &c. All this, coupled with the association of Aeddon with the names of these Gaelic settlers, lead me to conclude that he was a man of Irish origin, and that as he (probably) lived about 610, the Gael of Anglesey could not have been extirpated by Caswallon Law Hir; for, in addition to the contents of this poem, I shall presently adduce other evidence to prove that Aeddan was a man of some influence, power and authority. I was at one time of opinion that the verse

> When Aeddon came
> From the land of Gwydion,
>     The strong door of Seon,

would serve for a peg whereon to hang a pro-Gaelic argument, the land of Gwydion being interpreted to mean Ireland; but from the turn which I have now given to the words, it will be seen that that view is no longer considered tenable; yet, though this is one argument less in favour of that conclusion, I consider the view to be still quite sound.

In connexion with this, and the verses which follow it, there is a question of grave import. Coming from Mona, the land of Gwydion, who was king of Anglesey, and the bulwark of Caer Seon, against whom did Aeddon make war? Against whom were these four nocturnal enterprises directed? Surely against the king of Gwynedd. But history is silent upon this point, and speaks of no such war. Quite true – such history as we have is silent; but the history of Wales is written in its poetry; and there as yet it has never been sought. Let us now see if we cannot make a little history of this matter. The kings of North Wales, in the time of Taliesin, were Maelgwn Gwynedd, Rhun, Beli and Iago ab Beli. The latter was killed by *one of his own subjects*; and the notices respecting his death are as follows. One triad records the manner of his death:

> The three evil axe-blows of the isle of Britain: the axe-blow of Eiddyn in the head of Aneurin; the axe-blow in the head of Golyddan the bard; and the axe-blow in the head of Iago ab Beli.

Another triad states the political position of the striker:

> And thirdly, Iago the son of Beli, who was struck in the head by his own man (or subject).

And a third names the person:

> The axe-blow that Cadafael the Wild struck in the head of Iago ab Beli.

Again, we are further informed, that this assassin was made king, in consequence, perhaps, of the death of the monarch he slew:

> The three vassal-born kings of Britain: Gwriad the son of Gwrien, in the North; Hyvaidd the son of Bleiddig, in South Wales; and Cadafael the son of Cynfedw, in Gwynedd.

117

Why were these men made kings? Two out of three copies are silent; the third answers – for their good deeds. I incline to a less utopian view of this matter. Cadavael is named a wild man – a curious preface to good conduct; a vassal and subject of Iago ab Beli, and the slayer of his king – a still stranger kind of good conduct. And this man becomes king in Gwynedd. Mark the time, too:

> 613. – Gueith Cair Legion: et ibi cecidit Selim filii Cinan. Et Jacob filii Beli dormitatio.[31]

Again, in a blundering form:

> Cath Cairelegion, ubi sancti occisi sunt; et cecidit Solon M Conian rex Bretannorum; et Cetula rex cecidit ibi.[32]

Let us now put these facts together, connect them with the expeditions of Aeddon, and endeavour to discern their true significance.

We have here assumed that the Irish were not extirpated from Anglesey; and, in fact, there is no reason to think they were. Mr Jones has omitted one very important point in favour of his argument. Extirpation of races is an idea which has no foundation in fact, and only finds a local habitation in the minds of historians. To subdue a people is possible and conceivable; but extirpation is a thing unknown. The Romans subdued, but did not destroy; they did not drive the Gauls from France, nor the Britons from this island; and the Saxons did not drive the Britons from Lloegria. Conquerors want subjects, not dead bodies; tillers of the soil, not a soil untilled; men to do their work for them, not a place to work themselves. In like manner the Kymry wished to cripple the power of the Gael, but not to expel them; they defeated the Gael in Anglesey, but did not drive them out of it; the history speaks of conquest and subjugation; but expulsion is not upon the record: extirpation is not nominated in the bond. By abstaining from putting into the documents that which is not therein stated, we reconcile many seeming discrepancies, and arrive at a clearer conception of what may have been the actual facts. If this be a correct view – if the Kymry scotched the snake, not killed it – we may easily conceive that the people so subdued might have grown in power in the lapse of time, and have panted for an opportunity to emancipate themselves from vassalage, and to regain their independence.

Such I conceive to be a true view of the condition of the Gael in Gwynedd in 613. In that year, the defeat of Brochwel by Ethelfrid, at the battle of Chester, broke the power of North Wales, and presented the Gael with the wished for opportunity to rise in rebellion. Cadavael, after the death of Iago, might have been elected king (for Tigernach calls him *Rex*), not *of* Gwynedd, but of the Gael *in* Gwynedd; these vassals probably rose in rebellion; and it is probable that in checking this rebellion Iago ab Beli lost his life, for the Latin extracts above given clearly place his death posterior to, though in the same year as, the battle of Chester. Once before I called attention to the elegy of Taliesin on Iago ab Beli; and, here again, if we had it, it would prove of great service. If Lhuyd be correct, two copies of it exist in the Hengwrt Library. See *Arch. Britt.*, page 256, under the title of 'Hanesyn Hen,' and page 258, *sub. tit.* 'Y Kynveirdh Kymreig.' Cannot Mr

W. W. E. Wynne, Mr Wynne Ffoulkes, or some one of the northern antiquaries, furnish us with a copy of this poem?

There is a passage in Nennius which seems to be inconsistent with these views:

Osguid filius Eadlfrid regnavit XXVIII annis et sex mensibus. Dum ipse regnabat, venit mortalita hominum, Catgualart regnante apud Brittones post patrem suum, et in eâ periit. Et ipse (i.e. Oswy) occidit Pantha in Campo Gai; et nunc facta est strages Gai Campi, et reges Britonum interfecti sunt, qui exierant cum rege Pantha in expeditione usque ad urbem quae vocatur Iudeu. Tunc reddidit Osguid omnes divitias quae erant cum eo in urbe usque in Manau Pendae, et Penda distribuit ea regibus Brittonum; id est Atbret Iudeu. Solus autem *Catgabail, rex Guenedotae regionis*, cum exercitu suo evasit, de nocte consurgens; quapropter vocatus est Catgabail Catguommed.

Now if this Catgabail be the same person as Cadavael Wyllt, we shall have two kings of Gwynedd at the same time, viz., Cadavael, king of the Gael of Anglesey and Caernarvon, and Cadwaladr, king of the North Welsh; for it is quite clear that at this time (657) Cadwaladr was living; and as he is usually considered to have been king of all the Britons, it is possible that Cadavael may have been a vassal king of his. If so, Cadavael must have been at this time a man in years, for we find him a distinguished character forty-four years previously, when he had probably succeeded Aeddon as lord of Gwynedd, i.e. Mon and Arvon. But there are reasons for doubting that Cadavael was king for any long period; and it is possible that the Catgabail of Nennius may be another person. The poem called 'Kyvoesi Myrddin a Gwenddydd ei chewer,' contains a fuller account of this period than any other document; and in that poem we find the following verses:

G. – Who will reign after Kadwallon?
M. – A tall man holding council
    And *Britain under one sceptre*
    The best son of a Kymro, Kadwaladr.
G. – Who will reign after Kadwaladr?
M. – After Kadwaladr, Idwal (his son.)
G. – Who will reign after Idwal?
M. – Howel the son of KADWAL.

This may have been the person named by Nennius; but nothing more is known of him. But without further inquiry it is difficult to arrive at any satisfactory conclusion.

In this supposed rebellion Aeddon may have taken part, for the night expeditions referred to were clearly directed against Gwynedd; and the poem shows that Mon had cause to dread hostilities from thence, since the bard asks:

For the impetuous Aeddon,
What benign associate
    Will maintain Mon?

However this may have been, the success of the rebels was only temporary; for Cadvan, the son of Iago, restored the authority of the kings of North Wales over the subject Gael. Indeed we may, if necessary, assume these expeditions to have taken place afterwards, as it is probable that much bad feeling existed between the two districts; and it is quite evident that a considerable share of independence was enjoyed by Aeddan, possibly as the result of the rebellion, for he is designated as a rightful ruler in Britannia.

But leaving hypothesis, let us see if we can find any more biographical matter. The bard describes Mona to possess the manliness of Ervei. This Ervei was probably the father of Dillus ab Ervei, the greatest thief in Wales, according to the *Mabinogi* of Kilwch and Olwen; and we are told by Aneurin that Ervei, or Urvei, was at the battle of Cattraeth:

> Gnaut ar les Minidauc scuitaur trei
> Guarurut rac ut Eidin Urvei.

> Customary for the sake of Mynyddawg was a perforated shield;
> Red-speared was Urvei before the Lord of Eiddin.

And Aeddon was the son of Ervei. He is thus spoken of by Aneurin, not in the 'Gododdin', but in some of the later verses of that bard:

> Heavily in conflict he slew with the sword;
> Severe indications he brought from battle;
> A hundred new year songs he prepared.
> There served Adan the son of Ervei,
> There served Adan the presumptuous boar,
> A lady, a maid, and a nobleman;
> And when the son of a sovereign was a Ruler,
> The Lord of the Gwyndyd was a blood-stained protector.

They appear to connect Aeddon with the death of Iago ab Beli; but most probably 'the Lord of the Gwyndyd' was Aeddon himself, as Gwynedd was not used at that time in its present extended sense, and only included Anglesey and Caernarvonshire, instead of the whole of North Wales, as is now the case.

Here then let us for the present suspend our comment, satisfied if we have thrown some light upon one of our dark places, and if this tissue of speculation may be thought to contain some truth.

---

### Notes

1   Is this the Dorchester of Dorset, or of Oxfordshire?
2   *Heroic Elegies of Llywarch Hen*, page vii.
3   *Cyvrinach y Beirdd*, page 118.
4   *Ibid.*, page 76.
5   Or, – How great was their consumption
       And destruction,

When they came into the hands
Of the scatterer.

6   Is this Uch Aeron the name of the upper part of Cardiganshire, in which Cors Vochno occurs?

7   Probably the four sons of Cynvarch, Llew, Arawn, Keneu and Urien. Ceneu, through some rashness, appears in this conflict to have come to an untimely end.

8   See *Pughe's Dictionary, sub voce* Dwfr.

9   I do not know where these places are.

10  If this poem be ancient, the triple division of the Principality into Gwynedd, Powys and Deheubarth is very old.

11  We have here the pronoun *eu* with a singular signification, and it appears to have been so used in other parts of this poem.

12  Llyn Geirionnydd is in the upper part of Caernarvonshire.

13  See *Iolo MSS.*, page 457; and *Literature of the Kymry*, page 45, note.

14  *Myvyrian Archæology*, ii, page 515.

15  *Anglo-Saxon Chronicle*, A.D. 1063.

16  *Giraldus*, vol. ii, page 351.

17  Triugein mlyned a mil oed oet Crist pan dygwydawd Gruffud ap Llywelyn penn a tharyan ac amdiffynwr y Brytanyeit drwy dwyll y wyr e hun y gwr a uuassei gynt yn annorch-fygedic kyn no hynny yr awr hon a edewit y mywn glynneu diffeithon. – *Myv.*, ii, page 397.

18  Wendover says, August 5, 1064, (1063?).

19  Griffith was powerful at sea as well as on land, and it is recorded that Harold burned his ships and the stores at Rhuddlan (?)

20  *Myv.*, vol. ii., pages 397, 515, 516.

21  *Ynyt* is the word in the original, but *Ynys* is the proper reading.

22  This reading is from the MSS. of the Rev. E. Davies; the word in the *Myvyrian Archæology* is *rervintor.*[?]

23  *Yngohor.* – MSS. E.D.

24  *Myvyrian Archæology* – *ibid.*

25  Our learned correspondent is not quite correct in his statement; the word might be obsolete in South Wales, but certainly it is still very current in the northern portion of the Principality. – EDD. ARCH. CAMB.

26  This was Mona.

27  Caer Seiont in Caernarvonshire. The Segontium of the Romans.

28  This is Math ab Mathonwy, a celebrated character in Welsh romance, who was considered to have excelled all in his power of enchantment. Eunydd, also an enchanter, was the brother of Gwdion ab Don. – See Williams' *Biographical Dictionary* for further particulars of both.

29  Gwdion and Amaethon belonged to the Gaelic settlers in Anglesey. – See Williams' *Dictionary* for full particulars respecting them.

30  Sisters of our hero, it is probable.

31  *Monumenta Brit.*, page 832.

32  *Annal. Tigernach*, anno 613.

# 6

# MERLIN AND THE
# MERLINIAN POEMS

## JOHN VEITCH
### from the *Journal of the British Archaeological Association*

### PART I: MERLIN

ONE OF THE MOST obscure periods of British history, as regards details, is the epoch from 410 – the date of the Roman evacuation of Britain – to the close of the sixth century. During these 200 years there pass before us certain figures, dim and shadowy enough in some respects, yet typical of the historical, social, and racial forces at work; born of the past, and actively shaping the course of the future nationality and the story of the Island in which we live. The men of this epoch were, moreover, destined to influence not less, and in a very characteristic way, the feeling and the imagination of subsequent generations in the materials of its poetry and romance. The wail over a broken nationality, the mourning over beloved dead lost in a patriotic fight, the melancholy that broods over cairn and lonely mound on our moorlands, and the restful peace that touches the heart at the desolate caer on the windy hill – all this pathos and tenderness in our literature had its first, its best, its truest nourishment in the life and death of the men in those fifth and sixth centuries. And thus we are linked to them by the ties not so much of kinship as of our ever living and common human emotions. While the details of those times are obscure, we may, however, take three great facts in the epoch as standing out clearly enough:

1   There is the aggression of the Teutons and the pressing of the Celts westwards to the country now known as Devon, Cornwall, Wales, the English Lake District and a stretch of land northwards along a certain line to the rock Alcluith, or Dunbarton.

2   There is the splitting up even of this retreat of the Celts by the battle of Deorham, in 580, gained by Ceawlin. The result of this battle was the severance of the Celts south of the Severn from those of the north – briefly, Cornwall from Wales.

3    There is the second severance of the Celts by the battle of Chester, in 617, when they were defeated by Athelfrith, King of Northumbria.

There thus arose the division of the Cymri south of the Dee from those of the north – Cumbria and Strathclyde. The uniformity of the Cymric line of power was thus broken, and its continuance, as more than a series of isolated states, rendered impossible. The history of the period, if it could be written, would show a constant struggle between the disintegrated Celts and the gradually consolidating Teutons.

The story, the patriotism, the myth and the poetry of this period are associated chiefly with the names of Vortigern, Aurelius Ambrosianus, Myrdin Emrys or Merlin Ambrosius, Uther Pendragon, Arthur and Merlinus Caledonius, known also as Silvestris, or the Wylt. Since those early centuries, the greatest, most widespread historic interest has centred round the names of Arthur and Merlin.

The name of special interest to us at present is that of Merlin – a very shadowy figure, I admit; but still, I believe, the name of a person, or rather persons, one at least of whom has a certain sufficiently marked historical relief. Our question here is, Who and what was he? Were there more than one of the name? If he was historical, what was his work, and what his relation to the circumstances of the times? Was he an actor in them, or did he enact the often more powerful part of inspiring with motive and impulse the actors of his age?

Now all through those years from the time of Vortigern and Aurelius Ambrosianus down to a point beyond the burning of Uriconium – from shortly after 410 to 583 – we have floating before us the name *Merlin*. Merlin is associated with Vortigern; he is his *vates*, he stands in the same relation to Aurelius Ambrosianus, he is friend of Uthur Pendragon, and presides over the birth of Arthur. Still later he is the friend and associate of Gwenddoleu, who fell at the great and decisive battle of Ardderyd in 573. Then, even, he is referred to as having been met by Kentigern on the wilds of Drummelzier, on the Tweed, in the wood of Caledon. He is apparently referred to, under the name of Laloicen, as being present at the court of Rydderch Hael, the King of Strathclyde, who died in the same year as Kentigern, which was either in 603 or 614.[1]

I see no reason whatever for supposing that the name Merlin did not refer to a real person or persons more than that the other names of the time were purely fictitious, even such as Ninian, Kentigern or Columba. Direct evidence of a personality corresponding to the name will appear as we proceed; but I cannot concur in the opinion that there was but one person of the name, and that the same man who was contemporary with Aurelius Ambrosianus was also present at the battle of Ardderyd in 573. This, however, is the opinion of the Count Hersart de la Villemarqué in his very interesting book on *Myrddhin or Merlin*. But apart from other considerations, this seems to me impossible on the ground of the dates alone. Aurelius Ambrosianus comes into prominence as the successor of Vortigern about 457, and disappears in 465. If the Merlin of Ardderyd had been his contemporary, he must have been a great deal more than a hundred years old at the date of the battle; and yet we know that he survived this contest for many years. In the poem of the 'Avallenau', speaking of himself he says:

Ten years and forty, as the toy of lawless ones,
Have I been wandering in gloom among sprites.

Making allowance for poetical exaggeration, it is quite clear that the Merlin who was present at Ardderyd, and who wrote these lines, could not have been the Myrdin or Merlin the bard, soothsayer and enchanter, of Ambrosianus; or, for the same reason, of Vortigern himself. Nay, I go further, and say that he could not have been the original of that enchanter Merlin who was the ally of Uthur Pendragon, and who is credited with presiding over the birth of Arthur, and with the wondrous achievements of necromancy associated with this Prince and his exploits. A man who died in 623 or later, as appears from the 'Avallenau', could not be born in 470 or 480, as Villemarqué supposes. This date, I may observe, is too late for his connection with Aurelius Ambrosianus, and it is too early for the man who survived to the close of the sixth century. It follows either that the true Merlin and his exploits are antedated, or that there were two Merlins. The latter, I believe, is the true supposition; and the mythical attributes of the earlier Merlin have been assigned to the latter, while a third wholly legendary Merlin arose in the imagination of the romancers of the eleventh century.

That the Merlin of Ambrosianus and Vortigern was really distinct from the second Merlin is further proved by the circumstances of name and birth. The first Merlin, the *vates of Ambrosianus*, is called *Myrdyn Emrys* or *Merlinus Ambrosius*; the second is named by the Welsh *Merlinus Caledonius, Silvestris, Wylt* or *the Wild*; and in the *Polychronicon* these are regarded as wholly distinct persons. Myrdin Emrys is born of a nun or vestal virgin and an *incubus* or spirit of the air. He is a god or devil incarnate. Belief in relations of this sort was fixed in the popular mind of the time, and it is countenanced by St Augustine: indeed, the word *Myrdin* (or Merlin) is said to indicate this descent. According to Mr Nash it is originally *Mab-leian, Mac-leian, Mab-merchleian.* This was Latinized as *Merlinus, Mellinus, Merclinus.*[2] Villemarqué takes the same view as to the origin of the name, but runs it back to the classical Marsus. Now Merlin Caledonius had no such origin. He was clearly regarded as the son of Madog Morvryn, who was descended from the great Cymric family founded by Coel Godebawc, and was nearly related to the historical and famous Urien Reged. Merlin had, moreover, a twin-sister, Gwendydd, who is constantly associated with him in his life, sufferings and poetry. This by itself is sufficient to mark him off from Merlin Ambrosius.

If this be so, it follows that the second Merlin, or Merlinus Caledonius, is the author or reputed author of the poems attributed to the person of the name, as this author was undoubtedly present at the battle of Ardderydd, was the friend of Gwenddolleu who fell there, knew Rydderch Hael the King of Strathclyde, met Kentigern, and generally was identified with the civil life of the period towards the close of the sixth century. In this case he is brought very close to us as a person-age who lived within the bounds of the first known historical kingdom in the val-leys of the Clyde and Upper Tweeddale – a haunter, in fact, of the *Coed Celydon* or *Wood of Caledon*.

One word in passing regarding the first Merlin or Myrdin Emrys. He has been confounded with the King Aurelius Ambrosianus; but it is clear that he was quite a distinct person. The parentage of Aurelius Ambrosianus is obscure, but it would seem that he was of Roman descent; in fact, a Romanized Briton, and his mother probably a vestal virgin. Hence there arose regarding his birth, as respect-ing that of Myrdin Emrys, the notion that he too was born of a spirit of the air, which seems to have been the mode accepted at the time of accounting for certain irregularities. The Merlin of Ambrosius was also, and probably first of all, the *vates* of Vortigern. When Vortigern practically deserted the national cause, Merlin would seem to have attached himself to Ambrosius, the new leader, the leader, in fact, of the Romanized Britons who dwelt mainly in the Roman cities, as yet, in great measure, intact. Vortigern is said to have given to Ambrosius a city on one of the summits of Snowdon; but this is incorrect in point both of the gift itself and its actual locality. It was not a city, but a fort or *dinas* which was given; and it is not situated on a summit of Snowdon, but on an isolated eminence in the valley of Nant Gwynant (the Valley of Waters), on the south side of Snowdon, and about a mile from Beddgelert, and known even now as *Dinas Emrys*, or Fort of Ambrosius.[3] This eminence and fort are traditionally associated with Myrdin Emrys, and the probability is that it was he upon whom the gift was conferred either by Vortigern or Aurelius Ambrosianus. Certainly it was here, according to the legend, that Myrdin Emrys poured forth his prophecies and forebodings as to the future of his country,

Qui sua vaticinia
Proflavit in Snaudonia,

while Vortigern sat anxious and brooding by the stream which winds through the valley at the base of the hill. If stretch of lake and rush of stream below, grandeur of rock and peak above, the silence and the shadow that lie in the depths of cloven and precipitous *cwms* – the voice of the mountain as it sends its waters to the valley in the soft summer-tide, or as it swells in winter when the wind assails its changeless strength – could ever touch the heart of man, and link it to the supernatural, this must have been, in an impressionable age, especially the function of the land which nourished the bard and seer of Dinas Emrys.

Pierce then the heavens, thou hill of streams,
    And make the snows thy crest!
The sunlight of immortal dreams
    Around thee still shall rest!

Eryri, temple of the bard,
    And fortress of the free!
Midst rocks which heroes died to guard,
    Their spirit dwells with thee!
                Mrs Hemans, *Eryri Wen* [Snowdon]

Merlin Caledonius, then, the bard, was he who was present at the battle of Ardderyd in 573. How this arose is tolerably clear. Maelgwyn Gwynedd (or of Wales) was nominally at least King of all the Cymri of the time. These stretched in an unbroken territory from the estuary of the Severn to the Rock of Dunbarton. The second severance of the kingdom, consequent on the battle of Chester in 617, had not yet been effected. Maelgwyn was Christian, at least in name, and of fine presence, but a coarse sensualist in life. Somehow a pagan or semi-pagan party had grown up in the northern parts of his dominion – what was known afterwards as Strathclyde. This party had for its chief leader Gwenddoleu, of whom we know little more than his connection with this rising. His friend, prompter and counsellor in the matter would seem to have been Merlin Caledonius. On the other side was ranged, as a lieutenant of Maelgwyn, Rydderch Hael, or Rydderch the Liberal, who was then a lord or prince of Strathclyde, and whose original seat seems to have been on the Clyde, at Llanerch, now Lanark.

The result of the conflict on the banks of the Liddel, near Arthuret – where still may be seen a very ancient fortified position – was the complete defeat of the semi-pagan party, the death of Gwenddoleu, and the establishment of the kingdom of Strathclyde under Rydderch Hael. Merlin, said to be thus rendered insane, fled, after the battle, to a retreat in the heart of the wood of Caledon, where now rise from the valley of the Tweed the wild, bare, solitary heights of Drummelzier. His loss of reason was attributed not simply to grief at the result of the battle, but to his having seen in the air, before the close of the struggle, a monster of a terrific order:

> Silvestris dictus ideo,
> Quod consistens in praelio,
> Monstrum videns in aere,
> Mente coepit excedere.
> *Polychronicon*

Here, in the Wood of Caledon, he is said to have survived for many years; then to have met his death at the hands, or rather by the stones and clubs of the servants of Meldred, Prince of the place, who threw the body into the river. The Celtic Orpheus thus met the fate of the ancient Orpheus: 'Contigit ut eodem die a quibusdam pastoribus usque ad mortem lapidatus ac fustigatus casum faceret in mortis articulo, ultra oram Tuedae fluminis praeruptam, prope oppidum Dun Meller.'[4] His grave is still shown under a thorn-tree by the side of the Powsail Burn as it passes the mound on which stands Drummelzier Kirk, though another site, in a field a little to the east of the bank of the burn, is also pointed out as the resting-place of the bard and enchanter.

This, however, is not the only legend of the death of Merlin. The Welsh one of the Triads is that, with nine bards of Britain he went to sea in a ship of glass, and passed away beyond the horizon, disappearing in light, never to be seen again – an extremely likely result of such a venture. Then, again, in Cornwall he is regarded as having been enclosed by the wiles of a woman in

> a craige
> On Cornwall coast.[5]

Again, he is shut up in an enchanted bower or castle, whose walls, though of air, are to him of adamant; and while the wily woman, his lover, can go in and out to him, he cannot stir. There is difference of opinion, naturally, about the locality of this castle. Some place it in the Forest of Broceliande in Brittany, others set it in Cornwall.

Then, further, old Merlin is lying quietly in a cavern or hall under the Eildons, along with Arthur and his knights, in an enchanted sleep, from which, when it is broken some day by a vigorous bugle-blast, they will emerge to restore the Cymri, and redress the disorders of the world. I am sure we are all agreed that there never was a more fitting time for their reappearance than now.

## PART II: MERLINIAN POEMS

Whatever deduction we may make from the traditions regarding Merlin, on the ground of legend and myth, there remain in his relations to Ardderyd and Gwenddoleu, and his share in the battle – even his insanity – a substance of truth. This is clear from the Merlinian poems, which are traceable as distinctive compositions far back to the early centuries. They are preserved in MSS. written a considerable time after their actual composition, viz., the *Black Book of Caermarthen* (1154–89), time of Henry II; the *Book of Aneurin*, in the latter part of the thirteenth century; the *Book of Taliesin*, in the beginning of the fourteenth century; the *Red Book of Hergest* in the fourteenth and fifteenth centuries.[6] These poems are at least six in number:

There is (1) the dialogue between Taliesin and Myrdin (*Black Book of Caermarthen*, i; Skene, i, page 368).

There is (2) the 'Avallenau' in its oldest form (*ibid.*, xvii; Skene, i, page 370).

There is (3) the 'Kyvoesi Myrdin', a dialogue between Merlin and his sister Gwendydd (*Red Book of Hergest*, i; Skene, i, page 462).

There is (4) a 'Fugitive Poem of Myrdin in his Grave' (*Red Book of Hergest*, ii; Skene, page 478).

There is (5) the poem beginning 'Blessed is the birch in the Valley of the Gwy' (*Black Book of Caermarthen*, xvi; Skene, i, page 481).

There is (6) the poem beginning 'Listen, O little pig', etc. (*ibid.*, xviii; Skene, i, page 482).

The first two poems ('Dialogue between Taliesin and Myrdin', and the 'Avallenau') are regarded by Cymric scholars as the oldest, and as original, or very nearly so. The others, while containing original stanzas, are held to have been subject to interpolations by later hands; but all of them have characteristics and references in common, not possessed by the other poems in the *Four Ancient Books of Wales*. In nearly every one there is mournful reference to Ardderyd and Gwenddoleu; there is reference to the twin-sister Gwendydd; and they are characterized especially by a tone of wailing and regret for the past with its mournful memories, and a certain despair about the future which obtrudes itself on the vision of the seer. There is a constant sense of contrast between the happy life of the bard, gone for ever, and his present lot: 'Sorrow's crown of sorrow is remembering happier things.' There is, further, a feeling for nature of a remarkable, even delicate, kind; and there is a peculiar attitude to the Christianity, or rather ecclesiasticism, of the time.

The prevailing tone is the sadness I have indicated. Thus:

As Gwenddoleu was slain in the blood-spilling of Ardderyd,
And I have come from among the furze.

*Cyvoesi*, Skene, i, 462 *et seq.*

Has not the burden been consigned to earth?
Every one must give up what he loves.

*Ibid.*

Beneath my green sod is he not still?
The chief of sovereigns of the North, of mildest disposition.

*Ibid.*

*A bard authenticates the claim of Alexander III to the throne of
Scotland in 1249. (Corpus Christi College, Cambridge, Scoto-Chronicon,
MS 171. f205).*

The Creator has caused me heavy affliction:
Dead is Morgeneu, dead is Mordav,
Dead is Moryen: I wish to die.

*Ibid.*

The Merlinian poems, both earlier and later, contain very marked references to natural objects, especially trees and flowers. There is a distinct feeling for nature for its own sake. The Merlin of the poems seems to rejoice in wood and mountain. Others of the poets in the *Four Ancient Books of Wales* enumerate natural objects not without regard; in the Merlinian poems there is a special feeling for them. Perhaps this is due to the nature-worship of the Cymri, of which Merlin was certainly a representative and embodiment. Such a form of worship necessarily led to careful, minute and loving observation of the forms of the outward world, and this must eventually end in a complacent and sympathetic regard for them. Merlin worshipped, we are told, 'woods, fountains, stones and more or less the spirits of the air, water, fire and earth; he interrogated the stars, predicted the future, as his predecessors had done, and gave himself up to the magical practices of the time forbidden by Councils and punished by the Church. He was, if baptized, Christian only in name.' (Villemarqué, *Merlin*, pages 33–4.)

In this relation the apple-tree is the favourite, a constantly recurring object of address and regard in the Merlinian poems; and this is a very singular fact – showing a feeling for bloom and blossom, the early life of spring – symbolizing, I think, the heart of hope which waited patiently until autumn touched the tree with its ripened gold – a hope not always fulfilled, for the bloom was often untimely frayed.

Great apple-tree of delightful branches,
Budding luxuriantly, and shooting forth renowned scions.

Again:

Great apple-tree, a green tree of luxurious growth;
How large are its branches, and beautiful its form!

Again:

Great apple-tree, and a yellow tree,
Grew at Tal Ardd, without a garden surrounding it.

The 'yellow tree' here, the 'pren melyn', is the barberry, appropriately pictured as yellow, and growing beyond the garden-garth, free in the wilds. Then we have:

Sweet apple-tree, that grows by the river side.

Sweet apple-tree, and a tree of crimson hue,
Which grew in concealment in the Wood of Celyddon.

Can the tree of 'crimson hue' be the rowan? I have little doubt that it is. If so, we have in this and other points evidence of a feeling for objects in nature, on the part of these old Cymri, which wholly disappeared from Scottish, even English poetry for hundreds of years subsequent to their time.

His sister addresses him as 'the fosterer of song among the streams'. What finer touch could there be than this, or what more direct, reference to a soul yearning for, delighting in, the music of the hills? Then the following show the heart of one out amid the wilds, and therein rejoicing:

> Listen, O little pig! Is not the mountain green?

> Listen, O little pig! Are not the buds of thorns
> Very green, the mountain beautiful, and beautiful the earth?

Then we have references to the notes of birds:

> Listen to birds whose notes are pleasant.

> Listen, O little pig! Hear thou the melody
> And chirping of birds by Caer Reon!

But the notes of birds had a significance for him more than the merely pleasing. They were symbolical, prophetic:

> Listen, O little pig! thou little, speckled one!
> List to the voice of sea-birds! Great is their energy!
> Minstrels will be out, without their appropriate portion;
> Though they stand at the door a reward will not come,
> I was told by a seagull that had come from afar.
> > To me it is of no purpose
> To hear the voice of water-birds whose scream is tumultuous.
> Thin is the hair of my head; my covering is not warm.
> The dales are my barn; my corn is not plenteous.

Merlin's relation to the Christianity of the time is tolerably clear. He was more or less influenced by it; perhaps at one time or other, partially at least, embraced it. But he obviously wavered; probably gave it up for his original nature-worship and his power of enchantment and prophecy. Merlin was essentially a bard and seer, the product and reflection of his age, and this he in substance remained to the end. We must disregard the mythical and comparatively Christian character assigned to him in the later poems and traditions of the Welsh.

We find his true position depicted in the old 'Avallenau' and by himself. There he appears on the pagan side at the battle of Ardderyd. He is not in favour with the conqueror, Rydderch Hael, who appears in a somewhat later Merlinian poem as

> the enemy
> Of the city of the Bards in the region of the Clyd.[7]

Then, as he himself tells us, he is hated for his creed by the foremost minister of Rydderch, and this we know was the Christian Bishop Kentigern. Even in the famous interview between Merlin and Kentigern on the wilds, related in the *Scoto-Chronicon* (the details of which are, of course, fabulous), Merlin is represented, after making a formal acknowledgment of the Trinity, as at once relapsing into soothsaying, and offering to prophesy three events of importance to the incredulous Kentigern, who thinks it right, however, to dismiss him with a blessing.

Then there are the pleadings of his sister Gwendydd with him in the name of God and Christ, and his reference, in reply, to God as 'the Chief of Creatures'. She urges him, before he dies, to partake of the Communion; but he indignantly refuses to accept this at the hands of 'excommunicated monks',[8] whatever this phrase may mean, and says 'May God Himself give me communion.'[9] Then the loving sister says to him finally,

I will commend my blameless
Brother in the supreme Caer.
May God take care of Myrdin!

And he replies –

I, too, will commend my blameless
Sister in the supreme Caer.
May God take care of Gwendydd!
                            Amen.[10]

Merlin's references to priests, monks and bishops, are almost uniformly disparaging – even bitter. He foresaw the rise of this to him unworthy class into power and social importance, and the corresponding disparagement of the bards; and he bewails it beforehand as one of the evils of his country, and a source to him of personal grief. The priest was to be inside, and hospitably entertained; the bard was to be left standing outside the threshold, without his portion.

Merlin detested the rising ecclesiasticism of his time, and at the same time he had, to a certain extent, supplemented his feeling of nature-worship, and his belief in the grasp of supernatural powers, by a theism and some dim hold of a Trinity of Persons. His faith in the omnipotence, if it ever existed, of the supersensible powers at his command, was rudely shaken by the disaster to his party and himself sustained at Ardderyd, and he passed the remainder of his life a doubting, broken-hearted, and despairing man. This, I believe, was the true Merlin of the Wood of Caledon, of the wilds of Drummelzier and the Myrdin Wylt of the early Welsh bards and historians. In one of the Merlinian poems there is reference to

The single, white-bearded person who exhausted Dyved,
Who erected a chancel in the land for those of partial belief,
In the upland region and among wild beasts.[11]

The chancel in the upland region is characteristic, and the phrase 'partial belief' conveys precisely the attitude of Merlin to the Christian faith.

The later conception of Merlin, as developed in the Middle Ages, and to be found in the pages of Malory, and accepted by Tennyson, has nothing in common with the reality. It is the view of a wholly inferior character; it is simply that of the wise man entrapped and overcome through the vulgar wiles of a woman – a kind of temptation to which others than the wise are not less subject.

We must add to the features of the original Merlin his wizard power. Of what sort this was, or was supposed to be, we may learn from the traditions regarding the Welsh Gwydyon ap Don. He could call up before the eyes of men a fair woman from the blossoms of the tree; the springing plants were changed into forms of heroes seated on prancing horses. If his castle were attacked he could call up, with a wave of the hand, the stream of the rainbow to encircle the stronghold, and scare away the assailants; every sieger fled surprised and awed. Toiling spirits were ever ready at his command.[12]

Whatever we may think of this pretension, it is true that the people of the time profoundly believed in the wizard as a real power;and what is more, those who were supposed to possess it were not conscious impostors. It was the form in which the sphere of the supersensible appeared to the early, sensitive, and imaginative Cymric race; the supernatural power was not wholly divorced from the world, it was incarnate in some men. But the gift was accompanied by some awesome conditions. This same Gwydyon ap Don is represented by the bard as engaged in a fearsome and mysterious struggle:

> I saw a fierce conflict in Nant Frangcon
> On a Sunday, at the time of dawn,
> Between the bird of wrath and Gwydion.[13]

We thus see how it was that mediaeval personages in the Lowlands of Scotland were credited with supernatural powers; that Lord Soulis had his familiar *Red-Cap*, that Michael Scott sought to rule rebellious sprites, and how the whole feeling of Scotland during the Stuarts was tinged with awe of the supernatural and belief in faëry, ending in witchcraft and its attribution to the Devil's power. This, in its essence, was a Cymric inheritance, transmitted through the mediaeval romancers.

This conception of the higher world was, no doubt, sensuous and inadequate; but it was not wholly groundless or without its elevating power. The natural, as it is called – the part of the world presented to the senses, and unwarrantably emphasized as the whole – is but a clothing, an incarnation of the soul beyond and in it; as such it is truly symbolical. It manifests a mind analogous at least to our own; thus we know it, feel it, are able to put meaning into it. Sometimes it shows emotion, as it were, by sympathy with us in our moral and spiritual moods. Again, it appears to be in contrast and in conflict with our mental and moral processes; it seems to scorn and to spurn our individual aspirations, efforts and purposes. It passes by and over the individual, as if in pursuit of some far off divine event, towards which it is eagerly moving. The old Cymric view which spiritualized the world and the powers of earth and air, even the erroneous faith in the capacity of the individual to grasp, master and wield certain of those powers, were but dim precursors of that higher faith which finds the Divine in nature, which regards the so-called *natural* as by itself a mere fragment of what is, and of that insight into the life of things, based on openness of vision and reverential waiting on the revelation to be found there, which brings the world of heaven and earth, of light and shadow, of hill and stream and flower, into the heart of man, and thus truly enables him to make it his own.

---

## Notes

1     In the Life of Kentigern the Saint is said to have met at the court of Rydderch Hael one named Laloicen, who prophesied, 'In curia ejus quidam homo fatuus vocabulo *Laloicen.*' This Laloicen, according to the *Scoto-Chronicon,* was Myrdin Wylt, the Caledonian Merlin. (See Price in Skene, ii, page 424.)

2     Introduction to Merlin, page ix.

3     In the *Polychronicon* the site of the 'Collis Ambrosii' is erroneously given as at the source of the Conway.

4     *Vita Kentigerni*, page 157; Fordun, *Scoto-Chronicon,* 1, iii, c. 31.

5     *Ancient Scottish Prophecies*. Edinburgh, 1833.

6     Skene, *Four Ancient Books of Wales*, i, page 3. 1889 vol. 45, pt 3.

7     *Dialogue between Merdin and His Sister,* later form of the *Avallenau,* Skene, i, page 463.

8     The same contempt for the monks is found in the *Book of Taliesin* (xxx), Skene, i, page 264:

       Monks congregate like dogs in a kennel.
       From contact with their superiors they acquire knowledge.

       Monks congregate like wolves.

9     Skene, i, page 477.

10     *Ibid.,* pages 477–8.

11     Skene, i, page 483; *B. B. of Caermarthen,* xviii.

12     *The Chair of Ceridwen, B. of Taliesin,* xvi; Skene, i, page 296.

13     *Ibid.*

# 7

# SATIRISTS AND ENCHANTERS IN EARLY IRISH LITERATURE

## FRED NORRIS ROBINSON
### from *Studies in the History of Religion*

IT WOULD APPEAR from various references in Elizabethan writers that the feature of Irish literature which most impressed Englishmen of the time was the supposed power of Irish poets to work destruction with their verse. Sidney, at the end of his *Defense of Poesy*, in his parting curse upon the disdainer of the art, will not wish him 'the ass's ears of Midas, nor to be driven by a Poet's verses, as Bubonax was, to hang himself, nor to be rhymed to death, as is said to be done in Ireland.'[1] Again, in Reginald Scot's *Discovery of Witchcraft*, it is said that Irishmen, speaking of their witches, 'will not stick to affirm that they can rhyme either man or beast to death.'[2] And a number of writers refer to the destruction of rats by means of such potent verses. In the Epilogue to Ben Jonson's *Poetaster*,[3] the author declares that he will

> Rhyme them to death, as they do Irish rats,
> In drumming tunes;

and Rosalind, in *As You Like It*, humorously compares Orlando's rhymes to those which had released her soul from a lower existence and helped it to achieve its transmigration. 'I was never so berhymed,' she declares, 'since Pythagoras' time, that I was an Irish rat, which I can hardly remember.'[4]

The story of the destruction or expulsion of rats or mice is told of a number of Irishmen in different periods. In fact Eugene O'Curry, who made a report on the subject in 1855, for the Royal Irish Academy,[5] remarks that he once tried to perform the feat himself, but failed, perhaps because his words were too hard for the vermin to understand! The most famous early instance, probably, is that of the poet Senchan, who lived in the seventh century. According to the 'Proceedings of the Great Bardic Institution' ('Imtheacht na Tromdháimhe'),[6] a tale of the Middle Irish period, an egg which had been saved for Senchan's meal was eaten up by the 'nimble race', namely, the mice. 'That was not proper for them,' said Senchan; 'nevertheless there is not a king or chief, be he ever so great, but these mice would wish to leave the traces of their own teeth in his food; and in that they err, for food should not be used by any person after (the print of) their teeth; and I will satirize them.' Then follow stanzas in which Senchan threatens the mice with death, and they beg him to accept compensation instead. As a result of his verses, ten mice fell dead in his presence; whereupon he said to them: 'It is not you that I ought to have satirized, but the party whose duty it is to suppress you, namely, the tribe of cats.' And then he pronounced a satire on Irusan, the chief, lord and Brehon of all the cats. But the victim this time took the attack less meekly. Irusan came – 'blunt-mouthed, rapacious, panting, determined, jagged-eared, broad-breasted promi-nent-jointed, sharp and smooth-clawed, split-nosed, sharp and rough-toothed, thick-mouthed, nimble, powerful, deep-flanked, terror-striking, angry, extremely vindictive, quick, purring, glare-eyed.' In this guise he came and carried off Senchan on his back; and the poet, after trying flattery without avail, was barely saved by St Kieran, who killed Irusan as he passed his cell.

Exploits like these doubtless appealed to the English as being particularly appropriate to poets of the 'wild Irish', whose extraordinary character and cus-toms were a favourite topic with British writers from Giraldus Cambrensis down to Edmund Spenser.[7] And the story of Senchan itself is old enough to have been known in England before the days of Elizabeth.

The Middle Irish account of the 'Great Bardic Company' will be discussed again later. But it is already clear from the passages quoted that 'satire', or the Irish term which is so translated, is not employed in the ordinary English sense of the word. The poet's victims, whether rats and cats, as in the tale of Senchan, or men, as in many stories to be mentioned later, are not destroyed by the natural opera-tion of literary art. The verses used are magic spells, and the whole procedure belongs in the realm of sorcery. This was recognized by Reginald Scot, who classed the Irish rat-spells with other performances of witches or 'eye-biters'; and by Sir William Temple, who associated the Irish practice in question with the magic runes of the ancient Teutons.[8] The use of incantations to accomplish supernatural ends, whether of good or evil, is so familiar the world over that this obvious inter-pretation of the Irish story needs no defence or illustration; and one might at first be disposed to dismiss the whole matter with the suggestion that 'satire' is not a suitable translation of the Irish term for such verses as those of Senchan. There is manifestly a 'long and large difference' between these talismanic spells, often half-meaningless in content, and the highly acute and intellectual form of poetry which has been chiefly known in Europe by the name of satire. It seems like an unjusti-fiable looseness in language to use the same word for such dissimilar things. But as soon as one begins to examine the so-called satirical material in Irish literature, one finds difficulties in dispensing with the name. In the first place, the Irish lan-guage itself employs the same words (most commonly *aer* and its derivatives) for the rat-spells of Senchan and for the stricter satire of a later age. Furthermore, the persons described as pronouncing satires, even of the old destructive sort, were by no means always mere enchanters, but in many cases poets of high station, either in history or in saga. And finally, the subjects of their maleficent verse – often, for example, the inhospitality or other vices of chieftains – are such as might form suitable themes of genuine satire; and the purpose of the poets is frequently described as being to produce ridicule and shame. In short, it seems impossible in old Celtic literature to draw a line between what is strictly satire and what is not; and one ends by realizing that, for the ancient Celts themselves, the distinction did not exist. Just as their poets were not clearly separable from Druids and medicine-men, but often combined in one person the functions of all three,[9] so they freely mingled natural and supernatural processes in the practice of their arts. Destructive spells and poems of slander or abuse were all thought of together as the work, and it sometimes seems almost the chief work, of the tribal man of letters. And the retention of one term for all these products, at least while speaking of a literature where such conditions prevailed, is certainly defensible, and may be positively instructive in emphasizing the continuity of literary development.

Of course it is not to be supposed that Irish literature is peculiar in the respects that have been described. The combination of the functions of poet and magician is characteristic of early stages of civilization and appears in many parts of the world. Among various peoples, too, the satirical office of the poet has been given special prominence; and where this is the case, in simple states of society, a certain amount of sorcery may always be suspected in the poet's work. But in the literature of the *Kulturvölker* evidence is not always preserved of the lower civilization that went before, and the relation between sorcery and satire is by no means everywhere apparent. In Greek and Latin, for example, there are comparatively few traces of the magician-poet, though the use of incantations was common enough in ancient classical civilization and the terms ἐπαοιδή and *carmen* have a well-recognized magic association.[10] The familiar story of Archilochus, whose iambics led to the death of Lycambes and his daughters, shows, to be sure, the destructive power of satire. But it is hardly a case in point, unless it be assumed that an original story of magical destruction has been rationalized into an account of death from shame; and there is no necessity for such an assumption.[11] In general, the satire of the Greeks and Romans cannot be easily traced back beyond a fairly sophisticated age;[12] and the satire of modern Europe, it may be added, is in large measure classical and literary in origin.

Better parallels to the Irish situation are furnished by the popular poetry of ancient Arabia. There, according to an opinion which has found favour with Arabic scholars, the common name of the poet, Shā'ir, meant originally 'the knowing one, the one possessed of supernatural knowledge.'[13] There, as in Ireland, the satirical function of the order is very conspicuous. Men give the poets rich gifts to escape disfavour, or place them under restraint and punishment as dangerous persons. In one instance, it is said, the Calif Al-Mansur abandoned marriage with a noble woman of the Taghlib for fear of the effects of a satire which Djarir had pronounced against her. A large number of the old Arabic satires have been preserved, and with regard to them, as with regard to the Irish poems, it is hard to say how far they are real lampoons and how far incantations.[14] The supernatural element, so far as the present writer has observed, is less emphasized in the Arabic than in the Irish, and there is more real satire, more genuine mockery or criticism, in the Arabic verses. The Arabs had perhaps advanced a step farther than the Irish from the stage of the magician-poet.[15] But, on the whole, the similarity between the two literatures in the matters under discussion is most striking and instructive.

Among the peoples of central and northern Europe it can hardly be doubted that conditions like those of the Irish once prevailed, though evidence on the subject is comparatively scanty. Incantations make up an important element in the popular poetry of the Finns, and Comparetti has argued effectively to show that the primary sense of the Finnish *runo* was a magic spell.[16] But it is not clear that there was much development in the direction of personal satire. In old Germanic poetry there can be no question as to the prevalence of the *Zauberlied*,[17] and there is also testimony, though not so abundant as one could wish, to the existence of the *Spottlied* from a very early time.[18] That the two types probably stood in close relation, it is one of the purposes of the present discussion to show. But the existence of the destructive satirists on Germanic territory is not altogether a matter of inference. Their practices seem to be contemplated in an ecclesiastical canon of the year 744.[19] A definite case also seems to be furnished by the story of *Hug timidus*, in the ninth century, whose servants sang against him and inspired such terror that the victim did not dare step out of doors.[20] Coming down to later ages, it is well known that in Iceland of the saga period, satirical poems were greatly feared and the poets were strictly dealt with in the laws;[21] and even in the seventeenth century Isaac de la Peyrère, a French traveller in Iceland, testified to the belief that the wound given by a mad dog was 'scarce more dangerous than [the] venomous satyrs' of the poets.[22] It is possible, moreover, that the common name for a poet in the West Germanic languages (Anglo-Saxon *scop*, Old High German *scof*) contains the same root as the verb 'to scoff.' The etymology is not well enough established to be used as proof of the importance of satirical verse among the West Germanic peoples; but on the other hand, such evidence from other literatures as has here been presented removes any serious objection, on semasiological grounds, to the association of the two groups of words.[23]

The poets of the Celts seem to have been famous, even in antiquity, for their use of satire and malediction. One of the oldest classical references to Celtic literature, a well-known passage in Diodorus Siculus, perhaps derived by him from Posidonius, says that the bards, 'singing to instruments like lyres, praise some men and abuse others.'[24] And down to modern times, in both the main branches of Celtic literature, the Gaelic and the Brythonic, the twofold function of the bards, to praise and to blame, has been well recognized and freely exerted. Their supernatural power, too, has never ceased to be feared; and it was related of no less a poet than Dafydd ap Gwilym, almost a contemporary of Chaucer, that he killed a literary antagonist by the virulence of his verse.[25] On the whole, as might be expected, the magic aspect of the satirist's work was more emphasized in the early ages of lower civilization, and it is consequently conspicuous in Irish literature, which preserves most abundant evidence concerning those periods. Irish also exhibits very clearly the close connection between the poetry of magic malediction and the poetry of mockery and abuse, and shows the importance of satire, of whatever sort, as an element in the life of simple peoples. Numerous provisions concerning satirists appear in the ancient law of the land; their maledictions are even recognized among the sanctions of treaties; rules for the making of satires are laid down in the native treatises on poetry; and in the ancient popular sagas the part of satirist is played again and again by important poets, whose power often determines the fate of great national heroes.

Some of the evidence of these peculiar conditions will be taken up in the pages that follow. But a brief explanation of the Irish terms for satire ought perhaps to be given first. Satirists are often referred to in Irish texts by the general words for poet (*file, bard, licerd, aes dana*, etc.), Druid (*drui*), or seer (*fáith*); and it has already been pointed out that the classes named are freely confused, or at least exchange their functions, in the older sagas. With specific reference to satire the terms most frequently employed are *aer* and *cáined* and their derivatives. Common use is also made of *ainmed*, 'blemishing', *imdergad*, 'reddening', and *rindad*, 'cutting'; all of which seem to have reference primarily to the physical effects of the satirist's attack. Somewhat less frequent in occurrence are *ail*, 'disgrace', *aithgiud*, 'sharpening' (?), *aithisiugud*, 'reviling', *ainfhialad*, 'dishonouring', *cuitbiud*, 'laughter, ridicule', *ecnad*, 'reviling' (sometimes used in the religious sense of 'blaspheming'), *mifhoclad*, 'speaking ill', and *sinnad*, of which the primary sense is not clear. The word *glám*, especially in the phrase *glám dichenn*, usually refers to a special form of incantation which will be described later, but it is sometimes more loosely employed;[26] and *groma*, likewise, appears in the laws to be associated with a particular process called the *glas-gabail*.[27] Of only occasional, or even rare, occurrence are *dul*, explained in Cormac's Glossary as *cainte*, 'satirist';[28] *runa*, once used in the laws for satires;[29] and *bired* or *berach*, uncertain both in form and in meaning, but apparently applied to a woman-satirist in a passage of the laws.[30] The word *crosan*, also, of which the usual meaning is 'juggler' or 'buffoon', sometimes means 'satirist' as well.[31] Names for satire and the practitioners of the art are thus seen to be rather numerous in the Irish language, and they describe various aspects of the satirists' work. Some of them are restricted in application, but the majority are used loosely, and appear frequently in combinations of two or three even when referring to a single satirical performance. It is noteworthy, moreover, that in their use no distinction is made, or at all events steadily maintained, between the natural and the supernatural, between the satire of magic malediction and the satire of mockery or abuse.

To come to the actual accounts of the Irish satirists, frequent mention of them is made in the various tracts of the Brehon laws, which preserve, as is well known, most valuable evidence of the conditions of ancient Irish life. It is clear that satirical attacks were a common form of injury in all classes of society.[32] In the law of distress (i.e. the law relating to the seizure of property to be held for the enforcement of a claim) it is provided that three days' stay shall regularly be allowed in cases of ordinary satire, slander, betrayal, or false witness;[33] but five days' stay is the prescribed period for other offences, among which are the blemish of a nickname, satirizing a man after his death, and satire of exceptional power (?).[34] In these passages satire is classified with 'crimes of the tongue'. Elsewhere, as in the law relating to *eric*-fines, satirizing and assault are treated together,[35] and again, these two forms of injury are associated with the stealing of a man's cattle or the violation of his wife.[36] The damages allowed for satire, as for other injuries, depend in part upon the rank of the person injured. It is more serious to satirize a king's son than a lower chief,[37] and a henchman has a smaller indemnity than a chief of *aire-fene* rank.[38] From several places it appears that satire was in some way to be resisted;[39] and a distinction is made between lawful and unlawful satire, comparable, as O'Curry has pointed out, to the distinction in the English law of libel.[40]

Just as in the case of fasting against an enemy or a debtor – a familiar old Irish method of enforcing a claim or extorting a benefit[41] – so in this matter of persecution by poets, the law seems to have recognized, and to have sought to regulate, an ancient custom which was liable to dangerous abuse.

In the treatise on Customary Law there is a general analysis of crime (Irish *eitged*, a term which apparently had the general meaning of 'excess' or 'abnormality'), and several kinds of satire are mentioned, though the distinctions among them are not made very clear.[42] *Eitged* of words is said to comprise spying, satirizing and nicknaming. 'White *eitged*' is distinguished from the 'black *eitged*', the white of flattery from the black of satire. 'Speckled *eitged*' is explained as referring to the three words of warning, *gromfa gromfa, glamfa glamfa, aerfa aerfa*, which the English translator of the laws, for lack of specific equivalents, renders 'I will *grom*-satirize, I will *grom*-satirize; I will *glam*-satirize, I will *glam*-satirize; I will satirize, I will satirize.' *Aeraim* (future *aerfa*) is the most usual word for 'satirize', as already stated; *glamfa* is said by the Irish commentator on the passage to refer to the *glam dichenn*, which will be described later; and *gromfa* is similarly connected with the *glas-gabail*, a procedure of uncertain character.[43] That 'speckled *eitged*' is fundamentally of magical nature is clear from the whole account of it.

Another legal compilation, the Heptads,[44] designates seven kinds of satire and discusses the 'honour-price' appropriate to each: 'There are with the Feine seven kinds of satire for which *dire* is estimated; a nickname which clings; recitation of a satire of insults in his absence; to satirize the face; to laugh on all sides; to sneer at his form; to magnify a blemish; satire which is written by a bard who is far away, and which is recited.'[45] This classification, which is clearly the product of custom rather than of pure logic, is not altogether clear, even with the glosses of the native commentators. But the passage shows the usual association of mockery, invective, and magical injury. It is followed by regulations, which need not be repeated here, concerning the payment of honour-price to the aggrieved man and his descendants.

In decidedly the greater number of passages in the laws satire is treated as a kind of misdemeanour and the satirist condemned. Thus satirists are classed among the men for whom no one may go surety;[46] and woman-satirists, along with thieves, liars and bush-strumpets, are said to have no claim to an honour-price.[47] Similarly, the son of a woman-satirist, like the son of a bondmaid, is declared to be ineligible to chieftaincy.[48] And the same disparagement of the class appears in the definition of a demon-banquet as 'a banquet given to the sons of death and bad men, i.e. to lewd persons and satirists, and jesters, and buffoons, and mountebanks, and outlaws, and heathens, and harlots, and bad people in general; which is not given for earthly obligation or for heavenly reward – such a feast is forfeited to the demon.'[49] In all these places reference seems to be made primarily to a low sort of sorcerers and traffickers in personal abuse. But the satirist was not always so conceived by the makers of the laws. Just as there was a distinction, already referred to, between lawful and unlawful satire, so the poet was sometimes praised and rewarded, rather than blamed, for his exercise of the satirizing function. It may be doubted whether an honour or a reproach to the order is implied by the law that puts the house of a satirist, along with that of a king and that of a thief, among those into which it is forbidden to drive cattle seized in distraint;[50] but other references are less ambiguous. Because of his office as eulogist and satirist alike, the poet is mentioned among the men who have the special privilege of speaking in public.[51] In another place, poets are declared to have peculiar rights and claims because of their services in composing lawful praise on the one hand, and on the other hand, in levying taxes in territories where 'points of satire' are regarded and where 'points of weapons' are not.[52] And the same power of the poets which is reckoned as a means of enforcing tribute, is also invoked in treaties as a sanction of their observance.[53] The satire employed for such purposes was doubtless for the most part wizardry, but it may have included some ridicule and some appeal to the public opinion of the tribe.[54] At all events, by virtue of its exercise, the satirists obtained a considerable degree of recognition as public servants.

The formal recognition, and even the Christian adoption, of the old satire, with all its magic elements, is further strongly implied in the prescription of the ceremony for the *glámdichenn*. This is preserved, not in the laws, though the *glámdichenn* is frequently named there, but in one of the Middle Irish treatises on versification,[55] which describes the procedure against a king who refuses the proper reward for a poem. First there was fasting on the land of the king, and a council of thirty laymen and thirty bishops and thirty poets as to making a satire; and it was a crime to prevent the satire after the reward for the poem was refused. Then the poet himself with six others, on whom the six degrees of poets had been conferred, had to go at sunrise to a hill-top on the boundary of seven lands; and the face of each degree of them toward his own land, and the face of the ollave there toward the land of the king whom he would satirize, and the backs of them all toward a hawthorn which should be on the top of the hill, and the wind from the north, and a slingstone and a thorn of the hawthorn in every man's hand, and each of them to sing a stave in a prescribed metre into the slingstone and the thorn, the ollave singing his stave before the others, and they afterwards singing their staves at once; and each was then to put his stone and his thorn at the butt of the hawthorn. And if it were they that were in the wrong, the earth of the hill would swallow them up. But if it were the king that was in the wrong, the earth would swallow up him and his wife and his son and his horse and his arms and his dress and his hound. The curse (*glám*) of the *Mac fuirmed*[56] fell on the hound; the curse of the *fochloc* on the dress; the curse of the *doss* on the arms; the curse of the *cano* on the wife; the curse of the *cli* on the son; the curse of the *anradh* on the land; the curse of the *ollave* on the king himself.[57]

Whether this elaborate ceremony was actually in common practice does not matter fundamentally to the present discussion. It may have been largely invented, or at least embellished, by some *file* with a turn for magical liturgy. Certainly the thirty bishops are suspicious participants; and references to the *glám dichenn* in Irish literature do not usually suggest such a complicated affair. The bishops, however, it is to be observed, do not actually have a part in the *glám dichenn*, but only in the preliminary council which sanctions the proceedings. There is plenty of evidence, moreover, as will appear later, that Irish poets did join in companies for making or pronouncing satires; and the characteristic features of the ceremony here described – the fasting, the sympathetic magic, and the assumed retroaction of the unjust curse – are all unassailable elements of popular practice or belief.

The passages cited from the Brehon laws, or used in explanation of them, seem to show pretty clearly the importance of poetic malediction and satire in the life of the ancient Irish; and the impression derived from the laws is borne out by frequent references in the heroic tales and historical documents. In texts of the strict Old Irish period – that is, those preserved in Old Irish manuscripts – no actual accounts of satire have been noted by the writer, though some of the words regularly used for it already occur in documents of the time.[58] In view of the fact that the Old Irish texts are chiefly glosses, the lack of such material is not surprising. But Cormac's Glossary, which is generally conceded, though the manuscripts of it are Middle Irish, to be a work of the ninth or tenth century, and which is therefore one of the earliest documents preserving any considerable quantity of native Irish tradition, contains a score or more of references to the custom. Several words are there explained as having to do with the satirist or his work. *Leos* is defined as 'a blush wherewith a person is reddened after a satire or reproach of him'; and one meaning of *ferb* is said to be 'a blotch which is put on the face of a man after a satire or false judgment.'[59] A similar conception of the physical effect of satire (which will be discussed again later) appears in the definition of *rinntaid*, 'nomen for a man of satire, who wounds or cuts each face.' Both *groma* and *glam* are defined, and the latter explained as coming *ab eo quod est clamor*. The etymology, like that proposed for *cainte*, satirist, – 'i.e., *canis*, a dog, for the satirist has a dog's head in barking, and alike is the profession they follow' – has no value in the eyes of modern science, but such comments are of some incidental interest. And this is particularly true of the etymology proposed for *file*, poet, 'from poison (*fi*) in satire and splendour (*li*) in praise.' The derivation is again impossible, but in associating the word for poet with the 'poison of satire' Cormac anticipates, on the semasiological side, the modern theories, already mentioned, with regard to the Germanic words 'scop' and 'scoff.'[60]

More interesting, however, than any of these definitions[61] are four actual pieces of old satirical verse which Cormac has preserved among his citations. Under *riss*, 'story', a line is quoted and declared to come from the poem of Coirpre mac Etaine against Bres mac Elathain, the first satire which was made in Ireland. Under *cernine*, 'dish', another line from the same poem is cited; but Cormac nowhere gives the rest of the satire. In the saga of the 'Second Battle of Moytura',[62] however, the whole story is told to which allusion is made in the passages cited. According to this account, Coirpre, the poet of the 'Tuatha Dé Danann', once came a-guesting to the house of Bres. 'He entered a cabin narrow, black, dark, wherein there was neither fire nor furniture nor bed. Three small cakes, and they dry, were brought to him on a little dish. On the morrow he arose, and he was not thankful. As he went across the garth, he said:

> Without food quickly on a dish;
> Without a cow's milk whereon a calf grows;
> Without a man's abode under the gloom (?) of night;[63]
> Without paying a company of story-tellers – let that be Bres's condition.

As a result of the verse it is said that nought save decay was on Bres from that hour.

Under the word *Munnu*, interpreted as *Mo Fhinnu*, a pet name, the following quatrain is quoted and said to come from, the satire of Maedoc Ferna against Munnu, the son of Tulchan:

> O little vassal of mighty God!
> O son of Tulchan, O Shepherd!
> She bore a troublesome child to a family,
> The mother that bore thee, Fintan!

Other evidence concerning this satire has apparently not been preserved; in fact some very similar lines are quoted in the commentary on the 'Martyrology of Oengus' and attributed to Columbcille.[64]

A third quatrain, which also appears, as Stokes points out, to be of satirical character, is quoted under the word *rer*, 'blackbird.'

> Hard to thee[65] the little stripling,
> Son of the little blackbird!
> Have thou every good thing ready before him,
> O little head (that is, O head of a little goose)!

The son of the little blackbird is doubtless the poet Flann MacLonain, whom the Four Masters call 'the Virgil of the race of the Scots'; and the person addressed is Finnguine, King of Cashel, known as Cenn-gegain, 'head of a little goose'. The lines contain little more than word-play on the diminutive formations in the names, and the circumstances referred to are unknown.[66]

A typical story of satire, as it was employed among the Irish, is attached to a fourth stanza, quoted by Cormac under the word *gaire*, 'shortness (of life)'. The lines are said to have been uttered by Nede, the son of Adnae, against Caier, his uncle, the king of Connaught, and the whole episode is narrated in the version of Cormac's *Glossary* in the *Yellow Book of Lecan*.[67] 'Caier', as the tale goes, 'had adopted Nede as his son, because he had no son at all. The mind of Caier's wife clave unto Nede. She gave an apple of silver unto Nede for his love. Nede consented not, and she promised him half the realm after Caier, if he would go in unto her. 'How shall this happen to us?' said Nede. 'Not difficult', said the woman, 'make thou a satire on him, so that a blemish come upon him. Then the man with the blemish shall be no longer king.' 'Not easy to me is this thing; the man will not make refusal to me. There is nothing in the world in his possession that he will not give me.' 'I know,' said the woman, 'a thing that he will not give thee, namely, the dagger that was brought him from the lands of Alba he will not give thee; he is forbidden to part with it.' Nede asked Caier for the dagger. 'Woe is me,' said Caier, 'I am forbidden to part with it.' Nede made a *glám dichenn* upon him, and three blisters came forth on his cheeks. This is the satire:

> Evil, death, short life to Caier!
> Let spears of battle wound him, Caier!
> Caier . . .! Caier . . .! Caier under earth,
> Under ramparts, under stones be Caier![68]

Caier arose next morning early (and went) to the well. He put his hand over his countenance. He found on his face three blisters which the satire had caused, namely, Stain, Blemish, and Defect, to wit, red, and green, and white. Caier fled thence that none might see the disgrace, until he was in Dún Cermnai with Cacher, son of Eitirscél. Nede took the realm of Connaught after him. He was there till the end of a year. Grievous unto him was Caier's torment. Nede went after him to Dún Cermnai, seated in Caier's chariot, and Caier's wife and his greyhound were with him. Fair was the chariot that went to the fort! His face told how it was with him. 'Whose is that colour?' said every one. Said Caier: 'Twas we that rode on his high seat by the seat of the charioteer.' 'That is a king's word,' said Cacher, son of Eitirscél. (Caier was not known to him up to that time.) 'No, truly, I am not,' said Caier. With that Caier fled (?) from them out of the house, till he was on the flagstone behind the fort. Nede went in his chariot into the fort. The dogs pursued Caier's track until they found him under the flagstone behind the fort. Caier died for shame on seeing Nede. The rock flamed at Caier's death, and a fragment of the rock flew up under Nede's eye, and pierced into his head.' The exact manner of Nede's punishment is differently described in a stanza on the justice of his fate, with which the account ends:

> A stone that happened to be under Caier's foot
> Sprang up the height of a sail-tree,
> Fell – not unjust was the decree –
> On the head of the poet from above.

A number of elements in this story are of interest to the student of early institutions and beliefs: the symbolical use, for example, of the apple of silver,[69] or the peculiar prohibition (Irish *geis*, a kind of taboo) which forbade Caier to part with his dagger,[70] or the provision that a king with a bodily blemish must abdicate his throne.[71] But attention must here be called rather to what concerns the satire itself – to the poet's effort to find an excuse for his attack, to his final punishment for unjust satire, in spite of his ruse, and to the detailed account of the blemishing effect of his maledictory verse. The pimples, blushes or other kinds of disfigurement produced by satire have been several times referred to in passages previously cited. Here in the story of Caier three blotches, red, green and white, are definitely mentioned, and called Stain, Blemish and Defect. The allegorical interpretation may be relatively late, though such treatment of abstract qualities is by no means without parallel in early Irish literature. But the general conception of facial disfigurement as the result of magic persecution or even as a punishment for some form of misbehaviour is very widespread. Among the Irish the affliction was visited not only on the victim of an incantation, as in the case of Caier, but sometimes on the poet himself,[72] if his satire was unjust, and also on a judge who rendered an unjust verdict.[73] Somewhat similar is the case of Brieriu, mentioned in the Scéla Conchobair maic Nessa, who had a boil rise from his forehead whenever he tried to withhold a secret.[74] And many readers will recall, what is at bottom the same idea, the Greek belief, mentioned by Bacon in his essay 'Of Praise', that 'he that was praised to his hurt should have a push rise upon his nose; as we say that a blister will rise upon one's tongue that tells a lie.'[75] That there is a physiological basis for all such notions no one, in these days of psychotherapy, will be disposed to deny.[76]

Of the four satirical pieces that have been quoted from the *Glossary of Cormac*, two, it is to be noted, are really incantations, and two are rather mocking than maledictory in tone. Thus the examples of satire in an early document show the same confusion of different types that was observed in the references to the subject in the laws. And this close association of incantational verse with other forms of poetry will frequently appear in the accounts of satirists to be cited from Irish sagas.

In the further illustration of the subject from these sources no attempt will be made to follow a strict chronological order of events. Some of the saga material to be used is doubtless older, at least in substance, than Cormac's *Glossary*, and the examples taken from that work have fully established the existence of satire, in the senses under discussion, in the Old Irish period. The practice of it has survived among the Gaels, as will be shown later, down to the present time. Beyond these general statements of chronology it is not necessary to go. And there is, in fact, no reason for insisting on the antiquity of the evidences with regard to this custom, since nobody will contend (as is often contended with regard to the much-debated elements of Celtic and Arthurian romance) that the Irish borrowed it from other peoples of mediaeval Europe.

It is noteworthy, as has already been remarked, that tales of destructive satire are associated with some of the most conspicuous poets in Irish history and saga. The man who was perhaps most famous for the exercise of this dangerous power was Aithirne the Importunate, who was so representative a satirist that in the metaphorical language of poetry *sciath Aithirni*, 'the shield of Aithirne', became a 'kenning' for satire.[77] His ruthless exactions, from which he derived his sobriquet, are described in the saga of the Siege of Howth,[78] where he is declared to have been 'a hard, merciless man', 'a man who asked the one-eyed for his single eye, and who used to demand the woman in child-bed.' So much was he feared that when, in the course of his bardic circuit, he approached the borders of Leinster, the people came forth to meet him and offered him jewels and treasures not to come into their country, so that he might not leave invectives. And any man would give his wife to Aithirne, or the single eye out of his head, or whatever Aithirne might desire of jewels and treasures. As the result of an enforced contribution of women and cattle, levied by him on the men of Leinster, came about the siege of Howth and a war between Leinster and Ulster.[79]

That Aithirne sometimes met his match appears from a short story in the Book of Leinster, which describes his defeat at the hands of another poet.[80] Because of his niggardliness, it is declared, Aithirne never ate his full meal in a place where any one could see him. He proceeded, therefore, on one occasion to take with him a cooked pig and a pot of mead, in order that he might eat his fill all alone. And he set in order before him the pig and the pot of mead when he beheld a man coming towards him. 'Thou wouldst do it all alone', said the stranger, whilst he took the pig and the pot away from him. 'What is thy name?' said Aithirne. 'Nothing very grand,' said he:

> *Sethor, ethor, othor, sele, dele, dreng, gerce,*
> Son of Gerluscc, sharp sharp, right right, that is my name.

Aithirne neither got the pig, nor was able to make rhyme to the satire. It is evident that it was one come from God to take away the pig; for Aithirne was not stingy from that hour forth.

The use of the ordinary Irish word for satire (*aer*) here, where no personal attack or invective is involved, shows the range of its employment. The lines of the strange visitor are of course to be regarded as a spell, and the contest to which Aithirne is invited is really a contest in magic power. In fact, many of the stories of verse-capping, with which popular literature abounds,[81] are something more than tests of poetical skill, and the whole literary type known as the debate, or *Streitgedicht*, owes more than is commonly recognized to the ancient practice of competition between rival magician-poets. But that matter must be left for investigation and discussion at another time.

To return to Aithirne, the usual result of refusing his requests is seen in the saga of Aithirne and Luaine, which belongs to the cycle of King Conchobar of Ulster.[82] After the death of Deirdriu, it is related, Conchobar was in great sorrow, and no joy or beauty could appease his spirit. The chief men of Ulster urged him to search the provinces of Erin, if perchance he might find therein the daughter of a king or a noble, who would drive away his grief for Deirdriu, and to this he assented. After a long search his messengers found Luaine, the daughter of Domanchenn, the one maiden in Ireland who had upon her the ways of Deirdriu in shape and sense and handicraft; and when Conchobar beheld her there was no bone in him the size of an inch that was not filled with long-lasting love for the girl. She was betrothed to him, and her bride-price was bound upon him. When Aithirne the Importunate and his two sons heard of the plighting of the maiden to Conchobar, they went to beg boons of her. At sight of her they gave love to her, and besought her to play the king false. On her refusal they made three satires upon her, which left three blotches on her cheeks, namely Stain and Blemish and Disgrace, which were black and red and white. And thereupon the maiden died of shame. When Conchobar learned of her death, great silence fell upon him, and his grief was second only to his grief for Deirdriu. He took counsel with the Ulstermen concerning the punishment of Aithirne and his sons. Luaine's father and mother urged revenge, but Cathbad, the Druid, gave warning that Aithirne would send beasts of prey against them, namely Satire and Disgrace and Shame and Curse and Fire (?) and Bitter Word. In the end they decided upon Aithirne's destruction; and after the funeral rites had been celebrated for Luaine, the Ulstermen followed Aithirne to Benn Aithirni, and walled him in with his sons and all his household, and killed Mor and Midseng, his two daughters, and burnt his fortress upon him. But the doing of that deed, it is said, seemed evil to the poets of Ulster. Although the magician in Aithirne so much outweighs the poet, yet the bards took up his cause, and Amairgen, the chief poet, Aithirne's fosterling and pupil, made a lamentation upon him.

Aithirne and the kings with whom he is associated belong distinctly to the field of saga, but similar tales are told of poets who lived within the historical period or in relation with historical persons. Dallan Forgail, of the sixth century, the traditional author of the 'Amra Choluimb Chille', is said to have composed both songs of praise and satirical verses upon Aed mac Duach in an effort to obtain from him, by fair means or foul, his famous shield, the *Dubh-Ghilla*.[83] And the death of Niall of the Nine Hostages, one of the chief leaders of the marauding Scots at the beginning of the fifth century, was directly due, according to one account,[84] to strife engendered by a satirist. Echu, the son of Enna Censelach, the tale relates, when on his way from the house of Niall to his own people in Leinster, sought food at the house of Laidchenn, Niall's poet. Laidchenn refused Echu hospitality, and Echu revenged himself later by destroying the poet's house and killing his son. Thereupon for a whole year Laidchenn kept satirizing and lampooning and cursing the men of Leinster, so that neither grass nor corn grew with them, nor a leaf, to the end of a year. Niall also went to Leinster, and forced the people to give him Echu in bonds as a hostage; but Echu broke his chains, and slew nine champions who came up to kill him, and rejoined his people. A second time Niall demanded that the Leinstermen give up Echu, and when this was done, Laidchenn began to revile Echu and the Leinstermen, so that they melted away before him. But Echu let fly a champion's stone, which he had in his belt, and it hit Laidchenn in the crown of his forehead and lodged in his skull. Echu was exiled from Ireland, but this did not put an end to the feud, and afterward, in Alba, Niall himself fell by an arrow from Echu's hand. While the satires of Laidchenn are plainly of the nature of spells, it is clear that he was regarded in Irish tradition as a real poet, and not a mere pronouncer of charms. Poems on the history of the kings of Leinster, ascribed to him, though not to be taken as authentic, will be found in the Rawlinson Manuscript B 502.[85]

With the satires of Laidchenn, which blighted the whole face of Leinster, may be compared the spells attributed to Ferchertne, another great poet of the heroic age, before whom, according to a passage in the 'Táin Bó Cúalnge' ('The Cattle-Spoil of Cooley'), the lakes and streams sank when he blamed them and rose when he praised them.[86] They bring to mind also the threat of Forgoll, the poet, in the Voyage of Bran, when upon occasion of a disagreement with Mongan, he declared that he would satirize Mongan and his father and his mother and his grandfather; singing spells upon their waters so that no fish should be caught in their river-mouths, and on their woods so that they should bear no fruit, and on their plains so that they should be barren of produce.[87]

Enough has been said to show the association of satire and malediction with Irish poets of high station. The frequency of the practice in the life of the people is further indicated by many passages in the sagas. In the great central tale of the Ulster cycle, the 'Táin Bó Cúalnge', for example, satirists appear in several important episodes. The account of Ferchertne and his spells has just been referred to. Redg, another satirist, is employed against Cuchulainn when the latter is holding at bay all the army of Connaught. He is sent to ask Cuchulainn for his spear; and upon Cuchulainn's refusal he threatens to take away his honour. Then Cuchulainn lets him have the spear in the back of his head, and kills him.[88] Again, when Ferdiad, the companion of Cuchulainn's youth, refuses to take part against him, Medb sends the Druids and the satirists and the hard-attackers to him, that they may make three satires to hold him, and three imprecations (*glamma dicend*), that they may raise the three blotches on his face, Shame and Blemish and Disgrace, so that if he does not die at once he may die before the end of nine days, if he will not go into the fight. And Ferdiad yields, preferring to fall before the spears of bravery and warfare and prowess rather than before the spears of satire and insult and abuse.[89] On another occasion two female satirists from the camp of Connaught stand over Cuchulainn and weep in hypocrisy, predicting the ruin of Ulster.[90] And again, the Morrigan herself, the battle-goddess, appears to Cuchulainn in a similar guise.[91] In the text of the 'Táin Bó Cúalnge' she is not called a satirist, but she applies the name to herself in the 'Táin Bó Regamna', where she plays the same part.[92]

A few more illustrations of destructive satires may be cited from the great collection of early Irish topographical legends which is known as the 'Dindsenchas'.[93] In the account of Mullaghmast,[94] Maistiu, by whose name that of the place is explained, is said to have refused certain demands of Gris, the female rhymester, who so maltreated her with blemishing satires that she died thereof before her. 'The Dindsenchas of Dublin'[95] affords another instance of death from the verse of a poetess, but in this case the poem is described as a sea-spell. Dub, the wife of Enna, discovered that her husband had another wife, Aide, the daughter of Ochenn. In jealousy, then, Dub chanted a sea-spell before Ochenn's house, so that Aide was drowned with all her family.[96] In still another case, in the 'Dindsenchas of Fafaind',[97] the result of the satirist's verses is not death but disfigurement, as has been noted several times before. Aige, the sister of Fafne, the poet, was transformed into a fawn by her enemies, and then slain by the king's men. Thereupon Fafne went to blemish the king, and raised the customary three blotches upon him. In punishment for this Fafne was arrested and put to death.

It is apparent from a number of passages cited, and particularly from the description of the *glám dichenn*, that satirists often plied their work in companies. A whole body of 'druids and satirists and hard-attackers' were sent by Mebd to force Ferdiad into battle. Kings had bands of satirists in their employ,[98] and poets are sometimes grouped with other forces to be counted upon in war.[99] In the tale of the 'Second Battle of Moytura', for example, when the leaders of all the crafts are asked in turn what help they can give against the Fomorian enemies, the *file* promises, on behalf of his fellow-poets, to make a *glám dichenn* which will satirize them and shame them and take away their resistance.[100] And in the 'Dindsenchas of Carman', hostile enchanters appear in open opposition.[101] Carman and her sons, according to the story, came from Athens, and she ruined the land with spells and songs and incantations while the sons destroyed by plundering and dishonesty. But the Tuatha Dé Danann sent Ai of their poets and Cridenbél of their satirists and Lugh Laebach of their Druids and Bé Cuille of their witches to sing upon them, and the men were driven out, and Carman held as a prisoner behind them. The joint action of enchanters seems also to be referred to in the 'Dindsenchas of Laigen', which says that the Druids of Ireland nearly exterminated by their songs the tribe of the Gaileoin.[102]

In the light of so many accounts of maledictive work of poets it will not appear strange that Cormac thought the 'poison of satire' to be one element in the composite of *file*, or that Ferchertne and Nede, in a highly technical 'Colloquy' on the poets' profession, several times refer to satire among its characteristic features.[103] Nor is it to be wondered at that the poets as a class came to be greatly feared. In some verses ascribed to St Columba it is written, 'Blessed is he who is praised; woe to him who is satirized!' And again, 'Woe to the land that is satirized!' [104] And Ferchertne, in an interesting and typically Irish elaboration of the familiar list of signs before judgment, predicts, among other calamities, that 'every man will buy a lampooner to lampoon on his behalf.' [105] It was a general belief, sometimes explained by reference to the sacredness of the poet's person, that no request of his should ever be denied, and there was undoubtedly a strong feeling that poets were entitled to be rewarded for their work. But the real motive for yielding to their exactions seems often to have been the fear of their attacks, whether in maledictive verse or in some other form of magic persecution. And that they had other means than the poetic of enforcing their demands is suggested by Cormac's description of the *briamon smetrach*, [106] an operation which they performed on a man who refused them aught. They ground his ear-lobe between their fingers until he died. The supernatural power of the poets was even conceived as lasting beyond their own lives; and it is related of Cuan O'Lothchain, a famous poet who was murdered in 1024, that his murderers became putrid in a single hour. 'That,' the annalist says, 'was the miracle of a poet!' [107]

As a result of the terror they inspired, the poets commonly got what they asked for, even from the boldest of saga heroes. Thus Cridenbél the satirist regularly obtained on demand the best bits of the Dagda's supper, though the Dagda's health was the worse for it; and it was only by a trick that the importunate sorcerer was disposed of. [108] So also Lugaid the king, when solicited by Ban-bretnach, the woman-satirist of the Britons, complied with her demand and lay with her, and became the father of Conall Corc; [109] and it is related of a certain MacSweeney that, when unable to remove a ring which a poet had asked for, he hacked off finger and all rather than not grant the request. [110] Of Leborcham, the nurse of Deirdriu, it is said that she was a woman-satirist and no one dared refuse her aught; [111] and of MacConglinne, who was great at both eulogy and satire, that he was called *Anéra* (the negative of *era*, 'denial') because there was no denial of his requests. [112]

Even the Christian Saints, it would appear, were not exempted from such demands or by any means superior to the fear of them. For when St Columba was cutting wood for the church of Doire, certain poets came to him to seek a boon. He told them he had no gift for them there, but that if they would come home with him they should receive one. They replied that if he did not give the gift then and there they would satirize him; and Columba was seized with such shame at this threat that smoke rose from his forehead and he sweated exceedingly. He put up his hand to wipe away the sweat, and it became a talent of gold in his palm, and he gave the talent to the poets. 'Thus,' the narrator concludes, 'did God save the honour of Columbcille.' [113] In a story of similar purport the honour of St Patrick is saved by the miraculous provision of food for a company of minstrels or jugglers; but in this instance the petitioners, after receiving their boon, are swallowed up by the earth in punishment for their insolence. [114] Vengeance of like character is visited on three poets who threaten to defame St Laisren; [115] and, in general, when the satirists confront the saints, their sorcery is forced to succumb to a higher power.

The community as a whole also sometimes found means, according to the historians, of resisting the demands of the poets, and Geoffrey Keating reports traditions of at least three banishments of the order. [116] On the first occasion, in the time of King Conchobar of Ulster, when the poets were about to set out for Alba, they were taken under protection by Cuchulainn and retained by him for seven years. On their second banishment they were retained by Fiachna mac Baedan, and on their third by Maelcobha mac Deamain, both also kings of Ulster. A fourth attempt to expel them from the country was made by King Aed mac Ainmiri at the celebrated assembly of Drumceat. But St Columba intervened on the poets' behalf and arranged that they should be allowed to remain, though with their numbers reduced. His action, Keating observes, is commemorated in the stanza:

The poets were saved by this means,
Through Colum of the fair law;
A poet for each district is no heavy charge, –
That is what Colum ordained.

The same abuses of the poets which stirred up hostile legislation called forth much unfavourable comment in Irish literature, and in one case they produced a counterblast which ranks among the best pieces of humorous writing in Middle Irish. This is the 'Imtheacht na Tromdháimhe' ('Proceedings of the Great Bardic Institution'), which has been several times referred to. The account of Senchan and the mice, already quoted from it, shows the spirit of extravagant burlesque which pervades the whole, and which can hardly be reproduced in a condensed summary of the story. The chief episodes are as follows: The bards, under Senchan, their newly elected chief, decided to make a professional visit to Guaire, the king of Connaught, who had never been satirized for lack of hospitality; and out of special consideration for him they took with them only thrice fifty poets, thrice fifty students, thrice fifty hounds, thrice fifty kinswomen, and thrice nine of each class of artificers. Guaire greeted them all cordially, only regretting that he could not give a personal welcome to each member of the large company; and they were quartered in a great mansion and told to ask for whatever they might desire. 'It was, however, a great difficulty to procure all things for them; for it was requisite to give to each of them his meals apart and a separate bed; and they went to bed not any night without wanting something, and they arose not a day without some of them having longing desires for some things that were extraordinary, wonderful, and rare, and difficult of procurement. It was a task for all the men of Ireland to find that which was longed for, and unless the person who desired it obtained it within twenty-four hours, it was useless ever after to procure it for him.' Muireann, the wife of Dallan Forgail, on the very first night moaned aloud and declared that she should die unless she could have 'a bowl of the ale of sweet milk, with the marrow of the ankle-bone of a wild hog; a pet cuckoo on an ivy tree between the two Christmases; her full load on her back, with a girdle of yellow lard of an exceeding white boar about her; and to be mounted on a steed with a brown mane, and its four legs exceedingly white; a garment of the spider's web around her, and she humming a tune as she proceeded to Durlus.' Another woman of the company desired a skirt full of blackberries in January, and also that Guaire's people might all be stricken down with disease. For the fulfilment of these and other equally preposterous demands Guaire sought the aid of Marban, his brother, the holy hermit; and by miracles of heaven the king's honour was saved, like that of the saints in the stories previously related.

When all the desires of the company had been fulfilled, they sat down to a great feast. Senchan, however, took whimsical offence at the hearty eating of the servants, and refused all food. Guaire in distress sent a favourite steward to prepare a wild goose and serve it to Senchan with special care. But Senchan refused it because the young man's grandfather was chip-nailed. And when a favourite damsel of Guaire's household was sent, Senchan would not take food from her hands because her grandmother had once pointed out the road to lepers. At last, after several days' abstinence, Senchan consented to eat a hen's egg, but the mice got at it, with results that have already been described. When Senchan was saved by St Kieran from the clutches of Irusan, the great cat, he complained at his release, for he would rather by his death have given occasion for the satirizing of Guaire.

Marban, in the meantime, though a saintly hermit, had lost all patience with the unreasonable demands of the poets, and determined to obtain some redress. Accordingly he made his way to their mansion, declared that he was connected with poetry through the grandmother of his servant's wife, who was descended from poets, and claimed his choice of music from the company. Then he demanded the performance of a *cronán* (a low humming tune) till he should declare that he had enough. He would not be satisfied with the ordinary *cronán*, but insisted on the bass or guttural *cronán*, in the hope that they would break their heads, feet, and necks, and that their breathing would be the sooner exhausted. One company of singers after another was worn out by the performance. Efforts were made to put off Marban with riddle contests, but he always defeated his antagonists in questions, and then reverted to his first demand: 'Perform as much *cronán* as we desire.' At last, when no one else could respond, Senchan himself had to perform, and he made such exertions at the guttural *cronán* that his eye burst out upon his cheek. Marban was satisfied with this revenge, and restored the eye to its place. Then he laid bonds upon the bards to obtain for him the saga of the 'Cattle-Spoil of Cooley'; and the rest of the story is taken up with their adventures in discharge of the obligation.

In this way the 'Imtheacht na Tromdhaimbe' is brought into connection with the old saga-cycle. But it is really a comparatively late work,[117] and in effect, as has already been said, a satire on the satirists. Satire in the loose or primitive sense furnished material for satire in the stricter definition of the word. It would not be fair to say that the one passed over into the other, and no such suggestion is here intended. The 'Imtheacht' is cited rather as a significant piece of testimony to the extensive development of the old satire of malediction.

It would be easy to multiply references to satire from all branches of early Irish literature, but the passages which have been discussed illustrate the more important aspects of the subject. And it is beyond the compass of the present study to trace the history of satire through Irish literature of the modern period. Suffice it to say, of this later development, that although real satire, as opposed to incantational verse, increases as time goes on, the old conception of the destructive satirist, the poet with superior power, whom it is dangerous to displease, has never disappeared among the Gaels of either Ireland or Scotland.[118] But the village rhymester of today, though he may, like Chaucer's Somonour, have

In daunger . . . at his owene gyse
The yonge girles of the diocyse,

is far less important in power or influence than the magician-poet of saga times. He represents, so far as one can judge, the expiration of a tradition or custom which in mediaeval Ireland was still vigorous and productive of results in literary development.

For the practices of the old Irish satirists have, in addition to their merely curious interest, a wider bearing on literary history. Attention has already been called to their connection with the development of the 'flyting', or verse debate, a matter which cannot further be treated at this time. And their obvious relation to the beginnings of ordinary satire also deserves more consideration than it has received from students of the subject.[119] One might hesitate just now, when fashion among critics and scholars is turning against *Liedertheorien* and doctrines of popular origin, to lay stress upon such a development. The folklorists and ballad collectors are charged, not unjustly, with many extravagances: with ill-judged enthusiasm for poor productions, just because they are popular; with wild speculation about popular composition; and with a kind of easy-going satisfaction in the collection of popular parallels as if they explained the mature products of art. Nevertheless, in spite of its peccant humours, the study of folk literature has yielded solid results, and the 'thrice-battered Grimm', as Mr Gummere once called him, is not to be abjured as a Philistine god. Popular or communal composition, in some such reasonable sense as Mr Gummere also has most fully defined and illustrated, must be recognized as a significant fact in the history of poetry. Popular material, in various forms of mythology and tradition, has entered into the highest products of art, and the understanding of it is often essential to the comprehension of Chaucer or Shakespeare or Goethe. In a word, the historian of poetry will never again be at liberty to disregard the popular basis of the poetry of art.

Now satire, which belongs conspicuously to the poetry of art, doubtless owes little, in its developed phases, to such simple products as the quatrains of Nede and Coirpre. Yet it is unquestionably a very old poetic form, originating in early stages of society and having definite relations with various kinds of popular verse. On one side a source has been found for it in the rude, rustic songs of mockery which exist among many peoples.[120] In another aspect its connection with gnomic writing is well recognized; and one scholar has gone so far, in discussing old Germanic poetry,[121] as to assume that people who possessed a gnomic literature must also have had satire. The close association of these two types could also be admirably illustrated from Irish literature, which furnishes, in such collections of proverbial morality as the ancient Instructions of Cormac, many passages of well-developed satire.[122] But a still more intimate and essential relation seems to exist between satire and the kind of verse that has been described in this paper. And it is interesting to find that an observation by M. Brunetière, whom nobody will accuse of undue partiality for popular literature, points towards its recognition. He concludes an admirable survey of the general history of satire with the following definition:[123] 'Opposer, en nous moquant d'eux, ou en les invectivant, – c'est affaire de tempérament, – notre manière de penser, de sentir, ou de voir à ceux qui ne voient, ni ne pensent, ni ne sentent comme nous, tel est, on l'a pu voir, le

151

trait essentiel et commun qui relie les unes aux autres toutes les formes de la satire. Le poète Archiloque, ayant sur la fille de Lycambe des vues que Lycambe n'approuvait point, il les exprima d'une façon si virulente que Lycambe, et même sa fille, dit la légende, s'en pendirent. Voilà le fond de toute satire.' The French critic, though chiefly concerned in his essay with the more elaborate and literary forms of satire, yet finds its essential nature to be personal invective. If his observation is sound, and it is certainly not unreasonable, the old Irish satirists were in the main line of development, though very far up the line; and the evidence with regard to them shows that the poetry of enchantment must also be included in the reckoning. For in the days of the magician-poet invective, mockery and malediction are seen to have been almost inseparably bound together.

## Notes

1  Sidney's Works, ed. 1724, 3, 52.

2  Ed. 1665, page 35.

3  Jonson's Works, ed. Gifford (1875), 5, page 518.

4  *As You Like It*, act iii, scene 2. Other references to the subject, some of them of considerably later date, will be found in Ben Jonson's *Staple of News*, act iv, scene 1 (Gifford's ed., 5, 271); *Randolph's Jealous Lovers*, act v, scene 1; *Rhymes against Martin Marprelate*, cited by Nares from Herbert's *Typographical Antiquities*, page 1689 (the whole poem printed in D'Israeli's *Quarrels of Authors*, 2, 255–63); Sir William Temple's *Essay on Poetry*, in his works (ed. 1757), 3, 418; Swift's *Advice to a Young Poet* (ed. Scott, 9, 407); and Pope's version of *Donne's Second Satire*, line 23. Most of these passages were cited in *Nares' Glossary*, under *Rats Rimed to Death*; for further discussion see an article by Todd, Proceedings of the Royal Irish Academy, 1855, pages 355 ff.

5  O'Curry's materials were presented in Dr Todd's paper in the Proceedings for 1855. He mentions one instance of rat-rhyming in 1776, and another about 1820. Cases of the same sort among the Highland Gaels are cited by the Rev. Alexander Stewart in *Twixt Ben Nevis and Glencoe* (Edinburgh, 1885). A long spell said to have been composed and successfully used by a farmer on the Island of Lismore is given by Stewart on pages 4 ff. Somewhat different from these stories of rat-rhymers is the case related by Giraldus Cambrensis (*Gemma Ecclesiastica*, Rolls Series, 161) of St Yvor the bishop, who by his curse expelled the rats (majores mures, qui vulgariter rati vocantur) from an Irish province because they had gnawed his books. This was conceived by Giraldus as a Christian miracle, and is cited, along with the story of St Patrick and the snakes, to illustrate the fearful effects of excommunication. Still another method of disposing of rats is familiar to everybody in the legend of the Piper of Hamelin.

6  Edited and translated by O. Connellan in the *Transactions of the Ossianic Society*, vol. 5, Dublin, 1860. The Irish title means simply the Circuit of the Burdensome Company, but the tale is usually referred to in English by Connellan's rendering, as given above.

7  British treatment of Irish history has long been a grievance to Irish writers. Perhaps the best way of getting at the traditional accounts of the 'wild Irish' is by consulting the rejoinders of such native writers as Keating in his *Forus Feasa air Eirinn*, or Lynch in his *Cambrensis Eversus*. See also the Rev. Dr T.J. Shahan's survey of the subject in the *Am. Cath. Quarterly Review*, 28, 310ff.

8  For references to Temple, see note 4 above.

9  The confusion among these different classes is well set forth, with illustrative passages, by C. Plummer, *Vitae Sanctorum Hiberniae*, 1, pages clx–clxii.

10  For a convenient survey of the evidence concerning the use of incantations in Greek and Roman civilization, see an article on 'Graeco-Italian Magic', by F.B. Jevons, in *Anthropology and the Classics* (Oxford, 1908), pages 93 ff.

11　The story seems more likely to have been a late invention. For the authorities, and a possible explanation of its origin, see Croiset, *Histoire de la Littérature Grecque* (1890), 2, 180. And the death of Bupalus, the victim of Hipponax, of which Sidney's *Bubonax* (see above) seems to show a confused memory, is of similarly doubtful authority.

12　For certain evidences of ancient popular *Spottlieder* in Greece and Italy, which suggest conditions similar to those among Germans and Celts, see Usener, Rheinisches Museum, 56, 1 ff.; Hirt, *Die Indogermanen* (1905), 2, 478–9, 728. One cannot help suspecting in the light of the Irish material to be here discussed, that there was more of a magic element than Usener recognized in the old Italic poems of abuse.

13　For a full statement of the theory see Goldziher, *Abhandlungen zur Arabischen Philologie* (Leiden, 1896), pages 1–105. Goldziher's article contains much material of interest to students of European popular poetry. His main conclusion is briefly restated and indorsed by M.J. de Goeje, *Die Arabische Literatur, in Kultur der Gegenwart, Orientalische Literaturen*, pages 134 ff. Compare also Brockelmann, *Geschichte der Arabischen Litteratur* (1901), pages 7 ff.

14　Professor G.F. Moore called the writer's attention to the fact that Rückert, in his translation of the *Hamâsa*, employed the term *Schmählieder* for all such poems, just as writers on Irish have called them 'satires'. Freytag, similarly, in his edition of the *Hamâsa*, translated the Arabic subtitle (*Bâb el-Hija'*) as *Caput Satyrarum*, and the Arabic *Hija'* has acquired this general sense. But Goldziher (see particularly pages 26 ff. of his article) argues that it meant originally a curse or spell; thus it constitutes an interesting parallel to the development of the Irish *aer*.

15　This is consistent with the view expressed by De Goeje, *op. cit.*, page 134.

16　See Comparetti, *Il Kalevala, o la Poesia Tradizionale dei Finni* (Reale Accademia dei Lincei, Roma, 1891), pages 23 ff.

17　See E. Mogk, *Kelten und Nordgermanen*, page 12; also his article in the *Arkiv for Nordisk Filologi*, 17, 277 ff. In the latter place he even argues that the *Zauberlied* was the chief form of early Germanic poetry, and that the oldest Germanic names for poems (ljoõ, galdr, and the Finnish *runo*, borrowed from Germanic) had reference primarily to spells.

18　For evidence concerning early *Spottlieder* see Kögel's *Literaturgeschichte*, vol. 1, part i, pages 55 ff., 208; vol. 1, part ii, pages 164–5; also Kögel's article in Paul's *Grundriss* (2nd ed.), 2, pages 48ff., 68ff. The very early instance mentioned in Ausonius (Moselle, 167), of the *probra* sung against *seris cultoribus* among the Treviri has been counted by some scholars as Germanic, and by others as Celtic, or even as Roman. See Kögel, vol. 1, part i, page 55; C. Jullian, *Rev. Arch.*, 40, 321; Martin, *Gött. Gel. Anz.*, 1893, page 128. Brandl, in his article on 'Altenglische Literaturgeschichte', in Paul's *Grundriss*, 2nd ed., 2, 974, mentions the Anglo-Saxon *dreamas*, *'gesellschaftliche Lieder'*, and conjectures that the *Spottlied* (*bismerléop*) must have figured prominently among them.

19　On the canon see Müllenhoff in Haupt's *Zeitschrift*, 9, 130. There is some doubt, it should be said, concerning its application to Germanic conditions; and in general, as Professor Wiener has collected material to show, it is necessary to be cautious in deriving from ecclesiastical canons, which were taken over literally from one council to another, evidences as to local beliefs and practices.

20　The story is told in Thegan's Life of Louis the Pious, chapter 28, and is cited by Kögel, *Literaturgeschichte*, vol. 1, part i, page 208.

21　Cf. Weinhold, *Altnordisches Leben*, pages 341 ff., 465; Finnur Jonsson, *Den Oldnorske og Oldislandske Litteraturs Historie*, 2, 18, 133–9; and for a number of references to sagas, Vigfusson's Dictionary, under *danz*, *flim* and *niõ*.

22　The quotation is from the English version of the 'Relation de l'Islande of La Peyrère' (in Churchill's Collection of Voyages and Travels) (1704), 2, 437. See Farley, Scandinavian Influences in the English Romantic Movement (*Harvard Studies and Notes*, vol. 10), pages 19 ff.

23　On the etymology of *scop* there is still considerable difference of opinion. The word was formerly held to have a long vowel and was brought into connection with *scieppan* (compare the relation of ποιητής and ποιέω). When the vowel was seen to be short, this etymology became harder to support; but Kögel in his *Literaturgeschichte*, vol. 1, part i, pages 140 ff., still defended it, assuming a theoretic *skupó- with *Tiefstufe* of the *Ablaut*. In Paul's *Grundriss*, 2nd ed., 2, 34, however, he changed his explanation and proposed to connect the word with the root *seq-*, *sqe-* in ξυνεπε, Lat. *insece*, and perhaps the Anglo-Saxon *specan*. In favour of the association with 'scoff' see Kluge, *Engl. Stud.*, 8, 480, quoted with approval by Gummere, *Old English Ballads* (1894), page xxxii. This explanation is adopted in the *New English Dictionary*, under *scop*, and in Torp's *Wortschatz der Germanischen Spracheinheit* (Fick's *Wörterbuch*), 3. 469. The Irish *fáith*, 'poet' (cognate with Lat. *vates*), and the Welsh *gwawd*, 'mockery', perhaps show a similar relation in meaning. See Zimmer, 'Die Keltischen Literaturen' (in *Kultur der Gegenwart*), page 77 n. The old Norse *skald*, if related to *scold*, *schelten*, etc., would furnish another parallel. This etymology, defended in Vigfusson's Dictionary, page 541, is rejected by several later writers, though no other has been clearly established in its place. Compare Lidén in Paul and Brauné's *Beiträge*, 15. 507 ff.; Mogk, in Paul's *Grundriss*, 2nd ed., 2, 657; and F. Jonsson, *Litteraturs Historie*, 1, 329 ff.

24 Diodorus, v. 31.2. Ουτοι δε μετ' ὀργάνων ταῖς λύραις ὁμοίων αδουτες ους μὲν ὑμνοῦσιν, ους δὲ βλασφημοῦσι. M. Camille Jullian, in a discussion of this passage (in Revue Archéologique, 40, 321), cites also classical testimony on the use by the ancient Celts of invectives in battle. This custom, which is frequently referred to in both Celtic and Germanic sagas, is closely related to the other forms of satire under consideration. See Goldziher, *Abhandlungen zur arabischen Philologie*, pages 26–7, for similar observations with regard to Arabic.

25 For the strife between Dafydd and Rhys Meigen see *Barddoniaeth Dafydd ap Gwilym* (1789), pages xi ff., 452 ff.; also L.C. Stern in the *Zeitschrift für Celtische Philologie*, 7, 26 ff

26 For the *glám dichenn* see page 108, below; for other uses of the word, and some suggestions as to its fundamental meaning, see Windisch's edition of the 'Táin Bó Cúailnge' (Irische Texte, Extraband), page 241.

27 On the *glas-gabail* see note 47.

28 For references to satire see Cormac's *Glossary* .

29 *Ancient Laws*, ed. O'Curry, 5, 230.

30 *Ibid.*, 5, 456 ff.

31 See Todd's edition of the Irish version of 'Nennius' (Irish Archaeological Society, 1848), page 162; also Kuno Meyer's Contributions to Irish Lexicography, under crosan. A peculiar use of the word appears in the *Senadh Saighri*, ed. by Meyer in the *Gaelic Journal*, 4, 108.

32 With the references to satire in the Irish laws should be compared the treatment of the subject in Italic and Germanic laws, already referred to. See particularly *Usener* or *Italische Volksjustiz in Rheinisches Museum*, 56, 1 ff., and Weinhold, *Altnordisches Leben*, pages 341 ff.

33 *Ancient Laws of Ireland*, 1, 152, 162, 231 (published by the Government, Dublin, 1865–1901). The language of the English translation is quoted, except where there is special reason to depart from it.

34 *Ancient Laws*, 1, 185, 237. The last phrase is translated conjecturally. See d'Arbois de Jubainville, *Études sur le Droit Celtique*, 2, 181. For discussion of certain inconsistencies in the laws of distress, see the same work, 2, 159 ff.

35 *Ibid.*, 2, 156; 5, 143, 156.

36 *Ibid.*, 5, 512.

37 *Ibid.*, 2, 156.

38 *Ibid.*, 4, 348, 352.

39 *Ibid.*, 5, 168, 172.

40 *Ibid.*, 1, 58; 5, 168, 172, 388. For O'Curry's comment see the *Proceedings of the Royal Irish Academy*, 1855, page 357.

41 On fasting as a means of distraint, see an article by the present writer in the Putnam Anniversary Volume (Cedar Rapids, Ia., 1909), pages 567 ff.

42 *Ancient Laws*, 3, 92 ff.

43 The *glas-gabail* is mentioned, but not explained, in the *Ancient Laws*, 5, 216. In the same volume, page 230, it is glossed *glama gnuisi*, 'satirizing the face'. If this refers to

the disfigurement by blisters, the *glas-gabail* does not seem to be anything very different from the *glám dichenn*, at least in its effects.

44 *Ancient Laws*, 5, 228.

45 The last sentence contains one or two obscure words which are not translated. With regard to the distinction between author and reciter, it is to be noted that the Roman Twelve Tables provided for the punishment of both *(si quis occentauisset siue carmen condidisset)*. Cf. Usener, *Rheinisches Museum*, 56, 3.

46 *Ancient Laws*, 5, 225. Cf. also d'Arbois de Jubainville, *Études sur le Droit Celtique*, 2, 26.

47 *Ibid.*, 176. For the association with strumpets, cf. also pages 202–4.

48 *Ancient Laws*, 5, 456.

49 *Ibid.*, 3, 25.

50 *Ibid.*, 5, 266–8. Compare also the law (5, 235) which exempts poets, with kings, bishops, insane men, and others, from responsibility for paying their sons' debts.

51 *Ibid.*, 1, 19.

52 *Ibid.*, 5. 12.

53 See *Revue Celtique*, 16, 280; *Annals of Clonmacnoise*, page 39; and *Aislinge Meic Conglinne*, ed. Kuno Meyer, pages 44 ff.; all cited by Plummer, *Vitæ Sanctorum Hiberniae*, 1, cii–ciii.

54 An example of satire against a tribe, which was apparently of the nature of invective or insult rather than of incantation, is cited from the 'Leabhar Breac' in the *Miscellany of the Irish Archæological Society*, 1, 179 ff.; see also O'Donovan's edition of O'Daly's *Tribes of Ireland* (Dublin, 1852), page 17 n. The Cinel Fiacha of Westmeath are asserted to be of plebeian origin. In anger at the insult they murder the satirists.

55 Translated by O'Curry, *Manners and Customs*, 2, 216 ff.; Atkinson, *Book of Ballymote* (Facsimile), page 13a; and Stokes, *Revue Celtique*, 12, 119–20; and summarized and discussed by Thurneysen, *Mittelirische Verslehren*, pages 124 ff. Thurneysen questions the antiquity of the tradition, at least as part of the *Verslehren*. But the substance of the passage does not look like a late invention.

56 This and the following terms refer to the various degrees of poets.

57 Stokes's translation (in *Revue Celtique*, 12, 119), somewhat condensed, is followed in the present account.

58 See particularly Ascoli's *Glossarium Palaeohibernicum* under *air* and its compounds.

59 There is a similar explanation in the *Amra Choluimb Chille*. See page 114, below.

60 See page 102, above.

61 For other references to the subject in Cormac, not mentioned above, see the articles on *aithrinne, doeduine, dul* and *trefhocal*.

62 See Stoke's edition and translation, *Revue Celtique*, 12, 61. The quatrain is also given in some manuscripts of the Amra Choluimb Chille; cf. O'Beirne Crowe's edition, page 26 (from the Lebor na h-Uidhre), and Stoke's edition (from Ms. Rawl. B. 502) in *Revue Celtique*, 20, 158. The story is told separately in *Yellow Book of Lecan*, page 137b, and also (apparently) in Trinity College Ms. H. 3, 17. See the Catalogue of Mss. in Trinity College, Dublin, page 352.

63 The readings of this line differ in the manuscripts, and the translation is uncertain.

64 See the notes to the 'Martyrology', under 21 October (Stokes's edition for the Henry Bradshaw Society, page 226).

65 This is Stokes's rendering of *uindsi chucat*; perhaps it should rather be translated 'here comes to thee'.

66 On Flann mac Lonain see O'Reilly, *Irish Writers*, pages lviii ff.; O'Curry *Manners and Customs*, 2, 98–104; Todd's edition of the *Cogadh Gaedhel re Gallaibh* (Rolls Series), page x; Hennessy's edition of *Chronicon Scotorum* (Rolls Series), page 175.

67 See Stokes's *Three Irish Glossaires*, pages xxxvi ff. Stokes's translation, slightly condensed by the omission of doubtful words and of glossarial passages, is here followed. Part of Nede's satirical stanza is quoted at the end of the account of the *glám dichenn* in the metrical treatise already referred to. See pages 108, above, and Thurneysen, *Mittelirische Verslehren*, page 125.

68 Several words in the quatrain are of uncertain meaning.

69 Compare the gifts of Finnabair to Ferdiad, 'Táin Bó Cúalnge', L.W. Farraday's translation (London, 1904), page 100. See also Gaidoz, *La Réquisition d'Amour et le Symbolisme de la Pomme* (Annuaire de l'École des Hautes Études, 1902), with reviewer's remarks in *Revue Archéologique*, 1902, 1, 134; Lot, in *Romania*, 27, 560, n.; Foster, on the Symbolism of Apples in Classical Antiquity, in *Harvard Studies in Classical Philology*, 10, 43 ff.; and Leite de Vasconcellos, in *Revista Lusitana*, 7, 126 ff.

70 For illustrations of the *geis*, from early Irish sagas, see an article by Miss Eleanor Hull, in *Folklore*, 12, 40 ff.

71 For this requirement that the king shall be free from all deformities or blemishes see *Ancient Laws*, 1, 73; 2, 279; 3, 85. Compare also the story of 'Nuada of the Silver Hand', discussed by Rhys, *Hibbert Lectures*, page 120.

72 See *Revue Celtique*, 20, 422, and *Liber Hymnorum*, ed. Atkinson, page 173.

73 See *Ancient Laws*, 4, 16; also *Revue Celtique*, 24, 279.

74 See Ériu, 4, 21, 32.

75 Cf. Theocritus, *Idylls*, ix, 30; xii, 24. The Greek idea was apparently rather that the flatterer himself had the push rise upon him. For further illustration of the Irish belief, see D. Fitzgerald in the *Revue Celtique*, 6, 195 (citing a South African parallel).

76 Both Rhys (*Hibbert Lectures*, pages 324 ff.) and Zimmer ('Keltische Literaturen', in *Kultur der Gegenwart*, pages 50–51) have discussed the physiological side of the question.

77 See *Revue Celtique*, 26, 24.

78 Edited and translated by Stokes, *Revue Celtique*, 8, 47 ff. See also O'Curry's Manuscript Materials, pages 266 ff.

79 Rhys (*Hibbert Lectures*, page 325) observes in Aithirne's defence that the disparaging account of him comes from the Book of Leinster, and that the Leinstermen were his hereditary foes.

80 Quoted and discussed by Rhys, *Hibbert Lectures*, page 332.

81 General references on the subject of verse-capping are hardly necessary here. For some discussion and illustrations, see Gummere, *The Beginnings of Poetry*, pages 400 ff. Early Irish instances (with parallels from other literatures) are noted by Stokes in the translation of Cormac's *Glossary* (Ir. Arch. Society), page 138; see also *Irische Texte*, 4, 92 ff., 303.

82 Edited and translated by Stokes, *Revue Celtique*, 24, 272 ff.

83 See the 'Imtheacht na Tromdhaimhe', ed. Connellan (1860), pages 12 ff.

84 See the story of Niall's death, from Ms. Rawl. B. 502, edited and translated by K. Meyer, *Otia Merseiana*, 2, 84 ff. Cf. O'Curry, *Manners and Customs*, 2, 70 ff.

85 See the collotype facsimile, edited by Kuno Meyer, introduction, page ix., and text, pages 116 ff.

86 'Táin Bó Cúalnge', ed. Windisch (Irische Texte, Extraband), page 789.

87 The Voyage of Bran, Meyer and Nutt, 1, 49.

88 See the 'Táin Bó Cúalnge', Windisch's edition, page 273. And compare a similar episode in the 'Aided Conchulainn', *Revue Celtique*, 3, 78 ff.

89 'Táin Bó Cúalnge', Windisch's edition, page 441.

90 *Ibid.*, page 829.

91 See the 'Táin Bó Cúalnge', Lebor na h-Uidre version, Miss Farraday's translation (Grimm Library), page 74.

92 See the Irische Texte, ed. Windisch and Stokes, vol. 2, part ii, page 258.

93 References are made here to Stokes's edition and translation of the prose portion of the 'Dindsenchas' from the Rennes Ms., *Revue Celtique*, vols. 15 and 16. An edition of the metrical 'Dindsenchas' has been begun by E. Gwynn in the Todd Lecture Series of the Royal Irish Academy (vols. 7 and 8).

94 *Revue Celtique*, 15, 334 ff.

95 *Ibid.*, page 326.

96 A somewhat similar tale of a jealous wife is told in the Latin Vita Coemgeni (Plummer's *Vitae Sanctorum Hiberniæ*, 1, 250 ff.). Colman, the son of Carbre, finding his first wife incompatible, put her away and took another. But the rejected woman was powerful *in magicis artibus*, and sang spells which destroyed all the children of her successor. At last one of them (Faelan) was saved by a miracle of St Coemgen. The way in which different

magic arts were combined in these dangerous women of poetry is shown again by the tale of Dreco (Druidess and female poet), who prepared a poisonous liquor which killed the twenty-four sons of Fergus Redside. See the 'Dindsenchas of Nemthenn', *Revue Celtique*, 16, 34.

97  *Revue Celtique*, 15, 306; and compare Gwynn's Metrical 'Dindsenchas', 2, 66 ff.

98  Compare *Revue Celtique*, 22, 294.

99  At this point Arabic literature again furnishes interesting parallels. Cf. Goldziher's remarks on the use of the Hija' as an 'Element des Krieges' (*Abhandlungen zur Arabischen Philologie*, page 36).

100  *Revue Celtique*, 12, 91.

101  *Ibid.*, 15, 311.

102  *Ibid.*, 15, 299.

103  'The Colloquy of the Two Sages' (Agallam in da Suaradh), edited and translated by Stokes, *Revue Celtique*, 26, 23 ff.

104  *Revue Celtique*, 20, 44.

105  See the Colloquy, *Revue Celtique*, 26, 40.

106  See *Cormac's Glossary*, under *bri*; also *Revue Celtique*, 26, 55.

107  See *Annals of Ulster*, ed. B. MacCarthy (Rolls Series), under the year 1024.

108  See the 'Second Battle of Moytura', *Revue Celtique*, 12, 65.

109  See the 'Coir Anmann', under 'Conall Corc' (*Irische Texte*, 3, 310).

110  See the Publications of the Ossianic Society, 3, 297.

111  *Irische Texte*, 1, 71.

112  *Aislinge Meic Conglinne*, ed. Kuno Meyer, page 43.

113  See O'Donnell's *Life of Columbcille*, edited by R. Henebry, *Zeitschrift für Celtische Philologie*, 4, 296–8. The same life says later (*ibid.*, 5, 42) that Columbcille was weakly indulgent in rewarding poets and rhymers.

114  Compare Stokes, the *Tripartite Life of St Patrick*, pages lx, 204.

115  See De Smedt and Backer, *Acta Sanctorum Hiberniae* (1888), col. 796. Other instances of relations between the satirists and the saints are noted by Plummer, *Vitæ Sanctorum Hibernae*, 1, ciii.

116  See Keating's *Forus Feasa air Eirinn*, Irish Text Society edition, 3, 78 ff.

117  The text is late Middle Irish. In some parts old material is made use of. Compare, for example, the story of the leper, in the latter part of the 'Imtheacht,' with the similar narrative in Cormac's *Glossary*, under Prull.

118  An extended study of modern Irish satire is greatly to be desired. Interesting illustrations both of real literary satire and of the incantational type are referred to in O'Donovan's introduction to O'Daly's *Satire on the Tribes of Ireland* (Dublin, 1864). 'The Parliament Chloinne Thomáis', edited by Stern in the *Zeitschrift für Celtische Philologie*, 5, 541 ff., may also be mentioned as a representative satirical document of much interest. For the survival of destructive or incantational satire there is plenty of evidence in the editions of the modern Irish poets. See, for example, in addition to the references already given on rat-rhyming , Hardiman's *Irish Minstrelsy* (1831), 2, 358 n.; O'Daly's *Poets and Poetry of Munster* (Second Series, 1860), page 218, n.; Dinneen's edition of 'Egan O'Rahilly' (Publication of the Irish Text Society), pages xxxi ff.; Hyde's edition of Raftery, *Abhráin Atá Leagtha ar an Reachtuire* (1903), pages 15 ff.; Lady Gregory, *Poets and Dreamers* (1903), pages 8 ff.; and with special reference to Scotland, *Zeitschrift für Celtische Philologie*, 2, 28. Hyde points out that even the praise of the poets is feared, and it is believed that no man who has had a song made about him will live long.

119  This relation, which has been clearly involved in most of the preceding discussion, has doubtlessly been observed by nearly all scholars who are familiar with Celtic literature, but due account has not been taken of it in general discussions of satire. That it has not escaped the keen vision of Professors Kittredge and Gummere, in their investigations of popular poetry, is apparent from a note in Gummere's *Old English Ballads* (1894), page xxxiv.

120  Such, for example, as the Etruscan fescennina, and the Germanic *Schnaderhüpfl*. Compare Gummere, *Beginnings of Poetry*, pages 400 ff.; Hirt, *Die Indogermanen*, 2, 728; and Erich Schmidt, *Anfänge der Literatur* (*Kultur der Gegenwart*), pages 19 ff.

121 Kögel, in Paul's *Grundriss der Germanischen Philologie*, 2nd edn., 2, 48.
122 The Instructions of King Cormac Mac Airt *(Tecosca Cormaic)* have been edited by Kuno Meyer in the Todd Lecture Series of the Royal Irish Academy, vol. 15 (Dublin, 1909).
123 See *La Grande Encyclopédie*, under *Satire*.

# 8

# THE COOKING OF THE GREAT QUEEN

## DOUGLAS HYDE

### from *The Celtic Review*

THE PASSAGE FROM folio 10b of MS. V. Edinburgh, which the late lamented Professor Mackinnon printed at page 74 of vol. viii. of this Review, 'this very interesting piece of lore,' as he characterizes it, deserves a further study. There are, as he states, brief notices of the Great Queen's[1] 'Fulacht', or cooking, in the *Yellow Book of Lecan*, and H. 3. 18, Trinity College, Dublin. Petrie, in his *History and Antiquities of Tara Hill*, pages 213–14, prints all these notices in full. With the mention of the Great Queen's Fulacht, or cooking apparatus, is generally joined a mention of the Dagda's[2] 'Indeoin' and Deichen's Spit. Thus in one of the triads edited by Kuno Meyer,[3] we find the following: 'tréde neimthigedar gobainn, Bir Neithin, fulacht na morrígna, inneóin in Dagda,' which Kuno Meyer translates 'three things that constitute a blacksmith, Neithin's spit, the cooking hearth of the Morrigan, the Dagda's anvil.'

But the *n* of Neithin[4] is obviously the eclipsing *n* of the neuter word *bir*, a spit, and the Dagda's anvil is not an anvil at all but a cooking-machine. Professor Mackinnon also translates it by anvil, which, of course, is the general meaning, but the word *indeónad*, to broil or cook in some way, is of constant occurrence in the 'Agallamh na Senórach,' a thirteenth-century (?) text, and the Indeóin was obviously the utensil or gridiron upon which the indeónadh was carried out. It is quite plain from the passages I am about to quote, that it cannot possibly mean an anvil, as an anvil could not have 'twice nine spits and twice nine holes.'

My attention was called to the passages I am about to give by a MS. about a hundred-and-ten years old, which Mac Giolla Phádraig (in English Lord Castletown) gave me a few years ago, which he had picked up somewhere in Scotland. I found it contained amongst other things a quantity of matter belonging to the 'Agallamh na Senórach,' the longest and most valuable of all the Ossianic sagas, things, too, which, as they were neither in O'Grady's nor Stokes' edition, pointed to a completely different version, containing different matter. The

MS. of part of which this was a copy, I afterwards found. It is one of the Mac Adam MSS., which were bought by the late Bishop Reeves. At Reeves' death a number of these, mainly through the generosity of my late friend, the Rev. Maxwell Close, found their way into the Royal Irish Academy.[5] Many other most valuable MSS., however, were allowed to be scattered to the four winds of heaven. This particular MS., of which I have made a transcript in Roman letters, is apparently a seventeenth-century copy of a thirteenth-century (?) text. It is at least twice as long as the hitherto known versions given by O'Grady and Stokes.

I afterwards found a variant of these passages about the Great Queen's 'Fulacht' in the *Book of Lismore*. This MS. is in the possession of the Duke of Devonshire, but I possess a splendid facsimile transcript, line for line, word for word, and letter for letter, the same as the original, made by the great scribe O'Longan, and afterwards carefully compared with the vellum, and from this I transcribe the following passages, which I compare with the version in the Reeves MS.

As to this new edition of the 'Agallamh,' I may remark that there is probably not a century from the birth of Christ onwards that this story does not incorporate in itself some folk-lore or other concerning it, and in few pieces is this tendency to preserve ancient traditions more marked than in the following poems, which I have annotated as well as I could. I think many of the names mentioned represent real or mythological characters drawn from our literature. Probably nearly all the names would be found to represent real characters, if only we had the lost literature before us in which we might look for them.

It is hard to reconstruct a picture of the cooking hearth and the spit and the Indeoin. They seem to have all belonged to the same invention, continuously improved, by which water was used as a motive force to turn rows of spits, and perhaps gridirons, which were so arranged that they could keep at a due distance from the heat, rising when the fire was high, and falling when the fire was low, keeping hot what was already cooked, and cooking what was raw, and melting automatically a proper supply of butter for basting. According to the passage in the *Yellow Book of Lecan*, Nechin [Deichin] was the chief smith of the Tuatha De Danann at Tara. 'He made a spit with motion that it might reach the fire.' The MS. H. 3. 18 says that the Dagda's Indeoin 'used to lie with the cinders and rise with the flame'. The Indeoin is thus described: 'This is how it was, a stick at each end of it, and its axle was wood, and its wheel was wood, and its body was iron, and there were twice nine wheels on its axle that it might turn the faster, and there were thirty spits out of it and thirty hooks and thirty spindles, and it was as rapid as the rapidity of a stream in turning,[6] and thrice nine spits, and thrice nine cavities (or pots) and one spit for roasting, and one wing used to set it in motion.'

A further notice in the same MS. explains the Great Queen's Fulacht thus: 'Three kinds of victuals on it, dressed victuals and raw victuals and butter, and the dressed food was not burnt, and the raw food was dressed, and the butter was not melted but just as was proper.' The *Yellow Book of Lecan* adds 'even though the three were together on one spit'. This MS. describes the Indeoin, and says, 'It used to be raised to the height of a man when it was desired, and it was not higher over the fire another time than a fist, on the same legs, without breaking, without diminishing – that was natural, for its material was iron.'

In the *Yellow Book of Lecan* there is a picture of a single spit beside this description, with several joints spitted on it, their alternate sides being red, as if done over the fire. This redness of course does not show in the facsimile.

The Dagda, the Great Queen, and probably Deichen, are purely mythological characters, but surely there must have been some historical basis for the description of the spit, the cooking-hearth, and the Indeoin.

[The story has just been told of Caoilte's adventures, and how his servant and his two hounds had been swallowed up in Loch Gur. One of the Tuatha Dé Danann who lived in a *sidh* mound near had transformed himself into a deer and had tempted them to pursue him into the lake, where they were drowned. The name of the Dé Danann chief was Fer Aoi, who is undoubtedly the same being as Fer Fi, who is generally supposed to have lived in Cnoc Aine in the County Limerick. He was brother to Aine who bit off Oilioll Olum's ear, and his father was Eogabal, who had been killed by Oilioll Olum. It was in revenge for this that he brought about the battle of Magh Muchruime and the death of Eoghan Mór and of Oilioll's seven sons. There is a long unedited poem about him in the *Book of Leinster*, and about the enchanted yew tree which he made, which was really not a yew tree at all, and which raised the dispute between Eoghan Mór and Lughaidh Lágha. See the 'Battle of Magh Muchruime' in *Silva Gadelica*, also vol. ii, page 575. See also 'Kuno Meyer's Fianaigecht', Todd Lecture Series, R.I.A., pages 32–4, where he is called Fer I.]

[*Translation from the text in the* 'Book of Lismore']

They passed that night at the Rock of Loch Gair,[7] sorrowfully, until the early morning of the next day, and then they proceeded eastwards into Mairtine of Munster and the highway of Cnamhchoill[8] and into the old plain of Breogan, and into the Low Ford, and into Bealach na nGeinte mBandruagh across the Ford of Connath the son of Unéit, and from Findmagh Feimen[9] and Druin Dil meic da Chreaca and to Uaran Brain on one side of the fairy mound of Feimin,[10] and they remain there for it was an extensive thicket and an uninhabited wood. And Caoilte said, 'Let us hunt here.' And this they did. And [the loss of] their gillie was a calamity for them. Because it was they themselves who had to make[11] a bothy for themselves that night, and a broiling-of-food [indeónadh] was made by them. And Caoilte and Finnachaidh go down to the stream to wash their hands.

'This is a cooking-place,' said Finnachaidh, 'and it is a long time since it was made.'

'That is true,' said Caoilte, 'and this is the cooking-place [Fulacht] of the Great Queen. And it is not to be worked[12] without water, and the five sons of Eochaidh of the Red Eyebrows[13] it was who made it, Fat Fet Flann En and Enach, and he made the lay.'

The cooking hearth of the Great Queen over there
Escar Aonghabh prepared it,
The Indeoin of the Dagda that was strong
of the nice-workmanship of Grinne[14] son of Luchtar.

Of wood was its central-shaft, of wood its smooth wheel,
between water and strong fire,
Of Iron was its body, there was never its like,
with moving hooks[15] on one of its two forks.

Twice nine pulleys in its great centre-shaft
with ready activity a-turning,
Thirty spits used to project out of it,
Thirty pot hooks, thirty spindles.

The sail . . . wonderful its shape –
Through the vigour of Grinde . . .
On the opposite side were . . .
The activity of its spits the activity of its [master] spit.

Thrice nine spits, thrice nine perforations,[16]
From the Indeoin of the brown Dagda
One [great] spit used to sustain it for cooking[17] [?]
[There] Eochaidh Ollathuir fell.[18]

One wing,[19] its activity was manifest,
One man used to set-it-a-going
Against [?] a huge fire inside yonder;
It was a splendid piece-of-smiths-work.

The spit of Deichen made by clean Goibniu,
The cooking-hearth, the Indeoin, were perfected by him.
He promised that 'smiths triad,'[20]
There was no smith to be compared with Goibniu.

No smith in Magh Ai[21] is competent
after Loech after Ealcha,
my grief (?), it is not for them it is hard;
No more is the cooking-hearth capable of working.

'That is a joy for us [to hear], O Caoilte,' said Finnachaidh, 'and those were good men.' And they departed to their hunting-bothy after that to their companions, and they ate what-they-had-cooked ['fulacht'], and they slept on their couches.

They went forward then till they reached the Plain of Thorns and into *Máin-da-glas*, and into Slieve *Uighi*[22] of Leinster, into *Cubhat* of the druidesses, into Dun Cinn, into *Fotharta feda* and to *Rath Mháta mursci*, and into *Ess Gabhair*, and across the pool streams of *Grissi*[23] and to Maisten of the Kings. They came into Mullach Maisten[24] and to Goibniu's forge.

'Tell me, Caoilte,' said Finnachaidh, 'was it here the weapons for the Battle of Magh Tuireadh were made, and Deichin's Spit and the Great Queen's cooking-place and the Dagda's Indeoin?'

'In yonder glen, below there, Deichin's Spit was made, and Deichin the druid,
it was he who made it' [said Caoilte].

## I

It was Deichin who made Deichin's Spit
for (?) Goibhniu in Glen Treichim,
In the possession of Lugh [the Long-handed][25] of much valour,
It was made in the Tribe of Nuadha.[26]

## II

Eleven men in yonder house
of the fair children of Eithleann,
They made the manly cooking-place,
one of the eleven was their lord [i.e. Lugh].

## III

Lugh [the Long-handed], Angus óg of the Brugh,[27]
Cearmat,[28] Mider,[28] the son of Scala.
Cu and Cian[29] and Ceithean from the plain
Iucharba Uar and Iuchair.[30]

## IV

Lugair Tua Ten who was powerful
Confa, Aicher, most lovely the band,
Eni the small, and Eni the big,
Gola the stammerer, and Cessón.

## V

In the time of Eirimoin from the South[31]
In Tara, strong the conflict,
Nine men rose up to attend to it
of the children of Mile of Spain.[32]

## VI

In the time of Iugoine[33] the celebrated,
[Presiding] over Deichin's Spit belonging to the Daghdha
There were eight men in Tara of the flocks
who were able to keep it working.

## VII

Aighe and Lughaidh of the alos,
Croine and Erc and Eilleann [and]
Three sons of Glas from Glen an Scáil
Often used they come to it.

## VIII

With the king of celebrated beauty
whose name was Eochaidh Feidhleach;[34]
One man and six [i.e. seven], fair the lot,
were at the cooking of Goibniu's Spit.

163

### IX

Eoghan Eireann, Eochaidh the Rough
and Cobhthach who used to hurl weapons,
Lughaidh, Finn, Fiacha of the feasts,
Moran and Daire of the white teeth.

### X

King Conor in Emania[35] had
Deichin's spit after him [Eochaidh],
Five warriors and one woman, no lie,
Who were able to attend and work it.

### XI

Naoise[36] and Ceithirnn[37] with victory,
[King] Conor,[38] Cuchulainn the hardy,[39]
And Fedlim[40] [whom men used to . . .
Mesdeghadh [Mesgedràdh?][41] son of Amirgin.

### XII

Four men tended the cooking amongst the Fianna,
One of them was Finn himself,
Oisin, Caoilte, and loved Diarmid,
They used to set-going the Spit of Deichen.

### XIII

In the time of Lughaidh [the Long-handed] it had ten sides
And ten edges that were not thin,
These were in Deichin's Spit of which men used to speak,
Until the time of Eochaidh Feidhleach.

### XIV

In the time of Eochaidh Feidhleach son of Finn
Bernn a smith who was not feeble
Makes eight sides and eight edges, of a time, [they lasted]
Down to [the days of] King Conor of the Red Branch.

### XV

From Conor the high and renowned
Echelsach of Emania[42] makes
Six blades, six with sides thereto,
Until came Finn the Fenian Prince.

### XVI

A flock of sharp-points? Finn made,
A Spit of four sides, fine its points,
four edges . . .
Used to be [then] on Deichin's Spit.

# Notes

1 The Bellona, or war goddess of the Irish.

2 The greatest of the Tuatha Dé Danann, obviously a god.

3 R.I.A. Todd Lecture Series, vol. xiii, page 16.

4 In the *Yellow Book of Lecan* he is called Nechin, but in every other case that I have met with he is Dechen or Deichen.

5 See my *Literary History of Ireland*, note on page 376.

6 Caoilte says that it was not worked without water, i.e. that water was necessary to turn it.

7 Now Loch Gur, Co. Limerick.

8 Now Cleghill, near the town of Tipperary.

9 In Co. Tipperary.

10 This was probably Bodb's *sidh*.

11 Literally, 'made'.

12 Literally, 'to be made' or 'done'.

13 He is mentioned in the Dinnseanchas of Ath Liag Finn as having sons contemporaneous with Finn Mac Cumhaill. One of the two provinces of Munster was called the 'province of Eochaidh Abhradruaidh,' but in Stokes' *Agallamh*, page 33, he is called 'righ Uladh atuaidh.'

14 He is called Drinde mac Luchair in H. 3. 18. Luchté, or Luchtainé or Luchtain, was the carpenter of the Tuatha Dé Danann.

15 Literally, 'hooks of activity'.

16 Perhaps for holding the butter.

17 Or 'to the west'? *Fuine* = cooking, *fuined* = sunset.

18 This is obscure. It may allude to some story of E.O. (another name for the Dagda) being caught in the apparatus. His name occurs in the Cóir Anmann, and is explained as Oll-athair, i.e. greater was he than his father, or a great father to the Tuatha Dé Danann was he. See page 355 *Irische Texte*, iii, 2 heft.

19 Sciath, usually 'a shield,' is used for sciathan, a wing in 'Cuchulain's sick-bed'. Windisch, *Irische Texte*, page 207.

20 See the triad already quoted. Goibniu or Goibhnenn was the smith of the Tuatha Dé Danann.

21 Thus Reeves MS.

22 Aliter Sliabh Suidi Laigen, in the diocese of Leithghlinn, now Mount Leinster.

23 The river Griese flows into the Barrow three-and-a-half miles above the town of Carlow.

24 Mullaghmast, a name terrible in after times for the awful act of treachery there carried out against the O'Mores and their correlatives, is about five miles north-east of the town of Athy.

25 The leader of the Tuatha Dé Danann, the hero of the Battle of Moytura, whose father was the Eithleann mentioned in the next verse.

26 Nuada or Nuadu of the silver hand, king of the Tuatha Dé Danann. See 'Battle of Moytura'.

27 i.e. Angus of the Boyne, constantly mentioned in Irish romance.

28 These were sons of the Dagda himself.

29 Son of Diancecht, and father of the god Lugh the Long-handed according to some.

30 Gods of the Tuatha Dé Danann. 'Brian' is generally substituted for Uar. Their death is told in the saga of the 'Death of the Children of Tuireann'.

31 When the Milesians conquered the Tuatha De Danann, Eremoin, son of Milesius, took the north of Ireland. From him come the Eremonian families, i.e. the great reigning families of Ulster, Connacht and parts of Leinster.

32 i.e. of the Milesians in contradistinction to the Tuatha Dé Danann, who had made the spit.

33 Iugain or Ugaine the Great, celebrated for his division of Ireland into twenty-five parts. He died, according to the Four Masters, 594 B.C. There was evidently once a cycle of saga-telling centring round him and his sons Laeghaire, Lore, Cobhthach and Breàgh, and his grandson Labhraidh Loingseach. The names here mentioned are perhaps taken from such a cycle, now lost.

34     Eochaidh 'Feidleach', Eochaidh 'of the Long-sighs', as Keating uncritically explains the word, was father of Mève (Mebd), Queen of Connacht, who waged the celebrated war of the Táin Bo Cuailgn'e some time before the Christian era. He came to the throne, according to the Four Masters, a hundred-and-forty-two years before Christ.

35     King of Ulster and the Red Branch. Cuchulain fought under him.

36     He who eloped with Deirdre.

37     Cethern son of Fintan, for whom see Windisch's Táin Bo Cuailgn'e, pages 605 ff., where he figures conspicuously, a whole chapter of the *Tain* being given up to him under the title of 'Cethern's bloody wound'.

38     King of Ulster.

39     'Fortissimus heroes Scottorum.'

40     This is the 'one woman' mentioned in the last verse. She appears in H. 2. 17, a fourteenth-century vellum in Trinity College, Dublin, as one of the 'queens' of the Ulster folk, who by unrobing themselves before Cuchulainn caused him to look down out of modesty and so turn aside from the heat of his passion which King Conor feared he was about to wreak upon the men of Ulster. I do not know anything else about her, but from her being mentioned here she probably figured in some other saga.

41     Of whose brain the ball was made which lodged in King Concubhair's head.

42     This smith's son, Amargin Mac Ecelsalsaigh Goband, is several times mentioned in the Táin Bo Cuailgn'e. The name is variously spelt in the genitive Ecel-salaig, Ecet-shalaigh and, in Cormac's *Glossary*, Eculsaig (see under 'Greth'). He lived on the river, Buais or Bush. In the *Book of Leinster*, page 117b, his story is told *bái goba amra i n-Ultaib-i-Eccetsalach goba a ainm*, etc. His son Amargin afterwards became ard-ollamh of Ulster. See T. B. C. page 697.

# PART TWO

# THE
# CARPENTERS
# OF SONG

THE BARDIC POETRY of the Middle Ages to the seventeenth century, which is represented in this section, is, of its nature, more formal and consciously crafted than that of the first singers – hence their own descriptive epithet, which forms the title for this section. It is no less powerful for all that and, in fact, often preserves a close relationship to earlier works – as in the example of the powerful 'Shield of Fionn' (Chapter 16) or the poetry of the Gogynfeirdd found in Chapter 13.

In this period a complex system of patronage – always present but in simpler terms until the twelfth century – came to the fore. The bards of the thirteenth to seventeenth centuries were generally attached to the court of a particular nobleman and thus enjoyed a less nomadic life than their earlier counterparts. That this patronage was open to abuse, by both parties, is wonderfully illustrated in 'The Proceedings of the Great Bardic Institution' (Chapter 15), which, despite its length, is included here in full not only because it is an entertaining story but also because it gives a detailed glimpse into the whole system of the more ancient bardic colleges and their operation.

The wildly funny description of the bards' increasingly absurd requests for favours in return for poems, followed by the equally elaborate demands of their hosts, is one of the best examples of a late bardic story to come out of Ireland. It is placed here, because, although in its original state it probably dates from a much earlier period (perhaps as early as the seventh century), the form in which it has survived is from the seventeenth century. At that time it was recited as a prelude to the great Irish epic *The Tain,* which told the tale of the 'Cattle Raid of Cooley' and the war that arose as a result. In the 'Proceedings' this famous text is described as being unknown to the bards of Ireland – an ironic twist since this prime story would have been known to even the most junior student of the bardic colleges of the time.

This story is preceded by the mediaeval Welsh tale 'The Dream of Rhonabwy', which again derives ultimately from a far earlier period but which was not recorded until the thirteenth century. It was held to be a particularly challenging story for recitation because of the feat of memory required to recall the multiplicity of colours and variations of description that run through the text. It also very deliberately looks back to an earlier day, when King Arthur and his band of larger than life warriors held sway over what is perceived as a kind of golden age.

But this section begins, rightly enough, with a fine lecture on Bardic Poetry given before the National Literary Society of Dublin in 1912 by the great scholar Osborn Bergin. It is followed by an idiosyncratic account of the Welsh bardic institution by the eighteenth-century writer Edward Jones, who did much to revive an interest in bardic history among the general public in his two volumes of texts, notes and music, *Musical & Poetic Relics of the Welsh Bards* (1784) and *The Bardic Museum* (1802), which were hugely influential and prompted numerous imitations 'in the style of the bards' by popular composers of the time.

168

This is followed by an anonymous seventeenth-century text, preserved in the Library of Wales, which sets forth the nature of the bardic mysteries in terms of their preservation of the mystical heritage of the land. 'Tri Chof Ynys Brydain' ('The Three Antiquities of Britain'), already mentioned in the general introduction to this book, is reproduced here in its original spelling and orthography. This fascinating text outlines the nature and tasks of the bards, claiming immemorial descent for the continuity of the bardic tradition, then proceeding to set forth the various appropriate meters and forms to be used by practitioners of the art.

The idea of a Christian bardic tradition in the early Celtic world may seem unlikely, yet the next text included here in Chapter 12 suggests that there existed a curiously ambivalent relationship between the fili or poets of Ireland and the great saints who brought Christianity to that land. 'The Forespeech (of Foreword) to the Amra (Celebration of) Chohium Chille (Colum Cille)' dates from the seventeenth century in its present form, but derives, as do so many of these later bardic remains, from earlier time. More familiar to us as St Columba, Colum Cille is one of the premier Celtic Saints, whose life and deeds are related in the brief celebration, the 'Amra' itself, which originally followed this extract. Colum Cille himself had an ambiguous relationship with the indigenous bards. On the one hand he saw them as representatives of paganism and as a burden on the land – according to the 'forespeech' there were as many as thirty apprentice bards in the company of each *Olamb* or chief poet, and fifteen with each *Anrad* or junior poet, all of whom must be cared for and supported by their patrons – while on the other he seemed to respect them as inspired purveyors of the word of God. The account given here not only tells us of Colum Cille's own reluctance to be remembered in his own lifetime, in case he became swollen-headed, but also shows the author giving us a commentary on the meaning of various obscure poetic glosses – a rare glimpse into the mind of the working bard. The author of the 'Amra' is given as Dallan Forgail, who may well be the same Dallan who appears in a slightly less glamorous light in 'The Proceedings of the Great Bardic Institution' (see Chapter 15).

The Welsh court poets, or *Gogynfeirdd*, included some of the finest bards of their own or any time. There is less of a prophetic and incantatory nature about their work than that of their forbears; but the themes of nature, love and religion are still present. The brief selection that is contained in Chapter 13 includes Iolo Goch, Sion Cent and Dafydd ap Gwilym, whose works possess a richness, complexity and allusiveness seldom equalled before or since.

These, together with 'The Dream of Rhonabwy', and 'The Proceedings of the Great Bardic Institution', conclude this section, along with the wonderful mythic poem, 'The Shield of Fionn', which derives from a mediaeval cycle of poems, the *Duanaire Finn*, dealing with the life and deeds of the great hero Fionn Mac Cumhail. In this poem we learn of the long and complex history of the shield, its maker and its power, as well as, in the process, details of the battles in which it was used and the heroes (and their horses) encountered by Fionn while carrying it! This is a prime example of the kind of heroic material beloved of the bards from the earliest times and celebrated by contemporary Celtic poets to this day. One has only to look at the writings of one of the greatest modern Welsh poets, David Jones, to see the continuity that still exists within the Celtic tradition. Jones' long poem 'In Parenthesis' (1937), which deals with his experiences in the trenches during the First World War, is firmly rooted in the world of the ancient bards, with references to the Gododdin (see Part One) and the heroes of Arthur forming a glittering backdrop to the harsh realities of twentieth-century warfare. It is to this constant tradition that we turn in the third part of this collection.

# 9

# IRISH BARDIC POETRY

## OSBORN BERGIN
### from *Journal of the Ivernian Society*

A LECTURE ON THE SUBJECT of Bardic Poetry before the National Literary
Society implies, of course, a lecture on the bardic poetry of Ireland. That
is, no doubt, what you have expected. Yet after I had agreed to deliver this
lecture I began to doubt the wisdom of the choice. Irish bardic poetry differs so
widely from any form of literary expression that most of us have been accustomed
to, that it will be well-nigh impossible in a single evening to discuss its characteristic features. Few forms of composition suffer more in translation. The grace and
the elaborate polish of the original must disappear entirely, and even if I could suc-
ceed in the difficult task of producing an accurate though bald and prosaic version
of some of the finest work of the bardic schools, the world in which this kind of
poetry arose and flourished was so different from the world we live in today that
a running commentary would be needed to make that version intelligible. Such a
commentary would, I fear, leave little of the elusive charm of the original. In bringing specimens of the literature in question before your notice I have tried to do
two things – first, to select from the great mass of bardic poetry preserved in manuscript poems which have so far remained unedited, and are thus likely to throw
fresh light on the literary life of the period to which they belong; and, secondly, to
choose such poems as are likely to explain themselves.

By Bardic Poetry I mean the writings of poets trained in the Bardic Schools
as they existed in Ireland and the Gaelic parts of Scotland down to about the middle of the seventeenth century. In Scotland, indeed, they lingered on till the eighteenth century. At what time they were founded we don't know, for the Bardic
order existed in prehistoric times, and their position in society is well established
in the earliest tradition. You will understand that the subject is a vast one, but I
mean to deal only with a small portion of it – the poetry of the later Bardic
Schools from about the thirteenth century to the close – that is to say, compositions of the period known as Later Middle Irish and Early Modern Irish. For

171

this period the manuscript material is very plentiful, but very little has yet been printed.

Bardic Poetry of any period is easily distinguished by its form. A great deal of it is not really what a modern critic would call poetry in the higher sense. But though it may lack inspiration, it is never wanting in artistic finish. For we must remember that the Irish *file* or *bard*[1] was not necessarily an inspired poet. That he could not help. He was, in fact, a professor of literature and a man of letters, highly trained in the use of a polished literary medium, belonging to a hereditary caste in an aristocratic society, holding an official position therein by virtue of his training, his learning, his knowledge of the history and traditions of his country and his clan. He discharged, as O'Donovan pointed out many years ago, the functions of the modern journalist. He was not a song-writer. He was often a public official, a chronicler, a political essayist, a keen and satirical observer of his fellow-countrymen. At an earlier period he had been regarded as a dealer in magic, a weaver of spells and incantations, who could blast his enemies by the venom of his verse, and there are traces down to the most recent times of a lingering belief, which was not, of course, confined to Ireland, in the efficacy of a well-turned malediction. He might be a poet, too, if in addition to his training he was gifted with the indefinable power, the true magic, of poetry. But whether he was a poet in this higher sense or not, he always composed in verse.

It is a well known fact that verse comes before prose in the literatures of the world. In one sense, of course, we may talk prose all our lives. But most of us find it hard to write even passably good prose, although we have countless examples to show how it is done. In the literature of more than one nation we find that verse has been brought to the highest perfection of ease and grace and power, at a time when prose is still awkward and unattractive and obscure. It is not surprising, therefore, to find verse composition developed in Ireland before prose. The misfortune is, I think, that this state of things lasted too long. Until quite modern times we have no prose authors. Of course, there is prose of a kind – excluding such things as legal and medical tracts, annals and the like – there is a fairly large body of translations; above all there are the native romantic tales, the most important part of our literature.[2] These show that the early writers had full command of an admirable medium for plain vivid narrative. Unhappily it was not developed. Who were the authors of these tales? We cannot tell. No one thought of putting his name to a piece of prose. The copyist may deal with it as he pleases. And the copyist does so. He expands and condenses, combines two versions of a tale, recasts the language, and so on. Prose is common property; tales are made for telling, for public recitation, not for private study. This is what gives much of our romantic literature the incoherence, as well as the freshness and naiveté of the folktale. We have, then, practically no prose authors or stylists down to the modern period. Even in the seventeenth century we find two distinct recensions of Keating's *History*, quite different in style, in the same hand-writing, and we begin to ask which version did Keating write, and which is the work of the scribe, and did Keating object to this deliberate recasting of his sentences? If we want the personal note of the conscious literary artist we must go to the verse. I think this was a very unhealthy state of things for Gaelic literature, but that is beyond the scope of my subject.

I have already mentioned the fact that the *file* or *bard* – both terms had come to be used more or less indiscriminately in our period, though at an earlier time there was a technical distinction of rank between them – belonged to a hereditary caste. The Gaelic poet, we may say, had to be *both born and made*. In the same way the professions of history, law and medicine were confined to certain families. We must consider now how the poet was *made*. The best description of a Bardic School or College is in the *Memoirs of the Marquis of Clanricarde*, published in 1722, which gives us a fair idea of the training as practised in the early seventeenth century.[3] The manners of the professional classes in Ireland, indeed the whole structure of society, were so wonderfully conservative that Clanricarde's description will probably hold good for several centuries earlier. After a discussion of the custom of confining the professions to certain families, he continues:

> Concerning the poetical Seminary or School, from which I was carried away to clear other things that fell in my way, it was open only to such as were descended of Poets and reputed within their Tribes. And so was it with all the Schools of that kind in the Nation, being equal to the Number of Families that followed the said calling. But some more or less frequented for the difference of Professors, Conveniency, with other Reasons, and seldom any come but from remote parts, to be at a distance from Relations and other Acquaintances that might interrupt his Study. The Qualifications first requir'd were reading well, writing the Mother-tongue, and a strong Memory. It was likewise necessary the Place should be in the solitary Recess of a Garden or within a Sept or Enclosure far out of the reach of any Noise, which an Intercourse of People might otherwise occasion. The Structure was a snug, low Hut, and beds in it at convenient Distances, each within a small Apartment without much Furniture of any kind, save only a Table, some Seats, and a Conveniency for Cloaths to hang upon. No Windows to let in the Day, nor any Light at all us'd but that of Candles, and these brought in at a proper Season only. The Students upon thorough Examination being first divided into Classes, wherein a regard was had to every one's Age, Genius, and the Schooling had before, if any at all, or otherwise. The Professors (one or more as there was occasion) gave a Subject suitable to the Capacity of each Class, determining the number of Rhimes, and clearing what was to be chiefly observed therein as to Syllables, Quartans, Concord, Correspondence, Termination and Union, each of which were restrain'd by peculiar Rules. The said Subject (either one or more as aforesaid) having been given over Night, they work'd it apart each by himself upon his own Bed, the whole next Day in the Dark, till at a certain Hour in the Night, Lights being brought in, they committed it to writing. Being afterwards dress'd and come together into a large Room, where the Masters waited, each Scholar gave in his Performance, which being corrected or approv'd of (according as it requir'd) either the same or fresh subjects were given against the next Day. This Part being over, the Students went to their Meal, which was then serv'd up; and so, after some time spent in Conversation and other Diversions, each retir'd to his Rest, to be ready for the Business of the next Morning. Every *Saturday* and on the Eves of Festival Days they broke up

and dispers'd themselves among the Gentlemen and rich Farmers of the Country, by whom they were very well entertain'd and much made of, till they thought fit to take their leaves, in order to re-assume their Study. Nor was the People satisfied with affording this Hospitality alone; they sent in by turns every Week from far and near Liquors and all manner of Provision towards the Subsistence of the Academy, so that the chief Poet was at little or no Charges, but, on the contrary, got very well by it, besides the Presents made him by the Students upon their first coming, which was always at Michaelmas, and from thence till the 25th of March, during the cold season of the Year only, did that close Study last. At that time the Scholars broke up, and repair'd each to his own Country, with an Attestation of his Behaviour and Capacity from the chief Professor to those that had sent him.

The reason of laying the Study aforesaid in the Dark was doubtless to avoid the Distraction which Light and the variety of Objects represented thereby commonly occasions. This being prevented, the Faculties of the Soul occupied themselves solely upon the Subject in hand, and the Theme given; so that it was soon brought to some Perfection according to the Notions or Capacities of the Students. Yet the course was long and tedious, as we find, and it was six or seven Years before a Mastery or the last Degree was conferred, which you'll the less admire upon considering the great Difficulty of the Art, the many kinds of their Poems, the Exactness and Nicety to be observ'd in each, which was necessary to render their Numbers soft, and the Harmony agreeable and pleasing to the Ear.

As every Professor, or chief Poet, depended on some Prince or great Lord, that had endowed his Tribe, he was under strict ties to him and Family, as to record in good Metre his Marriages, Births, Deaths, Acquisitions made in war and Peace, Exploits, and other remarkable things relating to the Same. He was likewise bound to offer an Elegy on the Decease of the said Lord, his consort, or any of their children, and a Marriage Song when there should be Occasion. But as to any Epick, or Heroick Verse to be made for any other Lord or Stranger, it was requir'd that at least a Paroemion, or Metre therein, should be upon the Patron, or the Name in general. A pleasant Instance of this happen'd in the last Age, when Donough O Brian, Earl of Thoumond, was Lord President of the Province of *Munster*, to whom one of his Rhimers (to acquit himself of that Obligation) in a Panegyrical Poem compos'd by him in honour of a Gentleman of the MacCarthies, who had much signaliz'd himself in Martial Exploits, wish'd that some warlic Lord or Captain of the O Brians, then living, had by his Merit and Conduct acquir'd so excellent a Name. This immediately taking Wind, so disgusted the Earl, that in Revenge of the Slight or Affront he vowed his Chastisement whenever he fell into his Hands. Hereupon the Poet, dreading the consequences, disappear'd and kept out of the way for some Years. Notwithstanding, it happen'd that one time, going a Journey along with his Wife, they saw at a Distance the said Earl with his Equipage, and a great Company of Horse in his Attendance, coming towards them. There being no Probability of escaping, the Poet told his Wife that he would feign himself dead as of a sudden, which she should humour by crying over him; that if the Earl

ask'd the Reason she should not conceal his Name, but beg Forgiveness for
the great Folly he had been guilty of against his Lordship and Family. The
Woman acted her Part to the Life, and the Earl, when he was come up,
being told whose the Corps was, he had the Curiosity to put Questions
himself to her, and Ask'd whether the Poet had repented of his undutiful
Expression with relation to the O Brians. The Woman answer'd he did
heartily; and that being surpriz'd upon Sight of his Lordship's Equipage,
the Horrour of his own Guilt most sensibly touching him, he fell down
dead upon the Spot; but (in Addition) said farther, that since he was gone,
and had made some Attonement by the long Affliction he had suffer'd, his
Lordship would forgive him, which accordingly the Earl did, being moved
with Compassion, and flung down the Woman some Gold to bury her
Husband. This being over, the reputed dead Man springs up in an Instant,
and taking hold of the Reins of the Horse on which the Earl was mounted,
pronounced a very exquisite Poem in his Praise, which brought him into
full Favour again. It was pretended this Piece was Extemporary, and made
by the Poet whilst he lay there as dead. But 'tis more probable that he had
composed it before at his leisure, and that all that was acted in this Place
was only a Farce, design'd to gain a fit Opportunity to beg and obtain the
Earl's Pardon.

For the Nature of the Poem and great beauty of it shew that it was a
work of Study and Time.

The last Part to be done, which was the *Action* and *Pronunciation* of
the Poem in Presence of the Maecenas, or the principal Person it related to,
was perform'd with a great deal of Ceremony in a Consort of Vocal and
Instrumental Musick. The Poet himself said nothing, but directed and took
care that everybody else did his Part right. The Bards[4] having first had the
Composition from him, got it well by Heart, and now pronounc'd it
orderly, keeping even Pace with a Harp, touch'd upon that Occasion; no
other musical Instrument being allowed for the said Purpose than this
alone, as being Masculin, much sweeter and fuller than any other.

The bardic system, like the independence of the clans, lasted in Scotland into the
eighteenth century. Martin, in his *Description of the Western Islands of Scotland*,
published in London in 1703, describes it as he found it in its decay:

The Orators, in their Language called Is-Dane, were in high esteem in
these Islands and the Continent, until within these forty years they sat
always among the Nobles and Chiefs of Families in the *Streah* or Circle.
Their Houses and little Villages were Sanctuaries, as well as Churches, and
they took place before Doctors of Physic. The Orators, after the *Druids*
were extinct, were brought in to preserve the Genealogy of Families and to
repeat the same at every Succession of a Chief; and upon the occasion of
Marriages and Births they made *Epithalamiums* and *Panegyricks*, which
the Poet or Bard pronounc'd. The Orators by the force of their Eloquence
had a powerful ascendant over the greatest men in their time; for if any
Orator did but ask the Habit, Arms, Horse, or any other thing belonging
to the greatest Man in these Islands, it was readily granted them,
sometimes out of respect, and sometimes for fear of being exclaimed

against by a Satire, which in those days was reckon'd a great dishonour; but these Gentlemen becoming insolent, lost ever since both the Profit and Esteem which was formerly due to their Character; for neither their Panegyricks nor Satires are regarded to what they have been, and they are now allowed but a small salary. I must not omit to relate their way of Study, which is very singular. They shut their Doors and Windows for a Days time, and lie on their backs with a Stone upon their Belly, and Plads about their Heads, and their Eyes being cover'd they pump their Brains for Rhetorical Encomium or Panegyrick; and indeed they furnish such a Stile from this Dark Cell as is understood by very few; and if they purchase a couple of Horses as the reward of their Meditation, they think they have done a great Matter. The Poet or Bard had a Title to the Bridegroom's upper Garb – that is the Plad and Bonnet – but now he is satisfy'd with what the Bridegroom pleases to give him on such occasions.

I have never seen a description in Irish of life in a Bardic School. To the poets it was, of course, too familiar to need description; but there are many references to it which show that Clanricarde was well-informed. There is an anonymous poem, the utterance of an unknown poet looking back in his loneliness to the delights of his youthful studies, and the charm of a fellowship that has now passed away for ever:

> I am alone among men . . .
> *Aonar dhamhsa eidir dhaoinibh,* Poem 42

This poem probably belongs to the early seventeenth century – a time of upheaval, when the old Gaelic world was falling to pieces.

Whatever the students thought of the routine work of the schools, and the practice of 'lying in the beds of booths' – *lighe a leapthaibh both,* as one of the poets calls it – there are many indications that they greatly enjoyed the comradeship of school life. The fifteenth-century poet, Tadhg Óg Ó Huiginn, in an elegy on his elder brother, Fearghal, who was head of one of the schools, tells us that the students were sorry to hear the cuckoos, with the coming of the holidays they were to disperse. These bardic schools or colleges provided the nearest thing in Ireland to University life.

Yet some at least must have been willing to experiment for themselves outside the traditional limits. There is a curious poem, in which the writer, Ó Gnímh, pokes fun at Fearghal Óg for his defiance of convention:

> This is comfortable, o Fearghal Óg . . .
> *Cuimseach sin, a Fhearghail Óig,* Poem 27

This habit of composing in the dark no doubt did keep away distracting thoughts, and helped the poets to concentrate on the subject they had chosen. But I am inclined to think that in its origin it was something different. It looks very like a relic of some rite or ceremony of divination handed down from pagan times, long after its original purpose had been forgotten. We know that in early times the functions of the poet and the Druid or magician were very similar, and both practised magic. The whole subject of magic in ancient Ireland would repay a fuller investigation than has yet been made. There can be no doubt that even after the coming of Christianity the attempts to stamp out forbidden rites were not altogether a success, and the less dangerous had to be tolerated. In this connexion the following well known passage from Cormac's *Glossary* is instructive as showing the attitude of the most learned scholar and ecclesiastic of the ninth century. I quote from Whitley Stokes' translation, with a few corrections:

> *Imbas forosna*, 'Manifestation that enlightens': (it) discovers what thing soever the poet likes and which he desires to reveal. Thus then is that done. The poet chews a piece of the red flesh of a pig, or a dog, or a cat, and puts it then on a flagstone behind the door valve, and chants an incantation over it, and offers it to idol gods, and calls them to him, and leaves them not on the morrow, and then chants over his two palms, and calls again idol gods to him, that his sleep may not be disturbed. Then he puts his two palms on his two cheeks and sleeps. And men are watching him that he may not turn over and that no one may disturb him. And then is revealed to him that which is before him till the end of a nómad (a period of nine days) or two or three nómads, according to the long or short time he may arrange at the offering. Patrick banished that and the *Teinm láida* 'illumination of song', and declared that no one who shall do that shall belong to heaven or earth, for it is a denial of baptism. '*Dichetal do chennaib*', 'extempore incantation', however, that was left, in right of art, for it is science that causes it, and no offering to devils is necessary, but a declaration from the ends of his bones at once.

This last phrase is interesting. Sorcery that involved no offering to devils is regarded as a lawful branch of science.

Or take the description of the bull-feast in the *Sick-bed of Cuchulainn*, or the *Destruction of Da Derga's Hostel*. 'A bull-feast is gathered by the men of Erin (in order to determine their future king) – that is, a bull used to be killed by them, and thereof one man would eat his fill and drink its broth, and a spell of truth was chanted over him in his bed. Whosoever he would see in his sleep would be king, and the sleeper would perish if he uttered a falsehood.' Another way to procure a vision was to sleep in the hide of the newly-slaughtered bull – a means of invocation practised in the Highlands at a late period, and described by Scott in his 'Lady of the Lake'.

On the whole, I think this insistence on the dark room was originally due to other than literary motives. It must have been connected at first with some kind of pagan divination. Later on it was continued, with the professional reverence for precedent. It may have been found helpful. In any case it would never do to let people think poetry could be composed on horseback – that was contrary to all etiquette; it would rob poetry of half its mystery, and bring down its market value at once.

As to the length of the course, six or seven years, at the bardic schools, probably the first comment of a modern educationalist would be, 'Yes! but they got six months holidays in the year, not counting the weekend trips.' But the usual explanation of the length of time required is the extraordinary difficulty and complexity of the various metres in which the students were taught to compose. I think myself that the difficulty has been hugely exaggerated. Probably O'Molloy led the way by calling the *dán díreach* – that is, the straight or strict metre – 'the hardest of all that I have seen or heard – I might say the hardest thing under the sun.'[5] If O'Molloy, or any of those who continually copy him or one another at the present day, had reflected for a moment, it is hard to see how it could have escaped their notice that for many centuries, year after year, hundreds of poems in the most faultless metre had been written and recited all over Ireland by men who cannot all have been intellectual giants. The particular metre now generally selected as an example of the incredibly difficult is the *deibhidhe*,[6] which is actually the commonest metre of all, and was practised by the lowest grades of bards.

The truth is that worthy O'Molloy himself had not the knack of verse-writing, and most of his readers have simply taken his words as gospel. By flinging the rules of metre together, it might be shown that verse in almost any language is exceedingly difficult. But the poet is guided by his ear, and if he is composing in a well known metre, he unconsciously follows the model of number-less examples. Why, even at the present day thousands of fairly unintelligent schoolboys can be taught to write Latin verse, which has at least the one merit that it will scan, and that though they have to rely on their eyes for the metre, as the language is an utterly dead one to them, and as they pronounce it half the quantities are wrong.

Too much has been said about the difficulties of Irish metre. What is wanted is less amazement and more attention. The requisites of an Irish stanza are, curiously enough, often ignored by those who write about them. O'Donovan, for instance, wrote a description of Irish metres based on O'Molloy, but when he came to edit Irish poems he often disregarded the rules. The late Dr MacCarthy edited a tract on Irish metre, and in the same volume showed by his edition of certain Middle Irish poems that he had forgotten or ignored the rules, and frequently mistranslated lines where the metre would have kept him straight. Even O'Grady, in his brilliant Catalogue of Irish MSS. in the British Museum, often nods. In dealing with a faulty text the metrical test is almost unfailing. The poets *could* have mixed up their metres, just as Virgil could, if he liked, have ended his hexameters with a dactyl. But they never did so.

And besides the question of the difficulty of the metres, I think a wrong impression prevails with regard to the effect these metres had on style. We are told that the favourite metre allowed only seven syllables to the line, and four lines to the stanza, with a break after the second line. This must have led to a great condensation of thought. I admit that there is no room here for those long strings of alliterative adjectives which disfigure some Middle Irish prose and some eighteenth-century verse. But the break after the second line, though common, is not obligatory, the total number of syllables in a quatrain is twenty-eight, the same as in the ordinary English ballad metre, and the number of quatrains is quite unlimited. The fact is, some Irish poems are terse and epigrammatic, others are diffuse enough, no matter what their metre may be. Often in transcribing from manuscripts I have wished, before reaching the fortieth or fiftieth quatrain, that the poet had had enough restraint and good taste to stop at the twentieth.

Here I must join issue with my friend, Dr Hyde, who says in his *Literary History of Ireland*, page 537: 'Their chief characteristic is an intense compression which produces an air of weighty sententiousness . . . Accordingly O'Gnive calls the poets the schoolmen of condensed speech, and the Scotch bard, MacMuirich, in the Red Book of Clanranald, speaks of Teig Dall O'Higinn as putting into less than a half-rann what others would take a whole crooked stanza to express.' The phrase 'schoolmen of condensed speech' is one of those vivid sayings which stick in the memory and colour the thought. Dr Hyde has published O'Gnive's poem in his Mac Ternan Prize Essay on Irish Poetry [page 104]. The couplet with which we are concerned reads:

Ni clos sgoluidhe sgéil teinn
D'Uibh n-Dálaigh ná d'Uibh n-Uiginn.

Now, while it is doubtful whether *sgoluidhe sgéil teinn* could ever bear the mean-ing 'schoolman of condensed speech', it is quite certain that O'Gnive did not use these words at all. The text is corrupt, as the second line shows. There is a good copy of the poem in the *Book of the O'Conor Don* (in which, by the way, the author's name is given as Aonghus Ó Dálaigh), and this gives us the true reading: 'No scholar has been heard – a sorrowful tale! – of the O'Dalys or the O'Higgins.'

As for the lines in the *Red Book of Clanranald*, the only meaning I can extract from them is just the opposite to Dr Hyde's interpretation. In a bardic con-troversy someone quotes a line by Tadhg Dall Ó Huiginn, *Lámh dhearg Éirenn Íbh Eathach*, 'Iveagh is the Red Hand of Ulster.' Niall M'Vurich answers (Rel. Celt., ii, page 297): 'You hold that the straight verse of Tadhg Ó Huiginn is no authority concerning the Red Hand – I will put into a single crooked line more than Tadhg would into half a quatrain.'

The real difficulty was not so much the metre, for, though many elaborate metres are mentioned in the various metrical tracts, few of them were in common use. But, besides acquiring a thorough familiarity with the literature and history of the country, the student had to make a minute and careful study of the language itself. Practically all bardic poetry is written in one standard literary dialect, which remained almost unchanged for five hundred years. All this time the local dialects were diverging more and more, and there was no capital to set a natural standard. Yet the trained professional poet wrote in such a style that it is impossible to tell from his language to what part of Ireland or Scotland he belonged, or to fix his date even approximately. It is hard to say what they ought to have done, but what they actually did is clear. They made an artificial standard. They normalized the language by admitting into their verse only such forms and usages as had the sanc-tion of earlier poets of high repute, everything else being rigorously excluded. There is a grammatical tract compiled or revised about the beginning of the six-teenth century. This tract, which I hope to publish, gives models of declension and verbal inflection with thousands of examples, rules for aspiration and eclipsis, alternative forms, forms which must never be used, and so on. The most interest-ing thing about it is that the compiler gives hundreds of couplets from various poets as examples to prove his statements. In this he was like a modern scientific grammarian. He took the literary language as he found it and classified its usages. But it is unlikely that the compilation was due to scientific interest in the language. I believe it was intended as a practical text book for use in the schools. Without something of the kind the teaching of the standard dialect could hardly have been so successful. This dialect was somewhat archaic, as might have been expected, but it allowed a mixture of various periods, and indeed in some ways was less archaic than one or two of our twentieth-century writers. Thus a West Munster poet of the fourteenth century had no hesitation in writing *mar deir mé* when it suited his metre, though the spoken language of his district has not even now reached this stage of development. On the other hand a Scottish poet would write *atú*, 'I am', at a time when this form was certainly obsolete in Scotland, and only intelligible to the educated.

From their study of good models and their association with the best teachers the poets derived one characteristic which is common to the whole bardic order, and that is a sustained dignity of style. Their respect for their position, their hereditary pride, and their excessive devotion to traditional precedents, gave them at least a rooted dislike of vulgarity. They took their art seriously. It might be undignified to compose poetry on horseback, but what they thought of real buffoonery we can gather from a satire by the Scottish bard Cathal Mac Muireadhaigh on one who 'practised an art without difficulty': 'Good is the trade you have chosen, to win entertainment and revelry, the making of incorrect verses at the time of banqueting and assembly.'

The manners of this improvisator, he tells us, are as bad as his verse. He snatches up the food at table without waiting for grace. But, of course, however disorderly he may be, talking rambling nonsense in his cups – a thing more in his line than poetry – and throwing meat and butter at his host, he must never be deprived of the honourable title of scholar. For with all his buffoonery he manages to curry favour with the great!

> Being in the company of an earl is an omen of high honour to you, till you put one bite on top of another, while your tongue is grinding out words.
>
> Alas that I have never attempted to acquire your style, incorrect and formless in its import – not to speak of elementary scholarship.
>
> Let me forsake the snare of straight verse, as we have found it in tradition, and enter your order now in the new fashion – it will last longer than the track I have followed!
>
> *Sona do cheird, a Chalbhaigh, in Celtic Studies in Memory of*
> *Angus Matheson, pages 51–5*

Yet though times have changed and it would pay the poet to follow the bad example he has described, and adapt himself to circumstances, his professional pride is too strong, and he declines to pay the price of popularity.

This represents the attitude of the seventeenth century, when the old order was passing. In earlier times the position of the official poet was secure, and his confidence in it unshaken. He respected himself and demanded that others should respect him. Here is how the bard of the Maguires asks the chief to give him a new farm away from a disturbed neighbourhood:

> Attend to me thou chief of the descendants of Odhar . . .
> *T'aire riom-sa a rí ó nUidhir, Poem 33*

A good deal of the bardic poetry that has come down to us consists of elaborate panegyrics on patrons and benefactors. These compositions were greatly admired and treasured by the families of the recipients, but they are likely to leave the modern reader cold, for, while their technique is marvellous, there is naturally a want of freshness and variety about most of them. The earliest poem of the kind that has been preserved is addressed to a Leinster king of the eighth or ninth century. With a little touching up this might be passed off as a sixteenth-century panegyric. Allowing for the changes in the language, the style and mannerisms are almost identical.

All court poetry is more or less tainted by the voice of insincerity and formalism. A writer whose name is given as an *Pearsún Riabhach*, 'the Grey Parson', takes the Irish poets sternly to task for their extravagant flattery, accusing them of interfering with the dispensations of Providence:

> O ye who fashion lies in verse, when the judgment day comes ye shall
> repent it; if His anger arise, the Creator of the elements will take
> vengeance for the false witness that ye bear against Him.
>
> Ye put lovely graceful locks upon a bald forehead – for shame! – if a
> man's eyes are twitching and squinting, ye make them slow moving and
> clear as crystal.
>
> For one whose complexion is sallow and tawny you feign – though it
> is a pitiable saying – that the scion of lovely face has skin like the swan
> and a bosom like lime.
>
> From every man from whom you win a reward, you have
> deserved hatred and anger; because of your praise, alas! his last end
> will be hell.

> *A lucht chumas bréag sa dán, Measgra Dánta,* 21

I think the worthy Parson was a trifle severe. The Irish chiefs liked compliments, to be sure, but we need not suppose that they were so simple as to take them at their face value. For one thing, the practice was too common. When everyone in high place is addressed in superlatives, superlatives lose their force. The conventional language of ceremony tends to become obsequious in a formal way, and the formalities soon grow dull and petrified. We can see this even in a matter-of-fact age like the present; the language of public and private life is full of polite formalities which do not mislead anybody. What makes Irish panegyrics appear so extravagant and fantastic at the first glance is that they take us into a world of unfamiliar conventions. Thus, through mere habit we think it natural that a warrior prince should be termed a lion, though this is only a hackneyed literary metaphor to us, for few of us have ever seen a lion outside a cage, and, to judge by the reports of modern hunters, the lion at large has little in common with the king of beasts in Æsop's Fables. Well, the Irish poets used the word *lion* too, as a term of praise, though none of them could ever have seen a lion. But when they address a patron, in metaphors more familiar to them, as a *hound*, a *hawk*, a *salmon*, a *branch*, a *spreading tree*, a *cluster of nuts*, with much ornament in the way of mythological and geographical detail thrown in, the result to the modern reader is too quaint to be impressive.

Instead of one of these highly polished and difficult compositions let us take an anonymous poet's address to his old cloak. Here, at least, there is no room for flattery:

Are you my acquaintance, brown cloak?
*An tú m'aithne, a fhallaing dhonn?* Poem 41

Even an official poet could write simply and sincerely when his own feelings were touched. Here is an elegy on a young poet, written by his own father Gofraidh Fionn Ó Dálaigh, 'Ireland's Arch-professor of Poetry', who died in 1387. The writer, who was looked up to and quoted by later poets as one of the greatest of his period, was for a time devoted to the earls of Desmond.

O cross yonder upon the hill that art the cause of my weeping, whosoever is glad at thy completion, thy setting up is my casting down.

It is thou, my beloved son's cross, that hast made me cheerless to-night: O firm cross by which I mourn, it is thou that shalt quench my joy.

Should my mind wander from Eoghan, thou recallest to me his going hence: it is just that I should be as I am: it had been easy not to have erected thee.

Sad is thy recalling of grief, tho' thy shapeliness is lovely: with thee, cross of Eoghan, above me, my wealth will fade away.

When men pass thee on the road, tears shall fall to the ground: at the sight of thee, O cross, the face of women's hands will grow crimson.

Tho' they be the cause of a mighty grief, yet are they a goodly ornament to the world – thy four dark ridges, broad, even, and balanced.

O son for whom the cross has been framed as a bright and steady beacon, thou hast gotten a cross most fair and graceful, let an elegy be yoked thereto.

This cross which I see overhead is the cross of one who was best at winning goodly prizes: this cross, that is viewed like a banner, conceals the very flame of art.

There is no need to bear witness to it either in its neighbourhood or afar off: tho' it is a smooth jewel, it is sorrowful that it should be as a token before all.

His cross above the hill-side – omen of grief to men of my own craft! – there shall be a shower of tears upon dark eyebrows when poets recognize his cross.

For this it was raised above the ground, the student's cross, in that this wood will be to the fresh-cheeked lad a presage of alms and prayer.

A blessing upon the soul of him whose cross I see before me; better than a flood of grief is a prayer for the graceful comely one.

This cross whereby I have been tortured is fashioned after Thy cross, O Lord; may he thereby come to Thy house, he whose cross this is.

To stay behind Eoghan's cross will be an opening for my grief: it is a defence against a host, and yet, O God, it is no shelter against sorrow.

The delicately carved cross of the youth brings more honour to the holy churchyard, to reverence this cross a company comes which would fill a church.

He would have been the ollav of the men of Munster, tho' he never got the title of ollav, that we have no such ollav as he, O God, that is the want I feel.

I omit here a mythological narrative, which would seem far-fetched to modern taste, though it was not far-fetched or incongruous to the poet and his contemporaries. He concludes:

> A son in the father's place, that were a fitting ordinance: that his father should be his heir, O Lord, it is a cause of misery.
> While Eoghan lived, such was my love for him, I could not endure, tho' I do it now for ever, to be two nights parted from him.
> Had any other been his teacher, I should not feel his death as I do: it makes his departure more distant, O God, that I was Eoghan's teacher.
> This Eoghan, with his fair locks – I must do without him: his time is over – what more can I say? and yet what fate is harder?[7]
>
> *A chros thall ar an dtulaigh, D. Dána,* page 196

Some of you may have heard of the famous Contention of the Bards at the beginning of the seventeenth century. Such poetic debates were not uncommon. There are two graceful poems on the River Shannon. It is uncertain whether they belong to the fifteenth or to the end of the sixteenth century. The original in each case is in a pretty tripping measure, of which the technical name is *ae freslige*:

> A Shionainn Bhriain Bhóraimhe,
>     iongnadh is méd do gháire,
> mar sguire dod ghlóraighe,
>     ag dol siar isin sáile.
>
> Poem 12

The debate is continued, with more learning than poetry, in two other poems, and finally a third poet, Tadhg Mac Aedhagáin, sums up the case in favour of Tadhg Óg Ó Huiginn, deciding on historic grounds that the Shannon is a northern river.

In the Tudor period the shadow of impending change falls upon the classical poetry. The bards see to their dismay that even men of Gaelic race are found on the side of the foreigner and his foreign civilization. There is a poem by Laoiseach Mac an Bhaird, dating probably from the sixteenth century. It is apparently meant as a reproach to someone who has adopted the dress and manners of a Tudor courtier. He is contrasted with another, perhaps his brother, who has chosen the harder, but more adventurous, life of a rebel.

> O man who follows English ways . . .
>     *A fhir ghlacas a ghalldacht,* Poem 9

It is worth noting that our classical writers were no purists in the matter of vocabulary. They had no scruple about using the foreign word to denote the foreign thing. In this short piece we find several English loanwords – *loca, brísde, clóca, cóta, spor, buatais, stoca, ráipér, sgarfa.*

When the change came, it came suddenly. The old Gaelic world went to pieces, and numbers of highly trained educated men found that their once honourable profession had disappeared. There is a poem written by Fear Feasa Ó an Cháinte, a well known poet of the late-sixteenth and early-seventeenth century. It is addressed to the celebrated Finghean or Florence MacCarthy, 'the dangerousest man in all Ireland', who had learned at Elizabeth's court the diplomacy that so baffled her ministers, until Carew hit upon the expedient of trapping him by means of a safe-conduct, and then treacherously arresting him. It is not clear whether this appeal against a boycott by his clan was written during one of his earlier visits to London, or during the long years of imprisonment in the Tower. We know that Florence MacCarthy carried on correspondence and lawsuits throughout his imprisonment.

> Go, my letter, to London . . .
> *Gluais a litir go Lunndain,* Poem 39

I have already referred to a poem by an unknown writer who looks at an empty school. His fellow-students are scattered and his patrons are all gone. His lot must have been a common one, for we find many poetical begging letters composed about this period. Here is a specimen by Cian Ó Heachaidhén, a northern poet:

> Devise thou counsel for me O Cormac, in this difficulty, thou generous and most noble one: as thou art full of wisdom and learning, answer our hardship if thou canst.
> Here is thy poet – all that is left after the slaughter, 'tis fitting to listen to our address – thou salmon of the Mourne, thou fortress of wealth – seeking thy counsel, my chief.
> All men have hated the art of our fathers, since the glory of the Gaels has set, the end of our term has come alas! while English increases.
> O thou of mild glance and kindly eye, every one is full of hatred of the poets; it was foretold that they should be as they are, and that men should care only for howling and strolling jesters.
> Since generosity and honour have departed, all men – a tale of misery unmerited by us – have with hard hearts turned their backs upon listening to true art.
> The passing of the Gaels of the land of Fódla has made poetry an outlaw: alas for her helplessness to-day, a deed never expected under the old law.
> No Gael considers that we are alive, a thing which even the wicked deem marvellous: that alone is wretched, not to mention acknowledging literature.
> Moreover all that live of our artists have been made deaf mutes: who now listens to our music? The utter ruin of the nobles is the cause of this.
> The exile of the race of noble Niall, a woe which will long oppress our annals, has left me beyond all men powerless, this is the reason for my importunity.
> These new-fashioned Gaels of the bright field of Niall, it were more

fitting to call them Galls: they agree not with the sages of the schools. If they are Gaels, I know it not.

As thou art not one of this new company, devise thou for us a counsel, O Cormac, O potent salmon of Line's slopes, what craft would be best for me?

As it is thou, O darling of my heart, that art most quick and shrewd, make for me an exchange of profession, if perchance that would bring me into favour.

Search the markets, thou son of Art, let there be upon thy lips a bout of trafficking: refuse no exchange however bad; by thy luck let us find our relief.

We are weary of our tedious luck – coax his trade from the comb-maker: as we all know their proximity, get an exchange from the fuller.

Make for us an exchange betimes – hasten! gives us heed to our fortune, I beseech thee, O swift mighty star! – with the needle-makers.

Better for me, unless thou make an exchange of trade for me, O thou of the well-known form, to depart from the view of all men's senses, to leave Ireland and the sight of it.

Or a fourth time – a cruel hardship – I must go, thou tree of fortune with fair offspring, under the protection of the children of Rudhraighe.

Unless God and thou look upon the last of thy hereditary poets, alas for those of my noble craft who are gone – I am still left.

Thou descendant of Seaán, noble son of Brian, son of Feidhlim, whose foot was firm in hard fight, relieve, my prince, the destitution of the schools, it is fitting to magnify everything that is good.

If any lived of the blood of Brian Ballach, in the fashion that we have heard . . . I should not change my profession.

Thou offspring of the kings of Tara's rath, physician who dost banish drooping spirits, do thou loose the fetters of doom from her wrists, and put a new soul into Poetry.

The race of royal Niall of noble exploits, I should not speak of the woe of my profession – my sore plight has carried me beyond my purpose – if I saw them in their own sovranty.

*Cinn dúinn comhairle, a Chormaic, Leabhar Cloinne Aodha*
*Buidhe*, page 120

As this petition has been preserved in a fine and well written manuscript we may trust that it served its purpose, and that the author was not reduced to competing with 'rude mechanicals' in order to earn a living.

The last sample of bardic poetry to which I shall draw your attention deals with the same theme, the downfall of literature under the new regime. It was written by Mathghamhain Ó Hifearnáin, or Mahon O'Heffernan, who belonged to the early-seventeenth century, the time of confiscations and plantations. He was the author of the well known bitter verses beginning *A mhic, ná meabhraigh éigse* – 'My son, cultivate not the poetic art' [*BM Cat. of Irish MSS.* i, 392–3]:

Question! who will buy a poem?
*Ceist! cia do cheinneóchadh dán?*, Poem 37

These specimens will give you some idea of the scope and subject-matter of the poems produced in the bardic schools, though I cannot of course reproduce the elaborate polish or the idiomatic vigour of the original. Remember that they were made to be recited, or chanted in a kind of recitative to a musical accompaniment, but they are not songs; most of them are in an unrhythmical metre which could not be set to any regular melody. There must have been thousands of popular songs in mediaeval and early modern Ireland, but these songs have perished. There are several poems in praise of the harp, but the literary classes appear to have looked down upon the singer, whom they classed with the geócach or buffoon. Tom Moore's picture of the bard singing and playing in the intervals of draining bumpers would have shocked the real bard as something very vulgar indeed. O'Curry pointed out fifty years ago the existence of purely lyric measures in Middle Irish. He was mistaken in thinking that some verses in the *Book of Leinster* attributed to Cormac mac Cuillenáin, who died in the year 903, could be sung to the air of *Ar Éire ní 'neósainn cé hí*, for nearly all the lines in those verses are a syllable too short for that air. But there are some other examples of beautiful staves with a regular musical beat. Whatever be the reason, these song-measures are very rare in Middle Irish and then disappear entirely, until they reappear in modern songs. They must have been in use all along among the unlearned and unlettered. The earliest trace of a modern Gaelic song is, I think, the title of an air in *Queen Elizabeth's Virginal Book*, 'Callino Casturame'. It will be remembered that Shakespeare brings these words into *Henry V*. When Pistol calls upon a French soldier to surrender, the latter says '*Je pense que vous êtes le gentilhomme de bonne qualité*'. Pistol, who knows no French, answers 'Quality? *Calen O custure* me!' – ejaculating apparently the only foreign words he can think of. It is usual in Anglo-Irish circles to explain the words *Callino Casturame*, or *Calen O custure me* very simply as *cailín óg, a stór*, 'young girl, my treasure'. The words cannot bear this meaning, for *cailín óg* is not in the vocative. At a pinch we might translate them 'his sweetheart is a young girl'. But there are several difficulties in the way of identifying the Tudor English representation of sounds with these Irish words. There is the initial *c* of *casturame* (*custure me*), the *u* which does not correspond with the *ó* of *stór*, and above all there is the final *me*. No such difficulties stand in the way of the Scottish claim that the words represent *Chailin òig, an stiùir thu mi*? 'maiden, wilt thou guide me?' Here we have the loss of the pretonic particle *a* and the unvoicing of the *g* in the Scottish fashion, while the *u* and the final *mi* are correctly represented. In fact the words will read off with as close an approximation to the Highland pronunciation as can be expected from symbols with English sound values. *Chailin òig an stiùir thu mi?* is the first line of a 'waulking-song' published in the *Macdonald Collection of Gaelic Poetry*, 1911, page 246. To maintain that the Elizabethan English could not have heard any Scottish Gaelic songs is merely begging the question. For my part I am willing to admit the Scottish claim to this song, but there must, of course, have been many such songs at the time, in Ireland and Scotland. [See now G. Murphy, *Callen O Custure Me*, *Éigse*, 1, 125.]

To come back to my subject. Bardic poetry, like all Irish poetry, is lyrical in one sense, but the poems are not songs. They are compositions in verse of varying length, sometimes emotional lyrics, sometimes moral or didactic essays in verse, sometimes political pamphlets. They are addressed exclusively to members of the upper and educated classes. They sometimes lack genuine inspiration, but they are always dignified in style and carefully finished. And as they follow unswervingly the old traditional standards they form a great linguistic storehouse of classical Gaelic, unimpeachable in vocabulary, morphology and syntax. For the social history of Ireland it would be hard to exaggerate their importance. Until the various collections of bardic poetry have been published it will be impossible to fill in the outlines given by our annalists, for there is nothing corresponding to the romantic tales of an earlier period, and annals alone are dull and colourless things. I am glad to say that there are at least four important collections in the hands of editors at present, and much fresh material may be looked for in a year or two. But enough is now accessible to enable the critic to estimate the literary value of these compositions in general. We may regret the class prejudices of the bardic order. We may wish that their horizon had been widened by the freshening influences of the renaissance. But given the state of the country and the national and international relations in which they lived, that was impossible. They stood for the independence of the Gael, and they fell with it. While it lasted they were held in honour. Neither they nor their patrons dreamed that a change was needed. To serve one's own day and generation may not be the highest ideal for a man of letters, but it is an ideal worth attaining.

## Notes

1   The title 'bard' is rare in Irish. In early times the 'bard' was of lower rank than the 'file'. It is sometimes asserted that the 'file' died out and was replaced by the 'bard'. But all the writers with whom we shall deal called themselves 'fileadha', not 'baird', as far as I can remember. And 'file' is still the ordinary word. The supposed 'rise of the bard' is explained by the fact that the word 'bard' came to be used in English, not in Irish, to denote an official Celtic poet. It is in this English sense that I use the terms 'bard' and 'bardic' in this lecture.

2   It is noteworthy that the Irish epics – if we may use such a term – are all in prose, with occasional lyrics interspersed.

3   This account appears to be the work of Thomas O'Sullevane; see Flower, *BM Cat. of Irish MSS.*, iii, 16.

4   'Bard' is here used in the sense of 'reciter', for which the technical term was 'reacaire'; so 'reacaim' 'I recite'. It is to be regretted that modern revivalists have adopted the word 'aithriseóireacht' for 'recitation'; its ordinary meaning is 'mimicry'.

5   *Grammatica Latino-Hibernica* (Rome, 1677), page 144: 'De Metro, omnium quae unquam vidi, vel audivi ausim dicere, quae sub Sole reperiuntur, difficillimo.'

6   Miss Hull, *Text Book of Irish Literature,* ii, page 174, calls it 'the most difficult and scientific of all the classical forms of verse'. I do not understand the meaning of 'scientific' here.

7   It should be noted that the deliberate repetition of the word 'cross' is less monotonous in the original, where the form varies between *cros, crois* and *croise*.

# 10

# THE
# WELSH BARDS

## EDWARD JONES

B Y THE ROMAN INVASION, and the more barbarous incursions of the Saxons, the Danes, and the Normans, and the emigration of the Britons to Armorica;[1] by the frequent destruction of MSS.,[2] and the massacres of the Clergy,[3] and the Bards;[4] the Poetry and Music of Wales have suffered a loss, that has thrown a dark cloud over the history of those native arts, and for a long time threatened their total extinction. Yet from the memorials still extant, and the poetical and musical compositions which time has spared, we are enabled often to produce unquestionable evidence, and always to form a probable conjecture, concerning their rise and progress among us. There is no living nation that can produce works of so remote antiquity, and at the same time of such unimpeached authority as the Welsh.

Our historians, ever desirous to trace their subject to the utmost point of remote antiquity, have derived the name and profession of the *Bards* from *Bardus,* fifth king of Britain, who began his reign in the year of the world 2082. Berosus says, he reigned over the Celts, and was famous for the invention of Poetry and Music. Perizonius, as Vitus asserts, called the music of Bardus *not every music, but that which is poetical.*[5] Bardus, however, if other accounts may be credited, was not the first who cultivated the sister arts in this island. *Blegored,* king of Britain, who died in the year of the world 2069, was called, for his extraordinary skill in vocal and instrumental music, *the god of harmony.*[6]

The Bards were originally a constitutional appendage of the Druidical hierarchy, which was divided into three classes, priests, philosophers and poets.[7] At Llanidan in Anglesey, formerly inhabited by the Druidical conventual societies, we at this day find vestiges of *Tre'r Dryw,* the Arch Druid's mansion, and near it, of *Tre'r Beirdd,* the hamlet of the Bards.[8] Mr Mason, in his Caractacus, has adopted the ancient distinction of three orders of Druids. Having spoken of the arch Druid, he proceeds:

His brotherhood
Possess the neighb'ring cliffs:
   On the left
Reside the sage Euvates: yonder grots
Are tenanted by Bards, who nightly thence;
Rob'd in their flowing vests of innocent white,
Descend, with harps that glitter to the moon,
Hymning immortal strains.

Of the Bards, however, and of their poetry and music, at those remote periods, little more than a faint tradition is preserved: and that little we either derive from the poetical and fabulous remains of the British annals, or glean wherever it is scattered over the wider field of Roman history. There is no account, indeed, of Britain in any writer preceding Caesar; but as it is incredible that its ancient arts sprung up under the oppression of the Roman yoke, and as it has never been pretended that any part of them was borrowed from the conquerors; whatever mention of them is found in the Greek and Roman authors who succeeded the first invasion, may fairly be produced as in some measure descriptive of their state before it.

Those nations could not surely be rude in the construction of their poetry and music, among whom, as Caesar declares,[9] the supremacy and omnipotence of the gods was acknowledged, the immortality and transmigration of the soul was believed,[10] opinions were formed concerning the motion of the planets and the dimensions of the world, and whose youth was instructed in the nature and philosophy of things.

In all the Celtic nations we discover a remarkable uniformity of manners and institutes. It was the custom of the ancient Germans, when they marched to battle, to animate themselves with singing verses, prophetic of their success, which they called Barditus.[11] It was the honourable office of the Bards of Britain to sing to the harp; at their nuptials and funeral obsequies, their games and other solemnities, and at the head of their armies, the praises of those who had signalized themselves by virtuous and heroic actions.[12] This entertainment made a deep impression on the young warriors; elevated some to heroism, and prompted virtue in every breast. Among the Celts, says Diodorus Siculus,[13] are composers of melodies, called Bards, who sing to instruments like lyres, panegyrical, or invective strains: and in such reverence are they held, that when two armies, prepared for battle, have cast their darts, and drawn their swords, on the arrival and interposition of the Bards, they immediately desist. Thus, even among the rude barbarians, wrath gives place to wisdom, and Mars to the Muses.[14]

A fragment of *Posidonius*, preserved in Athenaenus,[15] enables us to exhibit the only specimen of the genius of the Bards that can be ascribed with certainty to a higher date than the sixth century. Describing the wealth and magnificence of Luernius, Posidonius relates, that, ambitious of popular favour, he frequently was borne over the plains in a chariot, scattering gold and silver among myriads of the Celts who followed him. On a day of banqueting and festivity, when he entertained with abundance of choice provisions and a profusion of costly liquors, his innumerable attendants; a poet of the barbarians, arriving long after the rest, greeted him with singing the praise of his unrivalled bounty and exalted virtues, but lamented his own bad fortune in so late an arrival. Luernius, charmed with his song, called for a purse of gold, and threw it to the Bard, who, animated with gratitude, renewed the encomium, and proclaimed, *that the track of his chariot wheels upon the earth was productive of wealth and blessings to mankind.*

The disciples of the Druidical Bards, during a noviciate of twenty years, learnt an immense number of verses,[16] in which they preserved the principles of their religious and civil polity by uninterrupted tradition for many centuries. Though the use of letters was familiar to them, they never committed their verses to writing, for the sake of strengthening their intellectual faculties, and of keeping their mysterious knowledge from the contemplation of the vulgar. The metre in which these poetical doctrines were communicated was called *Englyn Milwr*, or the Warrior's Song, which, as the reader will see in the annext specimen, is a stanza of three lines, each of seven syllables, the first and second containing the general subject of the poem, and the third conveying some divine or moral precept, or prudential maxim.[17]

### Druidical Triambics

Marchwiail bedw briglas,
A dyn fy nhroed o wanas;
Nac addef dy rîn[18] i wâs.

Marchwiail derw mwynllwyn,
A dyn fy nhroed o gadwyn:
Nac addef dy rîn i forwyn.

Marchwiail derw deiliar,
A dyn fy nhroed o garchar;
Nac addef dy rín i lafar.[19]

Eiry mynydd, gwyn pŏb ty;
Cynnefin brân a chanu;
Ni ddaw dâ o dra chyfgu.[20]

Eiry mynydd, gwynt ae tawl,
Llydan lloergan, glâs tafawl;
Odid dyn diriad, dihawl.[21]

Eiry mynydd, hydd ym mron;
Gochwiban gwynt uwch blaen on;
Trydydd troed i hen ei ffon.[22]

In the three first, the Druids seem to invoke their groves, and set forth their sacerdotal privileges and exemptions. In the other three, they apostrophize the mountain *Eryri* or Snowdon, the Parnassus of Wales. We learn from Gildas that the ancient Britains had an extraordinary veneration for mountains, groves and rivers.

When the Roman legions, after the invasion of Britain, and the conquest of the Gallic provinces, were recalled to oppose the power of Pompey in Italy, the exultation of the Bards, at recovering the secure possession and exercise of their ancient poetical function is described in a very animated manner by Lucan:

You too, ye Bards! whom sacred raptures fire
To chaunt your heroes to your country's lyre;
Who consecrate in your immortal strain
Brave patriot souls in righteous battle slain;
Securely now the tuneful task renew
And noblest themes in deathless songs pursue![23]

Such was the new but imperfectly discovered scene which the great Caesar's ambition opened in Britain. Nor are these accounts only imperfect; they are also partially delivered, as some bold spirits, even among the Romans, have hinted.[24]

The Druids, expelled from Britain by the legions, took refuge in Ireland and the Isle of Man, places which the Roman sword could not then reach. The theory of the British Music moved with them, and settled in Ireland, which from that period was for many ages the seat of learning and philosophy, till wars and dissentions buried almost every trace of them in oblivion.[25]

The Bards, having now lost their sacred Druidical character, began to appear in an honourable, though less dignified capacity at the courts of the British kings. The Oak Misselto[26] was deprived of its ancient authority, and the sword prevailed in its place. The Musick as well as the Poetry of Britain, no doubt, received a tincture from the martial spirit of the times, and the Bards, who once had dedicated their profession to the worship of the gods in their sylvan temples, the celebration of public solemnities, and the praise of all the arts of peace, and who had represt the fury of armies preparing to rush upon each other's spears: now

> With other echo taught the shades
> To answer, and resound far other song.[27]

If, while Britain remained a Roman province, the desultory wars produced any compositions that deserved to live, they were destroyed by the calamity that occasioned them. In the sixth century, the golden age of Welsh Poetry, the Bards resumed the harp with unusual boldness, to animate their country's last successful struggle with the Saxons.

Aneurin Gwawdrydd, called by his successors Monarch of Bards, lived under the patronage of Mynyddawg of Edinborough, a prince of the North, whose Milwyr, or men at arms, 363 in number, all wearing gold chains, were slain, except Aneurin and two others, in a battle with the Saxons at Cattraeth. His 'Gododdin' written on that event is perhaps the oldest and noblest production of that age. Being composed in a northern dialect, possibly the Pictish, it is at present in many places extremely difficult and obscure.[28] The following passage, verified by Mr Gray, from Mr Evans' specimens, will, though a fragment, give an ample proof of the genius of Aneurin.

### Ode
#### Selected from the Gododdin

Had I but the torrent's might,
With headlong rage, and wild affright,
Upon Dëira's squadrons hurl'd,
To rush, and sweep them from the
    world!

Too, too secure, in youthful pride
By them my friend, my Hoel, died,
Great Kian's son; of Madoc old
He ask'd no heaps of hoarded gold;
Alone in nature's wealth array'd,

He ask'd, and had the lovely maid.
Have ye seen the tusky boar
Or the bull, with sullen roar,
On surrounding foes advance?
So Caradoc bore his lance.

Vedel's name, my lay, rehearse,
Build to him the lofty verse,
Sacred tribute of the Bard,
Verse, the hero's sole reward.
As the flames devouring force;

191

As the whirlwind in its course,
As the thunder's fiery stroke,
Glancing on the shiver'd oak;
Did the sword of Vedel's mow
The crimson harvest of the foe.

To Cattraeth's vale, in glitt'ring row
Twice two hundred warriors go;
Ev'ry warrior's manly neck
Chains of regal honour deck,
Wreath'd in many a golden link:
From the golden cup they drink

Nectar, that the bees produce,
Or the grape's extatic juice.
Flush'd with mirth, and hope they
    burn;
But none from Cattraeth's vale
    return,
Save Aeron brave, and Conan
    strong,
(Bursting thro' the bloody throng),
And I, the meanest of them all,
That live to weep, and sing their
    fall.

Taliesin, who in one of his poems gives an honourable testimony to the fame of Aneurin,[29] was like him called Penbeirdd, king of Bards. He lived in the reign and enjoyed the favour of Maelgwn Gwynedd, king of Britain. He was found, when an infant, exposed in a weir, which Gwyddno Garanir, the petty king of Cantre'r Gwaelod, had granted as a maintenance to prince Elphin his son. Elphin, with many amiable qualities, was extravagant; and having little success at the weir, grew discontented and melancholy. At this juncture Taliesin was found by the fishermen of the prince, by whose command he was carefully fostered and liberally educated. At a proper age the accomplished Bard was introduced by his princely patron at the court of his father Gwyddno, to whom he presented, on that occasion, a poem called 'Hanes Taliesin', or Taliesin's History; and at the same time another to the prince, called 'Dybuddiant Elphin',[30] the consolation of Elphin, which the Bard addresses to him in the person and character of an exposed infant. Taliesin lived to recompense the kindness of his benefactor: by the magic of his Poetry he redeemed him from the castle of Teganwy (where he was for some misconduct confined by his uncle Maelgwn), and afterwards conferred upon him an illustrious immortality.

Taliesin was the master or poetical preceptor of Myrddin ab Morfryn: he enriched the British Prosody with five new metres; and has transmitted in his poems such vestiges, as throw new light on the history, knowledge, and manners of the ancient Britons and their Druids, much of whose mystical learning he imbibed.

The poem which I have chosen for a specimen of Taliesin's manner, is his description of the battle of Argoed Llwyfain, fought about the year 548, by Goddeu, a king of North Britain, and Urien Reged, king of Cumbria, against Fflamddwyn, a Saxon general, supposed to be Ida, king of Northumberland. I am indebted to the obliging disposition and undiminished powers of Mr Whitehead, for the following faithful and animated verification of this valuable antique:

### The Battle of Argoed Llwyfain[31]

Morning rose: the issuing sun
Saw the dreadful fight begun:
And that sun's descending ray
Clos'd the battle, clos'd the day.

Fflamddwyn pour'd his rapid bands,
Legions four, o'er Reged's lands.
The numerous host from side to side
Spread destruction wild and wide,

From Argoed's[32] summits, forest-
   crown'd,
To steep Arfyndd's[33] utmost bound.
Short their triumph, short their sway,
Born and ended with the day!

Flush'd with conquest Fflamddwyn
   said,
Boastful at his army's head,
'Strive not to oppose the stream,
Redeem your lands, your lives redeem.
Give me pledges,' Fflamddwyn cried,
'Never,' Urien's son replied
Owen[34] of the mighty stroke:
Kindling, as the hero spoke,
Cenau,[35] Coel's blooming heir
Caught the flame, and grasp'd the
   spear.

Shall Coel's issue pledges give
To the insulting foe, and live
Never such be Briton's shame,
Never,'till this mangled frame
Like some vanquish'd lion lie
Drench'd in blood, and bleeding die.

Day advanc'd: and ere the sun
Reach'd the radiant point of noon,
Urien came with fresh supplies.
'Rise, ye sons of Cambria, rise,
Spread your banners to the foe,

Spread them on the mountain's
   brow,
Lift your lances high in air,
Friends and brothers of the war,
Rush like torrents down the steep,
Thro' the vales in myriads sweep,
Fflamddwyn never can sustain
The force of our united train.'

Havoc, havoc rag'd around,
Many a carcase strew'd the
   ground:
Ravens drank the purple flood,
Raven plumes were dyed in blood;
Frighted crouds from place to place
   Eager, hurrying, breathless, pale
Spread the news of their disgrace,
   Trembling as they told the tale.

These are Taliesin's rhimes,
These shall live to distant times,
And the Bard's prophetic rage
Animate a future age.

Child of sorrow, child of pain,
Never may I smile again,
If 'till all-subduing death
Close these eyes, and stop this
   breath,
Ever I forget to raise
My grateful songs to Urien's praise!

Llywarch Hên, or Llywarch the aged, a Cumbrian prince, is the third great Bard of the British annals. He past his younger days at the court of King Arthur, with the honourable distinction of a free guest. When the British power was weakened by the death of Arthur, Llywarch was called to the aid of his kinsman Urien Reged, king of Cumbria, and the defence of his own principality, against the irruptions of the Saxons.

This princely Bard had four-and-twenty sons, all invested with the golden torques, which appears to have been the ancient badge of British nobility.[36] Many of them were slain in the Cumbrian wars, and the Saxons at length prevailed. The unfortunate Llywarch, with his few surviving sons, fled into Powys, there to revive the unequal and unsuccessful contest under the auspices of the prince of Powys, Cynddylan. Having lost, in the issue of these wars, all his sons and friends, he retired to a hut at Aber Ciog[37] in North Wales, to soothe with his harp the remembrance of misfortune, and vent with elegiac numbers the sorrows of old age in distress. His poems are in some places almost unintelligible: not because they want simplicity, which is their characteristic beauty, but from the antiquity of the lan-

The Bardic Source Book

guage, which is partly the Venedotian and partly the Cumbrian dialect, and from scantiness of information concerning the facts. The compositions of Llywarch are pure nature, unmixed with that learning and contrivance which appears in the writings of Taliesin: he did not, like that great Bard, extend the bounds of British poetry, but followed implicitly the works of the Druids, closing many of his stanzas with their venerable maxims. He writes in such a simple, undisguised, pathetic manner, that it is impossible to suspect him of misrepresentation; he has no fictions, no embellishments, no display of art; but gives an affecting narrative of events and circumstances.

The subsequent specimen, which is a close and literal prose translation of stanzas in the first and second poem of this princely Bard, will give my readers a relish for his excellence in natural, sentimental and martial description.[38]

**From Poem I**

The Cuckow sends forth her longing and complaining voice,
When she has fled from the pursuit of the Hawk,
And condoles with me at the waters of Ciog.

In spring all nature is beautiful and glad:
It is the season when heroes hasten to the field of war:
But I cannot go; infirmity will not suffer me.

The birds sing, and loud is the cry
Of the strong-scented hounds in the desart:
Again the birds are heard to warble.

The birds sing, the brooks murmur,
The moon shines out; it is the cold hour of midnight;
And my heart droops under its lingering cares.

Hear you not how the waves roar,
And dash from rock to rock?
O my weak heart! may my senses be granted me tonight!

**From Poem II**

Before I used a staff, I was comely and eloquent:
I was a free and welcome guest in the palace
Of Powis, the Paradise of Wales.

Before I used a staff, I was splendidly apparelled:
My spear was of the largest size; its thrust was terrible:
But now my years are many; I am feeble, I am miserable.

O my staff! in summer
The furrows are red, and the tender blades spring forth:
Thou art to me instead of my lost kindred, when I look upon thy beak.

Vallies were thrown up for the trenches of the fortress:
And I will arm myself with my shield.
My mind must be disordered ere I give way.

When danger overtakes thee, O Urien,
Blow thou the horn which I gave thee,
Whose mouth is tipped with gold.

Ghastly was the wound when Pyll was slain:
Blood streamed from his hair
On the bank of the rapid Ffraw.

Distinguished among all my sons
When they singled out their adversaries
Pyll rushed with the violence of flames through the streams of Llifon.

When, mounted on his prancing steed,
He halted at the door of his tent,
The wife of Pyll gloried in her husband.

Gwên! how joyous did I behold thee last night!
Thou hadst no roof to cover thee,
But didst traverse, cold, the banks of Morlas.

O Gwên! thou that wert dreadful in thine anger!
My thoughts are bloody because thou art slain:
Relentless was he that slew thee.

O Gwên! fire of a powerful progeny!
Thou wert the attack of an eagle
At the mouths of mighty rivers.

Let the waves cease to roar, the rivers to flow,
Since this fatal deed has been perpetrated!
Alas! my Gwên! in my trembling age have I lost thee.

My son was a hero: the sun was below Gwên.
He was the nephew of Urien
He was slain by the Ford of Morlas.

I had four and twenty sons;
All leaders of armies, all decked with the golden torques;
Gwên was the bravest of them all.

I had four and twenty sons,
All princely chiefs, all decked with chains of gold.
But compared with Gwên, the rest were children.

These were my sons,
The favourites of Bards;
And fair is their renown.

The British language, in which rhyme is as old as poetry itself, had, in the sixth century, attained such copiousness and musical refinement, that the Bards commonly composed in unirhythm stanzas of many lines. The rhymes of modern Italy are as famous for their number, as its language is admired for its pliability in yielding to all the inflections of the voice. Yet the Italian poets are constrained to change the rhyme more than once in a stanza, without producing any other effect than confusion from the diversity. The old performances of the Bards were therefore most happily calculated for accompanying the harp.

For this quality none of the remains of this remote period are more remarkable, than the works of Myrddin ab Morfryn, often called Merlin the Wild; whose reputation as a Bard, is not inferior to the prophetic and magical fame of his great predecessor; Myrddin Emrys.[39] He was born at Caerwerthefin, near the forest of Celyddon, in Scotland; where he possessed a great estate, which he lost in the war of his Lord Gwenddolau ap Ceidio, and Aeddan Fradawg against Rhydderch Hael. His misfortunes in Scotland drove him to Wales: and there is now extant a poetical dialogue between him and his preceptor Taliesin. He was present at the battle of Camlan, in the year 542, where, fighting under the banner of king Arthur, he accidentally slew his own nephew, the son of his sister Gwenddydd.[40] In consequence of this calamity, he was seized with madness, which affected him every other hour.[41] He fled back into Scotland, and concealed himself in the woods of that country, where, in an interval of recollection, he composed the following poem, which has many beauties, and is strongly tinctured with the enthusiasm of madness. He afterwards probably returned to Wales, where, in the disorder of his mind, he vented those poetical prophecies that pass under his name, and were translated into Latin, and published by Geoffrey of Monmouth. He was burried in the Isle of Enlli,[42] or Bardsey, on the coast of North Wales, where there was a college of Black cowled Monks.

### The Orchard [Myrddins Apple Trees]

Was ever given to man so acceptable a gift, as that bestowed on Myrddin ere age had overtaken him? a fair orchard, seven score and seven sweet apple trees, all equal in age, height, and magnitude: they possessed the slope of a majestic hill, branching high and wide, crowned with lovely foliage; a lovely nymph, whose hair flowed in beauteous ringlets, guarded them; her name Gloywedd, with the pearly teeth.

Sweet and excellent apple-tree! thy branches are loaded with delicious fruit; I am full of care and fearful anxiety for thy safety, lest the destructive woodman should dig thee up by the roots, or otherwise so injure thy prolific nature, that apples would no more grow on thy branches: for this I am wild with grief, torn with anxiety, anguish pierces me to the heart; I suffer no garment to cover my body. These trees are the inestimable gifts of Gwenddolau, He who is now, as if he was not.

Sweet apple-tree, of tall and stately growth! how admired thy shade and shelter, thy profitableness and beauty often will mighty lords and princes form a thousand pretences for frequenting thy recess, nor less eager the false and luxurious monks; and equally intent are the idle talkative youths: all hankering after thy apples; they all pretend to prophecy the warlike exploits of their prince, this their apology for robbing thee of thy fruit.

Sweet apple-tree, vigorous in growth, verdant in foliage! large are thy branches, beautiful thy form: ere the depredations of slaughtering war caused my thoughts to boil with grief, how beautiful was the sight of thy robe of vivid green! yet shall my prophetic song announce the day, when a mighty legion shall revenge my wrongs; the valourous armies of Pengwern, fierce in battle, animated by mighty mead.

Sweet apple-tree, growing in the lonely glade! fervent valour shall still keep thee secure from the stern lords of Rhydderch. Bare is the ground about thee, trodden by mighty warriors; their heroic forms strike their foes with terror. Alas! Gwenddydd loves me not, she greets me not; I am hated by the chiefs of Rhydderch; I have ruined his son and his daughter. Death relieves all, why does he not visit me? for after Gwenddolau no prince honours me, I am not soothed with diversion, I am no longer visited by the fair: yet in the battle of Arderydd I wore the golden torques, though I am now despised by her who is fair as the snowy swan.

Sweet apple-tree, covered with delicate bloom, growing unseen in the sequestered woods! early with the dawn have I heard that the high-commissioned chief of Meuwydd was offended with me; twice, three times, alas! four times in the same day have I heard this; it rung in my ears ere the sun had marked the hour of noon. O Jesus! why was I not taken away by destruction, ere it was the sad fate of my hand to kill the son of Gwenddydd?

Sweet apple-tree, appearing to the eye a large and fair wood of stately trees! monarch of the surrounding woods; shading all, thyself unshaded! yet shall my song of prophecy announce the coming again of Medrod, and of Arthur, monarch of the warlike host: again shall they rush to the battle of Camlan; two days will the conflict last, and only seven escape from the slaughter. Then let Gwenhwyfar remember the crimes she has been guilty of, when an ecclesiastical hero leads the warriors to battle. Alas! far more lamentable is my destiny, and hope affords no refuge. The son of Gwenddydd is dead, slain by my accursed hand!

Sweet apple-tree, loaded with the sweetest fruit, growing in the lonely wilds of the woods of Celyddon! all seek thee for the sake of thy produce, but in vain; until Cadwaladr comes to the conference of the ford of Rhëon, and Cynan advances to oppose the Saxons in their career. Then shall the Britons be again victorious, led by their graceful and majestic chief: then shall be restored to every one his own: then shall the founder of the trump of gladness proclaim the song of peace, the serene days of happiness.

These were the poetical luminaries of the sixth century. Their works are pregnant with feeling, with fancy, and enthusiasm; and do honour to the nation that produced them. Foreigners who shall read them, will be obliged to soften some of those dark colours in which they have usually painted our ancestors. The rays of genius that shone forth in the Britons, amid the gloom of the dark ages, are more valuable in the eye of reason, and contribute more to their glory, than all the bloody trophies they erected. But how can their poetry produce this effect, if their language remains unintelligible, if no one will translate it into the other languages of Europe?[43]

The writings of these ancient Bards deserve to be explored and published, not merely as sources of poetical and philosophical pleasures, but as stores of historical information. Their origin is not doubtful like that of some venerable works which we have reason to fear, were drawn together from fabulous records or vague tradition; these were composed on recent exploits, and copied immediately from their subjects, and sent abroad among nations that had acted or seen them. From a diligent investigation and accurate editions of them by learned Welshmen, many important advantages may be promised to the British history, which supplied and improved from these copious fountains, would no longer disgust with incredible fables of giants and magicians, but engage by a description of real events and true heroes. For early poetry has in all countries been known to give the fullest and most exact picture of life and manners.

The Druids, in their emigration to Ireland, had not left Britain, entirely destitute of its music, which though no longer communicated by the precepts of that learned order, was perpetuated by practice. It languished indeed for a time, but afterwards grew and flourished in Wales with the other surviving arts of Britain.

It seems to have been a prerogative peculiar to the ancient kings of Britain, to preside in the Eisteddfod or Congress of the Bards. Accordingly we find that late in the seventh century Cadwaladr sat in an Eisteddfod assembled for the purpose of regulating the Bards, taking into consideration their productions and performance, and giving new laws to harmony. It is recorded[44] that a Bard, who played on the harp in the presence of this illustrious assembly in a key called Is gywair ar y Bragod Dannau, was censured for the inharmonious effect he produced, interdicted under a heavy penalty from using it ever after; and commanded whenever he performed before persons skilful in the art to adopt that of Mwynen Gwynedd, the pleasing key of North Wales, which the royal associates first gave out, and preferred for its conformity with singing, and its superiority over the Is Gywair, which strikingly resembled the tone of the Pipes of Morfydd, a great performer on that instrument. They even decreed that none could sing with true harmony, but in Mwynen Gwynedd, because that key is formed of strings that make a perfect concord, and the other is of a mixed nature: of which superiority we have examples in the following tunes; Caniad Ceffyliwr, Caniad o Fawrwyrthiau, Caniad Jeuan ab y Góf, Caniad Anrheg Dewi, Caniad Cydwgi, Caniad Einion Delyniwr, Caniad Cryth ar y Carfi; and many others.

To this period may be referred, not without probability, those great but obscure characters in Welsh music, Ithel, Iorwerth and yr Athro Fêdd,[45] and the keys, and chromatic notes by them invented and still distinguished by their names.

From the era of Cadwaladr history is obstinately silent concerning the Welsh music and poetry to the middle of the tenth century, a period illuminated by the laws of Howel.[46] In these laws we do not find the musical or poetical establishment of the national Bards; but they contain such injunctions respecting the Bard of the palace, and the chief Bard of Wales, as in some measure compensate for that defect of information.

When the chief Bard appeared at the court of the Welsh princes, he sat next to the judge of the palace. None but himself and the Bard of the palace was allowed to perform in the presence of the prince. When the prince desired to hear music, the chief Bard sang to his harp two poems, one in praise of the Almighty, the other concerning kings and their heroic exploits, after which a third poem was sung by the Bard of the palace. He obtained his pre-eminence by a poetical contest, which was decided by the judge of the palace, who received on this occasion from the successful candidate, as an honorary fee, a bugle-horn, a gold ring, and a cushion for his chair of dignity. His poetical rights and authority were not subject to the control of the prince, and his privilege of protection lasted from the beginning of the first song in the hall of the palace, to the conclusion of the last.[47] But what remains to be said of the manner of his election, and the nature of his office, I must defer, till the institutes of Gruffudd ap Cynan enable me to speak more largely, and with greater certainty, of this dignified person.

The Bard of the palace, who was in rank the eighth officer of the prince's household, received at his appointment a harp and an ivory chess-board from the prince, and a gold-ring from the princess. On the same occasion he presented a gold-ring to the judge of the palace. At the prince's table on the three great festivals of Christmas, Easter and Whitsuntide, he sat next to the master of the palace, and publickly received from the hands of that officer the harp on which he performed. When he went with other Bards upon his Clera or musical peregrination, he was entitled to a double fee. He was obliged, at the queen's desire, to sing to his harp three pieces of poetry, but in a low voice, that the court might not be diverted from their avocations. He accompanied the army when it marched into an enemy's country; and while it was preparing for battle, or dividing the spoils, he performed an ancient song, called 'Unbennaeth Prydaia',[48] the 'Monarchy of Britain':

> The Bard who first adorn'd our native tongue,
> Tun'd to his British lyre this ancient song.
> > *Dryden*

and for this service, when the prince had received his share of the spoils, was rewarded with the most valuable beast that remained.[49]

In these constitutions we discover the first account of the *Clera*,[50] or triennial circuit of the Bards, as we before traced the origin of the Eisteddfod, their triennial assembly, in the annals of Cadwaladr. We likewise find that a vassal by the practice of Poetry and Music, which he could not adopt without the permission of his lord or prince, acquired the privileges of a freeman, and an honourable rank in society.[51] Nothing can display more forcibly the estimation and influence which the Bards enjoyed at this early period, than their remarkable prerogative of petitioning for presents[52] by occasional poems. This custom they afterwards carried to such excess, and such respect was constantly paid to their requests, that in the time of Gruffudd ap Cynan, it became necessary to control them by a law which restrained them from asking for the prince's Horse, Hawk, or Greyhound, or any other possession beyond a certain price, or that was particularly valued by the owner, or could not be replaced. Many poems of the succeeding centuries are now extant, written to obtain a horse, a bull, a sword, a rich garment, &c.

About the year 1070, prince Bleddyn ap Cynfyn, the author of another code of Welsh Laws, established some regulations respecting the musical Bards,[53] and revised and enforced those which were already made.

Towards the close of the eleventh century, the great prince Gruffudd ap Cynan invited to Wales some of the best musicians of Ireland;[54] and being partial to the music of that island, where he was born, and observing with displeasure the disorders and abuses of the Welsh Bards, created a body of institutes for the amendment of their manners, and the correction of their art and practice.[55] Accordingly I find in an old MS. of Welsh Music,[56] in the library of the Welsh school, a curious account of so remarkable a revolution, beginning with these words: *Here follow the four-and-twenty measures of instrumental Music, all conformable to the laws of harmony, as they were settled in a congress by many Doctors skilful in that science, Welsh and Irish, in the reign of Gruffudd ap Cynan, and written in books by order of both parties princely and principally, and thence copied, &c.*[57]

This grand reformation of the Bards was effected by dividing them into classes, and assigning to each class a distinct profession and employment. We have hitherto viewed them in a very various and extensive sphere. It was their office to applaud the living and record the dead: they were required to possess learning and genius, a skill in pedigrees, an acquaintance with the laws and metres of poetry, a knowledge of harmony, a fine voice, and the command of an instrument. This diversity of character is well expressed by Drayton in the sixth song of his Polyolbion:

> Musician, Herald, Bard, thrice may'st thou be renown'd
> And with three several wreaths immortally be crown'd!

Such variety of excellence was unattainable by human capacity. The Bards were now therefore distributed into three grand orders, of Poets, Heralds, and Musicians; each of which again branched into subordinate distinctions.

Neither of these orders or distinctions was any longer compatible with those with which it had been connected, or with any other profession. According to a more minute arrangement, there were of regular Bards, proceeding to degrees in the Eisteddfod, six classes: three of Poets and three of Musicians.

The first class of the Poets consisted of historical or antiquarian Bards,[58] who sometimes mixed prophecy with their inspiration: they were also critics and teachers: and to them belonged the praise of virtue and the censure of vice. It was their duty to celebrate the gifts of fancy and poetry. Of them it was required to address married women without the air of gallantry, and the clergy in a serious strain suitably to their function, to satirize without indecency, and without lampooning to answer and overthrow the lampoons of the inferior Bards.

The second class was formed of domestic or parenetic Bards,[59] who lived in the houses of the great, to celebrate their exploits and amiable qualities: they sung the praises of generosity, contentment, domestic happiness, and all the social virtues: and thus eminently contributed to enliven the leisure of their patrons. It was also their province to request presents in a familiar easy vein, without importunity.

The third class, though last, was probably not least in esteem: for it consisted of Herald Bards,[60] who were the national chroniclers, and were also well versed in pedigrees and blazonry of arms, and the works of the ancient Bards, such as Taliesin and the two Merlins. According to the account of them which Giraldus[61] has given in the succeeding century, they were admirably qualified for Poetry, if invention be one of its principal requisites: for he affirms that they could trace back the descents of their princes and nobles, not only to Roderic, but to Beli, Sylvius and Aeneas, and even to Adam himself. But their Poetry was of an humbler kind: it was usually confined to subjects of jocularity and mimickry, invective and reproach.

Of the musical Bards, the first class was appropriated to the performers on the Harp: concerning whom the reader may collect some information from the sequel of this short history, and from an account of the Welsh musical instruments in another part of this volume.

The second contained performers on the six-stringed *Crûth*; concerning whom also I refer the reader to the same places for information.

The third consisted of singers, whose employment was to sing to the harps of others the compositions of the poetical Bards; but from whom a variety of other qualifications was expected. 'A singer,' said the Laws, 'should know how to tune a Harp or Crŵth, and to play several essays and embellishments, two preludes, a cwlwm, a caniad, and the thirteen principal tunes, with all their flats and sharps.[62] He should understand likewise the thirteen principal styles of expression; and accenting them with his voice to several tunes: he should know the twenty-four metres of Poetry, and twenty-four measures of Music, and be capable of composing in two of the Englyn metres,[63] and one of the Cywydd metres. He should read Welsh with propriety and write it with exactness, and be skilful in correcting and restoring any old poem or song that has been corrupted by transcribers.'

At the nuptials of the prince or any of the princely blood, the singer waited upon the illustrious Bride, and at those entertainments was expected to carve dexterously every kind of fowl that might come before him.

Such, and so various were the regular Bards, who by a noviciate and probation of an appointed term of years, and the performance of poetical and musical exercises, acquired degrees in the Eisteddfod. As that venerable assembly existed long before the period I am describing, a description of it ought, perhaps, to have been already exhibited: but I chose to wait till, under the auspices of a prince to whom our Poetry and Music are forever obliged, I am enabled to display it to the eyes of the curious in its most perfect form.

The Eisteddfod was a triennial assembly of the Bards (usually held at Aberffraw, the royal seat of the princes of North Wales formerly, situated in Angelsey; likewise Dinefawr, the royal castle of the princes of South Wales, in Carmarthenshire; and Mathrafael, the royal palace of the princes of Powis, in Montgomeryshire). For the regulation of Poetry and Music, for the purpose of conferring degrees, and of advancing to the chair of the Eisteddfod by the decision of a poetical and musical contest some of the rival candidates; or establishing in that honourable seat the Chief Bard who already occupied it.

Wishing to convey to my readers a clear idea of this important subject, I annex an extract, faithfully translated, from the statute of prince Gruffudd ap

Cynan, concerning the manner of holding an Eisteddfod.

> When the congress hath assembled, according to notice and summons
> previously issued, at the place appointed, they shall choose as umpires
> twelve persons skilled in the Welsh Language, Poetry, Music, and Heraldry,
> who shall give to the Bards a subject to sing upon, in any of the 24 metres;
> but not in amaebean carols, or any such frivolous compositions. The
> umpires shall see that the candidates do not descend to satire or personal
> invective, and shall allow to each a sufficient interval for composing his
> Englyn or Cywydd, or other task that they shall assign. They shall
> moreover take down the names of the several Bards present intending to
> sing, that every one may be called by his name in order to the chair to
> perform his composition. The unsuccessful candidates shall acknowledge
> in writing that they are overcome, and shall deliver their acknowledgement
> to the chief Bard, that is, to him who shall win the chair: and they all shall
> drink health to the chief Bard, and all shall pay him fees; and he shall
> govern them till he is overcome in a future Eisteddfod.[64]

From this injunction it appears, that the duties which upon this occasion, in the
reign of Howel, belonged to the judge of the palace, were afterwards held in commission.

What served greatly to heighten the emulation of the Bards, if they wanted
any additional incitement, was the presence of the prince, who usually presided in
these contests. Their compositions delivered upon these occasions are frequently
upon historical subjects, and are valuable for their authenticity: for it was the business of the Eisteddfod, not only to give laws to Poetry and Music, but to extinguish falsehood and establish certainty in the relation of events. 'A custom so good
(says Drayton), that had it been judiciously observed, truth of story had not been
so uncertain: for there was, we suppose, a correction of what was faulty in form
or matter, or at least a censure of the hearers upon what was recited. Of which
course some have wished a recontinuance, that either amendment of opinion, or
change of purpose in publishing, might prevent blazoned errors.'[65]

Before any person could be enrolled in the Eisteddfod, the permission of the
prince or lord, within whose jurisdiction he lived, was necessary. If he desired to
proceed to degrees in Poetry, he was obliged at his presentation to explain the five
Englyn Metres, and to sing them in such a manner, that one of the principal Bards
would declare upon his conscience that he was competent to be admitted. He then
became the pupil of some one of the principal Bards, whom he was obliged to
attend annually in Lent, and without whose approbation he could make no composition public, and during three years, that is, till the next Eisteddfod, remained
a non-graduate, and was called Disgybl Yspas cerdd dafawd, a probationary student of Poetry.

At the next Eisteddfod, three years having expired, Disgybl Yspas was exam-
ined for the degree of Disgybl Disgyblaidd, or Bachelor of the Art of Poetry, and
was required to be versed in the five Englyn metres, the four Cywydd metres, and
three Awdl metres; and to produce, in a scholar-like manner, compositions of his
own, free from the fifteen common errors.

After the same interval, the Bard took the degree of Disgybl Penceirddiaidd, or Master of the Art of Poetry, for which he was required to understand the rules of Grammar and Rhetoric, and analyse and explain the alliterative concatenations of the language; to escape all the errors; and to sing with harmony and in parts, twenty-one of the metres.

To the Pencerdd, or Doctor of Poetry, who obtained his degree at the end of the same period, belonged the whole mystery of the art. He knew to sing in parts and concord, and was well versed in transposed alliteration. Among his qualifications are enumerated, fertility in poetical subjects, a store of matter and invention, authority of decision, and a facility in composing in praise of the great, what would be heard or read with most delight, and longest retained in memory.

If a Disgybl or disciple of any degree was discovered in taverns or secret places playing for money at dice or any other game, any person was authorized to take from him whatever money was found in his purse. For mockery and derision, and the invention or propagation of falsehood, the Disgyblion were also punished with lines and imprisonment. For, says the laws, the Bards shall be easy and peaceful in their manners, friendly in their disposition, and humble in their services to the prince and his adherents.

Those Bards alone who had acquired the degree of Pencerdd were authorized to teach: nor were more than a single pupil allowed to each Pencerdd. The pupils were expressly enjoined to refrain from ridiculing their teachers for that absence and inattention which is natural to a contemplative mind. But the most valued privilege of the Penceirddiaid was their exclusive right to the chair of the Eisteddfod. All those among them who aspired to the honour of presiding over the Bards, came forward (as the statute prescribes) at the triennial assembly, and contested it with each other, and with the Chief Bard who already possessed it. The successful candidate was seated in a magnificent chair, and was hence called Bardd Cadeiriog, the Chair-Bard. He was at the same time invested with a little silver or gold chair, which he wore on his breast as the badge of his office. As his rank was high, his emoluments were considerable: they arose from the Disgyblion or students, when they laid aside the hair strung harp, and were admitted to the practice of their art; from brides on their nuptials; and the marriage-fine of the daughters of all the Bards within his jurisdiction; likewise his own daughter had a marriage portion from the prince.

Whoever desired to proceed to degrees in Music, was presented to the Eisteddfod by a musical Pencerdd, who vouched for his capacity. During his noviciate of three years, he was called Disgybl Yspâs heb râdd, a probationary student of Music without a degree: and if he learnt to play the harp, was only suffered to use that instrument strung with horse-hair, that he might not (as I conjecture) by his rude attempt at harmony, torment the ears of the principality, and might pursue his studies with greater diligence, incited by the hope of relinquishing it for one furnished with strings of a more audible and pleasing sound.

His next step was to the degree of Disgybl Yspâs graddol, a graduate probationary student of Music, for which he was obliged to know ten cwlwms, one colofn, five cwlwms of cydgerdd, one cadair, and eight caniads.

He then commenced Disgybl Disgyblaidd, or Bachelor of Music, but was previously required to be master of twenty cwlwms, two colofns, ten cwlwms of cydgerdd, two cadairs, sixteen caniads, and the twenty-four measures of Music: and to play them with facility and correctness.

He next became Disgybl Penceirddiaidd, or Master of Music, a degree which implied a preparatory knowledge of thirty cwlwms, three colofns, fifteen cwlwms of cydgerdd, three cadairs, twenty-four caniads, and four gostegs: and skill in defining them properly and distinctly.

Lastly he was admitted Pencerdd, or Doctor of Music, and was obliged to know forty cwlwms, four colofns, twenty cwlwms of cydgerdd, four cadairs, thirty-two caniads, and four gostegs: to understand all the laws and modifications of harmony, especially the twenty-four Measures of Music, and to explain them as they were written in the book of musical division:[66] to compose a caniad pronounced faultless by the proficient Bards, and to show all its properties, its divisions and subdivisions, its licences and rests, the natural notes, all the flats and sharps, and every change of movement through the several keys. If the Pencerdd was a Harper, he was required to know the three excellent Mwchwls, which were equal to the four colofns, and the three new Mwchwls which were equal to the four cadairs. All this he was obliged to know and perform in a masterly manner, so that professors should declare him competent to be an author and a teacher of his art.

The Eisteddfod was a rigid school. The poetical or musical disciple who, at the expiration of his triennial term could not obtain a higher degree, was condemned to lose that which he already possessed.

We know that before Gruffudd ap Cynan the musical Bards were subject to the chief Bard of the Poets. But I have reasons for thinking that in his reign, and afterwards, they had a chair and a president of their own. In Mr Pennant's *Tour in Wales*, page 434, there is an engraving of the silver Harp in possession of Sir Roger Mostyn, 'which has been from time immemorial in the gift of his ancestors, to bestow on the chief of the faculty. This badge of honour is about five or six inches long, and furnished with strings equal to the number of the muses'. It was probably worn by the Chief Musician, as the silver chair was by the chief Poet.

The revenues of the Bards arose from presents at princely and other nuptials, and from fees in their annual circuits at Christmas, Easter and Whitsuntide, and in their triennial clera, or grand circuit. Their fees and presents were regulated with proportion to their degrees: and the number of visitants to the condition of the person that received them. Likewise in order to encourage the clerwyr to keep up the language, and the memory of the exploits and pedigrees of the Britons, they were allowed a certain sum out of every plough-land, and in proportion out of every half plough-land of their district. A month before each festival, the pupils enquired of their teachers what routs they should take in their approaching circuit, lest too many should resort to the same part of the country. A Pencerdd was not licensed to visit the commonalty, unless he chose to accept a fee beneath his station and dignity: nor could any Bard of an inferior degree appear before the gentry and nobles. The Bards were not suffered to request presents beyond a certain value, under penalty of being deprived of their musical instruments and practice for three years: when this happened, the present illegally requested became forfeit to the prince.

The Eisteddfod was followed by the grand triennial Clera, which was not limited, as the circuits of the festivals, to commots and cantreds, but extended through all Wales. Such was the benevolence of the Welsh institutions, that Bards afflicted with blindness, or any such natural defect, were indulged with the privilege of Clera, as well as the four poetical, and the five musical graduates. At a wake or festival a circuiting Bard was not suffered, during its continuance, to depart from the house he first visited, without the consent of the master of the house, or invitation given him by another. If he rambled from house to house, or became intoxicated, he was deprived of his Clera fees, which were applied to the uses of the church. If he offered any indecency to mistress or maid, he was fined and imprisoned, and forfeited his Clera for seven years.

Every art has its subordinate professors. Besides the four classes of regular or graduated Bards I have recounted, there were four other classes of inferior and unlicensed Bards (if that name may be given them without profanation): these were Pipers, Players on the three-stringed Crwth, Taborers and Buffoons. Of the pipe, the three-string Crwth and the tabor, the reader will find some mention near the trophy of the musical instruments of the Welsh. The performers who used them were looked upon among Bards as Weeds among Flowers; they had no connexion with the Eisteddfod, and their estimation and their profits were equally inconsiderable. One of their number, the Datceiniad Pen Pastwn, was a minstrel who rehearsed only, and played no instrument: on occasions of festivity, he stood in the middle of the hall where the company was assembled, and beating time with his staff, sung a poem to the sound. When any of the regular Bards were present, he attended them as a servant, and did not presume to sing, unless they signified their assent.

The only connexion that existed between the higher and lower orders of the Bards, we discover in the appointment of Cyff Clêr at the marriage of a prince, or any person of princely extraction. A year and a day before the celebration of the nuptials, notice was given to a Pencerdd to prepare himself to support that character. When the time came, he appeared in the hall, and a facetious subject being proposed, the inferior Bards surrounded him, and attacked him with their ridicule. In this extempore satirical effusions they were restrained from any personal allusion or real affront. The Cyff Clêr sat in a chair in the midst of them, and silently suffered them to say whatever they chose, that could tend to the diversion of the assembly. For this unpleasing service he received a considerable fee. The next day he appeared again in the hall, and answered his revilers, and provoked the laughter and gained the applause of all who were present, by exposing them in their turn, retorting all their ridicule upon themselves.[67]

At Christmas, in the year 1176, Rhys, prince of South Wales, gave a magnificent entertainment with deeds of arms, and other shows in his new castle of Cardigan or Aberteisi, to a great number of illustrious natives and foreigners; notice of which has been given a year and a day before by proclamation through all Britain and Ireland. The musical Bards of North Wales and South Wales, who had been expressly invited to the festival and a poetical contest, were seated in chairs with much ceremony in the middle of the great hall of the castle. Animated with their usual emulation, the presence of their noble audience, and expectation of the rich rewards promised to the victors, they pursued to a great length their generous strife, which terminated with honour to both parties, the pre-eminence in Poetry being adjudged to the poetical Bards of North Wales; and in music to the domestic musical Bards of Prince Rhys. In thus regaling his guests with poetry and music, the Welsh prince (as Lord Lyttelton remarks in his history of Henry II) kept up the ancient custom of his country, and by the number and skill of the Poets and Musicians he assembled together, did undoubtedly much excel what Henry could exhibit in the same way to him, and to the other chiefs of Wales, when he entertained them in his royal castle of Oxford.[68]

At this feast the Bards were confirmed by the prince's authority in the franchises and privileges granted them by former statutes. They were also recompensed with fees, settled by prescription, and proportioned to the order of their profession, and the degree they had obtained in it.[69]

Though the age of Rhys was thus propitious to the Bards, we should have remained unacquainted with the nature of the poetry and music for which they were so highly valued, if they had not found in Giraldus Cambrensis,[70] an historian worthy of their fame. He was a native of the country, and travelled in it in search of information with such an industrious and philosophical spirit of learned curiosity, as very rarely occurs in those early times. The manner in which the subject of Welsh Music is treated in the following quotation from his Description of Wales, will sufficiently justify its length.

> By the sweetness of their musical instruments they soothe and delight the ear: they are rapid yet delicate in their modulation; and by the astonishing execution of their fingers, and their swift transitions from discord to concord, produce the most pleasing harmony. This cannot be better explained than by what I have said in my *Topography of Ireland* concerning the musical instruments of the three nations. It is remarkable that in all their haste of performance they never forget time and musical proportion; and such is their art, that with all their inflexion of tones, the variety of their instruments, and the intricacy of their harmony, they attain the perfection of consonance and melody, by a sweet velocity, an equable disparity, and a discordant concord. The strings strike together fourths or fifths: they always begin with B flat, and return to it, that the whole may be completed under the sweetness of a grand and pleasing sound. They enter into a movement, and conclude it in so delicate a manner, and play the little notes so sportively under the blunter sound of the base strings, enlivening with wanton levity, or communicating a deeper internal sensation of pleasure, that the perfection of their art appears in the concealment of it. For

> > Art profits when conceal'd,
> > Disgraces when reveal'd.

Here I cannot refrain from interrupting this curious narrative of Giraldus, for the purpose of introducing from one of Philips' pastorals, some lines which are beautifully descriptive of those effects which the harp is peculiarly capable of producing, and for which it is universally admired.

> Now lightly skimming o'er the strings they pass,
> Like wings that gently brush the plying grass,

And melting airs arise at their command;
And now, laborious, with a weighty hand,
They sink into the chords with solemn pace,
And give the swelling tones a manly grace.

From this cause, those very strains which afford deep and unspeakable
mental delight to those who have looked far, and skilfully penetrated
into the mysteries of the art, fatigue rather than gratify the ears of others,
who, though they see, do not perceive, and, though they hear, do not
understand. By such the finest Music is esteemed no better than a confused
and disorderly noise, and will be heard with unwillingness and disgust.
The Welsh have three kinds of musical instruments, the Harp, the Crwth,
and Pipes.[71]
... They do not sing in unison, like the inhabitants of other countries:
but in many different parts. So that in a company of singers, which one
frequently meets with in Wales, as many different parts and voices are
heard, as there are performers: who all at length unite, with organic
melody, in one consonance, and the soft sweetness of B flat.

In the northern parts of Britain, beyond the Humber, and on the
borders of Yorkshire, the inhabitants use in singing the same kind of
symphonious harmony: but with less variety, singing only in two parts, one
murmuring in the base, the other warbling in the acute or treble. Neither
of the two nations has acquired this peculiar property by art, but by long
habit, which has rendered it familiar and natural: and the practice is now
so firmly rooted in them, that it is unusual to hear a simple and single
melody well sung. And, which is still more wonderful, their children, from
their infancy, sing in the same manner.[72]

After the account that has been given of the musical constitutions of the Welsh,
the testimony of Giraldus was not wanted to prove that they highly esteemed
and cultivated music, and that harmony must have existed among them in considerable perfection. But from the passages I have quoted concerning their art,
we may collect from the fairest presumption of certainty, that they possessed an
improvement of it, the first invention of which has always been attributed to
Guido.[73] They either were acquainted with counterpoint, and the method of
singing in parts, or Giraldus himself must have invented it, and given them the
merit of his discovery. I cannot, without feeling a repugnance, contradict the
opinion of so diligent an historian, and so ingenious a critic as Dr Burney:[74] but
I am persuaded, that if he had previously enquired into the musical studies of
the Bards, and their public establishment, in the preceding centuries, he would
not have suffered his unfavourable opinion of Giraldus' veracity to prevail
against the strong light of his evidence. If that the Bards understood counterpoint requires farther proof, it is to be found in the *Four and Twenty ancient
games of the Welsh;*[75] of which canu cywydd pedwar, singing an ode or song of
four parts is among the number: and in the MS. to which I have referred in page
12, which contains several Welsh tunes in full harmony that may be ascribed
with certainty to so early a date as the eleventh century, and some to remoter
periods.

Even at this day, our untaught native harpers, who are totally unacquainted with modern music, retain something of that skill for which the Bards were famous. For, like their great predecessors; from whom they have received their tunes by tradition, they perform, however rudely, in concert; they accompany the voice with harpegios, they delight in variations, and without deviation from their subject, indulge the sportive excursions of musical fancy:

Quales fuêre, cum tales sint reliquiae![73]

The Poetry, as well as the Music, of the Bards, has received much illustration from the pen of Giraldus: and of its adherence to truth, and its use in recording events to posterity, he has transmitted to us a memorable example. In his time the veracity of the Welsh Muse was made known by an extraordinary discovery to the world. Henry II was led to the churchyard of Glastonbury in search of the body of Arthur by some lines of Taliesin (describing the manner of his death, and the place of his interment) that had been repeated in his presence by a Welsh Bard (if I may borrow from Drayton, one of his beautiful apostrophes):

To Pembroke call'd before the English king,
And to thy powerful harp commanded there to sing,
Of famous Arthur told'st, and where he was interr'd,
In which those wreckless times had long and blindly err'd,
And ignorance had brought the world to such a pass
As now, which scarce believes that Arthur ever was:
But when king Henry sent th' reported place to view,
He found that man of men: and what thou saidst was true.
                    *Polyolbion, The Sixth Song*[77]

This is not fiction. The success of the investigation was not ungrateful to the monarch's poetic faith: and Henry had the satisfaction to view the stupendous remains, and to count the glorious wounds, of the last of Britons.[78]

To these incidents Mr Warton (with his usual skill and ingenuity) has given a new and poetical form in an ode called the 'Grave of Arthur', which possesses so many beauties as to perplex my choice, and deter me from a selection.

Of the use of our poetry in preserving the memory of events, and of the aid it has lent to history, the same period produced a similar example. Of the celebrated Madog ab Owain Gwynedd, and of his discovery of America,[79] we know nothing but what we gather from the poems of Cynfrig ab Gronw, and Meredydd ap Rhys, and the more express declaration of that learned herald and bard, Guttun Owain:[80] who all preceded the expedition of Columbus, and relate or allude to the expedition of Madog as an event well known and universally received, that had happened three hundred years before.

If Geoffrey of Monmouth, when he translated 'Tyssilio', had known the works of Taliesin and Llywarch Hên, he might have found in them abundance of historical passages that would have served better to enlarge and embellish that venerable and authentic history, than those legendary tales and incredible fictions he has adopted.

. . . Juvat integros accedere fontes.[81]

But lest the purity of these genuine sources yet unexplored should be doubted, let it be remembered that the desendants of the Celts could never be brought to think with the Greeks and Romans on the subject of heroic Poetry, which was held in such reverence by that primitive nation and its posterity, that fable and invention (the essence of the classical epopee) were never suffered to make any part of it. From this cause neither the Britons, the Irish, the Erse, the Cornish, nor the Armoricans, have ever to this day produced a poem similar in its structure to the 'Iliad' or 'Aeneid'; though most other nations have shown an inglorious pride in imitating them. What in one country is called an heroic poem, and the grandest performance of human art, is despised in another as a fabulous empty song, calculated to please a vain and boastful people, who have no actions of their own virtue and courage to be recorded, but are constrained to have recourse to fictitious gods, fictitious heroes, fictitious battles and such anachronisms as a grave British writer would have blushed to own. Historians who are acquainted only with the compositions of this character, may well regard Poetry with the contempt they have usually testified, as a vain art, that draws its materials more from fancy than nature, and delights in fiction rather than truth. But widely different is the Poetry of the British Bards, which has ever been from the first of times the sacred repository of the actions of great men.

The period which interfered between the reign of Gruffudd ap Cynan, and that of the last prince, Llewelyn, is the brightest in our annals. It abounds with perhaps the noblest monuments of genius as well as valour of which the Welsh nation can boast. It will be sufficient for me to mention a few illustrious names, who with veneration derived from their great predecessors, the Arts, Poetry and Music, and transmitted them with augmented honours to their posterity. I wish the limits of this essay would suffer me to give more than their names; or that my learned countrymen would show some of that enterprising spirit for which their ancestors are famed, and publish their remains to the world. The poems of Meilir, the Bard of Gruffudd ap Cynan; Cynddelw Brydydd Mawr; Owen Gyfeiliog, prince of Powys; Gwalchmai ap Meilir; Gwrgant ap Rhys; Llywarch, the Bard of Llewelyn the Great; Einion ap Gwalchmai; and Gruffudd ap yr Ynad Côch;[82] are now extant, and ascribed with certainty to their authors. But the harmonies of Albon ap Cynan, Rhydderch Foel, Cynwrig Bencerdd, Cybelyn[83] and Cadwgan, that oblivion has shared, are thinly scattered in our MSS. while the memory of their composers is only preserved by some slight mention in the pages of succeeding poets. 'Since Writing and practical Music have become separate professions, the celebrity of the poor Musician has died with the vibration of his strings. The voice of acclamation, and thunder of applause, pass away like vapours; and those hands that were most active in testifying temporary approbation, suffer the same of those who charmed away their cares and sorrows in the glowing hour of innocent delight, to remain unrecorded.'[84] Some of the musical productions of this period are to be found in the present collection ; and some far more ancient. I decline the task of pointing them out by any decisive opinion, because the original titles are lost, and they are now known by other names, substituted by later Bards in compliment to later patrons. This remark is minute, but necessary; for without it, the age of some of the best remains of Welsh Music might inadvertently be mistaken.

Early in the twelfth century, Harmony and Verse had approached their utmost degree of perfection in Wales. Nor, by the common fate of the Arts in other countries, did they suddenly fall from the eminence they had attained. If in the progress of the succeeding age they showed any symptoms of decay, remedy was so diligently applied by the skill of the Eisteddfod to the declining part, that they preserved their former vigour, and perhaps acquired new graces. And had not the fatal accident which overwhelmed, in the hour of its prosperity, the hereditary princedom of Wales, involved in the same ruin its Poetry and Music, our country might have retained to this day its ancient government, and its native arts, in the bosom of those mountains which protected them for ages. The Poets of these memorable times added energy to a nervous language, and the Musicians called forth from the harp its loudest and grandest tones, to re-animate the ancient struggle of their brave countrymen for freedom and the possession of their parent soil. What was the success of their virtuous and noble purpose, the history of the eras when they flourished, can best explain. It is no slight proof of their influence, that when the brave but unfortunate prince Llewelyn the last, after the surrender of his rights, and the sacrifice of his patriotism to his love,[85] was treacherously slain at Buellt, Edward I did not think himself secure in his triumph, till he added cruelty to injustice, and gave the final blow to Welsh liberty in the massacre of the Bards.[86] In this execrable deed Edward imitated the policy of Philip of Macedon, who demanded from the Athenians as a condition of amity the surrender of their orators. The massacre was general, and as some of our most eminent Bards must have perished, it is probable that many of their works, and of the remains of their predecessors, were also destroyed, and are for ever lost. This lamentable event has given birth to one of the noblest Lyric compositions in the English language: a poem of such fire and beauty as to remove, as a late writer has thought,[87] our regret of the occasion, and to compensate for the loss. But in heightening our regret consists the great merit of this admirable ode: and without bestowing on it any such extravagant praise, I may boldly affirm that the 'Polyolbion of Drayton',[88] and the Bard of Gray, have contributed no less to the reputation of their authors than to the glory of Wales, and are the only modern productions worthy to alleviate the loss we sustained, in so immense a waste of literary treasures, and such irreparable ruin of genius.

After the dissolution of the princely government in Wales, such was the tyranny exercised by the English over the conquered nation, that the Bards who were born 'since Cambria's fatal day', might be said to rise under the influence of a baleful and malignant star. They were reduced to possess their sacred art in obscurity and sorrow, and constrained to suppress the indignation that would burst forth in the most animated strains against their ungenerous and cruel oppressors. Yet they were not silent or inactive. That their poetry might breathe with impunity the spirit of their patriotism, they became dark, prophetic and oracular. As the Monks of the Welsh church, in their controversy with Rome, had written, to countenance their doctrines, several religious poems which they feigned to be the work of Taliesin: the Bards now ascribed many of their political writings to the same venerable author, and produced many others as the prophecies of the elder Merlin. Hence much uncertainty prevails concerning the genuine remains of the sixth century, great part of which has descended to us mutilated and depraved: and hence that mysterious air which pervades all the Poetry of the later periods I am now describing. The forgery of those poems, which are entirely spurious, though they may have past unquestioned even by such critics as Dr Davies and Dr J.D. Rhys, may, I think, be presently detected. They were written to serve a popular and a temporary purpose, and were not contrived with such sagacity and care as to hide from the eye of a judicious and enlightened scholar their historical mistakes, their novelty of language, and their other marks of imposture.

While the Bards were thus cramped in their poetical department, they had greater scope and leisure for the study of heraldry, and their other domestic duties. Every great man had under his roof and patronage some eminent Bard, who, at his death, composed on the subject of his descent, his dignities and the actions of his life, a funeral poem, which was solemnly recited by a Datceiniad in the presence of his surviving relations.[89] Hence it has happened that pedigrees are so well preserved in Wales.

By the insurrection, however, in the reign of Henry IV the martial spirit of the *Awen* or Welsh Muse was revived, to celebrate the heroic enterprises of the brave Glyndwr.[90] Like him the Bards of his time were 'irregular and wild': and as the taper glimmering in its socket gives a sudden blaze before it is extinguished, so did they make one bright effort of their original and daring genius, which was then lost and buried for ever with their hero in the grave. Yet though Poetry flourished, Learning suffered: for such was the undistinguishing fury of that celebrated partisan, and his enemies, against the monasteries that withstood them, that not only their cells, but also their libraries and MSS. were destroyed.[91]

The following 'Ode to Glyndwr', by his favourite Bard Gruffudd Llwyd, happily transfused into English verse by Mr Williams of Vron,[92] claims a distinguished place in this history, for the genius of the author, and the skill of the translator.

### Ode:
### The Praise of Owain Glyndwr[93]

Cambria's princely eagle, hail!
    Of Gruffudd Vychan's noble blood!
Thy high renown shall never fail,
    Owain Glyndwr, great and good!
Lord of Dwrdwy's fertile vale,
Warlike, high-born Owain, hail!
Dwrdwy, whose wide-spreading streams,
Reflecting Cynthia's midnight beams,
    Whilom led me to thy bower;
    Alas! in an unguarded hour!
For high in blood, with British beverage hot,
My awful distance I forgot;
    But soon my generous chief forgave
    The rude presumption of his slave.

But leave me not, illustrious lord!
Thy peaceful bow'r, and hospitable board,
 Are ill exchang'd for scenes of war,
 Tho' Henry calls thee from afar.
My prayers my tears were vain;
He flew like lightning to the hostile plain.
 While with remorse, regret, and woe,
 I saw the god-like hero go;
 I saw, with aching heart,
 The golden beam depart.
His glorious image in my mind,
Was all that Owain left behind.
 Wild with despair, and woe-begone,
 Thy faithful Bard is left alone,
 To sigh, to weep, to groan!

Thy sweet remembrance, ever dear,
Thy name, still usher'd by a tear,
 My inward anguish speak;
How could'st thou, cruel Owain, go,
And leave the bitter streams to flow
 Down Gruffudd's furrow'd cheek?
I heard (who has not heard thy fame?)
With extasy I heard thy name,
Loud echo'd by the trump of war,
Which spoke thee brave, and void of fear;
 Yet of a gentle heart possess'd,
 That bled within thy generous breast,
 Wide o'er the sanguine plain to see
 The havock of hostility.

Still with good omens may'st thou fight,
And do thy injur'd country right!
Like great Pendragon[94] shalt thou soar,
Who bade the din of battle roar,
What time his vengeful steel he drew
His brother's grandeur to renew,
 And vindicate his wrongs;
His gallant actions still are told
By youthful Bards, by Druids old,
 And grateful Cambria's songs.

On sea, on land, thou still didst brave
The dangerous cliff and rapid wave;
Like Urien, who subdu'd the knight,
And the fell dragon put to flight,
 Yon moss-grown fount, beside;
The grim, black warrior of the flood,
The Dragon, gorg'd with human blood,

212

The waters' scaly pride,
Before his sword the mighty fled:
But now he's number'd with the dead.
Oh! may his great example fire
My noble patron to aspire
To deeds like his! impetuous fly,
And bid the Saxon squadrons die:
So shall thy laurel'd bard rehearse
Thy praise in never dying verse;
Shall sing the prowess of thy sword,
Beloved and victorious Lord.

In future times thy honour'd name
Shall emulate brave Urien's same!
Surrounded by the numerous foe,
Well didst thou deal th' unequal blow,
  How terrible thy ashen spear,
   Which shook the bravest heart with fear.
    Yon hostile towers beneath!
More horrid than the lightning's glance,
Flash'd the red meteors from thy lance,
  The harbinger of death.
Dire, and more dire, the conflict grew;
Thousands before thy presence flew;
While borne in thy triumphal car,
Majestic as the god of war,
Midst charging hosts unmoved you stood,
Or waded thro' a sea of blood.

Immortal fame shall be thy meed
Due to every glorious deed;
Which latest annals shall record,
Beloved and victorious Lord!
Grace, Wisdom, Valour, all are thine,
Owain Glyndwrdwy divine!
Meet emblem of a two-edg'd sword,
Dreaded in war, in peace ador'd!
Steer thy swift Ships to Albion's coast
Pregnant with thy martial host.
  Thy robes are white as driven snow,
  And Virtue smiles upon thy brow:
But terrible in war thou art,
And swift and certain is the dart,
Thou hurlest at a Saxon's heart.

Loud fame has told thy gallant deeds;
In every word a Saxon bleeds.
Terror, and flight, together came,
Obedient to thy mighty name:

Death, in the van, with ample stride,
Hew'd thee a passage deep and wide.
Stubborn as steel, thy nervous chest
With more than mortal strength possess'd:
    And every excellence belongs
    To the bright subject of our songs.

Strike then your harps, ye Cambrian Bards;
The song of triumph best rewards
An hero's toils. Let Henry weep
His warriors wrapt in everlasting sleep:
    Success and victory are thine,
    Owain Glyndwrdwy divine!
Dominion, honour, pleasure, praise,
Attend upon thy vigorous days!
And, when thy evening sun is set,
May grateful Cambria ne'er forget
Thy noon-tide blaze; but on thy tomb
Never-fading laurels bloom!

Though heroic Poetry was afterwards no more attempted in Wales; a long series of Bards succeeded, who by their elegies and odes have made their names memorable to ages. Among these Dafydd ap Gwilym,[95] the Welsh Ovid, possesses a deserved pre-eminence. He often adds the sublime to the beautiful; of which his 'Cywydd y Daran',[96] or 'Ode of the Thunder', is a noble proof. It is the picture of a well-chosen scene admirably varied: it opens with placid ideas and rural images; a lovely maiden and a delightful prospect: then succeeds a sudden and tremendous change of the elements; the beauties of nature overshadowed and concealed; the terror of animals and the shrieks of the fair one. A thousand instances of similar excellence might be produced from the writings of this elegant Bard, and his contemporaries. Let those who complain that by the present scarcity of works of genius they are reduced to bestow on Horace, Pindar and Gray, a tenth perusal, explore the buried treasures of Welsh Poetry, and their search will be rewarded with new sources of pleasure, and new beauties of language and fancy.

The accession of a Tudor to the throne was the happy era destined to recall the exiled arts of Wales, and Henry VII, was reserved to be the patron and restorer of the Cambro-British Muses. If during the former inauspicious reigns the Eisteddfods had been discontinued, they were now re-established; and the Bards were employed in the honourable commission of making out from their authentic records the pedigree of their king.[97] Henry VIII the stern and cruel son of a mild father, did not, however, refuse to the Bards his smiles and favour.[98] I insert, as an instance, the following summons to an Eisteddfod by his authority.

'Be it known to all persons, both gentry and commonality, that an Eisteddfod of the professors of Poetry and Music will be held in the town of Caerwys, in the county of Flint, the 2nd day of July, 1523, and the 15th year of the reign of Henry the VIIIth, king of England, under the commission of the said king, before Richard ap Howel ap Ivan Vaughan, Esq. by the consent of Sir William Griffith, and Sir Roger Salsbri, and the advice of Griffith ap Ivan ap Llywelyn Vaughan, and the

Chair-Bard, Tudor Aled, and several other gentlemen and scholars, for the purpose of instituting order and government among the professors of Poetry and Music, and regulating their art and profession.'[99]

After a long interval of anarchy among the Bards, commissioners were appointed by Queen Elizabeth to assemble another Eisteddfod at Caerwys in 1568.[100] They were instructed to advance the ingenious and skilful to the accustomed degrees, and restore to the graduates their ancient exclusive privilege of exercising their profession. 'The rest not worthy' were by this commission commanded to betake themselves to some honest labour and livelihood, on pain of being apprehended and punished as vagabonds.[101]

About the end of Queen Elizabeth's reign, flourished Twm Bach (or Thomas Pritchard) who was the Orpheus on the Harp at that time. He was born at Coity in Wales; died (anno 1597) in London, and was buried in St Sepulchre's Church. That Poetry sympathized with the sister Art for the loss, we may be convinced by the following bipartite Englyn, written upon his death, the two first lines by Hugh Griffith, the sequel by Rhys Cain.

Ah, see! our last, best lyrist goes:
Sweet as his strain be his repose!
Extinct are all the tuneful fires,
And Music with Twm Bach expires:
No singer now remains to bring
The tone of rapture from the string.

In the reign of George II, Powel, a Welsh Harper, who used to play before that Monarch, drew such tones from his instrument, that the great Handel was delighted with his performance, and composed for him several pieces of Music, some of which are in the first set of Handel's Concertos. He also introduced him as a performer in his Oratorios, in which there are some songs *Harp Obligato*, that were accompanied by Powel: such as, 'Tune your Harps' and 'Praise the Lord with cheerful voice' in *Esther*, and 'Hark! he strikes the golden lyre' in *Alexander Balus*.

Having now conducted nearly to our own times the short history I intended; I make a little pause, before I bring it to its conclusion; and examine somewhat more minutely the causes that conferred such peculiarity and excellence on the Poetry and Music of Wales. The laws, manners, and fortunes of nations have a principal influence in giving an original character to national arts. The first care of the Welsh laws was the freedom of the people. They were free, and their manners accordingly were at once generous and impetuous; gentle, hospitable and social among their friends, and full of resentment and revenge against their enemies. They inhabited a country where they found in the works of nature what they afterwards copied into their own, the beautiful and the sublime. They were equally addicted to love and war: when they forsook the camp, they did not return to agriculture, commerce or the mechanic arts, but past their leisure in hunting and other manly sports and games, in converse with the fair, and in recounting their exploits amidst libations of mead at the tables of lords and princes. Hence they learnt to write verse and found the harp.

Another cause, which operated with equal power on our poetry, was the strength and beauty of the language in which it was conveyed: if it may not with greater truth be said, that by the Poetry those inherent properties of the language were called forth. The character of Welsh Poetry, and its dependence on the language, have been so well displayed in a dissertation on the subject by the Reverend Mr Walters,[102] that I am unwilling to make use of his sentiments in any other words than his own.

The Welsh language, he observes, is possessed of native ornaments, and unborrowed treasures. It rivals the celebrated Greek in its aptitude to form the most beautiful derivatives, as well as in the elegance, facility, and expressiveness of an infinite variety of compounds, and deserves the praise which has been given it by an enemy,[103] that notwithstanding the multiplicity of gutturals and consonants with which it abounds, it has the softness and harmony of the Italian, with the majesty and expression of the Greek.

> Of all the tissues ever wrought
> >    On the Parnassian hill,
> Fair Cambria's web, in art and thought,
> >    Displays the greatest skill.

The glory of a language is a copious rotundity, a vigorous tone, and a perspicuous and expressive brevity; of which a thousand happy instances might be produced from the Cambro-British MSS. Their compass reaches from the sublimity of the ode to the conciseness of the epigram. Whoever explores these ancient and genuine treasures, will find in them the most melodious numbers, the most poetical diction, the most nervous expression, and the most elevated sentiments, to be met with in any language.

A language, however fortunate in its original construction, can never attain such perfection without a very high degree of cultivation.[104] It is evident therefore that at some remote period the Welsh themselves were highly cultivated, and had made great progress in learning, arts and manners; since we discover such elegance, contrivance and philosophy in their language. Some authors have attributed this refinement of the Cambro-British dialect to the Druids. From this opinion I dissent: because I observe that Taliesin and his contemporaries, by whom they were followed and imitated, do not afford such specimens of polished numbers and diction as the Bards who lived under the later princes have exhibited. The Eisteddfod was the school in which the Welsh language was gradually improved, and brought at last to its unrivalled perfection. 'The Bards,' says the ingenious critic I have before quoted, 'have been always considered by the Welsh as the guardians of their language, and the conservators of its purity.'

The metre of Welsh poetry is very artificial and alliterative; possessing such peculiar ingenuity in the selection and arrangement of words, as to produce a rhythmical concatenation of sounds in every verse. To an English reader it may seem a laborious way of trifling: but every language has peculiar laws of harmony.

The ancient languages of Greece and Rome were not clogged with a superabundance of consonants, and were chiefly composed of polysyllabic words and vocal terminations. Their poets therefore made their metre consist in quantity, or the artful distribution of long and short syllables. The old British language abounded with consonants, and was formed of monosyllables, which are incompatible with quantity; and the Bards could reduce it to concord by no other means, than by placing at such intervals its harsher consonants, so intermixing them with vowels, and so adapting, repeating, and dividing the several sounds, as to produce an agreeable effect from their structure. Hence the laws of poetical composition in this language are so strict and rigorous, that they must greatly cramp the genius of the Bard, but that there is, in the language itself, a particular aptitude for that kind of alliterative melody, and is as essential as Harmony in Music, which constitutes the great beauty of its poetry. To the ears of natives the Welsh metre is extremely pleasing, and does not subject the Bard to more restraint than the different sorts of feet occasioned to the Greek and Roman Poets.[105] There are traces of Cynghanedd or alliteration in the poetical remains of the Druids. It was known to the Bards of the sixth century, but they used it sparingly, and were not circumscribed by rules. From the Norman Conquest to the death of Llywelyn the last, they were more strict. From Llywelyn to Elizabeth the laws of alliteration were prescribed and observed with the most scrupulous exactness. A line not perfectly alliterative was condemned as much by the Welsh grammarians, as a false quantity by the Greeks and Romans.[106]

The Bards, like other poets, were ostentatious of their wealth: for they had no sooner learnt the extent of their power, than they began to wander at will through all the mazes of Cynghanedd.

They gave other relative proofs of an unrivalled prosody. Not content with the mellifluence of this couplet, written on a harp.

> Within the concave of its womb is found
> The magic scale of soul-enchanting sound.[107]

They sought after more liquid measures, and produced such specimens as the following 'Englyn i'r Pryf Coppyn', or 'Epigram on the Spider', composed entirely of vowels.

> O'i wiw wy i weu ê â, – – a'i weuau
> O'i wyau y weua;
> E' weua ei we aia,
> A'i, weuau yw ieuau Jâ.[108]

In grandeur the following distich on 'Thunder' could not be surpassed:

> Tân a dwr yn ymŵriaw
> Yw'r taranau dreigiau draw.[109]

But it is exceeded in difficulty by the subsequent Englyn, composed of vowels and the consonant r:

Oer yw'r eira ar Eryri – – o ryw,
Ar awyr i rewi,
Oer yw'r i, ar riw'r Ri,
Ar eira oer yw 'Ryri.[110]

Such specimens deserve not to be read with ridicule or disgust: they were not designed to display the skill of the poet, but the powers of the language.

Something now remains to be said of Welsh Music. Though the supernatural power and effects, fabulously ascribed to the Music of antiquity, are now held in just derision; it is not difficult to conceive that (notwithstanding its known simplicity) by its association with poetry, which it rendered more articulate and expressive, it might operate with much greater success on the mind and affections, than the artificial melody and complicated harmony of modern times. The music, as well as the poetry, of Wales, was tinctured with its peculiar and original character by the genius of the country: they sprung out of the same soil, deriving from its delightful vallies their soft and tender measures, and from its wild mountainous scenes their bolder and more animated tones.[111]

And where could the Muses have chosen a happier residence? Now you are delighted with vallies at once wild and beautiful: in other parts, you are astonished with a continued tract of dreary cloud-capt country, 'hills whose heads touch heaven' – dark, tremendous precipices – swift rivers roaring over disjointed rocks – black caverns, and issuing cataracts. Did Salvata Rose's extravagant fancy ever indulge itself in such grand and savage prospects? Or has Claude Lorraine's inimitable pencil excelled the vale of Clwyd?

It is not to be wondered that the venerable Cambro songs possessed such influence on the minds of our ancestors, when we consider their beautiful and various change of style and time; transitions abrupt as the rocky prospects of the country, and sudden as the passions of the people.

The most ancient style of Welsh Music is the grave and solemn, which was consecrated to religious purposes and occasions.[112] The next, distinct from the former, is vehemently martial and magnificent.[113] Another is plaintive and expressive of sorrow, being appropriated to elegies and the celebration of the dead.[114] Another is of the pastoral kind, and of all perhaps the most agreeable; coming nearest to nature, and possessing a pleasing simplicity and soothing tranquility, suitable to genial love.[115]

Of these ancient melodies I have recovered some genuine remains; and their effects are not wholly lost or forgotten. A new era of Cambro-British harmony has risen in our times, and the wonderful things related of it in former ages have been already realized.

The trembling strings about her fingers crowd,
And tell their joy for every kiss aloud
Small force there needs to make them tremble so;
Touch'd by that hand, who would not tremble too?
*Waller*

The harp, in the hands of the British fair [sex],[116] has acquired new honours and a more irresistible influence; and never produced such transport and enthusiasm when struck by a Cyhelyn, or a Cadwgan, as it now excites, assisted by the liquid voice and distinguished beauty of our modern female Bards.

## Notes

1   About the year 383, a hundred thousand Britons, besides a numerous army of soldiers, followed the Emperor Maximus to Armorica, now Bretagne, in France, which he conquered, and placed Conan Meriadoc, a British lord and general, on the throne. See Jeffrey of Monmouth, book the 5th, chs. 11, 13, 14. Also *Drych y Prif Oefoedd* by Theophilus Evans. Likewise Wynn's *History of Wales*, page 8. And further particulars in Owen's *History of the Ancient Britons*, page 100, vol. I.

2   The Welsh nobles, who were captives in the Tower of London (formerly called the White Tower, and part of it now known by that name), obtained permission that the contents of their libraries should be sent them from Wales, to amuse them in their solitude and confinement. This was a frequent practice, so that in process of time the Tower became the principal repository of Welsh literature. Unfortunately for our history and poetry, all the MSS. thus collected were burnt by the villainy of one Scolan, of whom nothing more is known. Gutte'r Glyn, an eminent Bard of the fifteenth century, has in one of his poems the following passage:

> Llyfrau Cymru au llofrudd
> I'r Tŵr Gwyn aethant ar gudd
> Ysceler oedd Yscolam
> Fwrw'r twrr lyfrau i'r tan.

The books of Cymru, and their villainous destroyer,
Were concealed in the White Tower.
Cursed was the deed of Scolan,
Who committed them in a pile to the flames.

Also during the insurrections of Owen Glyndwr, the MSS. then extant of the ancient British learning and poetry were so scattered and destroyed, 'that there escaped not one (as William Salisbury relates) that was not incurably maimed, and irrecuperably torn and mangled'. See Evans' *Specimens*, page 160.

3   'The university of Bangor-ts-Coed, founded by Lucius king of Britain, was remarkable for its valuable library. It continued 350 years, and produced many learned men. Congellus, a holy man, who died A.D. 530, changed the university into a monastery, containing 2,100 Monks. At the instigation of Austin, the Monk, Ethelfred, king of Northumberland, massacred twelve hundred of the British clergy of this monastery: nine hundred, who escaped, were afterwards slain by pirates. This happened in the year 603. See Humphrey Lloyd's *Brittanica Descriptionis Commentariolum.* Lewis' *History of Great Britain.* Folio. London. 1729, b. 5, ch. I. And Rowland's *Mona Antiqua*; 2nd edition, page 151, &c.

4   See Guthrie's *Historical Grammar*, and the sequel of this history.

5   Lewis' *History*, b. 2, ch. 6.

6   'Ac yn ol Seisill y daeth Blegywryd yn frenhim, ac ni bu erioed Gantor cystal ag ef o Gelfyddyd Music na chwarydd cystal ag ef o hudol ac am hynny y gelwid ef Duw y Gwareu, A bwn a wladychawdd ar Ynys Prydein 28 nlynedd, ag yna a bu farw: fef oedd bunny wedi diliqw 2069 o flynyddoedd.' Tyffilio's *British History*, MS. Fabyan also, speaking of Blegored, names him 'a conynge musicyan, called of the Britons God of Gleemen'. Chron. f. 32, ed. 1533. See also Lewis' *History*, b. 3, ch. 35.

7   *Mona Antiqua*, 2nd edition, page 65, &c. Owen's *History of the Ancient Britons*, 8vo. London, 1743, vol. I. Introduction, page 16. And the 4th book of the *Geography of Strabo*, who lived under Augustus and Tiberius.

8   *Mona Antiqua*, pages 236, 239.

9   *De Bello Gallico*, lib. vi.

10    Thrice happy they beneath their northern skies
   Who that worst fear, the fear of death, despise;
   Hence they no cares from this frail being feel,
   But rush undaunted on the pointed steel,
   Provoke approaching fate, and bravely scorn
   To spare that life which must so soon return.
   *Rowe's* Lucan, *b. i*

11    Tacitus de Moribus Germanorum.

12    Retreated in silent valley, sing
   With notes angelical to many a harp,
   Their own heroic deeds, and haplets fall
   By doom of battle.
   *Milton*

13    H. Steph. edit. 1559, page 213.
   Bardi fortia virorum illustrium facta heroicis composita versibus cum dulcibus lyroe modulis cantitarunt. Ammian. Marcellin. 1. xv. Ammianus Marcellinus about the year 380.

14    Diodorus Siculus de Gest. Fabulos. Antiq 1. vi. See also the notes on the sixth song of Drayton's 'Polyolbion'.

15    See the Rev. Mr Evans' 'Specimens of Welsh Poetry', in *Dissert, de Bardis*; pages 65, 66.

16    *Caesar de Bello Gallico*, l. vi.

17    See *Mona Antiqua*, page 253, and Llwyd's *Archaeologia*, pages 251 and 221.

18    Cyfrinach, Arcanum.

19    Dyn fiaradus, Homo Garulus.

20    Melior vigilantia fomno.

21    Homo nequam litis occasione non carebit.

22    Seni baculus, tertius pes esto.

23    Rowe's *Lucan*, b. i.

24    Suetonii Vitae. Lucan Pharsalia.

25    An account of the British or Cambrian Music, by Mr Lewis Morris.

26    'Ad Viscum Druidae, Druidae cantare solebant'. Ovid. See *Mona Antiqua*.

27    Milton's *Paradise Lost*.

28    Evan's *Dissert, de Bardis*; pages 68, 69.

29    Taliesin, in his poem called 'Anrheg Urien', has the two following lines:
   *A wn ni enw Aneurin Gwawdrydd awenydd,*
   *A minnau Daliesin o lan Llyn Geirionydd.*
   I know the fame of the inspired genius Aneurin Gwawdrydd,
   And I am Taliesin, whose abode is by the Lake of Geirionydd.

30    See this poem published and translated in Evans' *Specimens*.

31    This is the last of the ten great battles of Urien Reged, celebrated by Taliesin in poems now extant. See Carte's *History of England*, pages 211 and 213. There is much valuable information relating to the Ancient Britons in the above history.

32    A part of Cumbria, the country of prince Llywarch Hên, from whence he was drove by the Saxons.

33    Some place on the borders of Northumberland.

34    Owen ap Urien acted as his father's general.

35    Cenau led to the assistance of Urien Reged the forces of his father Coel Godhebog, king of a northern tract, called Goadeu, probably inhabited by the Godini of Ptolemy. Owen ap Urien and Cenau ap Coel were in the number of Arthur's Knights. See Lewis' *History of Britain*, page 201.

36    *Hybarch iw mâb y marchog,*
   *(Yn aur) yn arian golerog Torchog.*

37    Now Dôl Giog near Machynlleth in Montgomeryshire. There Llywarch died, near the age of 150, about the year 634; and was buried at Llanfor near Bala in Merionethshire, where, in the west window of the church, is a stone with an inscription.

38    Those who shall be incited to a farther acquaintance with the beauties of Lywarch Hên, will shortly have access to them in an edition of all his extant works, with a literal version and notes, lately announced to the public by the Rev. Mr J. Walters of Jesus College,

Oxford; to whom I am much indebted for adding some notes to this preface.

39 Myrddin Emrys, or Merlin Ambrose, the prophet and reputed magician, born at Caermarthen, was the son of a Welsh Nun, daughter of a king of Denictia. His father was unknown. He was made king of West Wales by Vortigern, who then reigned in Britain. His prophesies, which were written in prose, were translated into Latin, and published by Geoffrey of Monmouth.

40 *Dissertatio de Bardis*, page 77. Lewis' *History of Britain*, page 206.

41 Awr o'i gôf gan Dduw ry gai
   Awr ymhell yr ambwyllai.
        S. Deifi, i, *Fyrddin*. MS.

42 Sir William Glynn, in *Cywydd y Ddraig Gôch*. MS.

43 The reader may see these reflections better expressed by M. Mallet, in his *Introduction à l'Histoire de Dannemare*.

44 *Cambro-Britannica Cymraeca Lingua Institutions* by Dr John David Rhys, page 303. Also *Grammadeg Cymraeg*. by John Rhyddreb. 12mo printed at Shrewsbury, 1728, page 134.

45 Mr Lewis Morris, in one of his MSS., which I have seen, supposes that they were Druids.

46 See 'Cyfreithieu Hywel Dda ac Eraill', or 'Leges Wallicae', translated in Latin by Dr Wotton and Mr Moses Williams; and published with a learned preface by Mr Clarke. Folio. London. 1730.

47 *King Howel's Laws*, page 68, 69.

48 *Howel's Laws*, page 35, 36, 37.

49 'Dr Wotton, the learned editor of *Howel's Laws*, in a note on this passage, conjectures that the title and subject only were prescribed, and that the choice and composition of the Poetry was left to the Bard. The Welsh, says he, always preserved a tradition that the whole island had once been possessed by their ancestors, who were driven into a corner of it by their Saxon invaders. When they ravaged the English borders, they dignified their incursions with the pretext of recovering their hereditary rights. Their poets therefore entertained them with descriptions and praises of the splendour and courage with which the monarchy of Britain was maintained by its ancient heroes, and inspired with an ardour of emulating their glorious example. If any thing can be added to the conjectures of so discerning a critic as Dr Wotton, it is, that probably an excellent old poem, called 'Unbennaeth Prydain', was constantly recited in the field, and accompanied by a tune of the same antiquity, till by a long interval of peace, or some other accident, they were both forgotten and that afterwards the Bards supplied what had been lost from their own inventions.' *Translated Specimens of Welsh Poetry in English verse*. 1782. page 33.

   But heed, ye Bards, that for the sign of onset
   Ye sound the ancientest of all your rhymes,
   Whose birth tradition notes not, nor who fram'd
       Its lofty strains.
            Mason's Caractacus

50 *Howel's Laws*, page 37, paras 11, 12.

51 *Ibid.*, page 307, 31st Triad.

52 *Ibid.*, page 37. para. 12.

53 Dr Rhys' *Grammatical Institutes of the Welsh Language*, page 295.

54 Dr Powel, in his notes on Caradoc informs us, that either our Music came hither with prince Gruffudd's Irish Musicians, or was composed by them afterwards. Mr Wynne, the other editor of *Caradoc's History*, mistaking this passage in Dr Powel, and not distinguishing instrumental music from musical instruments, hath milled his readers by asserting that the Harp and Crwth came from Ireland. See *Wynne's History of Wales*, edit. 1774, page 159.

55 *Ibid.* Also Powel's *History of Wales*, pages 115 and 191. Clarke's *Preface to the Welsh Laws*, page 25, and Rhydaerch's *Welsh Grammar*, page 177, &c.

56 'Some part of this MS., according to a memorandum which I found in it, was transcribed in the time of Charles the First, by Robert ap Huw of Bodwigen, in the isle of Anglesey from William Penllyn's Book.' Dr Burney's *History of Music*; vol. II, page 110. William Penllyn is recorded among the successful candidates on the harp, at an Eisteddfod at Caerwys, in 1568, where he was elected one of the chief Bards and Teachers of instrumental song.

Pennant's *Tour in North Wales*, printed 1778, page 438. This MS., Dr Burney informs me, 'contains pieces for the harp that are in full harmony or counterpoint: they are written in a peculiar notation, and supposed to be as old as the year 1100 at least, such is the known antiquity of many of the songs mentioned in the collection.' *History of Music, ibid.*

The 24 measures of Music are here annexed from the MS. in the original Welsh: for the purpose of assisting future enquiries, and shewing by the variety of its technical terms, what perfection the art had formerly acquired. As they have never been explained, I forbear attempting a translation, from apprehension of mistake, and misleading the reader.

### Y Pedwar Mesur ar hugain cerdd Dant

| | |
|---|---|
| Alfarch | Mac y mwn byr |
| Mac y mwnhir | Ffamgar Gwrgan |
| Cordia tytlach | Brâth yn Yigel |
| Cor-Aedan | Macy mawyrfaen |
| Cor-Finfain | Tudyr bâch |
| Carfi | Hatyr |
| Cor-wrgog | Brut Odidog |
| Wnfach | Cor-Ffiniwr |
| Toddyf | Aibantiyfaidd |
| Mac y Delgi | TrwsglMawr |
| Cor-Aichan | Cor-y-golofa |
| Rhiniart | Tresi nili |

In the same MS. are preserved the five principal Keys of Welsh Music, established by the same authority.

Is gywair, the Grave, or Bass Key.
Cras gywair, the Acute, or Sharp Key.
Lleddf gywair, the Flat Key.
Go gwair, a Secondary Key, or perhaps the Natural Key.
Bragod gywair, the Mixt, or Minor Key.

57  Ilyma'r Pedwar Misur ar hugain Cerdd dant, yn ol rl eol fesar oll, fal y eysansoddwyd mewn Eisteddfod, &c. MS.

58  Pryaydd, or Prifadd.

59  Truluwr, or Possardd. 'We find the King had always a civil judge to attend him, and one of the chief lords to consult with upon all emergencies. He had a Bard to celebrate the praises of his ancestors; a Chronicler to register his own actions; a Physician to take care of his health, and a Musician to entertain him. These were obliged to be always present, and to attend the King whither-forever he went. Besides these, there were a certain number of heroic men called Milwyr, who attended him, when he went on his progress, or marched out with his army, and were resolved to stand by him, even at the expense of their lives.' Owen's *History of the Ancient Britons*, pages 21 and 22.

60  Clerwr, ar Arwyddsardd.

61  *Cambria Descriptio*, cap. 3.

62  These technical terms of Welsh music are very obscure, and are too unintelligible to admit of a positive translation. If Dr Burney shou'd hereafter be able to decypher the notation of the ancient and very curious musical MS. I have quoted above, much light would be thrown on this dark subject. Till that desirable object is accomplished, the candid reader will accept the following imperfect attempt to explain it.

*Cwlwm*, a congruous piece of music, with words.

*Colofn*, pillar, or fundamental part.

*Cydgerad*, music in parts.

*Cadair*, a masterly piece of music, I conjecture, by the performance of which the musical Bards rose to the superior degrees, and to the chair; whence it probably took its name.

*Caniad*, a tune, or song.

*Gosteg*, a prelude, or overture.

*Dfr*, a measure, or a diverting air.

*Mwebwl*, this famous piece of music seems only was acquired by a pencerdd or Doctor of Music of the Harp. N.B. The three noble Mwchwls was equal to the four Colofns.

A Colofn was equivalent to 10 cwlwms.

A Cadair parallel with 5 cwlwms.

63  **Y Pedwar Mesur ar hugain Cerdd Dafod**
(The Twenty-four Metres of Poetry)

| | |
|---|---|
| *Englyn* | *Close Metre* |
| Unodl union | Unirythm direct |
| Unodl gyrch | Unirhythem incursive |
| Unodl grwch | Unirhythm inverted |
| Prost cyfarwidiog | Prosaic interchanged |
| Prost caderynodl | Prosaic concatenated |
| | |
| *Cyuydd* | *Parallel Metre* |
| Deuair birion | Long double distich |
| Deuair fyrion | Short double distich |
| Llosgyrnog | Tailed |
| Awdl gywydd | Multirhythm |
| | |
| *Awdl* | *Pindaric Metre* |
| Toddaid | Melting |
| Hir a thoddaid | Long and melting |
| Byr a thoddaid | Short and melting |
| Cybydedd fer | Short and of equal extent |
| Cybydedd hir | Long and of equal extnet |
| Cydydedd nawban | Nine syllabled and of equal extent |
| Huppynt hir | Long Brunt |
| Huppynt byr | Short Brunt |
| Gwawdodyn hir | Long Parenetic |
| Gwawdodyn byr | Short Parenetic |
| Cadwyn fyr | Short chair |
| Tawddgyrch cadwynog | Soft concatenated incursive |
| Cyrch a chwtta | Incursive with a little tail |
| Clogyrnach | Rugged |
| Gorcheft y Beirdd | Master-piece of the Bards |

Of all these metres specimens are exhibited by Dr Rhys, John Rhydderch, and the Rev. Mr Gronw Owen (see *Beirdd Môn* by Hugh Jones, 18vo, London, 1763); also in the constitutions of the Society of Cymmrodorion, reprinted 1778. There are other metres, now accounted obsolete and irregular; such as Triban or Englyn Milwr, 'The Warrior's Song'. *Engyln o'r hên ganiad*, 'The Song of the Ancient Strain'. *Englyn garrhir*, 'The Song of the Long Thigh'. *Englyn cildwrn*, 'The Song of the Clinched Fist'.

The Twenty-four Metres were probably antecedent to the twenty-four measures of Music, for the latter seem to have been adapted to, and founded upon them.

'The Cambro-British Muse hath, at the instance of her votaries, condescended to put on various other garbs wherein she hath appeared not only not ungraceful, but even with some degree of dignity and ease; yet the robes she hath ever gloried in, are the Twenty-four celebrated antient British Metres, unknown to every Muse besides, and wherein she hath always shone with unrivalled lustre.' (*The Rev. Mr Walter's Disseration on the Welsh Language*, page 51.)

64  John Rhydderch's *Welsh Grammar*, pages 188 and 189.

65  Notes on the 'Fourth Song of Polyolbion'.

66  This MS., called *Llyfr Dosparth*, is not now extant.

67 Dr Rhys' *Institutes of the Welsh Language*, page 296, &c. *Rhyddent's Grammar*, page 179, &c. and Pennant's *Tour in Wales*.

68 History of Henry II, 4to vol. III, page 302.

69 Powel's *History of Wales*, page 205. Dr J.D. Rhys' *Institutes*, page 296.

70 Sylvester Giraldus, or Giraldus Cambrensis, of a noble Flemish family near Tenby, in Pembrockshire, was born in 1145. He was secretary to Henry II, tutor to King John, and Bishop of St David's. In 1187 he accompanied Baldwin, Archbishop of Canterbury, into Wales, to preach the Crusade. He wrote an *Irish and Welsh Itinerary*, and other works. He died and was buried at St David's about the age of 70.

71 *Cambria Descriptio*, ch. 11.

72 *Ibid.*, ch. 13.

73 'It is well known that Guido's new invented counterpoint was expressed in long notes to protract and lengthen out his harmonious sounds; and that his movements were slow, but Giraldus Cambrensis, his contemporary, gives us an amazing account of the celerity, rapidity, execution, and correctness, with which the Britons played in parts their intricate and complicated music on their harps. If Guido's invention had then reached Wales, would they have been so expert so soon in the practice of it? or would they have written their music in the rude, clumsy, old-fashioned manner of the MS. you allude to, when a much better method had been found out? It may therefore be inferred that the Britons performed music harmoniously in parts, before the Italians.

'The characters in the Welsh MS. were probably chants or recitatives, used in bands of music, concerts, symphonies, and choruses, in great houses, or perhaps in divine worship. We read of Kor Alun, Kor Aedan, Kor Elfyw, Kor Finwr, &c. which signifies a body or number of voices and instruments joined in harmony.' *(A Letter from the Rev. Mr Evans, of Llanymynech, with which I was favoured in answer to my enquiries.)*

N.B. Also the name of the ancient and famous monastery of Bangor, in North Wales, seems to be derived from Bann gor, or famous choir.

74 *History of Music*, vol. II, page 108, &c.

75 I annex an accurate copy and translation of these celebrated games, consisting of twenty-four kinds of exercises, used by the ancient Britons, as they are printed in Dr Davis' *Welsh-Latin, and Latin-Welsh Dictionary*, folio, London, 1632.

**Y Pedair camp ar hugain**
(The Four and Twenty Games)

| 6 O rym Corph | 6 Feats of activity |
|---|---|
| Cryfder dan bwysau | Display of strength in supporting and hurling weights, such as pitching a bar of iron, throwing a sledge, quoits, or large stone. |
| Rhedeg | |
| Neidio | |
| Nofio | Running. |
| Ymafael | Leaping. |
| Marchogacth | Swimming. |
| | Wrestling. |
| | Riding, which perhaps extended to feats in chariots of war. |

| 4 O rym arfau | 4 Exercises of weapons |
|---|---|
| Sacthu | Archery, and throwing the javelin. |
| Chwarau cleddyf a tharian | Fencing with a sword and buckler. |
| Chwarau cleddyf deuddwrn | Fencing with the two-handed sword. |
| Chwarau ffon ddwybig | Playing with the quarter staff. |

| 3 Helwriacth | 3 Rural sports |
|---|---|
| Hela â Milgi | Hunting. |
| Hela Pyfg | Fishing. |
| Hela Aderyn | Hawking. |

| 7 *Gamp Deuluaidd* | 7 *Domestic and literary games* |
|---|---|
| Barddoniaeth | Poetry. |
| Canu Telyn | Playing the harp. |
| Darllain cymraeg | Reading Welsh. |
| Canu cywydd gan dant | Singing a poem with the Harp, or Crwth. |
| Canu Cywydd pedwar, ac accenu | Singing an ode of four parts, and accenting it with proper expression. |
| Tynnu arfau | Heraldry. |
| Herodraeth | Embassy. |

| 4 *Gogampau* | 4 *Inferior games* |
|---|---|
| Chwarau gwyddbwyll | Chefs. |
| Chwarau tawlbwrdd | Draughts, Back Gammon, or some similar game. |
| Chwarau ffriftial | Dice. |
| Cyweirio telyn | Tuning the harp. |

76 Phædrus.

77 See also the notes of the third song of Polyolbion.

78 Guthrie's *History of England*, vol. I., page 102.

79 For a candid enquiry into this subject, see Lord Lyttelton's notes on the 5th book of his *History of Henry II*. See also Owen's *British Remains*, 8vo, London, 1777. Likewise Carte's *History of England*, page 638.

80 Meredydd ap Rhys flourished 1470: Guttun Owain, 1480: and Cynfrig ap Gronw near the same period.

81 Lucretius.

82 The name and dates of these Bards are to be found in the catalogue of British authors published by Dr Davies and Mr Richard in their *Dictionaries of the Welsh Language*. Some extracts from their writings are inserted in Mr Evan's *Specimens of Welsh Poetry*, and his *Dissertatio de Bardis*. Likewise an extensive catalogue of the works of the Bards in Mr Lhudy's *Archaeologia Britannica*, page 254, &c.

83 Chwaer Cyhelyn befrddyn bach,
Chiwbanogl, chwe' buanach.
    *Dafydd ap Gwilym*

84 Dr Burney's *History of Music*, vol. II, page 70.

85 See Wynne's *History of Wales*, edit. 1774, page 283.

86 See Guthrie's *Historical Grammar*.

87 See the Hon. Mr Barrington's *Miscellanies*.

88 Mich. Drayton, by the communications of his friend, Mr John Williams, was extremely well informed respecting the Bards, and their institutions: and his accurate knowledge is conveyed in the 'Polyolbion' in the most elegant and spirited poetry.

89 *Dissertatio de Bardis*, page 92.

90 Owen's *Memoirs of Owain Glyndwr*, 4to, London, 1775, and Pennant's *Tour in Wales*, page 302, &c. The liberality and exploits of this daring chief are celebrated in the most animated strains by that famous and learned Bard, Jelo Gôch.

91 Evans' *Specimens of Welsh Poetry*, page 160. Pennant's *Tour in Wales*, pages 325 and 330.

92 Pennant's *Tour*, page 311.

93 Owain Glyndwr, descended from the ancient race of British princes, first appeared in arms against Henry IV in the year 1400. He directed his attack against the lands of his enemy Lord Grey, and immediately recovered what he had unjustly been dispossessed of by him, and soon after caused himself to be proclaimed prince of Wales. His chief Bard, Gruffydd Llwyd, regretting his absence, chants his praise, and predicts the success of the war in a Cywydd. This Cywydd, or Ode, is elegantly verified from the Welsh by the Rev. Mr Williams of Vron.

94 The omen alluded to was a star and fiery dragon; which according to the interpretation of Merlin, predicted the reign of Uther, afterwards surnamed Pendragon from having caused

two golden Dragons to be made, one of which he presented to the cathedral of Winchester; the other he carried along with him in his wars, or, what is more likely, wore by way of crest on his helmet. His son Arthur adopted the same. See Geoffrey of Monmouth, pages 254, 257 and 283.

95 He flourished about the year 1400. See the titles of some of his poems, in the catalogue of British MSS. in Mr Edward Llwyd's *Archaeologica Britannica*.

96 See his poem published by Mr Rice Jones, in Gorcheflion Beirdd Cymry. For the following remarks I am obliged to that excellent Welsh critic, the late Mr Lewis Morris. 'Mr Pope in his Preface to the *Iliad*, enumerating Homer's excellencies, next to his boundless invention places his imitative sounds, and makes them peculiar to him and Virgil, and says that no other poet ever reached this point of art.

'Dafydd ah Gwilym, if I mistake not, has also a strong claim to this excellency. You must either allow of the atomical philosophy; or that copying nature by its own light, he intended his Cywydd y Daran should sound what it really is – a description of thunder and lightning, though in his love poems, and other soft subjects (of which I have now by me near a hundred) he is as smooth, and glides as easy, as an Italian song.

'Let those who are not over partial to the school languages, and are proper judges of ours, compare this poem in its sounds, and the loftiness of its metaphors, with the best passages of this kind in the above authors, and I doubt not but they will deem this bold-ness of comparison excusable, let Homer's character be ever so sacred.' *Tyfen 'r hen erfadd.*

97 Wynce's *History of Wales*, page 325, edit. 1774.

98 See Mr Evans' address At y Cym y; *Specimens of Welsh Poetry*, page 107.

99 Rhydderch's *Welsh Grammar*, page 186.

100 'This Commission,' says Mr Pennant (*Tour*, page 433), 'is the last of the kind which was granted.' If he understands that this was the last Eisteddfod, he is misinformed. For the commissioners here mentioned, having in 1568 constituted Simmwnt Fychan Chief Bard, appointed another Eisteddfod to be held in 1569, the tenth year of queen Elizabeth's reign. See Evans' *Specimens of Welsh Poetry*, page viii, before the preface.

101 Rhydderch's *Welsh Grammar*, page 187. Evans' *Specimens of Welsh Poetry*, page v, before the preface. And Pennant's *Tour in Wales*, page 434. At this Eisteddfod the number of the poetical Bards was 17, and of their musical brethren 38.

102 *A Dissertation on the Welsh Language*, 8vo, Cowbridge, 1771.

103 The author of the *Letters from Snowdon*.

104 Dr Llewelyn ingeniously refers the curious and delicate structure of the Welsh language to its peculiar property of varying artificially, euphoniae gratiâ, its mutable initial conson-ants; making it superior in this respect to the Roman and the Greek. See *Historical and Critical Remarks on the British Tongue*, 8vo, London, 1769. page 58, &c. Likewise *Antique Languae Britanicae,* by Dr Davies, 8vo, London, 1621.

105 *Northern Antiquities*, 8vo, London, vol. I, page 401, &c.

106 *Ibid.*, vol. II, page 197, &c.

107 Walters' *Dissertation on the Welsh Language*, page 52.

108 Rhydderch's *Welsh Grammar*, page 141. See this Englyn ingeniously answered in another, composed in like manner of vowels, by the Rev. Mr Grony Owen; 'Diddanwch Teuluaidd, Gwaith Beirdd Môn', 18vo, London, 1763, page 35.

109 Walters' *Dissertation*, page 53.

110 Rhydderch's *Welsh Grammar*.

111 Whoever desires to see this idea pursued to some length, may find it ingeniously and philosophically developed with reference to the native music of Scotland in Dr Beattie's *Essays on Poetry and Music*.

112 The fine old Psalms, which are chanted in some of the churches in Wales, particularly in those where modern singing is not introduced.

Likewise, Côr-Aedan, Côr-finfain, Côr-wrgog, Côr-Alchan, Côr-Ffiniwr, Côr-y gwyfn &c. Some of the Côrs or holy songs are carefully displayed from an ancient manuscript in the original musical notes supposed to be Druidical, which the reader will see engraved on a book, delineated in the print of the muscial instruments, further in this volume.

113 Triban, or The Warriors Song, Triban Morganwg, Mynediad Cadpen Morgan, Erdaigan

tro'r tant, Cudyn Gwyn, Ymdaith Mwnge, Bleuddwyd y Frenbines, Blodeu'r Grug, Torriad y Dydd, Siendyn, P'ygiad y Bedol-fach, Wyres Ned Puw, Pen Rhaw, Farwel Ned Puw, &c.

114 Morfa Rhuddlan, Y Galon Drom, Dafydd Garreg-wen, Gorddi-nam, Confet Gruffudd ap Cynan, Anhawdd ymadael, Mwynen Môn, Symlen Ben bys, Yr Hen Dôn, &c.

115 Mentra Gwen, Glân Feddwdod mwyn, Codiad yr Hedydd, Hên Sibel, Merch Megan, Twll yn ei boch, Tôn y Fammaeth, Dewis Meinwen, Dylyn Serch, Consêt Dafydd ab Gwilym, Maldod Arglwyddes Owen, Mantell Siani, Nôi Galan, Ar Byd y nos, Tros y Garreg, Megen a golledd ei gardai, Blodw'r Drain, Cnott y Coed, Hob y dirif, Digan y Pibydd Coch, &c, &c.

116 'The harp is the favourite instrument of the fair sex, and nothing should be spared to make it beautiful: for it should be a principal object of mankind to attach them by every means to music, as it is the only amusement that may be enjoyed to excels, and the heart still remain virtuous and uncorrupted.'

*Dr Burney's* History of Music, *vol. I.*

'Their business should be to practice merely for the amusement of themselves, their own family, and particular friends, or rather for domestic comfort, which they were by providence designed to promote; viz. To calm the boisterous passion – to relieve the anxieties and cares of life – to inspire cheerfulness – to appease the nerves, when irritated by pain, sickness, or labour of mind or body, to soothe the peevishness of infancy and old age – and to raise the mind to a feeling and love of order. She who shall improve the natural talents, with which women are born, of doing all these things will not have misspent her time by applying a few years to music.'

*Stillingfleet's* Principle and Power of Harmony, *page 151.*

# 11
# TRI CHOF YNYS BRYDAIN

THE OFFICE AND FUNCTIONE of the Bruttish or Cambrian Bards was to keepe and preserve *Tri chof ynys Brydain*: That is the 'Three Records or Memorialls of Bryttaen', which otherwise is called the Bruttish antiquitie which consisteth of three parts and is called *Tri chof*. ffor the preservatione wheareof when the Bards were graduated at there comencements, they were rewarded wyth treble reward one reward for every *Cof*: as the auncient Bard Tudur Aled doth recite of this *Tri chof* and his reward for the same at his comencement and graduacione at the Royall wedding of Ieuan ap Davyd ap Ithel vychan of Northopp in Inglfield in fflintshire which hee vppon the *Cerdd marwnad* of the sayd Ieuan ap Davyd ap Ithel recited thus

> Cyntaf neuadd im graddwyd
> vy oror llys f'eryr llwyd
> am Dri chof im dyrchafodd
> yn neithior hwnn a thair rhodd

And soe you may see that hee was exalted and graduated at the sayd wedding for his knowledge in the sayd *Tri chof*, and was rewarded wyth thre severall rewards one for every *Cof*.

The one of the sayd three *Cof* is the History of the notable Acts of the kings & princes of this land of Bruttaen and Cambria;

And the second of the sayd thre *cof* is the languaige of the Bruttons for which thee Bards ought to giue accompt for every word and sillable therein when they are demaunded thereof and to preserue the auncient tonge & not to intermix ytt wyth any forrayne tonge or to bring any forrayne word amongest yt to the preiudice of there owne words wheareby they might eyther be forgotten or extyrped.

228

And the Thyrd *Cof* was, to keepe the genealogies or Descents of the Nobitie, there Division of lands and there Armes; for there Descents Armes and Divisione of lands were but one of the Three *Cof*.

The aunccient Bards had a stipend out of every plowland in the countrey for there mayntenance And the sayd Bards had alsoe a Perambulacione or a Visitacione once every three yeares to the houses of all the Gentlmen in the Countrey (which was called *Cylch clera*) for preservinge of the sayd *Tri chof*. At which Perambulacione they dyd collect all the memorable things that were donne & fell out in every Countrey that concerned there profession to take notice of & wrotte yt downe: soe that theye could not be ignorant of any Memorabl actes, the death of any greate persone, his descent, Division or porcione of lands, Armes and Children in any Countrey wythin theyre Perambulacione.

At which Perambulacione the sayd Bards receaved there Rewards beinge a sett and a certenn Stipend from every gentlman to whose house they were intertayned in there Perambulacione, which Stipend or Reward was called *Clera*.

*Cerdd foliant* is the Poemes of laude and prayse made in the Commendacione of a gentlman or gentlewoman in his liftime & *Cerdd farwnad*, are Mournfull Poems made in lamentacione of a gentlmans death after his decesse.

Those menn that I call & tearme heare by the title of Gentlman, is called in oure languaige *Gwr bonheddic*, and there is no mann admitted by the Lawe to be called *Gwr bonheddic*, but hee yt paternally descendeth from the Kings & Princes of this lande of Bruttaen for *Bonheddic* is as much as *Nobilis* in Laten.

And the Paternall ascent of every gentlman most asscend to Royall persons from whom every gentlman dyd hould his Lands and his Armes.

229

And if a gentlman be soe descendded by father & mother then is hee stiled or tituled by the Lawe *Bonheddic canhwynawl,* which signifieth a perfect Noblman, by father and by mother. And this Title *Bonheddic,* is the first title that a man hath and remayneth in his blood from his byrth to his death and this Title *Bonhedd* cann not be really given by any man whatsoever to any man or any that hath yt really deprived of yt. All other Titls may be taken from man & may extinguish by his death or other casualties but this can not for hee bringeth this Title into the world and is not extinguished by his death for yt remayneth in his blood to his posteritie soe that hee cannot be severed from ytt.

Comon persones of late yeares haue taken vppon them the title of *Bonhedd* or Genorositie, but they are not really *Bonheddic* but are soe called or tearmed for fashione sake by reason of theyre welth, Offices or behavioure which are but Transitory things And *Bonedd* consisteth in noe Transitory thing but in a permanent. Soe that hearby you may vnderstand the gentrie of the Countrey had a speciall Interrest in the *Tri chof,* for th[e] Histories were the Acts and deeds of theyre Ancestors and kinsmen; and the preservatione of the Languaige, Armes, descents, and Divisione of lands were theyre owne proper service, and therefor the Stipend payd by them to the Bards was not constituted wythout good cause therevnto nor there Intertaynments in ther perambulacione allowed vnto them but vpon good cause & reasone. And all the Histories and Acts of the kings and Nobilitie were Collected by them all the Battells were recorded by them, and expresly remembred, vppon the *Cerdd foliant* of such noble persones as had performed the service in feelde and vppon there *Cerdd farwnad* soe that there could be noe mistakinge of Truth in setting downe Histories from three yeare to three yeare.

And there was a greate punishment inflicted by the lawe vppon the Bards wyth long Imprisonement losse of place and dignitie wyth great disgrace if any of them should sett downe for truth but ye truth in any Historicall treatie whatsoever.

for noe man dyd treate of any Battell but such as was an eye witnes thereof for some of the cheefest of the Bards were the Marshalls of all Battells, and of Counsell for directinge the field and the kings or Generalls Inteligencers how the Battell went on, soe that they could not be ignorant of any passaige or thinge donne in field. They dyd not write of Battells by hearesay afarr of by relacione vnles yt were some suddayne fight or skirmish vnexpected, for in all Battells of moment they were present as I shall express yt at large in an other place and my warrant and authorytie to prove the same.

Our Histories were not written by Scoolmasters that trafayled noe further for his knowledge then a Childs iourney from his Brekfast to his lesson, nor by any munck that iourned no further then from masse to meate nor by any prentise that had noe other educatione but from shopp to market nor by any Base persone of byrth condicion or calling But by noble Bards noblie descended Barons and fellowes to lords and princes.

Kinge Arthur and Two of his knights Sr Trystam & Sr Lambrock were Bards as testifieth these fewe verses

Arthur aesdew a Thrystan
a llywarch benn cyfarch can.

And the *Penncerdd* or *Bardd teylu,* was of soe heigh a vocatione that hee sate at meate next to the *Pennteylu* (which is called *Princeps familiae*) & had such respecte and honor donn vnto hym that ytt was the office of the *Penteylu* (being the fowerth persone of the land) to lay his hand vppon his Harpe to hould yt hym while hee dyd play vppon ytt a songe to the Kinge in presence of the king (at the thre festivall times of the yeare, Chrismas, Ester, and whitsontyde) to grace hym.

And the cheef Bards was very often of the kinges Counsell. And the cheef Bard in the land was to sytt in a chayre in the kings house at ffestivall dayes when the king and his familie sate in State & nonn of the Bards but the cheef Bard in the land was admitted then to sytt in a Chayre.

And in figur of that when the comencement of Bards was, for there graduatione, ther chefest Title was *Pencerdd* and the cheefest *Pencerdd* of all the Bards had a Juell in forme of a Chayre bestowed vppon hym vppon his creacione or graduacione which he was to fix to his shoulder wyth a Rybend or such like thinge, and then was hee called *Bardd Cadeirioc,* that is a Chayred Bard and thys Chayred Bard was to sytt in a Chayre in the kings house or any wheare els that hee came which was not lawfull to any Bard els by vertue of his dignitie of Bardshipp to haue in the kings house or Courte or clayme ytt any wheare else, as his right but only the *Bardd cadeirioc* whoe had wonn the Chayre vppon disputacione openly before the kinge at comencement time (or at a Royall weddinge) when the *Bardd cadeirioc* was deade that formerly enioyed the sayd Juell, or els ytt was yalded vnto the cheef Bard of knowledge and worth, by the Bards wythout Disputacione (by reason of his knowen sufficiencie in his profession to surpasse all the rest of the Bards) and soe hee had yt *pro confesso* that hee was the cheef Bard of knowledge in that Dominion.

But if any Bard whatsoever challenge to dispute for ytt, yt could not be given *pro confesso* but hee most dispute for ytt, and accomplish the proverb at that time vizt (winne ytt and weare ytt) for hee should not weare yt vnles hee dyd winn yt vppon treyall or was yealded vnto hym by all the residue of the Bards vppon confessione of preheminent and singular knowledg and worth in hym aboue them all. for the dignitie of a Bard amongest the Bryttaens & Cambrians was a very honorable dignitie and the Bards were very honorable menn and of the blood Royall and called the kings and princes by the title of Cosons and fellowes as: Bleddyn vardd calleth Llew[el]yn ap Iorwerth (which the Engl[i]shmen doe call Leolinus magnus) the Prince of Cambria, his cosone in these verses folowing

Collais a gerais o gar ag arglwydd
erglyw en tramgwydd trymgwyn anwar
collais chwe theyrn cedyrn cydfar
chuech eryr cedwyr cadr y darpar
llewelyn ai blant blaengar/vrodorion
ae haelion wyrion oer eu galar

That was Llewelyn hymself and Davyd and Gruffyth his sonnes and Owen goch, Llewelyn and Davydd the three sonnes of Gruffydd ap Lewelyn.

And soe dyd Cynddelw the greate *Bardd* or Poet when hee called Madawc ap

Meredydd ye prince of Powys his lord and fellowe, or fellowe lord vppon his poems made in Comendacione of the sayd Madoc, thus

> Profi prydy
> Cyfarchaf im ri rhad fobeith
> cyfarchaf cyferchais e canweith
> y profi prydu o pieith/eurgerdd
> ym arglwydd cedymddeith

And in like maner the great Bard Iolo Goch dyd challenge his kinred wyth Ithel ap Rotbert of Coed y mynydd in Tegeingl vppon his poem made to the sayd Ithell wharein hee reciteth the kinred thus.

> kydwersog kof diweirsalm
> vum ag ef yn dolef dalm
> Gyd ar un athro clo clod
> an henfeistr gwys yn hanfod
> Or un llwyth o Ronwy llwyd
> post Drefrydd pais dryfrwyd.

And thus yw mae vnderstand yt the anncient Bards in the time of the kings & princes were there kinsmen, and for the next aige after the Princes they were kinne to the Nobilitie of the Countrey, as Iolo Goch to Ithell ap Rotbert of Coed y mynydd and Llewelyn Goch ap Meuric hên, to the noble familie o[f] Nanneu. Nether should any base persone in the times of the kings of Bryttaen & Cambria presume to Studdy or to enter into the learning or professione of a Bard. But when the lawe fell the limitatione of the lawe fell alsoe: and other meane menn of byrth havinge good qualities were admitted to studdy the doctrine of the Bards and to proceed in there profession to there graduacione, but vnder the Title and vocatione of *Prydyddion.*

After the dissolutione of the auncient Bruttish gover[n]ment of Cambria and the reducement thereof vnder the king of England in Edward the firsts time whoe not respectinge the honor nor the dignitie of the Bruttayne natione, Lawe, Antiquitie or Rights but endevored by all the meanes hee and all his successors could (vntyll Henry the Seaventh time) to destroy and extinguish both them, there honor and antiquities.

At which time the nobilitie & Barons of Cambria dyd receave such ould Bards after the death of the Princes (as were then beinge) into there protectione and encouraged them to take disciples vnto them that were fytt and apt for that professione, and gaue vnto them after the subuertione of the lawe all ther Stipends Rights, Privileges & Intertaynments amongest them as fully and as large as when the lawe was in force.

And at this time all the greate knowledge of the Bards, there credyt and worth is altogether decayed and worne out, soe that at this time they are extinguish[ed] amongest vs.

And the *Prydyddion,* at this time likewise are of noe estimatione for divers reasones neyther dyd the Bards write any continuance of the aforsayd History at all sythence the lawe was extinguished by the death of the princes whose acts they were bound to preserve soe that there is noe History written by the Bards sythence the death of Llewelyn ap Gruffyth ap Llewelyn the last prince of Cambria for they had noe princes of there owne to sett foorth there acts.

And all the worthie acts of the Cambrians sythence the death of there princes and there annexacione to the Crowne of England were all assumed by the kinges of England and by the Englishmen wth whom they dyd serve as subiects to the kings of England. Soe that all the acciones and deeds of the Cambrians were drowned vnder the English Title and shadowed by the English Banner, and therby the Englishmen got and assumed to themselves the honor due to the Cambrians and the reward for there deserts. as Vi[r]gill sayd

> Hos ego versiculos feci tulit alter honores
> Sic vos non vobis &c.

But as for the acts of some of oure countreymen sythence the time of the Reigne of oure princes I will god willing an other time and in an other place sett ytt foorth.

And in respect the Languaige of the Bryttaines is one of the *Tri chof*, and part of the Antiquitie of Bryttaen I will write a little concerninge the same for yw to vnderstand how to read ytt perfectly and vnderstand ytt rightly, and then I will proceed to the History of the kings of Bryttaen & Cambria as I haue found ytt in some of oure auncient bookes one wheareof I haue sett foorth at this time for a fundacione for a greater work hearafter to be sett foorth which most haue his cheef dependancie vppon this booke: and therefore before I doe enter into that parte of Antiquitie wch treateth of the Acts and Deeds of the kings and Princes of this land of Bryttaen and Cambria I will beginne wyth the fundacione of Gramer and Treate some things of the Letters and carecters (and the true & perfect sound tone & accent thereof) that is vsed in oure modern Languaige.

# 12

# THE FORESPEECH TO
# THE AMRA CHOHIUM
# CHILLE

THE PLACE FOR THIS forespeech, firstly, is Druimm Ceta, for it is in it was made the great meeting of Druimm Ceta: in a different place, however, was made the body of the hymn from that forth, as appears after. In the time of Aed, son of Anmere, it was made: author – Dallan Forgaill of the Masraige of Mag Slecht: cause – for reaching of heaven for himself and for others through it. Now there are three causes for which Colum Cille came from Alba to Eriu that time – namely, for the releasing of Scanlann Mór, son of Cend Faelad, king of the Osrarians, with whom he went in pledgeship: and for the staying of the poets in Eriu (for they were in banishment on account of their burdensomeness, for there used to be thirty in the company of each *Ollom,* and fifteen in the company of each *Anrad*): and for pacification between the men of Eriu and of Alba about Dal Riata. And it is it they say, that Colum Cille by no means saw Eriu that time, for there used to be a bandage over his eyes; and it is it that caused that, because he promised before that at going past it, that he would not view Eriu from that forth, saying:

> There is a grey eye
> That will view Eriu backwards:
> By no means will it see afterwards
> The men of Eriu or its women.

Colum Cille then came to the assembly, and several rose up before him for welcome to him. If it is according to another tradition, however, there rose not up one before him but Domnall, the king's son, for the king said that there should not rise up one before him; for he knew that about which he had come, and his coming was not thought well of by him, for the staying of the poets, or the releasing of Scannlan was not pleasing to him. So that it is then Columb Cille blessed this

Domnall, because he was reverent to that extent. So that his blessing was thought ill of by the queen, for he was a stepson to her: so that the cleric grew angry towards her, so that she said to the cleric: 'Very great is the craneing on which thou art.' 'Thou hast leave,' says the cleric, 'to be on a craneing on which thou art: thou hast leave,' says the cleric, 'to be on a craneing.' So that it is then she was turned into a crane, so that her handmaid took to reproaching the cleric, so that she turned into another crane: so that those two cranes are from that hither in Druim Ceta, as some say.

The poets after that came into the assembly, and a poem of praising with them for him, and *aidbsi* (chorus) is the name of that music; and a surpassing music was it, as Colman Mac Lenene said:

Blackbirds beside swans, ounces beside masses,
Forms of peasant women beside forms of queens,
Kings beside Domnall, a murmur beside a chorus,
A taper beside a candle [is] a sword beside my sword.

And together they used to make that music. Dignity of mind came for the cleric, so that the sky above his head was full from demons, so that this was manifested to Baithene; and that he rebuked the cleric, and that the cleric after that brought his head under cover, and that he did penance, and that he raised after that his head from its cover, and that a great fog sprang from his head, and that the demons scattered from it before that fog. And twelve hundred was the number of the poets as a certain one said:

As Mael Choba of the companies was once
At Ibar Chind Trachta in the west:
Twelve hundred poets – he them found
By the Yew in the north-west,
Refection of three melodious years
Mael Coba the chief gave to them:
It shall live to the day of pale judgment
For the well-formed race of Deman.

So that Columb Cille after that stayed the poets, and that he said to Aed:

Cormac well broke battle,
New [his] praisings, withered [his] jewels:
It is it I have read wheel-poetry –
A blessing that one is praised, woe that one is satirized, Aed!
Fair the juice which from its free lawns is sucked:
Woe the absent land that is satirized!
Renowned ladder: fair the course they living drive;
The treasures of praisers remain.

The refection of the poets was after that made over Eriu, and their companies were diminished after that – namely [only] twenty-four in the company of the Ollom, and twelve in the company of the Anrad.

It is after that Columb Cille was making the demand of Scandlan upon Aed, and he was not given to him; so that he said accordingly to Aed, that it is he [Scandlan] who would get his shoes about him [Columb] about midnight, whatever place he should be, and it was so fulfilled. Now, Colman, son of Comgellan, it is he who gave the judgment between the men of Eriu and of Alba, and he was of Dal Riata; and it is with him Columb Cille made the embrace the time the Colman was a little infant, as he said:

> O tree of hounds: O pure soul!
> This is a kiss to thee; deal thou a kiss to me.

And Columb Cille said, it is he who would make pacification between the men of Eriu and of Alba: and it is the judgment he gave, 'Their expedition and their hosting with the men of Eriu always,' for there is hosting with territories always: 'their tribute and their exaction with the men of Alba;' or, 'their sea-gathering only with the men of Alba, but from that forth with the men of Eriu.'

Then Dallan, chief Ollom of Eriu that time, came to converse with Columb Cille, so that it is then he recited the forespeech for him: and Columb Cille did not allow him the making of it beyond that, that he should make it in the time of his death; for he said, to one dead it was fitting: and it is of headlets [capitula] Dallan proceeded to make his poem. Now Columb Cille promised to Dallan the gifts and products of the earth for this praising, and he did not take them, but heaven for himself and for every one who would recite it each day, and would understand it between sense and sound, as a certain one said:

> Columb's Amra – every day
> Whoever will recite it completely,
> Will reach the good bright kingdom
> Which God granted to Dallan.

Now three signs Columb Cille gave him the time he should make it – namely, a rider of a speckled steed would announce to him the death of Columb Cille, and the first word the rider would utter, that it was to be the beginning of the praising, and that his eyes would be allowed to him, while he should be at the making of it. At Feni's Ford again in Mide [Meath] this praising was made, as Mael Suthain said: Ferdomnach, however, successor of Columb Cille, declares it is behind Assal's Way it was chanted, from where the Fort of the Balustrades is to the Cross at Lomman's House. *Anamain* between two *Ashes* this; that is, *Ash* in the beginning of the praising, and *Ash* in its ending; namely, *Ni dis [s]ceoil* and Nimuain. Or it is *fork of two*, that is, bi-rhyming narration; that is, to begin two sounds or three from one tree still; that is, one after another; and a sound from a tree which is different after that.

'God, God,' &c. It is why he doubles the first word – on account of the rapidity and avidity of the praising, as is, *Deus, Deus meus*, &c. But the name of that with the Goedel is 'return to a usual sound;' for there be three similar standards of expression with the poets of the Goedel; that is, *re-return to a usual sound*, and *renarration mode*, and *reduplication*, and this is the mark of each of them. The 'return,' indeed, is a doubling of one word in one place in the round, without adhering to it from that forth. The 'renarration mode,' again, is renarrating from a like mode; that is, the one word – to say it frequently in the round, with an intervention of other words between them, as is this:

> Came the foam [which] the plain filters,
>> Came the ox through fifty warriors;
> [So] came the keen, active lad,
>> [Whome] brown Cu Dinisc left.

But 'reduplication' is, namely, 'refolding;' that is, 'bi-geminating,' as is this:

> I ask, I ask, after long, long,
>> to be in pain, pain, not peace, peace:
> Like each, each, till judgment, judgment,
>> In each time, time, though fatigue, fatigue.

Two divisions of these in this forespeech: 'return to a usual sound,' and 'renarration-mode;' but 'renarration-mode' only in the body of the hymn.

GOD, GOD – I HAVE ASKED HIM ERE I COME TO HIS FACE – I implore of God, or I ask of God ere I come to his face, or the time, or the period I come.

FOR CHARIOTS THROUGH BATTLE.– 'Obscuration,' or 'superabundance,' here; and that appearances of 'obscuration' might not exist, the 'be-heading,' and 'bi-heading,' and 'head-changing' have been established, as some persons say. 'Neit' also means, that is, wound, as is said:

> May thy monument at dawn-breeze be
> After thy death-wound a sail ever to be driven;
> Borne may [she] be in a chariot after a horse
> Thy wife, O hero, to her beautiful church.

That is: as a serrated chariot goes through battle, may it be so my soul shall go through the battle of demons to heaven.

'Obscuration' here in a special way, for *cul* is the usual word; but the poet added .u. here for filling of the poetry; or for making the words hard to be known through diminution and through increase and through immutation being made in them. And there are three forms on it, [on 'obscuration,'] that is, 'be-heading,' and 'bi-heading,' and 'head-changing.' The 'be-heading' is – to cut its own head off the word and without anything else in its place, as some one said:

> A meeting I appointed – great the folly –
>> In the stand above Druimm:
> O my Lord, O king of noble mysteries!
> .    .    .    .    .    . &c

'Ru ra' – it is the example there; for it is 'run ran' that was lawful. But the 'bi-heading' is – two heads on it, that is, its own head and another head; and that its propriety may be the doubling of the last letter of the word, as if *benn* were made of what is *ben*, as is said:

> The desire of a man of battle [is] purple spoil;
> God's fire comes gloomy, not rare;
> A strong stroke [is] from a shaft of eight hands;
> Usual a head in the fist of Cu of deadliness.

So that it be in matter the example may be here, that is, his own head on that man, and the head of another one in his hand; but yet it is in speech these proprieties are viewed, and not in matter. So that it be the example here, '*ni tercda*,' for '*da*' was added to the proper word; but yet that is criticized, for the increase of a syllable is not 'bi-heading' according to propriety, but it is a 'super-abundance of poets;' and this is the example of that:

> Advance from lakes for a net of twists,
>     With celebrities – a fame not narrow this:
> Coming past horses in the end of a territory –
>     Good the life in which there is plentiness.

What, then, is the 'bi-heading' in the round we have spoken. 'Lainn fir, &c.' Not difficult. To make *tenn* of that which is *ten*, that is, *fire*, with a view that it may answer to *cenn*, and that is 'bi-heading' according to propriety. The following, however, is the way these divisions are exemplified in other books, that is, 'beheading' as is *dochusin*, that is, cutting its head off it; that is, the 'et,' for it is *docuis[i]net* it was formerly. But the 'bi-heading' is as is *maelan*, that is, *an* is the other head: the 'headlet-changing' is as is *senchas*, for it is *fenchas* it was former-ly. The following is the criticism of these examples, that is, diminution of a sylla-ble is not 'beheading' according to propriety, and anything else is not 'be-heading' according to the antiquity. Another thing in the case too – the usual words at pre-sent are – *dochusin* and *maelan*, and *senchas*. According to the ancients then examples are here; for the usual words with them were *docuisinet*, and *mael*, and *fencas*. But the 'head-changing' at present is to make fencas of the word which is *senchas*; for the usual at present is senchas, as is said:

> The poets of Fal have viewed here
> The Fenchas with illumination by Fergus:
> If it is in reference to the poet of every plain forth –
> Dubthach has surpassed men.

'Fenachas:' the example there is .*f*. for .*s*. It is alike in the beginning or in the end of a word the 'be-heading' and the 'head-changing' are made; but in the end only of a word it is usual to make the 'bi-heading.' We do not see again with the poets of the Goedelic a different name for diminution of a letter and of a syllable, as we see for increase of a letter and of a syllable, that is, 'bi-heading' increase of a let-ter, and 'superabundance' increase of a syllable.

THE GOD OF HEAVEN – MAY HE NOT ALLOW ME INTO THE HOST IN WHICH THERE

IS CRYING ON ACCOUNT OF SMOKE FROM ITS GREATNESS – For the manifestation of truth he says, 'God of heaven,' or from his knowledge that he is not a God who is an idol. 'May he not allow me into the host of the demons, with whom crying is made on account of the greatness of their smoke.'

GREAT GOD MY PROTECTION FROM THE FIERY RAMPART OF LONG EYES OF TEARS! – Great God for my protection against the fence of the fire, a place in which are shed tears for a long time a-looking on it. That is, for mur means *fence (immed)*, as is said:

> 'Mur' [means] *fence* beyond in the law.
> 'Coph,' *victory*, and a full-right *word*.
> 'Du' [means] *place*, 'du' *inheritance* with thee.
> 'Cul,' *protection*, and 'cul,' *chariot*.

'Diu-dere' accordingly is a noun compounded from Latin and Scotic. 'Diu,' that is, *long;* 'derc,' that is, *eye*: as Granne, daughter of Cormac, said to Find:

> There is a person,
> For a long look at whom I should feel grateful,
> For whom I should give the whole world,
> O Son of Mary, what a privation!

GOD RIGHTEOUS, TRULY NEAR, WHO HEARS MY SAD WAIL TO THE HEAVEN-LAND OF CLOUDS – Righteous God, or God of the righteous. 'Truly near,' that is, because God is everywhere, and near to all who invoke him. 'Mo do nuaill,' that is, my two wails; that is, the wail of my body and of my soul behind clouds to the land of heaven: or, the wail of the Old Law and of the New Testament. Or, 'mo do nuaill,' that is, 'my to him wail,' that is, my wail to him, that is, to God. 'Iath,' again, means a *diadem*, and 'iath,' a *territory*, as is said:

> 'Fo' [is] a name for *good* and for *honor*,
> 'Fi' [is] a name for *bad* and for *disobedience*:
> 'An' [means] *true*, and it is no weak knowledge,
> 'Iath' [is] a *diadem*, and 'iath' is a *territory*.

# 13

# POETRY OF THE GOGYNFEIRDD

## from *A Celtic Anthology* by
## GRACE RHYS

### Gwalchmai's Delight

Early rises the sun, summer draws nigh; sweet is the talk of the birds, bright and soft the air.

I am adorned with gold, fearless in the battle, I am a lion before the host, like lightning is my onset.

I have watched by night, keeping the confines of the fords of the murmuring waters of Dygen Freiddin.

Very green the untrodden grass, radiant the water, and the nightingale's rapturous song is an ode that ceases not.

*Gwalchmai (translated by H. Idris Bell)*

### The Delights of Howel ab Owen

A foam-crowned wave flows o'er the grave
Of Rhuvawn Bevyr, chief of men,
I love the land where I drank the mead,
Where the shores are in conflict with the sea;
I love its people living there at peace.

I love its sea coasts and its mountains,
Its cities bordering on its forests, its fair landscapes,
Its dales, its waters and its valleys,
Its white sea-mews and its beautiful women.
I love its warriors and its well-trained steeds,
Its woods, its strongholds, and its sheltering homes;
I love its fields clothed in the tender trefoil
Where glory and where triumph fell to me.

*Howel ab Owen*

## Howel's Choice

My choice of ladies is one bright and slender,
white and tall in her green wimple.

My choice of thoughts is to muse on a maiden as
she utters tenderly her seemly mind.

My choice is a fair one wave-white, even thou,
whose Welsh sounds sweetly in thy land.

My choice art thou; what am I to thee?
*Howel ab Owen (translated by H. Idris Bell)*

## Golden the Hair

Golden the hair on the head of Gwen,
Loose, flowing, fit for an Earl's daughter.
It falls down to her feet
Like the willow saplings, waving, wine-coloured.
How beautiful the long golden curls
That hang from a fair woman's brows, –
Smooth, clear, and purely white
As water spray on the top of the rocks.
Her head is bound about by a band of pure gold.
Beneath the long glistering white veil
Beam two gentle eyes, blue, radiant,
Two stars of love, gladdening to the sight.
Her cheeks are redder than the red wine of raspberries.
As the colour of wild roses in leafy woods
Is the bright glow of her buoyant health.
*Rhys Goch ap Rhiccert (translated by Ernest Rhys)*

## A Reproach to Morvyth

O calm, yellow-haired girl, all gold is the burden on thy head; white
is thy body and straight and shapely, richly endowed.

So long as thou art fair and sweet, radiant in loveliness, to be a cause
of grief to me, thy face, O gem among women, is before all to work
treachery; God has dyed thy tresses, thy golden hair, to beguile man.

To lift up thy delicate brows and make men sad for loving thee was
thine appointed task.

My body, though I spoke not of it, has wasted away for thy white
love-liness; thy beauty, all Gwynedd knows it, has stolen away my life and
my sense.

If I consider thy words, O thou of the wine-red cheek, I shall lay me down
to rest; better is the grave, where is true rest, than to live long in this pain.

Woe is me, I am in pain daily that ever I saw thy fair cheek. Lovely
flattery and laughter were ever on thy lips; thou evil one, less worth is thy
hue of enchantment than the foam on the shore.

Mine enemy, a boundless loss it were to me if thou shouldst depart;
nay, depart not against my will: never shouldst thou depart with it!
*Dafydd ab Gwilym (translated by H. Idris Bell)*

241

## A Snowy Day

There is no walking, no going abroad to-day, woe is me!

There is no world, no road or mountain side; no open place or ground to-day.

Where's the girl whose word shall cheat me forth, out into the driving snow.

Plague on it! The feathers hang on one's gown like a dragon's scales. My dress would seem the white coat of a miller.

'Tis no fable that after New Year's Day furred raiment is the only wear.

January's month, the leader of the Train, God clothes him like a hermit; he has dusted the black earth with white on every side.

Not a wood without white raiment, not a copse without its covering.

Finest flour is the down on every stump, flour of the sky like April blossoms.

On the lusty trees of the copse is a chilly veil, a load of chalk weighs down the wood. Like wheaten flour it comes; a coat of mail about the level ground, cold grit that covers the ploughed land, thick tallow on the earth's skin, a dense shower of foam, fleeces larger than a man's fists, white bees of heaven rushing through Gwynedd.

Where does God gather so many feathers? Where are they grown? – feathers of holy geese? Like bran they are; or a mantle of ermine.

The dust is drifted now where once stood May on the little pathways.

Who will tell me, in January, what host it is that is spitting from above?

White angels surely at their carpentry! See how they take up the flooring, how they lift the plank from the flour-bin!

A silver robe of ice for a season, quick-silver the coldest in the world, a cold mantle; dreary is the waiting, dreary to hill and hollow and ditch.

What a weight on earth's door! This pavement is vaster than the graveyard of the sea, a great mass fallen on my country, a pallid wall from sea to sea.

Where lives this white-robed plague? This plaster, who shall stay it? who will dare send it packing? A cold cloak of lead – O where is the rain?

*Dafydd ab Gwilym (translated by H. Idris Bell)*

## May

Many a one has sung of May,
The merry queen, and yesterday
She returned, to hold her reign,
Green and gold, on earth again.
Ah, my girl, what gifts of gold
In her hands the queen did hold, –
Florins of the field and tree,
Hazel flowers and *fleurs-de-lis*!
Stars, that in the dark do shine,
Do not gleam gold half so fine.
Blackbirds, in their burnish'd flight
From the branch, are not so bright.
Nightingales, you do not sing
Sweet enough for her to sing.
Make a name for minstrelsy,
Mirth and greenness, – May! 'Tis she.

> *Dafydd ab Gwilym (translated by Ernest Rhys)*

## The Love Messengers

Now, blackbird! fly, be gone
To greet her, cruel one!
Fly, let thy forest-strain
Cry, and complain.
Ah, specklebreast,
Now leave thy bough and nest, –
To her, the radiant maid
Sing, tell her what I said.
And lark too, daybreak-bard!
Thou shalt be heard.
Take her, my love, apart
To show my broken heart.
Next, repetend cuckoo,
With double love-notes too.
Thou shalt my trouble bear
To touch her ear!
My night's companion,
The nightingale alone,
Knows all my misery;
Now, let him fly
Southward until he sees,
Lime-white amid the trees,
A girl walk in the glade,
All alone, lovely maid:
There bid her think of me
Every leaf, every tree!

> *Dafydd ab Gwilym (translated by Ernest Rhys)*

### Morvyth's Winter House

Whoever, on a winter's day,
Saw step, green-sleev'd, the month of May?
I did, who saw this holly-house
Above the tallest birch-tree boughs, –
A forest harbour, green to see
As May in all her gaiety:
A palace, pack'd within a croft
With green leaves for an organ loft:
Song's House, whose eaves no painter could
Ever have painted – none but God.
Not Amon's generous son arrayed.
So fair a place in field or mead:
Crisp, curl'd, its leaves – curl'd like that man
In the song of Howel Vaughan,
Who chose his words, fit, bright, and few,
To bring the very man to view –
Short-hair'd, short-frock'd, a tabard on,
Marching erect there in the sun.
*Dafydd ab Gwilym (translated by Ernest Rhys)*


### The Ploughman and the Plough

Easy to the labourer of the smiling meads to put his trust in the Lord God.

He passes no judgment save on the plough-beam.

Ah! blessed is he as his hands guide the plough right straight, as its smooth coulter laces the field.

Lovingly do men sing its praise, the precious tool.

With its heron's bill it cleaves the shining furrows, lightly opening up the lay land, as with deft and stately motion the coulter moves on.

Forward it thrusts its unbending neck, cleaving a bed for the deep-soiled crop; ever diligent to follow the road that the feet of the oxen have trodden.

Many the hymn it has sung, following the plough-chain.

Lord of the fruitful acres, from its craft comes the grain in due order.

A servant 'tis of sturdy beam to feed a multitude; scatterer of the sods, shod with wood.

A strong whelp it is, gnawing the earth, calling forth the crops from the fertile ground.
*Iolo Goch (translated by H. Idris Bell)*

## A Lady

She who wore fine cloth, of green, of red and blue, – for her is the anguish on death's mourning;

She who wore fine gold on her cheeks, she who wore purple, is now shut within the choir.

*Gruffudd ab Maredydd (translated by H. Idris Bell)*

## Elegy for Lucy Lloyd

*(This poet loved the well-born maiden Lucy; during his absence, her parents having told her he had married another, Lucy died. Hence this famous* marwnad *of the fifteenth century.)*

Here's a summer, heavy and hard:
Here's a black world for the bard!
Ah, song, what summer should this be,
To break the heart of melody!
Now to the north, this mourning day,
Sun nor moon send any ray;
Since she, the moon of womankind
Lies in the clay now, cold and blind:
And, nailed in by the oaken lid,
Her comely lovely form is hid.

Ah, silver candle of the north,
How wert thou carried, earth to earth?
My soul, arise, and where I wait
Open to me the earthen gate, –
Forget thy grave and gravelled place,
And let me see thee face to face;
For truly by thy grave stands one
Who has no pleasure in the sun, –
Sad lingerer, that gave to thee
His heart, his hope, his melody.

*Llewelyn Goch (translated by Ernest Rhys)*

## Elegy on Gwenllian

Dead a long month? Dead a star,
Gwenllian the daughter of Rhys
In her virginity to Mary in heaven has gone.
The star of Blaen Tren sleeps in her grave.
More bitter than the salt foam is human life.
Alas that Gwenllian's life was cut off with May;
Longer she would not stay with us;
My beloved is the treasure of the saints;
As for me, I am grown old.

*Lewis Glyn Cothi (translated by Ernest Rhys)*

## The Birch Grove

Ah, the pleasant grove of birches,
A pleasant place to tarry all the day:
Swift green path to holiness;
Place of leaves well strung upon the branches,
A tapestry fit for the proudest princess;
Place of the thrush's voice, the king of song,
Place of the fair-breasted hill, green place of tree-tops,
Place set apart for two, far from jealous strife;
Veil that hides the maiden at the wooing,
Full of delight is then the green birch grove.

Lo, I possess the whole extent of the birches,
Each corner of the greenwood is my throne;
I have loved as my Saviour this building of Nature
Tapestried in tenfold royalty by the leaves of the grove,
The sweet-voiced nightingale beneath the green boughs,
Is the herald inhabitant of the wood,
Endlessly pouring his songs from within the forest,
From the jutting hill and the glistening green tree-top;
And so I pour forth songs in praise of my green enclosure,
My purest green parlour framed of leaves.

There is a chamber for us within the grove
Made all of young vines;
A gleaning of the birch boughs, fair in colour,
Makes in this chamber a fragrant bed.
A place for the gentle gift of love
Is the house of leaves made by God the Father.

Fair chapel, sacred from strife,
Of boughs and leaves in the green and airy May:
Be ye, O trees, my fitting consolation,
In that I am left houseless to-day.
O nightingale, with the grey wings trailing low,
That art from the beginning the love messenger in May,
Be a strong voice from the steep hillside;
Let the day bring the meeting between Morvyth and me!
        *Dafydd ab Gwilym (translated by Grace Rhys)*

## The Way of the World

I

A grievous burden is this body of clay; a sorry tale is all the way of the world.

To-day in golden splendour man heaps his wealth, his garlands, his rings, his gems, great store of scarlet and camlet of fine silk to wrap him from the cold, his gold-rimmed horn, his hawks, his falcons, his wine.

He seeks for fat tilth, and takes cruel rent for it, he casts down the house of the weak man, and brings his place into his own hand.

From the blind he takes his farmstead, he takes from that man his portion.

He takes the corn from under the ash-wood flails of the reapers, he takes the hay of the innocent.

He heaps up the money of many men; the wealth he bears off, and the men he binds in prison.

## II

Yesterday he would not give two fair cows of all his herds though God Himself should ask it; to-day he lies in earth and nothingness, and of all his wealth nought follows him.

Pain fills him when he goes thither, into his covering of gravel and pebbles, and low is his bed now.

Upon his brow presses the roof-tree of his house; a stone for a porter is by his head, and his dark clay is a dream to us.

The shroud clings about him in sickening folds, clad woefully in clay and pebbles.

His stout limbs are shut in an earthen coffer, his face is pinched and grey, his arms are folded on his breast, the dark earth is his coverlet.

Full soon is he broken beneath the stone. The whole field's weight is upon him who was so fair to look upon.

## III

Where now are his fair towers, his patrimony, his palaces so many, his sweet music?

Where are his high-chimnied houses, his land, his offices of honour? Where his mead-cellar, his kitchen under the hill, his stores of wine?

Where now his journeys into England, his loud feasting, his household bards, his tables of payment?

Where his new parlour, his dainties and roast meats, his cook to make ready the feast, his well-trained hounds, mighty in the hunt, his swanneries, his great horses, his much raiment, his treasures, his wide estates over land and sea, his lineage, his glory, his gleaming lances, his troop of henchmen, his hall of wood new-wrought, his mansions, his wainscottings?

This is the end of it, all the harbour that is left him, but seven feet of earth!

*Sion Cent (translated by H. Idris Bell)*

# 14

# THE DREAM OF RHONABWY

from *The Maginogion*
translated by
**LADY CHARLOTTE GUEST**

MADAWC THE SON OF MAREDUDD possessed Powys within its boundaries, from Porfoed to Gwauan in the uplands of Arwystli. And at that time he had a brother, Iorwerth the son of Maredudd, in rank not equal to himself. And Iorwerth had great sorrow and heaviness because of the honour and power that his brother enjoyed, which he shared not. And he sought his fellows and his foster-brothers, and took counsel with them what he should do in this matter. And they resolved to despatch some of their number to go and seek a maintenance for him. Then Madawc offered him to become Master of the Household and to have horses, and arms, and honour, and to fare like as himself. But Iorwerth refused this.

And Iorwerth made an inroad into Loegria, slaying the inhabitants, and burning houses, and carrying away prisoners. And Madawc took counsel with the men of Powys, and they determined to place an hundred men in each of the three Commots of Powys to seek for him. And thus did they in the plains of Powys from Aber Ceirawc, and in Allictwn Ver, and in Rhyd Wilure, on the Vyrnwy, the three best Commots of Powys. So he was none the better, he nor his household, in Powys, nor in the plains thereof. And they spread these men over the plains as far as Nillystwn Trevan.

Now one of the men who was upon this quest was called Rhonabwy. And Rhonabwy and Kynwrig Vrychgoch, a man of Mawddwy, and Cadwgan Vras, a man of Moelvre in Kynlleith, came together to the house of Heilyn Goch the son of Cadwgan the son of Iddon. And when they came near to the house, they saw an old hall, very black and having an upright gable, whence issued a great smoke; and on entering, they found the floor full of puddles and mounds; and it was difficult to stand thereon, so slippery was it with the mire of cattle. And where the puddles were, a man might go up to his ankles in water and dirt. And there were boughs of holly spread over the floor, whereof the cattle had browsed the sprigs.

When they came to the hall of the house, they beheld cells full of dust, and very gloomy, and on one side an old hag making a fire. And whenever she felt cold, she cast a lapful of chaff upon the fire, and raised such a smoke, that it was scarcely to be borne, as it rose up the nostrils. And on the other side was a yellow calf-skin on the floor; a main privilege was it to any one who should get upon that hide.

And when they had sat down, they asked the hag where were the people of the house. And the hag spoke not, but muttered. Thereupon behold the people of the house entered; a ruddy, clownish, curly-headed man, with a burthen of faggots on his back, and a pale slender woman, also carrying a bundle under her arm. And they barely welcomed the men, and kindled a fire with the boughs. And the woman cooked something, and gave them to eat, barley bread, and cheese, and milk and water.

And there arose a storm of wind and rain, so that it was hardly possible to go forth with safety. And being weary with their journey, they laid themselves down and sought to sleep. And when they looked at the couch, it seemed to be made but of a little coarse straw full of dust and vermin, with the stems of boughs sticking up therethrough, for the cattle had eaten all the straw that was placed at the head and the foot. And upon it was stretched an old russet-coloured rug, threadbare and ragged; and a coarse sheet, full of slits, was upon the rug, and an ill-stuffed pillow, and a worn-out cover upon the sheet. And after much suffering from the vermin, and from the discomfort of their couch, a heavy sleep fell on Rhonabwy's companions. But Rhonabwy, not being able either to sleep or to rest, thought he should suffer less if he went to lie upon the yellow calf-skin that was stretched out on the floor. And there he slept.

As soon as sleep had come upon his eyes, it seemed to him that he was journeying with his companions across the plain of Argyngroeg, and he thought that he went towards Rhyd y Groes on the Severn. As he journeyed, he heard a mighty noise, the like whereof heard he never before; and looking behind him, he beheld a youth with yellow curling hair, and with his beard newly trimmed, mounted on a chestnut horse, whereof the legs were grey from the top of the forelegs, and from the bend of the hindlegs downwards. And the rider wore a coat of yellow satin sewn with green silk, and on his thigh was a gold-hilted sword, with a scabbard of new leather of Cordova, belted with the skin of the deer, and clasped with gold. And over this was a scarf of yellow satin wrought with green silk, the borders whereof were likewise green. And the green of the caparison of the horse, and of his rider, was as green as the leaves of the fir-tree, and the yellow was as yellow as the blossom of the broom. So fierce was the aspect of the knight, that fear seized upon them, and they began to flee. And the knight pursued them. And when the horse breathed forth, the men became distant from him, and when he drew in his breath, they were drawn near to him, even to the horse's chest. And when he had overtaken them, they besought his mercy. 'You have it gladly,' said he; 'fear nought.' 'Ha, chieftain, since thou hast mercy upon me, tell me also who thou art,' said Rhonabwy. 'I will not conceal my lineage from thee; I am Iddawc the son of Mynyo, yet not by my name, but by my nickname am I best known.' 'And wilt thou tell us what thy nickname is?' 'I will tell you; it is Iddawc Cordd Prydain.'[1] 'Ha, chieftain,' said Rhonabwy, 'why art thou called thus?' 'I will tell thee. I was one of the messengers between Arthur and Medrawd his nephew, at the battle of

Camlan; and I was then a reckless youth, and through my desire for battle, I kindled strife between them, and stirred up wrath, when I was sent by Arthur the Emperor to reason with Medrawd, and to show him, that he was his foster-father and his uncle, and to seek for peace, lest the sons of the Kings of the Island of Britain, and of the nobles, should be slain. And whereas Arthur charged me with the fairest sayings he could think of, I uttered unto Medrawd the harshest I could devise. And therefore am I called Iddawc Cordd Prydain, for from this did the battle of Camlan ensue. And three nights before the end of the battle of Camlan I left them, and went to the Llech Las² in North Britain to do penance. And there I remained doing penance seven years, and after that I gained pardon.'

Then lo! they heard a mighty sound which was much louder than that which they had heard before, and when they looked round towards the sound, they beheld a ruddy youth, without beard or whiskers, noble of mien, and mounted on a stately courser. And from the shoulders and the front of the knees downwards the horse was bay. And upon the man was a dress of red satin wrought with yellow silk, and yellow were the borders of his scarf. And such parts of his apparel and of the trappings of his horse as were yellow, as yellow were they as the blossom of the broom, and such as were red, were as ruddy as the ruddiest blood in the world.

Then, behold the horseman overtook them, and he asked of Iddawc a share of the little men that were with him. 'That which is fitting for me to grant I will grant, and thou shalt be a companion to them as I have been.' And the horseman went away. 'Iddawc,' inquired Rhonabwy, 'who was that horseman?' 'Rhuvawn Pebyr the son of Prince Deorthach.'

And they journeyed over the plain of Argyngroeg as far as the ford of Rhyd y Groes on the Severn. And for a mile around the ford on both sides of the road, they saw tents and encampments, and there was the clamour of a mighty host. And they came to the edge of the ford, and there they beheld Arthur sitting on a flat island below the ford, having Bedwini the Bishop on one side of him, and Gwarthegyd the son of Kaw on the other. And a tall, auburn-haired youth stood before him, with his sheathed sword in his hand, and clad in a coat and cap of jet-black satin. And his face was white as ivory, and his eyebrows black as jet, and such a part of his wrist as could be seen between his glove and his sleeve, was whiter than the lily, and thicker than a warrior's ankle.

Then came Iddawc and they that were with him, and stood before Arthur and saluted him. 'Heaven grant thee good,' said Arthur. 'And where, Iddawc, didst thou find these little men?' 'I found them, lord, up yonder on the road.' Then the Emperor smiled. 'Lord,' said Iddawc, 'wherefore dost thou laugh?' 'Iddawc,' replied Arthur, 'I laugh not; but it pitieth me that men of such stature as these should have this island in their keeping, after the men that guarded it of yore.' Then said Iddawc, 'Rhonabwy, dost thou see the ring with a stone set in it, that is upon the Emperor's hand?' 'I see it,' he answered. 'It is one of the properties of that stone to enable thee to remember that thou seest here to-night, and hadst thou not seen the stone, thou wouldest never have been able to remember aught thereof.'

After this they saw a troop coming towards the ford. 'Iddawc,' inquired Rhonabwy, 'to whom does yonder troop belong?' 'They are the fellows of Rhuvawn Pebyr the son of Prince Deorthach. And these men are honourably served with mead and bragget, and are freely beloved by the daughters of the kings of the Island of Britain. And this they merit, for they were ever in the front and the rear in every peril.' And he saw but one hue upon the men and the horses of this troop, for they were all as red as blood. And when one of the knights rode forth from the troop, he looked like a pillar of fire glancing athwart the sky. And this troop encamped above the ford.

Then they beheld another troop coming towards the ford, and these from their horses' chests upwards were whiter than the lily, and below blacker than jet. And they saw one of these knights go before the rest, and spur his horse into the ford in such a manner that the water dashed over Arthur and the Bishop, and those holding counsel with them, so that they were as wet as if they had been drenched in the river. And as he turned the head of his horse, the youth who stood before Arthur struck the horse over the nostrils with his sheathed sword, so that, had it been with the bare blade, it would have been a marvel if the bone had not been wounded as well as the flesh. And the knight drew his sword half out of the scabbard, and asked of him, 'Wherefore didst thou strike my horse? Whether was it in insult or in counsel unto me?' 'Thou dost indeed lack counsel. What madness caused thee to ride so furiously as to dash the water of the ford over Arthur, and the consecrated Bishop, and their counsellors, so that they were as wet as if they had been dragged out of the river?' 'As counsel then will I take it.' So he turned his horse's head round towards his army.

'Iddawc,' said Rhonabwy, 'who was yonder knight?' 'The most eloquent and the wisest youth that is in this island; Adaon, the son of Taliesin.' 'Who was the man that struck his horse?' 'A youth of forward nature; Elphin, the son of Gwyddno.'

Then spake a tall and stately man, of noble and flowing speech, saying that it was a marvel that so vast a host should be assembled in so narrow a space, and that it was a still greater marvel that those should be there at that time who had promised to be by midday in the battle of Badon, fighting with Osla Gyllellvawr. 'Whether thou mayest choose to proceed or not, I will proceed.' 'Thou sayest well,' said Arthur, 'and we will go altogether.' 'Iddawc,' said Rhonabwy, 'who was the man who spoke so marvellously unto Arthur erewhile?' 'A man who may speak as boldly as he listeth, Caradawc Vreichvras, the son of Llyr Marini, his chief counsellor and his cousin.'

Then Iddawc took Rhonabwy behind him on his horse, and that mighty host moved forward, each troop in its order, towards Cevndigoll. And when they came to the middle of the ford of the Severn, Iddawc turned his horse's head, and Rhonabwy looked along the valley of the Severn. And he beheld two fair troops coming towards the ford. One troop there came of brilliant white, whereof every one of the men had a scarf of white satin with jet-black borders. And the knees and the tops of the shoulders of their horses were jet-black, though they were of a pure white in every other part. And their banners were pure white, with black points to them all.

'Iddawc,' said Rhonabwy, 'who are yonder pure white troop?' 'They are the men of Norway, and March the son of Meirchion is their prince. And he is cousin unto Arthur.' And farther on he saw a troop, whereof each man wore garments of jet-black, with borders of pure white to every scarf; and the tops of the shoulders and the knees of their horses were pure white. And their banners were jet-black with pure white at the point of each.

251

'Iddawc,' said Rhonabwy, 'who are the jet-black troop yonder?' 'They are the men of Denmark, and Edeyrn the son of Nudd is their prince.'

And when they had overtaken the host, Arthur and his army of mighty ones dismounted below Caer Badou, and he perceived that he and Iddawc journeyed the same road as Arthur. And after they had dismounted he heard a great tumult and confusion amongst the host, and such as were then at the flanks turned to the centre, and such as had been in the centre moved to the flanks. And then, behold, he saw a knight coming, clad, both he and his horse, in mail, of which the rings were whiter than the whitest lily, and the rivets redder than the ruddiest blood. And he rode amongst the host.

'Iddawc,' said Rhonabwy, 'will yonder host flee?' 'King Arthur never fled, and if this discourse of thine were heard, thou wert a lost man. But as to the knight whom thou seest yonder, it is Kai. The fairest horseman is Kai in all Arthur's Court; and the men who are at the front of the army hasten to the rear to see Kai ride, and the men who are in the centre flee to the side, from the shock of his horse. And this is the cause of the confusion of the host.'

Thereupon they heard a call made for Kadwr, Earl of Cornwall, and behold he arose with the sword of Arthur in his hand. And the similitude of two serpents was upon the sword in gold. And when the sword was drawn from its scabbard, it seemed as if two flames of fire burst forth from the jaws of the serpents, and then so wonderful was the sword, that it was hard for any one to look upon it. And the host became still, and the tumult ceased, and the earl returned to the tent.

'Iddawc,' said Rhonabwy, 'who is the man who bore the sword of Arthur?' 'Kadwr, the Earl of Cornwall, whose duty it is to arm the king on the days of battle and warfare.'

And they heard a call made for Eirynwych Amheibyn, Arthur's servant, a red, rough, ill-favoured man, having red whiskers with bristly hairs. And behold he came upon a tall red horse with the mane parted on each side, and he brought with him a large and beautiful sumpter pack. And the huge red youth dismounted before Arthur, and he drew a golden chair out of the pack, and a carpet of diapered satin. And he spread the carpet before Arthur, and there was an apple of ruddy gold at each corner thereof, and he placed the chair upon the carpet. And so large was the chair that three armed warriors might have sat therein. Gwenn was the name of the carpet, and it was one of its properties that whoever was upon it no one could see him, and he could see every one. And it would retain no colour but its own.

And Arthur sat within the carpet, and Owain the son of Urien was standing before him. 'Owain,' said Arthur, 'wilt thou play chess?' 'I will, lord,' said Owain. And the red youth brought the chess for Arthur and Owain; golden pieces and a board of silver. And they began to play.

And while they were thus, and when they were best amused with their game, behold they saw a white tent with a red canopy, and the figure of a jet-black serpent on the top of the tent, and red glaring venomous eyes in the head of the serpent, and a red flaming tongue. And there came a young page with yellow curling hair and blue eyes, and a newly-springing beard, wearing a coat and a surcoat of yellow satin, and hose of thin greenish-yellow cloth upon his feet, and over his hose shoes of parti-coloured leather, fastened at the insteps with golden clasps. And he bore a heavy three-edged sword with a golden hilt, in a scabbard of black leather tipped with fine gold. And he came to the place where the Emperor and Owain were playing at chess.

And the youth saluted Owain. And Owain marvelled that the youth should salute him and should not have saluted the Emperor Arthur. And Arthur knew what was in Owain's thought. And he said to Owain, 'Marvel not that the youth salutes thee now, for he saluted me erewhile; and it is unto thee that his errand is.' Then said the youth unto Owain, 'Lord, is it with thy leave that the young pages and attendants of the Emperor harass and torment and worry thy Ravens? And if it be not with thy leave, cause the Emperor to forbid them.' 'Lord,' said Owain, 'thou hearest what the youth says; if it seem good to thee, forbid them from my Ravens.' 'Play thy game,' said he. Then the youth returned to the tent.

That game did they finish, and another they began, and when they were in the midst of the game, behold, a ruddy young man with auburn curling hair and large eyes, well-grown, and having his beard new shorn, came forth from a bright yellow tent, upon the summit of which was the figure of a bright red lion. And he was clad in a coat of yellow satin, falling as low as the small of his leg, and embroidered with threads of red silk. And on his feet were hose of fine white buckram, and buskins of black leather were over his hose, whereon were golden clasps. And in his hand a huge, heavy, three-edged sword, with a scabbard of red deerhide, tipped with gold. And he came to the place where Arthur and Owain were playing at chess. And he saluted him. And Owain was troubled at his salutation, but Arthur minded it no more than before. And the youth said unto Owain, 'Is it not against thy will that the attendants of the Emperor harass thy Ravens, killing some and worrying others? If against thy will it be, beseech him to forbid them.' 'Lord,' said Owain, 'forbid thy men, if it seem good to thee.' 'Play thy game,' said the Emperor. And the youth returned to the tent.

And that game was ended and another begun. And as they were beginning the first move of the game, they beheld at a small distance from them a tent speckled yellow, the largest ever seen, and the figure of an eagle of gold upon it, and a precious stone on the eagle's head. And coming out of the tent, they saw a youth with thick yellow hair upon his head, fair and comely, and a scarf of blue satin upon him, and a brooch of gold in the scarf upon his right shoulder as large as a warrior's middle finger. And upon his feet were hose of fine Totness, and shoes of parti-coloured leather, clasped with gold, and the youth was of noble bearing, fair of face, with ruddy cheeks and large hawk's eyes. In the hand of the youth was a mighty lance, speckled yellow, with a newly sharpened head; and upon the lance a banner displayed.

Fiercely angry, and with rapid pace, came the youth to the place where Arthur was playing at chess with Owain. And they perceived that he was wroth. And thereupon he saluted Owain, and told him that his Ravens had been killed, the chief part of them, and that such of them as were not slain were so wounded and bruised that not one of them could raise its wings a single fathom above the earth. 'Lord,' said Owain, 'forbid thy men.' 'Play,' said he, 'if it please thee.' Then said Owain to the youth, 'Go back, and wherever thou findest the strife at the thickest, there lift up the banner, and let come what pleases heaven.'

So the youth returned back to the place where the strife bore hardest upon the Ravens, and he lifted up the banner; and as he did so they all rose up in the air, wrathful and fierce and high of spirit, clapping their wings in the wind, and shaking off the weariness that was upon them. And recovering their energy and courage, furiously and with exultation did they, with one sweep, descend upon the heads of the men, who had erewhile caused them anger and pain and damage, and they seized some by the heads and others by the eyes, and some by the ears, and others by the arms, and carried them up into the air; and in the air there was a mighty tumult with the flapping of the wings of the triumphant Ravens, and with their croaking; and there was another mighty tumult with the groaning of the men, that were being torn and wounded, and some of whom were slain.

And Arthur and Owain marvelled at the tumult as they played at chess; and, looking, they perceived a knight upon a dun-coloured horse coming towards them. And marvellous was the hue of the dun horse. Bright red was his right shoulder, and from the top of his legs to the centre of his hoof was bright yellow. Both the knight and his horse were fully equipped with heavy foreign armour. The clothing of the horse from the front opening upwards was of bright red sendal, and from thence opening downwards was of bright yellow sendal. A large gold-hilted one-edged sword had the youth upon his thigh, in a scabbard of light blue, and tipped with Spanish laton. The belt of the sword was of dark green leather with golden slides and a clasp of ivory upon it, and a buckle of jet-black upon the clasp. A helmet of gold was on the head of the knight, set with precious stones of great virtue, and at the top of the helmet was the image of a flame-coloured leopard with two ruby-red stones in its head, so that it was astounding for a warrior, however stout his heart, to look at the face of the leopard, much more at the face of the knight. He had in his hand a blue-shafted lance, but from the haft to the point it was stained crimson-red with the blood of the Ravens and their plumage.

The knight came to the place where Arthur and Owain were seated at chess. And they perceived that he was harassed and vexed and weary as he came towards them. And the youth saluted Arthur, and told him that the Ravens of Owain were slaying his young men and attendants. And Arthur looked at Owain and said, 'Forbid thy Ravens.' 'Lord,' answered Owain, 'play thy game.' And they played. And the knight returned back towards the strife, and the Ravens were not forbidden any more than before.

And when they had played awhile, they heard a mighty tumult, and a wailing of men, and a croaking of Ravens, as they carried the men in their strength into the air, and, tearing them betwixt them, let them fall piecemeal to the earth. And during the tumult they saw a knight coming towards them on a light grey horse, and the left foreleg of the horse was jet-black to the centre of his hoof. And the knight and the horse were fully accoutred with huge heavy blue armour. And a robe of honour of yellow diapered satin was upon the knight, and the borders of the robe were blue. And the housings of the horse were jet-black, with borders of bright yellow. And on the thigh of the youth was a sword, long, and three-edged, and heavy. And the scabbard was of red cut leather, and the belt of new red deer-skin, having upon it many golden slides and a buckle of the bone of the sea-horse, the tongue of which was jet-black. A golden helmet was upon the head of the knight, wherein were set sapphire stones of great virtue. And at the top of the helmet was the figure of a flame-coloured lion, with a fiery-red tongue, issuing above a foot from his mouth, and with venomous eyes, crimson-red, in his head.

And the knight came, bearing in his hand a thick ashen lance, the head whereof, which had been newly steeped in blood, was overlaid with silver.

And the youth saluted the Emperor: 'Lord,' said he, 'carest thou not for the slaying of thy pages, and thy young men, and the sons of the nobles of the Island of Britain, whereby it will be difficult to defend this island from henceforward for ever?' 'Owain,' said Arthur, 'forbid thy Ravens.' 'Play this game, lord,' said Owain.

So they finished the game and began another; and as they were finishing that game, lo, they heard a great tumult and a clamour of armed men, and a croaking of Ravens, and a flapping of wings in the air, as they flung down the armour entire to the ground, and the men and the horses piecemeal. Then they saw coming a knight on a lofty-headed piebald horse. And the left shoulder of the horse was of bright red, and its right leg from the chest to the hollow of the hoof was pure white. And the knight and horse were equipped with arms of speckled yellow, variegated with Spanish laton. And there was a robe of honour upon him, and upon his horse, divided in two parts, white and black, and the borders of the robe of honour were of golden purple. And above the robe he wore a sword three-edged and bright, with a golden hilt. And the belt of the sword was of yellow gold-work, having a clasp upon it of the eyelid of a black sea-horse, and a tongue of yellow gold to the clasp. Upon the head of the knight was a bright helmet of yellow laton, with sparkling stones of crystal in it, and at the crest of the helmet was the figure of a griffin, with a stone of many virtues in its head. And he had an ashen spear in his hand, with a round shaft, covered with azure-blue. And the head of the spear was newly stained with blood, and was overlaid with fine silver.

Wrathfully came the knight to the place where Arthur was, and he told him that the Ravens had slain his household and the sons of the chief men of this island, and he besought him to cause Owain to forbid his Ravens. And Arthur besought Owain to forbid them. Then Arthur took the golden chessmen that were upon the board, and crushed them until they became as dust. Then Owain ordered Gwres the son of Rheged to lower his banner. So it was lowered, and all was peace.

Then Rhonabwy inquired of Iddawc who were the first three men that came to Owain, to tell him his Ravens were being slain. Said Iddawc, 'They were men who grieved that Owain should suffer loss, his fellow-chieftains and companions, Selyv the son of Kynan Garwyn of Powys, and Gwgawn Gleddyvrudd, and Gwres the son of Rheged, he who bears the banner in the day of battle and strife.' 'Who,' said Rhonabwy, 'were the last three men who came to Arthur, and told him that the Ravens were slaughtering his men?' 'The best of men,' said Iddawc, 'and the bravest, and who would grieve exceedingly that Arthur should have damage in aught; Blathaon the son of Mawrheth, and Rhuvawn Pebyr the son of Prince Deorthach, and Hyveidd Unllenn.'

And with that behold four-and-twenty knights came from Osla Gyllellvawr, to crave a truce of Arthur for a fortnight and a month. And Arthur arose and went to take counsel. And he came to where a tall, auburn, curly-headed man was a little way off, and there he assembled his counsellors. Bedwini, the Bishop, and Gwarthegyd the son of Kaw, and March the son of Meirchawn, and Caradawc Vreichvras, and Gwalchmai the son of Gwyar, and Edeyrn the son of Nudd, and Rhuvawn Pebyr the son of Prince Deorthach, and Rhiogan the son of the King of Ireland, and Gwenwynwyn the son of Nav, Howel the son of Emyr Llydaw,

Gwilym the son of Rhwyf Freinc, and Daned the son of Ath, and Goreu Custennin, and Mabon the son of Modron, and Peredur Paladyr Hir, and Hyveidd Unllenn, and Twrch the son of Perif, and Nerth the son of Kadarn, and Gobrwy the son of Echel Vorddwyttwll, Gwair the son of Gwestyl, and Gadwy the son of Geraint, Trystan the son of Tallwch, Moryen Manawc, Granwen the son of Llyr, and Llacheu the son of Arthur, and Llawvrodedd Varvawc, and Kadwr Earl of Cornwall, Morvran the son of Tegid, and Rhyawd the son of Morgant, and Dyvyr the son of Alun Dyved, Gwrhyr Gwalstawd Ieithoedd, Adaon the son of Taliesin, Llary the son of Kasnar Wledig, and Fflewddur Fflam, and Greidawl Galldovydd, Gilbert the son of Kadgyffro, Menw the son of Teirgwaedd, Gwrthmwl Wledig, Cawrdav the son of Caradawc Vreichvras, Gildas the son of Kaw, Kadyriaith the son of Saidi, and many of the men of Norway, and Denmark, and many of the men of Greece, and a crowd of the men of the host came to that council.

'Iddawc,' said Rhonabwy, 'who was the auburn-haired man to whom they came just now?' 'Rhun the son of Maelgwn Gwynedd, a man whose prerogative it is, that he may join in counsel with all.' 'And wherefore did they admit into counsel with men of such dignity as are yonder a stripling so young as Kadyriaith the son of Saidi?' 'Because there is not throughout Britain a man better skilled in counsel than he.'

Thereupon, behold, bards came and recited verses before Arthur, and no man understood those verses but Kadyriaith only, save that they were in Arthur's praise.

And lo, there came four-and-twenty asses with their burdens of gold and of silver, and a tired wayworn man with each of them, bringing tribute to Arthur from the Islands of Greece. Then Kadyriaith the son of Saidi besought that a truce might be granted to Osla Gyllellvawr for the space of a fortnight and a month, and that the asses and the burdens they carried might be given to the bards, to be to them as the reward for their stay and that their verse might be recompensed during the time of the truce. And thus it was settled.

'Rhonabwy,' said Iddawc, 'would it not be wrong to forbid a youth who can give counsel so liberal as this from coming to the councils of his lord?'

Then Kai arose, and he said, 'Whosoever will follow Arthur, let him be with him to-night in Cornwall, and whosoever will not, let him be opposed to Arthur even during the truce.' And through the greatness of the tumult that ensued, Rhonabwy awoke. And when he awoke he was upon the yellow calf-skin, having slept three nights and three days.

*And this tale is called the Dream of Rhonabwy. And this is the reason that no one knows the dream without a book, neither bard nor gifted seer; because of the various colours that were upon the horses, and the many wondrous colours of the arms and of the panoply, and of the precious scarfs, and of the virtue-bearing stones.*

## Notes

1     Agitator of Britain.
2     Blue Slab.

# 15

# THE PROCEEDINGS OF THE GREAT BARDIC INSTITUTION

edited and translated by
**OWEN CONNELAN**

*In which is explained how 'The Tain' (or an account of the Cattle Raid of Cuailgne) was first discovered, etc.*

A NOBLE, WORTHY, KING ruled Airgiall at one time whose name was Hugh son of Duach the Dark. Contemporaneous with him was Hugh the Fair, son of Fergna, son of Fergus, son of Muredagh Mal, king of Brefney, and those two were at strife. In every good act performed by one, the other would endeavour to excel him; yet both were not equally circumstanced; for one was hundred fold more (wealthy), just, and prosperous, namely Hugh the Fair; whilst the other was valiant and warlike, namely Hugh the son of Duach the Dark, king of Oirgiall. It was, indeed, far easier for him to be the more warlike of the two, for he had a shield and the name of the shield was Duv-Gilla (the Black Attendant), and one of its properties was this, that whosoever was opposed to it in the field of battle became as enfeebled as an old woman, and all fled before it in every conflict it entered into, even when there was present but the shield itself and its bearer.

It was at that very period and time that Eohy the chief Professor was staying with the king of Brefney, and this was Dallan Forguil. He was accompanied by a numerous professional body, and the quarter he liked best was Brefney, for numerous were its flocks and cattle herds.

It happened that the king of Brefney was one night in his festive chamber, and he said to Dallan: – 'Thou hast great honour and privilege from me.' 'That is not to be wondered at,' said Dallan, 'for great is my honour in Alban (Scotland), in Saxonland, in Britain (perhaps Wales), and in France, because I hold the chief professorship of all those countries.' 'Notwithstanding all that,' said Hugh the Fair, 'I give you more than all those kings and noble chiefs together, for whenever thou goest on a professional visit into distant foreign countries, and if thou shouldst

257

lose a cow I send you a cow in its place, and if thou shouldst lose goods I send you goods instead of them, and if thou losest a penny I put a penny in its place, in order that thou mayest find thy cattle, goods, and wealth whole on thy return.' 'Why sayest thou this, O king?' says Dallan. 'For this reason,' said the kind, 'that thou shouldst obtain whatever thou wouldst ask from that person whom thou honourest as much as me, and that is the king of Oirgiall.' 'He has nothing,' says Dallan, 'excepting his sovereignty, that he would not give me.' 'He has surely,' says Hugh the Fair. 'What is that?' asked Dallan. 'A shield which he has; its name is Duv-Gilla, and by it he has hitherto gained sway and will ever gain it, and by it he has defended the territory of Oirgiall and its borders, and he would not give it to thee.' That is not the request of a truly learned man, and if it were I would ask it.' 'I will reward you for going to ask it,' said Hugh the Fair, viz., one hundred of each kind of cattle.' 'I will go to ask it,' said Dallan, 'and if I shall not obtain it, I will satirize the king of Oirgiall.' They passed over that night.

Dallan arose early, and his steeds were got ready for him, and he took along with him his thrice nine Professors to the *Dun* of the king of Oirgiall. When the king was informed that Dallan was on the lawn, he came forth to meet him and gave him three kisses. In like manner he welcomed his accompanying professors, after which Dallan was borne into the fortress. 'I will not stay,' says Dallan, 'till I know whether I shall obtain my request.' 'What is the request?' asked the king. 'Thy shield,' replied Dallan, 'namely Duv-Gilla.' 'That is not the request of a truly learned man,' said the king, 'and if it were thou shouldst obtain it.' 'I have brought you a poem for it,' said Dallan. 'I would like to hear your poem,' said the king. He then recited the poem as follows:–

> A hero of fortune (art thou) O Hugh
> Thou daring, determined foe (or venom),
> Thy goodness as the great ocean;
> Thou canst not be subdued,
> Thou canst not be impeded,
> O Hugh, son of Duach the Dark.
> Good and great is his substance,
> Without censure, and without reproach,
> Thou sun after leaving its stars
> Which is awful to me,
> Thou white chess-board
> We will return, O hero.

'That is a good poem,' says the king, 'whoever could understand it.' 'That is true for you,' says Dallan, 'and whosoever composes a poetic remonstrance, it is he himself who ought to explain it; and as it was I that composed it, it is I that will interpret it. "A hero of fortune art thou O Hugh," I have addressed to thee, that is, thou art the hero of valour and of singular deeds of (the men of) Ireland. "Thou venom, daring and firm," I addressed to thee, that is *Daigh* is a name for *poison*, and daringly enters thy venom, namely thy shield, into battle and conflict. "Thou goodness as the great ocean," that is to say that if the wealth of the ocean belonged to thee thou wouldst distribute it amongst the professors of arts and sciences. "Thou sun after (leaving) its stars," that is, the sun after leaving its stars is the time its figure appears best, and its figure is not better than your figure. "Thou white chess-board," that is, if any person should have seven sets of chess-men they would be of no use to him if wanting a board. Thou art the board for the support and protection of the men of Ireland, &c.'

'That is good,' said the king, 'and I will give money and cattle for it.' 'Give it if it be taken from thee,' says Dallan, 'and I have composed another poem for the shield as follows:–

> O Hugh, generous and worthy,
> Chasing is thy shield
> As the wave which runs its course;
> Thou art head of our tribes and chiefs.
> We will convey thy mighty fame
> Beyond every clear and productive stream.
> Honour, without envy, to the prince,
> My magnificent shield is his shield;
> A speckled shield, the feeder of ravens,
> Wards off the foe from his borders.
> Surprising and beautiful shield
> Is with Hugh the son of Duach;
> We will bear it away from the son of Duach
> Ere we should depart in sorrow;
> A surprizing and beautiful shield
> Will be given to me by Hugh for praise.

'That is a good poem, O Dallan,' said Hugh, 'and whatever is meet, viz., gold, silver, jewels and substance, thou shalt have them from me.' 'I will not have them,' said Dallan, 'because it was for the shield I composed my poem, and I have composed another poem, also for the shield, viz.:'–

> Bright as the speckled salmon of the wave!
> Dubh-Ghiolla! panic of the banded brave;
> With thee would I combine in deathless praise,
> Proud Aodh, whose arm of might thy burthen sways.
>
> Fenced with its thorny mail the holly stands –
> So round the prince the guardian shield expands:
> The bull's strong hide the needle's point defies –
> Thus vainly round him baffled ranks arise:
>
> That shield at once his panoply and blade.
> He scorns the spear, the falchion's feebler aid.
>
> As chafing storms too long in durance pent
> Sweep through the forest, finding sudden vent;
> Such is the voice of Aodh, when with his shield
> Compassed, he stands bright terror of the field.

'That is a good poem, O Dallan,' said Hugh, 'and I will give good payment for it of gold and silver; I will, moreover give a hundred of each flock for it.' 'That is very good,' said Dallan, 'however nought of all the gold, the silver, and the jewels of the world, that have been expressed by the mouth of man, will I accept from thee but the shield.' 'I will not give you the shield,' said Hugh. 'I will satirize you,' said Dallan. 'The powers and miracles of the king of Heaven and earth be on my side to save and protect me against thee! And dost thou remember, O Dallan,' said Hugh, 'that when the saints of Erin made peace between us (the kings) and you the bards of Erin, it was agreed that whosoever of you should compose a satire on us unjustly, three blotches of reproach should grow upon him; and if we should deserve it and that you should compose it justly, the same number should grow upon us; and the following are (the names of) the saints: – Columbkill, son of Feidlim; Kieran of Cluain; Kieran the senior, of Saigir; Finnen of Clonard; Finnen of Moyville; Seanagh son of Caitin; Ruadan of Lothra; Brendan of Birr; Brendan son of Finnlogha; the holy Mocholmoge; Comgall; Dalua of Derry; and the holy Caillen.' 'All those will not save you from being satirized by me; and it is no satisfaction to me to satirize you except I do so in your presence' – and this is what he said: –

> O Hugh, son of Duach the Dark,
> Thou pool not permanent;
> Thou pet of the mild cuckoos;
> Thou quick chafferer of a blackbird;
>
> Thou sour green berry;
> Swarms (of bees) will suck the herbs;
> Thou green crop like fine clothes;
> A candlestick without light;
>
> Thou cold wooden boat;
> Thou bark that will give dissatisfaction;
> Thou disgusting black chafer;
> Thou art more disgusting, O Hugh.

'We must confess,' said Hugh, 'that we do not know whether that is better or worse than the first poem you composed.' 'No wonder for a man of your intellect to say so,' said Dallan, 'and as it was I that composed the satires, it is I that will interpret them.

'"O Hugh, son of Duach the Dark, thou pool not permanent;" that is equivalent to a summer pool when it experiences a great drought and that persons trample in it; its water entirely evaporates, and it is not replenished till the flood comes again; you are similarly circumstanced, for no matter how highly you may be praised, the same hospitality shall not possess you again in consequence of these satires. "Thou captive of a tamed cuckoo;" that is equivalent to a pet of a cuckoo, for there cannot be in a house a worse pet than this. It ceases to sing except a little, and he will as soon do so in winter as at any other time. And some assert that another bird nurses for it; its name is Cobcan, and he puts away his own bird and feeds the cuckoo's bird till it is able to provide for itself, when the cuckoo takes it away with her, and she has no more regard for that Cobcan than she has for any other bird. Similar to that is your case and of the learned professors of Erin, for they will not remember any good thou hast done after these satires. "Thou quick chaffering blackbird;" that is equivalent to a blackbird which is roused by the approach of a person in the night; he gives a whistle or cry of alarm, and he is silent for that night through the terror that seizes him. Similar to that is your case; your hospitality has been heard of far off, but since you have been satirized no one will hear of it in consequence of these satires. "Tribes will suck the herb;" like to the bee, for if seven horse-loads (of it) were put into one vessel upon the fire it only blackens after the bees have sucked it.'

'Be done, O Dallan,' said the king, 'do not satirize me any more in my presence, for I will now excuse you from further professional attendance.' 'I'll take it for granted,' says Dallan; 'get my steeds ready that I may depart.' Their steeds were brought to them, and (Dallan and his ollavs) leave the place. 'The might of God and the saints pursue you if ye have wrongfully satirized me,' said Hugh.

They had not come far from the township when Dallan said to his professors: 'It is a wonder to me,' said he, 'what the publishers of stories have related, for they assert that whosoever composes satires wrongfully it will be worse for himself; and I believe that never have been made satires more unjustly or wrongfully than the satires I myself have composed, and yet I am now the better for uttering them, for I was without an eye on my coming to the place, and I have two good eyes now.' 'O chief professor,' said they, 'it is good news thou tellest, although it is not easy to believe it.' 'It is a fact,' said Dallan. 'If so,' said the professors, 'tell us our order in the way before thee and after thee.' 'There are,' said he, 'twice nine of you before me, and nine of you after me.' 'True for you, O chief professor,' said they. 'I know not if these be good signs,' said Dallan, 'for I had an assurance from Columbkille, the son of Feidhlim, that I should have an extraordinary forewarning before my death, and what more wonderful sign could I get than, being blind on my coming to the town, and to have the use of my two eyes now? therefore take me to my home.' They then took him to his house, and he lived three days and three nights, after which he died.

The professors assembled together, and these were their names: – Maolgedic, son of Firgoboc, Bard of Alban; Arrachtan, son of Onsclann, Bard of Britain; Srubchaille, son of Sreabchaille, Bard of Saxan; Niamchaemh, Bard of Ulster; Dael Duileadh, professor of Leinster; Ollmhor, the arch sage of the professors of Desmond; Oircne Aiteamain, professor of Thomond; (and) Seanchán, the learned Fileadh and chief Bard of Connaught. These bards having assembled together they debated amongst them as to whom they should appoint arch Bard in the place of Dallan. 'Let the foster-mother of the literati be brought to us,' said they, 'namely, Muireann, daughter of Cuain-Cuilli, the wife of Dallan, together with the learned aged females, namely, Grug, Grag, and Grangait.' They were convened accordingly, and they enquired of them who ought to be appointed chief Bard. Muireann said: – 'You formerly went on a professional visit to Alban, and I then asked Dallan that whensoever he himself would die, who should be appointed chief professor in his place. He then said that if any person in this world could substitute a stanza for a stanza and a word for a word of his own (composition), it is

Seanchan, the aged poet, that can do so.' 'Well, then,' said the professors, 'let Seanchan be elected our prophetic chief professor.' Whereupon Seanchan was then inaugurated chief Bard by them; and they desired him to go over Dallan and compose an Elegy for him. Seanchan went and made this Elegy, and recited it over Dallan:–

Beloved is the body that here lies dead,
Although a weighty man he was a light man;
Light in body he was mighty in mind,
Great was the clan over whom he was chief.

Thrice fifty of us were along with him,
Of learned men of letters of superior knowledge;
If our numbers had been greater
We would have new instruction from him each day.

The sound of the Deluge which hosts could not comprehend,
The mighty rushing flow of Eassa-Roe,
The overwhelming flood of the Red Sea,
To these may be compared the intellect of Dallan [incomprehensible].

Till the brilliant sun shall cease his course
Which God ordained for him over the elements,
No poet north or south shall ever excel
The fluent Eohy, chief of learned men.

He was a philosopher, O God of Heaven!
He was illustrious, he was chief poet;
Until the wave of unhappy death came upon him,
Oh! he was splendid, he was beloved.

The entire of the Bardic Association declared that they had a sufficiently competent Professor in the person who composed that Elegy. It was then they deliberated as to what province in Ireland they should first proceed on a professional visit; and each one of them was desirous to go to his own province. Seanchan said it would be more meet to visit the person who was never satirized or reproached about (his liberality of) gold or abundance of valuable goods. 'Who is he?' said each of them. 'Guaire, son of Colman, son of Coffey, son of Gabneann, son of Connell, son of Owen, son of Eohy Breac, son of Dathy, son of Fiachra.' The entire of the great Bardic Association declared it would be proper to go there since Seanchan desired it. 'Let messengers be despatched from us to Guaire' (said they). They (the messengers) went and informed him (Guaire) that Seanchan along with his professors and poets were coming to him. 'My respect for them,' said Guaire. 'My respect for their good and for their bad; my respect for their nobles and their ignobles; my respect for their women and for their men.' Guaire, after that, made a mansion for them, which had eight sides to it, and a door between every two sides (or divisions); and there were eight first class beds between every two doors, and a low bed (or truckle bed) beside every chief bed. The reason he made that arrangement was, that whosoever of those that occupied the beds, in case they should have a quarrel or strife and get out of them, he might find the lower bed ready for him. And he constructed eight fountains (or lavatories) for their men; and eight fountains for their women; for he did not wish that the water used in washing the hands of the professors should touch the hands of the women, nor the water of the hands of the women should be used in washing the hands of the professors; and feasts and banquets were ordered for their entertainment, and he then sent messengers to invite them.

Seanchan said: – 'Though excellent the hospitality of Guaire may be, I will not take all that are here to him to spoil Connaught, for I consider it enough to take the two-thirds of them to him, and to let one-third remain,' and he acted accordingly. He did not take to Guaire but thrice fifty of the professors; thrice fifty students (or second class of professors); thrice fifty hounds; thrice fifty male attendants; thrice fifty female relatives; and thrice nine of each class of artificers; and that number arrived at Durlus.

Guaire went forth to meet them, and he bestowed kisses on their chiefs, and gave welcome to their learned men. 'My regards to you, said Guaire; 'my regards to your nobles and ignobles; I have great welcome for you all, both professors and poets; both scientific men and students; both sons and women; both hounds and servants; only you are so numerous, but not deeming you too many, I would give each of you a separate welcome; however, my respects to you all on every side.' And they were led into the large mansion, and viands were laid out before them, and Guaire told them that whatever they would desire they might ask for it and they should have it.

It was, however, a great difficulty to procure all things for them, for it was requisite to give to each of them his meals apart and a separate bed; and they went not to bed any night without wanting something, and they arose not a day without some one of them having longing desires for some things that were extraordinary, wonderful, and rare, and difficult of procurement. It was a task for all the men of Ireland to find that which was longed for, and unless the person who desired it obtained it within twenty-four hours, it was useless ever after to procure it for him.

An extraordinary wish occurred that very night, in the mansion of the learned association; and the person to whom that longing happened was Muireann, daughter of Cuan Culli, the wife of Dallan, who was the foster-mother of the literati; and she uttered a great moan aloud. Seanchan answered her, and what he said was: – 'What is the matter with you, chieftainess?' 'A desire that has seized me,' said she, 'and unless it be procured for me I will not live.' 'What is that wish,' asked Seanchan. She told him the wish which seized her, namely, 'a bowl of the ale of sweet milk (or common Tormentil), with the marrow of the ankle-bone of a wild hog; a pet cuckoo on an ivy tree in my presence between the two Christmases (Christmas-day and Twelfth-day or Epiphany) at that time; and her full load on her back, with a girdle of yellow lard of an exceeding white boar about her; and to be mounted on a steed with a brown main, and its four legs exceedingly white; a garment of the spider's web around her, and she humming a tune as she proceeded to Durlus.' 'It is difficult to procure that wish,' said Seanchan; 'that is not one but a number of strange wishes which are not easily gratified.'

They bore away that night 'till the morrow; Guaire was in the habit of visiting the mansion every day, and used to enquire how they fared; and he enquired 'how fares it with this great and good people to-day.' 'We never had,' said they, 'worse times than we now have.' 'How is that?' asked Guaire. 'A longing that has happened to one of us,' said Seanchan. 'To whom did that occur?' asked Guaire. 'To Muireann, daughter of Cuan Culli,' replied Seanchan, 'namely the wife of Dallan, the foster-mother of the literati.' 'What is the wish?' said Guaire. Seanchan told him. 'That is not one wish but a variety of bad wishes, and the easiest is difficult of procuring;' and Guaire departed sad and sorrowful. None of his people accompanied him at that time but one attending servant, and Guaire asked him, 'are you a good secret keeper.' 'For what purpose do you ask,' said the servant. 'I would wish to go to Seasgan-Uar-Beoil,' said Guaire, 'where dwells Fulachtach the son of Owen; for it was I that slew his father, his six sons, and his three brothers; and I would rather he should kill me in order that my hospitality may endure after me, than that I should survive my liberality, for those wishes can never be obtained.' 'My secrecy is good,' said the servant, 'and should you be seen to proceed thither, there is not a person in this house that would not be around you.'

That was displeasing to Guaire, and he proceeded to Finn-Aragal of hospitality, where he knelt and prayed and supplicated Jesus Christ, and here he obtained from God every thing he desired through the efficacies of his bounteous liberality, and it was on that account that it was called Aracul of Hospitality. Guaire was kneeling and praying, and imploring God that he might die ere he should hear himself satirized and defamed by the great Bardic Association. To be sure, no favours were ever asked of him more difficult to be procured than the wishes desiderated by the old dame, and he prayed God most fervently to deliver him from that strait, and that he might obtain from the Supreme Being whatever wish any of the Bardic Institution might desire; and he made the following little Lay, in sadness, at Finn-Aracul of Hospitality: –

Here is my sorrow, O Son of my God!
Through all that happen'd me yesterday;
Thrice fifty learned men, a vexatious clan,
Who came to this place with Seanchan.

Though great is the number of austere bards
That came to Durlus of Guaire,
Each enjoyed pleasure and entertainment
Until the old woman intruded.

Great was the task I took in hand,
To administer to the learned of sumptuous living;
Should any depart from my house unsupplied,
In vain to this day has been my generosity.

Why hath the king of the brilliant sun
Conferred on myself his likeness,
Should he of his bounty not grant to me
Means to protect my countenance.

I have promised to the son of Mary
Not to refuse the face of man;
Should any such person deprive me of my good fame.
Even to him it will be no sorrow.

Guaire passed over that night till the morning came, and he heard the bustle and paces of an individual advancing towards him in the early morn, but his grief was so great that he did not look on him. He afterwards, however, recognized him, and he who happened to be there was Marvan the swine-herd, the prime prophet of heaven and earth, he was son of Guaire's mother, and swine-herd to Guaire. His object in this occupation was that he might the more advantageously devote himself to religion and devotion in the capacity of swine-herd, in woods and desert places. He saluted Guaire; 'the same compliments to you, chief prophet of heaven and earth,' said Guaire. 'What is the cause of your sadness?' asked Marvan. 'A yearning that has seized a person in the house of the great Bardic Association.' 'What is the wish?' enquired Marvan, 'or to whom did it happen?' 'To Muiran, daughter of Cuan Culli,' replied Guaire, 'the wife of Dallan, and the foster-mother of the Bards.' 'That is she, whom we desire to be the first of them that should die; and what is the wish?' asked Marvan. 'A bowl of the ale of sweet milk, together with the marrow of the ankle bone of a wild hog.' 'It is difficult to procure that wish,' said Marvan, 'and although difficult it will be found with me in Glen-a-Scail.'

'She seeks another thing,' said Guaire, 'namely, a pet cuckoo cooing on an ivy tree in her presence.' 'It is a strange time (of the year) to desire that now,' said Marvan, 'and although strange we know the place where that is.'

'She desired another thing,' said Guaire, 'namely, a bay steed, with a red mane and its four legs purely white.' 'In one house those two are to be had,' said Marvan, 'the pet cuckoo and the bay steed.' 'Who has them?' asked Guaire. 'Derdavna, daughter of Iuvdan, your own powerful sprite (or protectress,) it is she possesses them.' 'If she has them I will obtain them,' said Guaire.

'She desired another thing,' said Guaire, 'namely, to have about her a garment of many colours (made) of the spider's silk.' 'That will be found with me in Glen-a-Scail,' said Marvan.

'She desired another thing,' said Guaire, 'namely, her full load on her back and a girdle about her of the yellow lard of a purely white boar.' 'Did she request that?' asked Marvan. 'She did request it,' replied Guaire. 'My malediction on the person who desired that,' said Marvan, 'and I implore the King of Heaven and earth that that wish may not serve her. Sure it is I who have that boar and it is a hardship for me to kill him, for he is to me a herdsman, a physician, a messenger and a musician.' 'How does he perform all that for you?' asked Guaire. 'In the following manner,' replied Marvan: 'When I return from the swine at night, and that the skin is torn off my feet by the briars of Glen-a-Scail, he comes to me and rubs his tongue over my feet, and though I should have all the surgeons and healing ointments in the world his tongue would cure me soonest; in that manner he is a physician to me. He is herd to me, for when the swine wander through Glen-a-Scail, and that I am wearied, I give him a blow with my foot, and he goes after the swine. There are nine passes leading into Glen-a-Scail, and there is no danger of any hog of them (being carried off) by a thief, vagrant, or wolf of the forest, until he drives in the very last hog of them. He is a musician to me, for when I am anxious to sleep I give him a stroke with my foot and he lies on his back with his belly uppermost and sings me a humming tune, and his music is more grateful to me than that of a sweet toned harp in the hands of an accomplished minstrel. The blackbird is the most variable in his notes of all birds, yet he (the boar) is still more varied. It is hard for me to kill that animal,' said Marvan, 'and do thou thyself send messengers for him, for I cannot kill him, and I pledge my word to you,' said Marvan, 'that I will pay a visit some day to the mansion of the great bardic body to be avenged of them for the white boar, and may they never be the better for it.'

Howbeit, all those objects of desire were procured through the instrumentality of Marvan. The white boar was afterwards killed, his lard was put on the old dame's back, and she hummed her tune as she proceeded on her way to Durlus. While passing over an unsettled causeway that led to the place her steed fell and she happened to be under it, by which her thigh bone, fore arm, and neck were broken, and she died after that manner; and thence originated (the adage,) 'The Hag's load of lard.'

Another longing desire seized a person in the mansion of the great Bardic Association, namely Meve Neidigh, the daughter of Seanchan, and she uttered a great moan. Her father responded to her. 'What ails thee my daughter?' said he. 'A yearning wish that has possessed me,' answered she, 'and unless it be procured I will not live.' 'What is the wish?' asked Seanchan. 'That I might have the full of the skirt of my mantle of large blackberries; (the season being that of January,) and that I might be on my way to Durlus, and that on my arrival there I might find the people of Guaire in sickness and distemper.' 'Why sayest thou that, my daughter,' said Seanchan, 'since Guaire is our consoler and comforter.' 'Dost thou know, father, how I am like unto the *Fidat*, that is the nettle, for he who would construct a house about it would as soon be stung by it as any other person. Similar is my case, for I do not desire that any other should die sooner than he who gives me wealth and great substance.' They wore away that night.

Guaire came to the mansion of the bards on the morrow, and he asked, 'How does it fare with this great and worthy people to-day?' said he. 'We never have had,' replied Seanchan, 'so bad a day as we have had, for a longing desire has seized my daughter, namely Meave Neidigh.' 'What is the desire?' asked Guaire. Seanchan told him. Guaire was sorrowful for that. 'It is not in the comprehension of man to gratify these wishes,' said Guaire. He departed from the mansion, but had not proceeded far when he met Marvan. 'My love to thee, Guaire,' said Marvan. 'The like to thee, chief prophet of Heaven and earth,' responded Guaire. 'What sadness is this over you, Guaire?' asked Marvan. 'A wish that has seized one of the great bardic body,' replied Guaire. 'After the white boar?' exclaimed Marvan. 'Yes,' responded Guaire. 'What is the wish, and to whom did it occur?' asked Marvan. 'To Meve Neidigh, the daughter of Seanchan, viz., the full of the skirt of her mantle of large blackberries.' 'They will be found with me in Glen-a-Scail,' said Marvan. 'How may that be?' asked Guaire. 'One day that you had been hunting in Glen-a-Scail, you held a hound by the leash, and the hound having espied an animal, he made a pull at you; a bush of briars which was adjacent to you, caught and pulled off your cloak, which you readily let go, for you never refused a favour to any; you were just departed from it when I came up, and found a great large quantity of berries on the bush; I spread the cloak over it, so that neither storm nor rain has touched them ever since, through the powers of God and my intercessions; and such of them as were red on that day, are black to-day, and those that were black have the taste of honey.'

'She desired another thing,' said Guaire, 'namely, that my people might be in sickness and disease on her arrival.' 'It is hard to ask that,' said Marvan, 'and do thou proceed to-night to Finn-Aragal of hospitality, and I will go to Glen-a-Scail, and let us conjointly implore the Supreme King of Heaven and Earth, that your people may be in sickness and disease, and be restored immediately after.'

They proceeded forward and they both prayed to God fervently that night. Meave got the blackberries; she came to Durlus, and the condition she found the people of Guaire in, was that each of them had the symptoms of death through the united prayers of Guaire and Marvan; and she had only left the place when all of them both men and women recovered their health; and such was the manner in which those things wished for were obtained by God's means and Marvan.

Another longing desire seized a person in the house of the great Bardic Association, namely, Bridget, daughter of Onithkerne, the wife of Shanchan, and she uttered a loud moan. Shanchan responded – 'What is the matter with thee, chieftainess?' asked Shanchan. 'A wish that has seized me,' said she, 'and unless it be obtained I will die.' 'Say the wish,' said Shanchan. 'To get my fill of the fat of a water blackbird; and again my fill of a red-eared and purely white cow without a liver, but having tallow in place of her liver; also my fill of red strawberries and of purple berries, and that the drink I may get after them shall be *Fethnait Feagha Fuinn*, viz., the honey of the woodbine.' 'It is difficult to procure these wishes,' said Shanchan. That night wore on.

Guaire came early on the morrow to the bardic mansion, and enquired – 'How fares it with this great and excellent people to-day?' 'We never have been,' replied Shanchan, 'at any time so badly off, for a longing desire has seized one of us, namely, Bridget, daughter of Onithkerne, my own wife.' 'What is the wish?' asked Guaire. Shanchan informed him. 'There is no possibility of procuring those wishes,' said Guaire.

He went away in sorrow from the mansion, but did not proceed far when he met Marvan. They greeted each other. 'What is the matter with thee, O Guaire?' asked Marvan. 'A wish that has happened to a person in the dwelling of the Bards,' replied Guaire. 'After the white boar, eh?' exclaimed Marvan. 'Yes,' responded Guaire, and he told him the wishes. 'I know the place where those are, viz., with the Nuns of Tuaim-daghualan, for there are nine score nuns in one house, and they all get a sufficiency (of milk) by one milking from that cow; and it is they who have that blackbird, and when the last of the nuns retires to sleep he sings music for them which would lull to sleep wounded men and parturient women; and it is certain that should you give them nine score, red-eared, purely white cows, their one cow would be more valuable than them all; and should you give them nine score blackbirds, their one blackbird would be better than they.

'She desired another thing,' said Guaire, 'namely, shrub-berries and tree-berries and the honey of the woodbine.' 'Those will be found with me,' said Marvan. All those wishes were procured as Marvan predicted. Nine score kine, and nine score blackbirds, were given to the nuns for their one cow and one blackbird; and the nobility of the men of Ireland, declared that the entire of the great Bardic Association were not worth those two (animals) that were killed.

Another longing desire seized one of the great Bardic Association, namely, Shanchan, and he uttered a great moan. The whole of the great Bardic Association simultaneously responded, and they asked what was the matter with him. 'A longing desire that has seized me,' replied he, 'and unless it be procured I shall die, namely, that I myself, my Bardic Association and the nobles of Connaught may get our fill of the fat of hogs that have not yet been farrowed, and also of ale (the produce) of one grain (of corn), and except these be obtained within the period of twenty-four hours I shall be dead.'

That (circumstance) was revealed to Guaire in the night, and he did not wait for the day, but came directly to the mansion, and he asked – 'How does it fare with this great and good people to-night?' 'We never,' said they, 'have had a worse night.' 'How so?' asked Guaire. 'A longing desire that has seized one of us.' 'To whom did that longing happen?' asked Guaire. 'To Shanchan the aged poet, the arch bard himself.' 'What is the wish?' asked Guaire. He was told it. Whereupon Guaire was sore troubled, for he considered that those wishes could not be gratified.

He turned away out from the mansion but proceeded not far when Marvan met him. 'What is it troubles thee, O Guaire?' asked Marvan. 'A longing desire that has seized one in the mansion of the learned.' 'After the white boar?' exclaimed Marvan. 'Yes,' replied Guaire. 'What is the wish,' asked Marvan, 'and to whom did it happen?' 'To Shanchan, the aged poet,' replied Guaire, 'namely, a sufficiency for himself and for his associates, and for the nobility and gentry of Connaught, of the ale of one grain (of corn).' 'That will be found with me in Glen-a-Scail,' said Marvan. 'How so?' asked Guaire. 'One day that your own agriculturist, namely, Guaire Beiceinigh (or of little hospitality) had been returning from sowing seed, he felt a substance (literally a prominence) under the sole of his shoe, and he found a grain of wheat in it, and an acorn was not larger than it; this he brought to me. It was planted by me in the ground that year, and seven and twenty prime ears sprung forth in the second year. But eleven years have elapsed since then, and no other corn has been allowed to mix with it during that period, and I have (now) seven prime stacks (of corn) which are the produce of that one grain. I have given directions to prepare a great excellent banquet in Glen-a-Scail, and I am confident,' said Marvan, 'that should all the nobles of Connaught assemble, they can have plenty of food and drink from the produce of that one grain.'

'He desired another thing,' said Guaire, 'namely, to have plenty for himself and for his bardic associates and for the nobles of Connaught of the fat of a hog that has not yet been farrowed, and unless it be procured within the space of a day and a night it need never be procured.' 'That will be found with me in Glen-a-Scail,' said Marvan. 'How?' asked Guaire. 'One day that the chief sow of your swine had wandered through Glen-a-Scail to farrow, she encountered a wolf in the forest, and the wolf having torn her, her litter and bowels gushed out. The sow made a charge at the wolf and took off her head, and they had only fallen by each other when I came up to them and found the holder (or matrix) of the piglings on the ground, and each pigling making a forward effort. I let them out, there being nine boar piglings and one sow pigling. I then killed the sucking pigs of a hog of an inferior breed to these, in order to rear them. Nine years have since then elapsed, and they are now nine full grown boars with curved tusks; and it is my opinion,' said Marvan, 'that should the nobility and gentry of Connaught assemble together, they shall have their full sufficiency of the fat of those hogs; and do thou give them their choice to have the feast conveyed to them or come and partake of it at Glen-a-Scail.'

The choice of selection was submitted to the Bards. They replied, that they had a mind to satirize the nobles of Connaught for presuming to think that they would leave their own mansion. That feast was brought to them, and they were seated in conformity with the decision of Shanchan. They drank and made merry, and every guest present was entertained by the great Bardic Association with the choicest music and professional accomplishments. That feast was continued for three days and three nights. When Shanchan perceived the extraordinary quantity of food and drink that was being consumed by the servants he became very churlish, and said, that he would not taste of food or drink until the nobles of Connaught were dismissed from the mansion, and forthwith they were sent away.

Shanchan, however, continued three days and three nights without food or drink. Guaire said. 'It is grievous to us that the whole Bardic Order should be taking food around Shanchan while he himself fasts.' He then sent a favourite domestic of his to Shanchan, and he instructed him to procure a long white hazel spit, to put a goose on it, to keep two-thirds of the spit before him, and one-third behind him, and to hold it in that manner in the presence of Shanchan. The young man went into the place where Shanchan was. 'What do you intend to do with that goose?' asked Shanchan. 'To prepare it for thee, O Royal Bard,' replied the youth. 'Why have you been sent with it?' asked Shanchan. 'As a person of mild manners and of cleanliness, selected by Guaire to bring you your food.' 'We believe,' said Shanchan, 'that he could not find in the locality a more uncomely person than thyself.' 'For what cause; O Royal Bard?' asked the youth. 'I knew your grandfather and he was chip-nailed, and since he was so, I shall not take food out of thy hands.'

The youth came away sorrowfully, and he related to Guaire what had happened. Guaire was dissatisfied with that; and they passed away the time till the termination of three days and three nights. Guaire then called another favourite (or foster child) of his to him, namely the daughter of Bec Bainig, and he said to her. 'Lady take with thee wheaten flour and the roe of a salmon to Shanchan, and knead them in his presence.' The maiden went. 'What do you intend to do with that, young girl?' asked Shanchan. 'To prepare it for thee, O Royal Bard,' she replied. 'Why hast thou been sent with it?' asked Shanchan. 'As a person of cleanliness and comeliness whom Guaire desired to send with thy food to thee.' 'Indeed I am sure,' said Shanchan, 'that there is not in the place another young girl more unseemly than thyself.' 'How so, O Royal Bard?' asked the maiden. 'I knew thy grandmother, who was seated (one day) on a high rock whilst giving instructions to lepers about their way, and she stretched her hand forth to point out the way for them, and as she did so, how could I take food from thy hands.'

The maiden went away in sorrow, and informed Guaire. Guaire exclaimed: 'My malediction upon the mouth that uttered that, and I implore the Supreme

King of Heaven and Earth that ere Shanchan shall depart this world, his mouth may kiss a leper's mouth.'

Shanchan continued for a day and night after that without food or drink. Bridget, the daughter of Onithcerne, desired her maid servant to give Shanchan her spare food. 'What leavings hast thou?' enquired Shanchan. 'A hen egg,' replied Bridget. 'It is almost enough for me,' said Shanchan, 'and it will suffice for the present.' The maid servant went for the egg, Beaidgill was her name, and she searched for the remnant of the food a long time and did not find it. Shanchan said: 'I believe it is thyself that art eating the leavings.' 'Not I, O chief Bard,' replied Beaidgill, 'but the nimble race that have eaten it, namely the mice.' 'That was not proper for them,' said Shanchan; 'nevertheless there is not a king or chief, be he ever so great, but these (mice) would wish to leave the traces of their own teeth in his food, and in that they err, for food should not be used by any person after (the prints of) their teeth, and I will satirize them,' said Shanchan; and he began to satirize them, and said:–

SHAN    The mice though sharp are their beaks,
        Are not powerful in the battles of warriors;
        Venomous death I'll deal out to the tribe,
        In avengement of Bridget's leavings.

MOUSE   Small were the leavings you left,
        It was not abundance you retired from;
        Receive payment from us, receive compensation,
        Don't satirize us all, O learned bard.

BRIDGET Thou mouse that art in the hole,
        Whose utterance is opposition;
        'Twas thou, whose claws are not short,
        That ate my leavings in your ambling.

MOUSE   My own son Bianan (sleek skin'd) of the white breast,
        Thou art the non-observer of ordinances;
        To the mighty and luxurious bardic body,
        Is the knowledge of it, thou little doomed being.

SHAN    Clear ye out of your spacious abodes,
        As we are prepared to convict you,
        Come ye all out of the hole (or burrow)
        And lie down (here) O ye mice!

And it is stated that ten mice fell dead in the presence of Shanchan; and Shanchan said unto them – 'It is not you that I ought to have satirized but the party whose duty it is to suppress you, namely, the tribe of cats; and now I will satirize them effectually, as also their chief, lord and Brehon, namely, Irusan, son of Arusan, and I know where he is, viz., in the cave of Cnogda, on the eastern side of Clonmacnois of St Kieran; and (also) Riacall-rinn-fiaclach (or of the sharp-pointed teeth), the daughter of Clab-aithine (or fiery mouth), his spouse; Reang-gearfiaclach (of the sharp teeth), his daughter; the Crónánach (or the purrer) of Croaghan, and Gruaman-garv-fiaclach (or the surly looking fellow with the rough teeth), her brothers. And I will satirize Irusan himself, for he is the chief and most responsible of them, and is their lord,' – and he said:–

'Hirusan, monster of claws. Remnant food of the Otter. With beauish tail like that of a cow. Similar to a horse watching another horse. A monster is Hirusan. Hirusan of the monstrous claws,' (said he); 'that is to say, that when the mouse gets into the hole he misses him, and only darts his claws at the hole. "Refuse of the food of the Otter," (said he) for the progenitor of the cats had been formerly on the margin of a lake at a pool of water asleep, and the otter came up to him and bit off the tops of his two ears, so that every cat ever since has been defective and jagged-eared. "Hanging down cow tail," (he said) for no quicker does a cow's tail fall downward than does his tail when the mouse escapes from him. "A horse watching a horse," viz., the mouse and cat are similar to two horses yoked together, for there is a close attention between them; the ear of one is listening to the other, and the ear of the other is listening to him; and those are the satires,' said Shanchan.

Their influence reached Irusan while in the cave of Cnogda, and he said, – 'Shanchan has satirized me,' said he, 'and I will be avenged of him for it.' Reang of the sharp teeth, his daughter, said unto him, 'we would rather,' said she, 'that you would bring Shanchan alive to us that we ourselves may take revenge on him for the satires.' 'I shall bring him in due time,' said Irusan. He made ready to go on, and told his daughter to send her brothers after him.

It was told to Shanchan that Irusan was on his way coming to kill him; and he requested Guaire to come with the nobility of Connaught in order to protect him against Irusan. They all came around him, and they had not been long there when they heard a vibrating, impetuous and impressive sound similar to that produced by a tremendously raging fiery furnace in full blaze; and it appeared to them that there was not in Connaught a plough bullock larger than he.

His appearance, viz., that of Irusan's, was as follows: – Blunt-snouted, rapacious, panting, determined, jagged-eared, broad-breasted, prominent-jointed, sharp and smooth clawed, split-nosed, sharp and rough-toothed, thick-snouted, nimble, powerful, deep-flanked, terror-striking, angry, extremely vindictive, quick, purring, glare-eyed; and he came towards them in that similitude. He passed amongst them generally, but did not stop till he came to the place where Shanchan was. He took hold of him by one arm, jerked him on his back, and he proceeded by the same way (he had come), for he had no other object in view but to come for Shanchan.

Shanchan, however, had now recourse to flattery of Irusan, praising his leap, his progress in his running, his power, strength, and activity; and he said, 'Hirusan, son of Arusan, of the race of *faigli fithise* (probably the remnant of the food of the otter); I invoke God between you and me; I implore him to deliver me.' But, however, Shanchan was not let down until they reached Clonmacnois of St Kieran. As they were passing by the door of the forge, in which forge Kieran happened to have been, he beheld Irusan with Shanchan on his back, and he said: 'It is a great pity that Guaire's hospitality should be tarnished, and there goes the chief Bard of Erin on the back of the cat.' There was at the time a flaming bar of iron held by the pincers, and Kieran made a fortunate brave throw at the cat, with which he hit him on the flank, and it passed out on the other side, and left him lifeless.

Shanchan dismounted from him, and he uttered a vindictive expression. 'My curse on the hand that gave that throw,' said he. 'Why so?' asked Kieran. 'I am so dissatisfied that I have not been let go with Irusan to be eaten by him, that thereby the great Bardic Association might satirize Guaire; for I would rather that Guaire would be satirized than that I should live and he not satirized.' He then proceeded to Durlus where the nobility of Connaught desired to welcome him, but he would not have a kiss or welcome from any of them; he went to the Bardic mansion, where they passed away the time with abundance of the best of viands and in feasting.

Marvan, the swineherd, said one day in Glen-a-Scail – 'It is long since I proposed going to be avenged of the great Bardic Association for the (loss) of the white boar.' Now Marvan's position was this – He was a saint, a prophet, and a poet; and he was a man who kept a prime house for general hospitality in Glen-a-Scail. He was brother to Guaire, and it was he that used to relieve Guaire from all his difficulties; it was he that originally aided him in obtaining the sovereignty of Connaught; also, every wrong deed that Guaire committed, it was Marvan that redressed or atoned it, he was moreover a zealous servant to God.

In the course of time he came to the abode of the great Bardic order, and on his proceeding to the mansion he perceived the ladies of the great Institution washing their hands at the fountain, and the first lady he met was Meave Neitigh, the daughter of Shanchan. He saluted her and enquired where was the mansion of the great Bardic Institution. 'It is evident, young man,' says Meave Neitigh, 'that you have been sea-faring away from the house in which you were reared, since thou knowest not where the palace of the great Bardic community is, nor heard of its stories and music.' 'That is not what I attend to,' said Marvan, 'but herding swine is my calling; I have, however, been informed that every person obtains whatever music he chooses in the palace.' 'He does not,' replied Meave, 'except he has a connection with arts and sciences.' 'I am connected with the arts,' said Marvan, 'viz., through the grandmother of my servant's wife, who was descended from poets.'

Marvan arrived at the Bardic mansion, and it was not to the open door he came but to the best closed door of the building, and the door rose open before him. The manner by which he entered was thus, having the skirt of his mantle full with wind, and there was not one within that a portion of the wind did not blow into his bosom. The entire of the great Bardic assemblage rose up simultaneously; Shanchan also rose and enquired who it was that came to him against the wind. 'You are mistaken in that,' said Marvan, 'it is not so, but with the wind I came, and in proof thereof I have brought much of it along with me.' 'Is it a contention you desire to enter upon?' asked Shanchan. 'It is,' answered Marvan, 'if I get any to contend with me.' 'If so then,' replied Shanchan, 'say from what did the first cause originate?' 'From blind nuts,' answered Marvan. 'True,' said Shanchan, 'and art thou Marvan the swineherd, chief prophet of heaven and earth?' 'I am, indeed,' replied Marvan. 'What is thy pleasure?' asked Shanchan. 'I heard,' replied Marvan, 'that every person gets his choice of music or of arts from you, and I am come to ask my choice of the arts.' 'You shall obtain that,' said Shanchan, 'if you can show your relationship to the arts.' 'I can do so,' said Marvan, 'namely, that the grandmother of my servant's wife was descended from poets.' 'You shall obtain your choice of the arts, though very remote is your connection with them,' said Shanchan, 'and say what art is it you prefer.' 'I desire no better at present than as much *Cronan* (a monotonous chaunting tune often used as a lullabi) as I like,' says Marvan. 'It is not easier for these to perform any other art for thee than that,' says Shanchan.

The Cronan performers came to them, thrice nine was their number, and they wished to perform the regular Cronan. That, however, was not what Marvan desired, but the bass (or hoarse) Cronan; and the reason he chose that was, in the hope that they might break their heads, feet and necks, and that their breathing might the sooner be exhausted by it than by the regular Cronan.

The three nines were singing the Cronan after that manner; and, whenever they wished to stop, it was then that Marvan would say – 'Give us as much of the Cronan as we desire in accordance with your promise.' The three nines soon became exhausted, and Marvan again desired that more of the Cronan should be sung for him. Nine of them, who were inefficient, only answered to his call, and these continued a shorter time to sing it than the three nines previously; and Marvan said – 'Perform as much Cronan as we desire.'

A person within, in answer to him, said – 'I will perform an art for thee, O Marvan.' 'Who art thou?' says Marvan. 'I am Dael Duileadh, Professor of Leinster.' 'What is the art thou wouldst perform for me?' asked Marvan. 'I am a good disputant (or wrangler),' said Dael Duileadh. 'Thou wilt not propose to me a question that I will not solve; and there is not a problem which I would propose, that the entire of the great Bardic Association could solve; and do thou tell me,' said Dael Duileadh, 'what goodness did man find on the earth which God did not find? Which are the two trees whose green tops do not fade till they become withered? What is the animal which lives in the sea-water, whose drowning it would be if taken out of the sea-water, and whose life would be preserved by putting him into it? And what is the animal which lives in the fire, and whose burning it would be if taken out of it, and whose life would be preserved by putting him into it?'

'These are good problems, Dael Duilidh,' said Marvan, 'and though excellent I will solve them. That which man found on earth, and which God did not find, is his sufficiency of a Lord; for there has not been a man, be he never so bad or so good, who, if he could not find his sufficiency of an earthly lord, would find the King of heaven and earth to be his Lord, because He is himself Lord of lords. The two trees whose green tops do not fade are *Eo-Rosa* and *Fidh-Sidheang*, namely, Holly and Yew. The animal, whose drowning it is to take him out of the sea, is named *Gnim-Abraen*; and the beast, whose burning it is to take him out of the fire, is *Tegillus*, which was its original name, and its name at present is *Salmandar*. And these are the solutions of the problems you proposed to me, Dael Duilidh,' said Marvan. 'I crave thy mercy, prime prophet of heaven and earth,' said Dael Duilidh; 'Ask me no question and I'll ask thee no more questions.' 'Perform as much Cronan for me as I desire, ye great Bardic Association,' says Marvan.

One of the bardic body answered him and said: – 'I will perform an art for thee,' says he. 'Who art thou?' says Marvan. 'I am Oircne Aitheamuin,' says he,

'Professor of Thomond.' 'What art wilt thou perform for me?' asked Marvan. 'It is easy for me to perform a good art for thee, for I am skilful and highly learned.' 'It is clear to me,' says Marvan, 'that, though many an ignorant person there be in the house of the great Bardic Association, there is not of the entire one person more ignorant than thyself.' How so?' said Oircne. 'There are two men paying their addresses to thy wife, and thou knowest neither of them; and these two men are the son of the king Findfhaltaigh (of fair hair), and the son of Fraigid Dairine, that is, the foster-son of Guaire; and the gold ring which thou receivedst from Guaire, she has given it to one of them, and she gave your sword to the other man.' Oircne Aithemuin arose, looked for his gold ring and sword, and he discovered he had neither of them; and, as he did not find them, he said: – 'I beseech thy mercy, O prime prophet of heaven and earth; do not disturb me and I will trouble thee no more.' 'I will not,' said Marvan, 'but let me have a sufficiency of Cronan.'

A person in the mansion said: – 'I will submit an art unto thee,' said she. 'Who art thou?' says Marvan. 'I am Crinliath Caillidhe' (Withered Hag) she replied. 'What is the art thou wouldst perform for me?' 'The most noble of all the arts in the world, namely, to become thy spouse. 'It is evident to me,' said Marvan, 'that thou art an ill-disposed old woman, and possibly had been so in your younger days, since thou speakest so immodestly at this advanced period of thy life. As for me,' said Marvan, 'as I did not wed in my youthful days, neither shall I do so now, particularly a withered, emaciated, and decrepid old hag as thou art.' 'Be merciful to me, O prime prophet of heaven and earth. Forgive me, and I shall say no more.' 'I will, said Marvan, 'but let a sufficiency of Cronan be performed for me.'

'I will perform,' said a man in the house, 'an art for thee.' 'What is the art?' says Marvan, 'and who art thou?' 'I am a good professor in my art to Seanchan, and Casmael the harper is my name.' 'I question thee, Casmael,' said Marvan, 'whence originated the science of playing the harp; who was the first that composed poetry, or whether the harp or the timpan was the first made?' 'I don't know that, prime prophet,' said Casmael. 'I know it,' says Marvan, 'and I will tell it thee. In former times there lived a married couple whose names were Macuel, son of Miduel, and Cana Cludhmor (or of great fame) his wife. His wife, having entertained a hatred for him, fled before him through woods and wildernesses, and he was in pursuit of her. One day that the wife had gone to the strand of the sea of Camas, and while walking along the strand she discovered the skeleton of a whale on the strand, and having heard the sound of the wind acting on the sinews of the whale, she fell asleep by that sound. Her husband came up to her, and having understood that it was by the sound she had fallen asleep, he proceeded into an adjacent forest, where he made the frame of a harp, and he put chords in it of the tendons of the whale, and that is the first harp that ever was made.

'And moreover, Lamiach had two sons – Bigamus, namely, Jubal and Tubalcain. One of them was a smith, that is, Tubalcain; and he conceived that the tones of the two hammers in the forge denoted the quantities of metre, and on that measure he composed a verse, and that was the first verse that ever was composed.'

'Be merciful to me, prime prophet of heaven and earth; do not annoy me and I shall not annoy thee.' 'I will not,' said Marvan, but let there be plenty of Cronan performed for me.'

A person in the mansion said: – 'I will perform an art for thee, O Marvan.' 'Who art thou?' says Marvan, 'and what is the art thou hast?' 'Coirche Ceoilbhinn (performer of melodious music) is my name,' said he, 'Professor of Timpanism to the great Bardic Institution.' 'I question thee, Coirche Ceoilbhinn,' says Marvan, 'why is the Timpan called the "Saint's Timpan," and that no saint ever performed on a Timpan?' 'I really do not know,' replied the Timpanist. 'I will tell thee,' said Marvan; 'it was as follows: – When Noah, the son of Lamiach, went into the ark, he brought many musical instruments with him, and in particular he brought a Timpan, and he had a son who was accustomed to play on it. They remained in the ark during the time that the deluge had been over the world; and when Noah and his family were coming out of it, the son wished to take the Timpan with him. 'Thou shalt not take it,' said Noah, 'unless I obtain a request.' The son asked him what was the request. Noah said he would be satisfied by naming the Timpan after himself. The son granted him that favour, so that the Timpan of Noah has been its name ever since; and that is not what you ignorant Timpanists call it, but the Saint's Timpan.'

'Be merciful unto me, prime prophet of heaven and earth; do not interfere with me, and I shall interfere with thee no more.' 'I will not,' said Marvan, 'but let me have enough of Cronan performed for me;' and Marvan called for the Cronan three times and did not obtain it.

Seanchan was ashamed of that, and as he found no other person to comply with Marvan's request, he said he would himself perform the Cronan. 'It will be more melodious to me from thyself,' said Marvan, 'than from any other person.' Seanchan raised his beard up high, and Marvan would have no other from him than the guttural Cronan. Whenever Seanchan would wish to cease, then would Marvan say – 'Perform enough of Cronan for me.' Seanchan was ashamed of that, and, by an overstrained effort of his in performing the Cronan, one of his eyes gushed out and lay on his cheek. When Marvan beheld that he was afraid that he might get blame from Guaire, and he said his Pater in his right hand, and he put the eye back into its own place, and he afterwards said: – 'Perform ye a sufficiency of Cronan for me.'

A person in the mansion said: – 'I will myself perform an art for thee, Marvan.' 'Who art thou?' says Marvan, 'and what is the art?' 'I am the best *scelaidhe* (story-teller) in the great Bardic Institution,' said he, 'and in all Ireland; and Fis Mac Fochmarc is my tribe (or family) name.' 'If thou art the best sgeulee in Erin,' said Marvan, 'thou knowest the principal stories of Erin.' 'I do, indeed,' replied the sgeulee. 'Well then,' said Marvan, 'relate to me "Tain-Bo-Cuailgne"' (or the Cattle Prey of Cooley). Silence seized the sgeulee and he is reproved for it. 'What are you about,' says Seanchan, 'in not telling the story to Marvan?' 'Have patience, O arch Professor,' said the sgeulee, 'I have not heard that that Prey was ever executed in Erin, nor do I know who took it.' 'Since that is the case,' said Marvan, 'I put thee under *geasa* (enchantment) until thou relatest the "Tain" to me; and I put the entire of the great bardic body under injunctions that they shall not remain two nights in the same house until they discover the story of the Tain. I also deprive you all of your poetic faculties, by the will of my God, that henceforth you shall not have the power of composing verse, excepting one poem only until you find for me the "Tain-Bo-Cuailgne"; and there am I now going away, and, upon my word, were it not for Guaire well would I avenge myself on you for the white boar, you indolent, ignorant, bardic clan.'

Marvan proceeded on his way, and left the great Bardic Association wearied, downcast, gloomy, and in sorrow. Then Shanchan said: – 'Marvan bound us under *geasa,* that we should not remain two nights in one place, until we would procure the *Tain;* and it was in this place we were last night, and we must not be here to-night, that we may fulfill our *geasa;* we must, therefore, proceed on our way in quest of the *Tain* till we discover it.' It was then that every individual of the great Bardic Institution started up simultaneously, both professors and students, both poets and scientific persons, both men and women, both hounds and servants, both young and old. But, notwithstanding their being called the great Bardic Institution, and though greatly they were abhorred, yet small was their consumption of food; for Brigit, daughter of Onitcerne, the wife of Shanchan, was the person among them who did eat most, and she usually did eat only a hen egg at a meal, and therefore she was called Brigit of the great appetite.

The great Bardic Association then proceeded on their journey, until they arrived at the residence of Guaire. Guaire went forth to meet them, for he wondered at seeing them all on the plain, and he bid them a welcome in general. He gave three kisses to Shanchan, and said – 'What news hast thou, arch Ollav ?' said he; 'why have you departed from your own mansion?' 'Bad is our story, O king,' said Shanchan. 'Marvan the swineherd, prime prophet of heaven and earth, came on a visit to us to take revenge of us for the white boar. He requested his choice art and music, which was granted to him, and the choice he made was to have his sufficiency of Cronan. Thrice nine of us went to chaunt the Cronan for him, and I myself,' said Shanchan, 'finally went to sing it for him; and whenever I chanced to cease he then desired to have more Cronan sung for him; and by an over-strained effort I made I put out my eye on my cheek, but he healed me by the power of God. A person in the mansion then told him he would entertain him with Sgeuleeaght (story-telling), and he (Marvan) chose to have 'Tain-bo-Cuailgne' (the 'Cattle Raid of Cooley'). The *Sgeulee* said he had not that story, and he bound us and the story-teller by *Geasa* (solemn injunctions) so as not to have the power of composing one stanza of our poetry, and that we are not to remain two nights in the same house till we procure for him the story of the *Tain.* In this place we were last night, and we cannot be in it to-night.'

'To what place do you propose to go in quest of the "Tain"?' said Guaire. 'To Albain' (Scotland), replied Shanchan. 'Don't go there, said Guaire, 'because in Alba you have the least chance of information, for in Erin itself that Tain was effected; and I know,' added Guaire, 'what you ought to do.' 'What is that?' asked Shanchan, 'to remain with me,' said he; 'and the honour which you have been receiving from me and from the men of Erin unto this day, you shall now have it from me in consideration of your poetry.' 'That would be no better than a compliment of alms,' said Shanchan. 'If you think so,' says Guaire, 'then let your women, sons and servants remain with me, and let your professors, poets and musicians go in quest of the Tain.' They all approved of that proposal and determined on that resolution.

*'The Harp' by Sulamith Wülfing*

It was then Shanchan said: – 'The only poem of our poetry which has been vouchsafed to us, it is fit we compose it for Guaire, for we have been with him a month, a quarter and a year, in this place, namely at Durlus.' The great Bardic Association agreed that that would be proper; 'for truly' (said they) 'we had no want of food or drink, of gold or silver, or of jewels and substance; the yearning of no individual amongst us was unprovided for during that period; and there will not be found to the end of the world, in the residence of a king of Ireland or of a provincial king, an entertainment equal to the entertainment he gave us,' as Shanchan said –

We depart from thee O spotless Guaire,
We leave with thee our benedictions;
A year, a quarter and a month
We have been with thee O exalted king.

Thrice fifty acute professors,
And thrice fifty students;
Two women, a valet, and a hound with each man
Were all supplied with food in one mansion.

Each person had his own meals apart,
Each one had a separate bed;
We rose not on an early morning
Without debate or without complaint.

I say unto you as an inference,
That the prophecy will be fulfilled;
If our numerous body will reach the destined place
We shall return again, though we now proceed.

'Where do you intend to be to-night?' said Guaire. 'At Naas of the kings if we can arrive there,' replied Shanchan, 'in the fortress of the king of Leinster, Connra Caech' (Connra the Blind).

They proceeded on their journey to Naas, and when they were coming to the place they met a leper on the way who said unto them – 'From what place did this large rustic crowd come?' says he. 'They are none such who are here,' said one of them, 'but Shanchan the sage poet with his bards and noble company.' 'Your names are familiar to me, though long it would take to repeat them; and the country into which you come is the worse for it, and the country whence you came is the better for it. How far do you intend going to-night?' asked the leper. 'To the fortress of Connra Caech, king of Leinster,' they replied. 'You have no business going there since you have not (the power of composing) one stanza of your poetry.' 'Who told you that? you mangy fellow,' said they. 'Now is the time to prove it,' said the leper, 'for it will be necessary for you to compose a poem for the king of Leinster, as it is he that is to give you a passage to Alpa' (Scotland). 'What the leper says is true,' said the professors; 'and it is better for us to try if we can compose a poem for the king of Leinster.' They accordingly set about composing it, viz., a verse by each professor of them; but however had it been only one word (by each) they could not arrange them properly.

The leper said – 'If you would be pleased to grant me a consideration I will compose a poem for the king of Leinster in your stead.' They said they would grant him his choice favour. 'Pledge your troth to that,' said the leper. They all pledged their word to him. 'Well then,' said he, 'the reward I ask of you is that Seanchan will give me a kiss.' Shanchan said that should he and his professors be forfeited for it he would not give a kiss to the scabby fellow. The professors declared they would return to Guaire again, and that they would not accompany him unless he would give a kiss to the leper. Shanchan thereupon gave a kiss to the scabby man, though loathsome it was to him.

They came to the gate of the fortress and they knocked (with) the hand-wood. The porter asked who was at the door. The leper replied that it was Shanchan with his professors that was there. The door-keeper asked 'had they a poem for the king of Leinster?' 'They have,' said the leper, 'and I am its reciter.' 'Bad is your appearance as a reciter,' said Shanchan, 'and it is worse for us to have you along with us.' They went into the Dun, and the king of Leinster bid them a hearty welcome, and asked them 'to what place they desired to go.' 'To Alban,' they replied, 'and we wish to obtain a ship and stores from thee.' The king of Leinster asked them if they had a poem in praise of himself? 'They surely have,' answered the leper, 'and I am to deliver it,' and he recited the poem.

O Connra Caech, son of Dairbre of the strand,
Thou friend of the fair-haired women of Inis Fail;
Give us a ship to convey us over the waves
Of the boisterous sea of the ports of fortresses.
O purest man we have come by thy renown
To the fertile land of the delightful plain;
To praise thee well, O king, O chief,

Of the bounteous hands, convey us away from thee,
Speedily over the sea
With wind and favour, O generous man.

After that poem they were supplied with bed-chambers; and they passed that night in cheerfulness and great mirth, without want of entertainment or attendance, till the morning on the morrow came.

A ship was soon cleared out for them, and provision stores were put into her. The leper asked might he go along with them in the ship. Shanchan replied that should he (the leper) go, he himself would not go into it. Then Shanchan with his professors went on board the ship, and they left the leper on land. They proceeded on their voyage over the sea till they came near the rocks of Mann. They beheld an individual on the rock, and at the very same time they saw the leper in the foremost part of the ship, and he singing the bass Cronan.

The person who was on the rock above them asked: – 'Who is in the ship?' said he. The leper answered him. 'Shanchan with his bardic company.' 'If that be so,' said the man, 'I put you under *geasa* (or injunctions) that not one of you shall come on land until you furnish a half stanza in reply to this half stanza.' 'Recite it,' said the leper. Shanchan said: – 'It is unfortunate for us to have the leper among us, for he is regardless what destruction may befall us.' 'Thou canst not land here, O royal professor,' said the leper, 'until a half stanza be produced in reply to his. Recite your verse, man,' said the leper, 'since Shanchan has no premium that I would accept from him.' The man recited his half stanza as follows:–

Every mariner of the sea has a crew under his command:

The leper replied:

Snow will fall, lightning will flash,
The voice of mild Caireall will be loud.

'That is the correct half stanza,' said the man above, 'and there is not in the ship a person who could give it a correct half stanza but thyself; and I have another half stanza,' quoth he. 'Recite it,' says the leper.

The learned will be severe on opponents;
They will excite their anger and increase their toil.

The leper replied:

On the borders of the rock of the sea of Mann,
Thou hast made much salt there.

'That is the half stanza,' said the man above, 'and I have another half stanza,' said he. 'Recite it,' says the leper.

On (or by) my burning, on my mixing,
On my cutting on the wave.

The leper replied:

O Woman-doctor that followest the profitable trade,
Great is thy weariness on the wave.

'That' (said the leper) 'is a Female-Doctor (or Doctoress) who has been hitherto conversing with you (or carrying on a dialogue with you). Every alternate year she is (a practicing) female-doctor, and the other year a maker of salt. She has a stone dwelling place and has a treasure in that house; she has three score marks in it, and she will share it with you to-night, and will give you the half of it; that shall be your provision during your stay in Alban; and it is not her you are to thank,' says the leper, 'but me.' The leper then departed from them, and they could not see in what direction he went. They afterwards landed and remained with the Doctoress during that night, who gave them the choicest entertainment and attendance till the morrow morning. She gave thirty marks to Shanchan, and said to him: – 'This is your last largesse, O Shanchan,' said she, 'till you again recover your poetic faculties; and your sojourn in Alban would be a state of contempt for you whilst you had not the power (of composing) one stanza of your poetry.'

They then went on board their ship and sailed on till they reached Alban. The chief professor of Alban had a feast prepared for them on their arrival; Mael-Gedhic Mac Fir-Goboc was his name, and they remained with him that night; they had the best of entertainment and attendance, and that was the most friendly night's reception they obtained in Alban. They traversed Alba from South to North, and from East to West; and remained there a year, but, notwithstanding, they got no tidings about the 'Tain'. Shanchan was troubled at not discovering the history of the *Tain*, and he said that he desired to return to Erin.

Their ship was cleared out by them, and they came along the sea until they entered port at *Ath-Cliath*. When they landed there they beheld St Caillin coming towards them; he was Shanchan's mother's son, and he gave three kisses to Shanchan, and asked him for news, and Shanchan told him that he got no account about the *Tain*. 'That is but right,' said Caillin, 'for great is the injustice and trespass thou hast committed on Guaire; and he prayed God that thou mightest give a kiss to a leper, and knowest thou the leper to whom thou gavest a kiss?' 'I do not know,' said Shanchan. 'To me thou gavest it,' said Caillin, 'and you were obliged to give it me.' 'Well, then, my beloved brother, give me assistance to get the 'Tain'.' 'I shall,' said Caillin, 'and will go with thee to Durlus, where Guaire resides; and we shall get Marvan the swineherd to come to us from Glen-a-scail, for it is he who knows how the 'Tain' may be obtained.'

They proceeded with one accord, namely, Caillin and Shanchan with his great bardic company, until they arrived at Durlus, where Guaire was. He gave a kiss to Caillin and another kiss to Shanchan, and he gave a general welcome to the bardic body altogether. He asked news of Shanchan, and Shanchan told him that he had got no account of the 'Tain' since he had left him. They then sent an invitation to Marvan at Glen-a-scail. Marvan came to them to Durlus, and they asked him who could relate to them (the story of) the 'Tain'. Marvan told them that there was not living in Erin, nor was there among the dead any who could relate the 'Tain' but one person only. 'Who is that individual person?' asked Shanchan. 'Fergus Mac Roy,' replied Marvan, 'for it was he had a knowledge of the exploits of the men of Erin and of Uladh (Ulster) in the 'Tain', as it was from his own pupil (Cuchulain) the 'Tain' (or Cattle Prey) was carried off.' 'How are we to act?' said they. Marvan told them to send invitations and messages to the saints of Erin, and to bring them with them to the tomb of Fergus, and to fast three days and three nights to the Godhead (or Holy Trinity), that He may send Fergus to narrate unto them the (story of) 'Tain-bo-Cuailgne' (or the 'Cattle Raid of Cooley'). Caillin went forth and brought the saints of Erin to Durlus, where they feasted for a night. They went on the morrow to the tomb of Fergus, and they supplicated Jesus Christ to send them Fergus to narrate the 'Tain' unto them.

Fergus came to them, and he was about relating the 'Tain' to them standing up, but they would hear none of it until they had him seated, and in that position he narrated the 'Tain' to them. Kiaran of Cluan (Macnoise) was he who wrote it from him; and the place in which he wrote it was on the hide of the *Huidhre*. Fergus was narrating the story until the story came to its termination, after which he returned to the same tomb. The saints offered up thanksgiving to God for their petition being granted regarding the question that Shanchan proposed to them, through the powers of the saints of Erin and through the instructions of Marvan.

The following were the saints who went thither: – Columbkille the son of Feilim; the holy Caillin (or St Caillin); Kiaran of Clonmacnoise; Kiaran senior of Saigir; Finnen of Clonard; Finnen of Moville; Seanach son of Gaitin; Brennan of Birr; and Brennan son of Finnlogha. They proceeded to Durlus of Guaire, and they feasted with Guaire for three days and three nights. Then Marvan departed for Glen-a-Sgail, and all those saints went to their own holy (or consecrated) places.

Shanchan the aged poet, with his professors, attendants, and household, proceeded on a professional visitation to the territories of Munster; and Shanchan made a vow and promise to Marvan and to all the fore-mentioned saints, that none of the great Bardic Institution should seek for a wish from any person in the world, from thenceforth unto the day of judgment and the termination of life (literally to the womb of Judgment and of life).

So far for the Proceedings of the great Bardic Institution.

It is now our purpose to treat of the 'Tain', the undertaking of which originated with a curtain conversation that happened between Oilioll More and Meave (King and Queen of Connaught about the commencement of the Christian era).

# 16

# The Shield of Fionn

## translated by
## E. MACNEILL

Ah me! thou shield of my bright king, 'tis hard that thou shouldst be defaced: woe that thy sturdy lord no longer lives, thou foreguard of the shields of Ireland.

Many a spoiling, many a brave battle thou and thy lord have given: good was the cover of thy chalk round spearheads, thou staunch protection against strokes.

There was not on the firm earth in the time when he possessed thee, there seized not shield a braver man than thy chieftain and thy lord.

He was a poet, a man of science, a battle-hero of assemblies: none was found like him for gifts: he was a brave warrior in stern battles.

He was a craftsman, an excellent metal-wright, a happy ready judge: woe to him that met him in anger: he was a master in every free craft.

Hardly is there on solid earth, unless there be some seer or sage, thou shield of the king of frosty Sígear, one that knows thy career.

Scarce are they too on the same earth, man or woman, that can tell the reason why thy name abroad is called the Dripping Ancient Hazel.

There is not, except myself and Caoilte, man of wisdom, and Fionntan of Dún Fearta, one that knows thy career.

From of old the shield of my king – I tell you it is a true matter – is unknown of men, grieves me no man, until the great battle of Magh Tuireadh.

'Twas Balor that besought Lugh a short time before his beheading: 'Set my head on thy own comely head and earn my blessing.

'The triumph and the terror that the men of Inis Fail found in me, well I wish that henceforth they may be found in my daughter's son.'

That blessing nevertheless Lugh Longarm did not earn: he set the head above an eastern wave in a fork of hazel before his face.

A poisonous milk drips down out of that tree of strong hardness: through the drip of the bane of no slight stress, the tree splits right in two.

For the space of fifty full years the hazel remained unfelled, but ever bore a cause of tears, being an abode of vultures and ravens.

Manannán of the round eye went to the wilderness of the White-hazel Mountain, where he saw a leafless tree among the trees that vied in beauty.

Manannán sets workmen at work on this tree without slackness: to dig it out of the firm earth: this were a mighty deed.

A poisonous vapour rises up incessantly from the root of that tree until it killed – perilous consequence – nine men of the working folk.

It killed nine others of them of the people of smooth Manannán – the story of the tree well I wot – and blinded a third nine.

Now I say to you, let the prophecy be sought out: around that mighty hazel uncontemned was found the source of many an 'ah me!'

Lucra was the wright that wrought the plaited blossom-light shield – lord of the Marannmháls of the plain – for Manannán the warrior.

Two virtues of the virtues of the shield, to be untouched in battle or in fray – few were the shields its equal – before it 'twas a rush of utter rout.

A battle in Pict-land that was not weak was the first battle fought by thee, when Mothla son of Meilge was slain, the mighty high-king of Egypt.

Not inferior was the next battle fought by thee, whereof the grief was great, when Dubhthach son of Daire was slain, the mighty high-king of Spain.

'Twas a quest on which noble Manannán went into Asia with a numerous host, when he slew Fiodhabhlach the active, the many-weaponed high-king of Asia.

These were noble Manannán's share in thy struggles south and north, till he gave thee, that wert a beloved goodly screen, a marriage-gift to the king of Sigear.

Cairbre made a song of praise on the beauty-scarlet shield – a man of sweetness and delight was he – for the king of the noble island of Sigear.

Fifty ounces of the pure gold Gola gave him for his praising: the better was his worth and the greater his fame, both his and the beauty-clear shield's.

Cairbre the generous prince, son of Eadaoin, whose honour was good, bestowed the shield on the brave lord on whom it brought no sorrow, on the Daghdha of majestic face.

The Daghdha gave to tall Eitheor the hue-ruddy brown-red shield – to the rod of many a feat in fight, to the son of Conn son of Cearmaid.

It was from that shield that Eitheor of smooth brown face was called 'Son of Hazel' – the man of deeds whereof the fame was not feeble – for this was the hazel that he worshipped.

On the day when MacCuill was slain in the battle of Taillte of the great muster, a man whose heavy slaughters abroad were not slight, Sgorán possessed that shield.

For the space of two hundred full years was the golden ancient shield, after a still longer life, in the possession of the kings of Fir Menia (Armenia?).

Manannán of the heroes went after it into the country of Fir Menia, where he gained nine glorious battles over the people of shield-bright Sgorán.

He killed three brave battalions of the splendid oversea army: it was a great affair beyond despite, whereof arose cause for cries of 'ah me!'

Fifty ounces of the red gold, fifty horses of waving mane, brown-red, a [chess] board that was not shaky (?) in his house, and the chessmen of shield-bright Sgorán [were paid by him].

He gave him a still greater ransom – for Manannán it was no distress – for giving battle with the fifty battalions, thrice fifty shields along with that same shield.

Manannán himself kept it, the much-adorned terrific shield: the cunning man of never feeble deed kept it till Tadhg, son of Nuadha came.

Manannán gave to Tadhg the hue-ruddy, brown-red shield, to Nuadha's son the well-knit craftsman, together with the chessmen.

The day that comely Cumhall carried off Muirn of the lovely neck by force, the lord of every manly honour, he obtained the shield of onsets.

When comely Cumhall fell in Cnucha above Liffey of the Leinster-men, the smooth steady prince of no small frame, Criomhall obtained that shield.

When Fionn the manly succeeded (?) to handsome, splendid Criomhall, that bright great grasp to which each battle yielded took from Tréanmhór the stout shield.

What of battles were fought by thee under Cumhall's son of the bright hands, thou brightest shield that hast not been defamed, 'twere hard to number them.

By thee was given the battle of Ceann Cluig, when Dubhthach, son of Dubh, was slain: the battle of Móin Mafaidh without woe, when Déidgheal hard-mouth was slain.

The battle of Luachair, the battle of Ceann Aise, and the battle of Inbhear Dubhghlaise, the battle of Teathbha, stiff was its entanglement, the battle of Cluain Meann of Muirisg.

The battle of Lusga, the battle of Ceann Cláire, and the battle of Dún Maighe, the battle of Sliabh Fuaid, whose heat was tense, the rout in which fell rough grey-eyed Garbhán.

The battle of Fionntráigh, whereby the warsprite was sated, where blood and booty were left behind, two bloody battles round Ath Móna, and eke the battle of Cronnmhóin.

The battle of Bolgraighe of great deeds, in which fell Cormac the exact, the battle of Achad Abhla that was not slack, the battle of Gabhair, the battle of the Sheaves.

The battle of Ollarbha, where the strife was fierce, wherein generous Fathadh was slain, the battle of Eise, great were its deeds, and the battle of Ceis Corainn.

The battle of Carraig, the battle of Srubh Brain, and the battle of Beann Eadair, the battle of Sliabh Uighe that was not slack, and the battle of Magh Málann.

The battle of the brave Colamhnaigh, and the battle of Inbhear Bádlma, the battle of Ath Modhairn, clear to us, and the battle of Beirge above Boyne.

The battle of Magh Adhair not belittled, and the battle of Dún Fraochán, the battle of Meilge of the mighty struggle, that caused loud cries and wails of woe.

The battle of Beirbhe, great was its deed, the after-battle with the King of Lochlainn of the ships, the battle of Uighe, undoubtful were its tidings, and the battle of the Isle of Gaibiel.

The battle of Móin, the battle of Ceann Tíre, and the fortunate battle of Islay; the battle of the Saxons, great was its glory, and the battle of sturdy Dún Binne.

The battle where tall Aichil was slain, the ready-handed high-king of Denmark, the battle of Inbhear Buille in truth, and the battle of fierce firm Buinne.

Twenty battles and twelve outside of Ireland in full sooth as far as Tír na n-Dionn of fame not small, Fionn fought of battles with thee.

Eight battles in Leinster of the blades thou and thy side-slender lord fought: in thy space of grace, no falsehood is this, sixteen battles in Ulster.

Thirty battles without reproach thou gavest in Munster of MacCon – it is no lie but sooth – and twelve battles in Connacht.

Twenty-five victorious battles were fought by thee, thou hardy door, eighteen battles, a rout that was not slack, thou didst gain over the Tuatha De Danann.

Not reckoning thy fierce indoor fights and thy duels of hard swords, these while thy success lasted strong were thy share of the battles of Ireland.

Broken is my heart in my body: I have mourned for many a good equal: thou undefended on the plain, burned by the swineherd.

Thrice nine were we on Druim Deilg after the blood-red battle: sad to relate was our plight: we raised three cries of '*ochán*.'

Since the forbidden tree that was in Paradise on account of which, alas! transgression was done, never was shaped tree on ground that caused more cries of '*uchán*'.

The King of Heaven save me, the good Son of Mary maiden, from Hell of sharpest peril that has caused laments and *ucháns*.

# PART THREE

# THE
# CONSTANT
# TRADITION

OWARDS THE END of the Middle Ages the bardic tradition suffered something of an eclipse. The publication of works such as Gruffydd Roberts' *Grammar* in Wales in 1567 meant that students could study the arts of poetry without the need of a tutor. In Ireland the composition of works in the native tongue and even the speaking of Gaelic were proscribed, and although this had the effect of heightening the nationalistic response among poets in hiding, the quantity of work produced inevitably declined.

Interest in the bardic remains waned for a time from the middle of the seventeenth century. Few scholars had either the necessary knowledge or, indeed, the interest to examine the older documents, and the more recent were considered crude and unsophisticated. Two things changed this. One was the publication in 1760 of the 'Ossian' poems by James Macpherson. The other was the restoration of the national Eisteddfod in Wales, largely through the activities of Iolo Morgannwg. Between them, these two men, Macpherson and Morgannwg, probably did more to keep the bardic traditions alive than any one else since the Middle Ages. Yet both are now acknowledged to have been forgers, and few of Macpherson's works are still read.

Macpherson's books, which purported to be the remains of ancient Scottish poetry, became worldwide best-sellers and promoted a tremendous renewal of interest in the ancient bards. That they were, by and large, forgeries, did not come to light until much later. In the meantime everyone wanted to know about them and wanted more of the same.

Macpherson was born at Ruthven, in the parish of Kingussie, Inverness-shire, on 27 October 1736. His father was a poor farmer, and his mother was a more well-to-do woman, and when James showed an aptitude for learning she saw to it that he was educated to a standard that would enable him to study for a degree in law. He entered King's College, Aberdeen, in 1753 but soon after went on, probably as a student of divinity, to Edinburgh University. But, although he prepared for the clergy, he almost certainly never took Holy Orders. He seems to have drifted through life after this, acting at various times as a private tutor – work he apparently hated – as a hack writer for Edinburgh booksellers, and as a teacher at village schools, and it was at this time that he composed over 4,000 poems, some of his own devising, others 'translations' of old Gaelic songs and ballads.

In 1759 he met John Home, a successful Scots author, who read some of Macpherson's works and saw fit to encourage him – even showing them to Carlisle who urged him to publish them. With some reluctance James agreed, and eventually published a volume under the title *Fragments of Ancient Poetry Collected in the Highlands of Scotland* and 'Translated from the Gaelic or Erse Language' (1760). Dr Hugh Blair, an eminent literary figure, wrote the foreword, in which he referred to a longer epic poem on the subject of the great hero Fionn or Fingall. This created so much interest that a subscription was taken up to allow Macpherson to make two long journeys around the Highlands to 'collect' further information and sufficient versions of the story to compose not only the dramatic poem, 'Fingal: An Ancient Poem', but other 'epics' as well.

It may well have been Macpherson's extraordinary success that inspired another, roughly contemporary writer, to emulate his work and to rediscover the bardic heritage of Wales in much the same way as Macpherson had done for Scotland. Iolo Morgannwg (1747–1826), who was born Edward Williams, called himself Iolo from 1785. A wanderer and a poet in his own right, he became fascinated by the ancient Welsh poetic remains after he met the bard Evan Evans, 'Ieuan Fardd', in 1784. A few years later, while in prison for debt in Cardiff, Iolo began to study the fragmentary materials to which he could get access, and to translate them, first into modern Welsh and later into English. Unfortunately, he was not content with this important and valuable contribution to scholarship. He hungered for something more, for a completeness that no longer existed. And so, just as Macpherson had done a few years earlier, he began to add to the material from his own imagination, forging dozens of manuscripts that he later claimed to have copied from works in the possession of various Welsh families. Unfortunately, for those engaged in the deciphering of the original poems, he also really did copy some documents, since lost, so that it is hard at times to tell what is real and what is the product of Iolo's fertile imagination.

A vast and complex bardic system is described in Iolo's work, and two extracts from this, 'The Voice Conventional' and 'The Book of Bardism', are included here. Much of this is almost certainly the invention of his brilliant mind – one may see this clearly enough once one has become sufficiently familiar with the material. One question we should also ask is: if the texts to which he constantly refers were forged, who forged them? Not necessarily Iolo. It has been suggested that the bardic system is purely the invention of the Bards of the fourteenth and fifteenth centuries, and this view has some credence – although one may well ask why they should have done so. It is possible that the decline in the status of the bard may have had something to do with it, as we see from even a brief glance at the changing social status of the poet.

Whatever the truth, Iolo's contribution to the continuing tradition of bardism is considerable, not only through his published work, but in his tireless efforts in promoting the restoration of a national Eisteddfod in Wales from 1791. This annual gathering, which has become an established event since that time, has kept alive the heritage of bardism until the present and has prompted a number of more recent writers to explore and add to the canon of bardic work.

In this third and final part of the present anthology we begin with an account of the ancient Gorsedd or Bardic Enclosure and its restoration, and this is followed by the two extracts from Iolo Morgannwg already mentioned. This is followed by a brief essay by the Irish-American writer Charles de Kay, who traces elements of Celtic bardism to the Finnish epic cycles of the *Kalevala*.

The last part of the volume is taken up with a powerful story, 'The Druid Path', by Marah Ellis Ryan, taken from a long-forgotten book of the same name, and a brief selection of poems by William Sharp, who, under the pseudonym Fiona Macleod, penned a large number of poems and plays, including the famous *Immortal Hour*, which was set to music by Rutland Boughton in 1925 and became among the most successful musical plays of its time.

To bring the collection up to date are a poem from a longer cycle describing the knowledge and wisdom possessed by Taliesin, written by the editor, a selection of powerful poems on bardic themes by Caitlín Matthews and two extracts from a remarkable sequence of dramatic re-workings of the *Four Branches of the Mabinogion* (the most famous mythic cycle to come out of the medieval Welsh bardic tradition) by the contemporary poet Martin Ludgate.

With this the collection ends. As noted in the introduction, this is only a very small portion of the total range of material that has survived. Those who would explore further are referred to the Further Reading, which follows this section.

# 17

# THE ANTIQUITY OF THE WELSH GORSEDD

from *The Bards of the Isle of Britain* by
**WILLIAM EVANS**

IN THE YEAR 1791 a Welsh Gorsedd and Bardic Circle was held at London. There were present Edward Williams (Iolo Morgannwg), Dr David Samwel, famous otherwise as Captain Cook's physician on his voyages of exploration, and other noted Welshmen. Previous to this, we have no historical record of any Gorsedd held this side of the Roman invasion. But there is an overwhelming probability that it was on the one hand a perfectly true claim of the Bards of Glamorgan that they had passed the tradition down secretly among themselves until the late Middle Ages, when the ancient rites became permissible again; and that on the other, from that time down to the instance recorded in 1791 the Gorsedd had become the principal feature of every Eisteddfod recorded in history. The mere fact of this being the principal ceremony of the festival and so obviously included in the term Eisteddfod itself, made it unnecessary to give it especial mention amongst those who were acquainted with the institution from their childhood. But the instance quoted above, happening, as it did, away from home among a strange people, was an exception and required to be explained for the edification of the English spectator, who had never previously witnessed such a sight. In proof of this supposition a verse of Goronwy Owen, a celebrated Welsh poet of the eighteenth century, may be cited. It was written long before the year 1791 and is culled from an ode in memory of Lewis Morus (Llywelyn Ddu o Fôn), a late-lamented benefactor of Welsh art and literature.

Glyw defodau
Eisteddfodau
Eu hynodau a'u hynadon.
(The master of Eisteddfodic ceremonies and their wonders and their
    adjudicators.)

291

What Eisteddfodic ceremonies could there be other than a performance of the ancient Gorsedd rites? For apart from the holding of the Bardic Circle, the term Eisteddfod includes nothing more than a round of artistic, musical and literary competitions; and the connection of the subject of the poem with these departments is mentioned additionally under the term 'adjudicators'.

There was a period, that is from the introduction of Christianity into Britain down to the late Middle Ages, when even the very name of Druidism was abhorred in the land as that of rank Paganism, and great battles culminating in the field of Argoed Llwyfain were fought on account of the survival of the ancient creed. Under these circumstances the mediaeval Bards must have been hard pressed for opportunities to perform their rites in secret and it is probably not irrelevant to mention here an observation included in the Iolo MSS., that it is permissible to form a Bardic Circle even with such small stones as might be carried in the pocket, which in itself suggests that at some time or another in the history of the Gorsedd and the performance of the Bardic rites there has been occasion for clandestinity.

It was in its Druidic, that is to say from the religious standpoint in its Pagan aspect, that the cult was persecuted. Mere Bardism, divorced from any religious significance, was never disallowed. Indeed the Bard, up to the Saxon subjugation of the country, was held in the highest esteem at the Welsh court. To quote from the Welsh Mediaeval Laws – 'He,' the Bard, 'sits second nearest to the chief of the household. He has a harp from the King, and a gold ring from the queen, when his office shall be given to him; and the harp let him never part with.' And again: – 'He has his land free, and his horse regularly from the King. He also sings the Monarchy of Britain in front of them in the day of battle and fighting.'

But alas, subsequent to the fateful fall of Prince Llywelyn in 1282 and the consequent absorbtion of the Welsh nobility, who had once supported him, into the English court in London, where they hibernate to this day, the Bard was left destitute at home and roamed from place to place, a beggar and a social pariah. He had nowhere to lay down his head and apparently in the end, so troublesome and obnoxious to the community had he become in his mournful wanderings and solicitations, that King Henry IV issued an edict forbidding his presence as bard or minstrel in the land under a penalty of imprisonment for one year (see 'Ordinance de Gales' enacted A.D. 1403). So it appears on the face of it, but one may read between the lines and conjecture that a darker motive was concealed; for more than once, if tradition be true, the English government had had occasion to round up and massacre the patriotic Cymric Bards wholesale, for encouraging and instigating their fiery countrymen to rebellion. For a like reason, probably, and in like manner, the venerable Druids of Mona were annihilated by the Roman General Suetonius.

Even the prehistoric or Druidic Eisteddfod, but in its purely artistic and competitive aspect, had been allowed to survive and flourish to their own glorification by the Christian priesthood. Culling again from the old Welsh Laws we find: – 'A Bard, when he shall have won a chair such is the chief of song.' A chair apparently, as now, has always been the chief coveted prize to be won at an Eisteddfod, for it is on record in Welsh History that a Chair Eisteddfod was held by Urien Rheged in A.D. 517 or some four-hundred years before the Welsh Laws were codified by King Howel the Good. Another was held at Conway by Maelgwyn

*Sgrôl y Cyhoeddi*
*The proclamation scroll of the Welsh Gorsedd*

293

Gwynedd in A.D. 540 or thereabout, and thereafter the pages of history are punctuated with records of celebrated Chair Eisteddfodau, down to that held at Carmarthen in A.D. 1451. Dafydd ab Edmwnt won the Silver Chair, whence arose the famous schism among the Bards concerning the authenticity of some of their alleged ancient records, which persists and gains adherence from a certain class of supposedly learned Welsh scholars to this day.

But these were times when the Catholic faith was fiercely upheld and the word of the Pope was law throughout the land, and it must not be thought for an instant that an open performance of the pagan Druidic rites and Bardic Circle would have been allowed at any of the above Eisteddfodau. Yet the term 'Gorsedd' is used as a title in connection with them from A.D. 1460 when a 'Gorsedd of Song' was 'held on the Mountain of Garth Maelwg' in Glamorgan, and it is met with at a very much earlier date in the *Mabinogion*, the wonderful mediaeval romances. Richard's *Dictionary* makes the name signify an ancient cairn or tumulus, which is a meaning not very far removed. Giraldus Cambrensis only two centuries earlier wrote that some of the ancient Druidic doctrines were still taught in secret.

Under English rule, all Bardic meetings in Wales were forbidden. But in the year 1567 in the reign of Queen Elizabeth a Royal Warrant, which is extant, to hold a Grand Eisteddfod at Caerwys was granted to Sir Richard Bulkeley and divers other 'trustie and well beloved' knights and Gentlemen. That an open and public performance of the ancient Druidic Gorsedd and rites, devoid of pagan significance, was ventured on, at least, in this Eisteddfod is more than likely. For the ancient Druidic Cult had been, relative to Christianity, so dead and forgotten for centuries, as to render the possibility of a revival of its teaching laughable, and with the crown's warrant and under the patronage of the nobility there would have been no temporal objection to the business either.

The book of *Mediaeval Welsh Laws* is a most valuable compendium of the settled laws and customs of the Welsh people, descendants of the Ancient Druids, and these customs were those to which they reverted on the departure of the Roman legions and the cessation of the Roman rule here. Yet in the whole code, the term Druid or Druids, as Caesar and the Roman authors designate the followers of the ancient cult, is not to be met with; so most writers cite this fact as an incontrovertible proof that such a name never existed in Wales outside the imagination of the Bards of Glamorgan. This argument is more facile than weighty; for had this ancient name, which was then abhorred as the badge of the pagan priesthood, been admitted into the new code of laws with which King Howel the Good journeyed to Rome that he might have it purged by the Pope himself of any lurking heresies that could have possibly escaped the searching vigilance of his Christian scribes, this fact would have only been ten times more a proof of the unimportance of the Druids.

But as a matter of fact while the word itself is rigorously excluded the Druids hold their place under a thin disguise, even as do all the fundamental elements of Druidism. For Christianity at its inception had no social framework of its own and the sacred doctrines had to be applied and coupled on to the pre-existing pagan institutions of the land, the latter of course bereft of any attribute that might run directly counter to the ruling precepts of the former. Hence the elimination of the term 'Druid' or 'Priest' in favour of 'Scholar' or 'Clerk in Holy Orders' side by side with the continuance unchanged of the terms 'Ovate' and 'Bard' which never could have borne any religious significance.

More than these names continues. The entire structure of the ancient Druidic organization with its triad of Druids, Ovates, and Bards and its duodecimal sub-orders was confiscated by Christianity and caused to serve even to this day as the social frame-work of reorganized Britain. 'Three Arts,' – we quote again from the priceless heirloom left us by the good old Welsh King of the tenth century – 'which a bondman may not teach to his son without his Lord's permission, "Ysgoleictod" meaning Scholarship or a Clerkship in Holy Orders, the "Druidism" of old; "Barddoniaeth" or Bardism and "Gofanaeth", Smith-craft,' embracing of course the liberal arts. 'For if his lord be passive until the tonsure be given to the Scholar, or until the Smith enters his smithy or a Bard with his song, no one can enslave them after that.'

Thus by merely substituting 'Druid' for 'Scholar' we get the three ancient classes of Druids, Ovates and Bards of Roman times, losing little but name, intact in their relations to each other and to the system, continuing to function in a Christianized civilization; for 'gof': the root of 'Gofanaeth' or Smithcraft is but too obviously synonymous with the ancient term 'Ovate', with a Welsh radical as prefix.

# 18

# THE VOICE CONVENTIONAL

## IOLO MORGANNWG

Of the bards of the Island of Britain, extracted from Meyryg of Glamorgan's Book, at Ragaln Castle, by me, Llywelyn John of Llangewydd, in Glamorgan: – that is,

AN ACCOUNT OF THE RIGHTS and usages of the bards of the Island of Britain, as exercised in the times of the primitive bards and princes of the Cimbri; and no one can attain the privileged grade of Chief Bard, unless initiated into this system, which was instituted for that order, and for bardism, because of the duties prescribed by ancient usage to them, and other persons of vocal song, according to the immunities and customs of the Bards of Britain.

### The Voice Conventional of the Bards of the Island of Britain

I. Before the time of Prydain, the son of Aedd the Great, no persons existed who were versed in national and genealogical knowledge, except the Gwyddoniaid; and because neither ordinance nor voice conventional was known to that order, much knowledge, traditional lore, and national information became lost to the Cimbric race. But after they had attained national order, under the protection of Prydain's government, and had fully conformed to his wise and benign regulations and laws, anarchy ceased, and tranquillity prevailed. Prydain, now, ordered diligent search to be made throughout the Island for any persons who might possibly have retained in memory the primitive knowledge of the Cimbri, so as to secure the traditional preservation of such information; and three persons of genuine Cimbric origin, nobility, and ordination, were found, called Plennydd, Alawn, and Gwron, who were of the order of Gwyddoniaid, and professed to know, traditionally, much of the learning that had appertained to the Cimbric race, from time immemorial. These persons having communicated what they knew, the whole was recited in national audience, before commons and lords, proclamation being made, under a year and a day's notice, that patronage would be extended to all persons possessing any traditional knowledge, however limited, of ancient lore, who should assemble in privileged Gorsedd, and there declare it. That object being effected, a second Gorsedd was similarly announced, and numerously held, at which the whole information obtained was traditionally recited by Voice Conventional; whereupon it was submitted to the consideration of a third Gorsedd, convened in like manner, and which, this time, consisted of all the wise men of the nation, to whom a well digested system of ancient Cimbric learning was shown, together with the poetical institutes of Tydain the father of genius, who first composed a regular Cimbric poem. The system here produced having been judicially ratified, as well as every other branch of knowledge and tradition relating to early science; the three superior bards, already named, were requested to perpetuate the whole by means of song and traditional recitation, so as most conveniently and systematically to impart oral instruction; and at the succeeding Gorsedd they presented their recitative compositions, which were referred to the consideration of three additional and consecutive bardic chairs, to be held under prescribed observances. Having, at the expiration of the requisite three years, again assembled in Gorsedd, and no voice, whether native or alien, being raised either against them or their compositions, degrees were conferred on those three bards, who now framed laws for the regulation of bards, and the confirmation of privileges and usages, from thenceforward, in perpetuity; – which immunities are called the privileges and usages of the bards of the Island of Britain; these bards, also, being each designated 'bard according to the privileges and usages of the bards of the Island of Britain.'

The aforesaid three primitive bards, having fully established their regulations, took aspirants in poetry under their tuition, as students in progression, to be instructed and perfected in the mystery of Bardism; – and endowments were granted to all bards, and their disciples, – whence they were designated 'endowed bards by right,' and 'endowed disciples by claim or protection;' the whole being legally substantiated by the assent of country and aristocracy. The preceding immunities and usages, and the mode by which they are sustained by oral tradition and voice conventional, are explained as follows.

A Gorsedd of the bards of the island of Britain must be held in a conspicuous place, in full view and hearing of country and aristocracy, and in the face of the sun and the eye of Light; it being unlawful to hold such meetings either under cover, at night, or under any circumstance otherwise than while the sun shall be visible in the sky: or, as otherwise expressed, –

A chair and Gorsedd of the British bards shall be held conspicuously, in the face of the sun, in the eye of Light, and under the expansive freedom of the sky, that all may see and hear.

Bards bear no naked weapon against, nor in the presence, of any one; and on one is permitted to do so in their presence; for a bard is the minister of peace, refuge, and justice.

The judgment of a bardic Gorsedd must be given, either by ballot, or in any other way by which a majority of votes may be collected and ascertained, in accordance with the prescribed rights.

The manner by which the judgment of a Gorsedd may be known, is as follows: – Any application or claim whatever, must be submitted to the consideration and decision of a Gorsedd; and if protected thereby, it must consecutively undergo the deliberation of a second and a third Gorsedd; and if again adopted by the protective judgment of each, it shall thereupon acquire the full force and efficiency of authority: and the judgment of a Gorsedd cannot be otherwise determined.

A convention, held for the primary consideration of any thing, is called a Gorsedd of greeting; and if it pass a protective judgment on the subject, the same shall be submitted to a second convention, called a Gorsedd of claim; and if the decision of that be equally favourable, a third convention, called a Gorsedd of efficiency, shall duly ensue; and if that again pronounce its judgment in affirmation, the measure so passed shall be finally received as possessing forcible and efficient authority; but unless the affirming and protective decisions of such three Conventions be obtained, no production or circumstance whatever, whether it be a song, or anything else, shall be admitted to the privileges of the Gorsedd of British bards. No production or circumstance, whether it be a song, tradition, instruction, notice, or anything else, shall be deemed of legal importance, or constitute any authority, unless ratified by the protective adoption of a Gorsedd of efficiency of the bards of Britain; but when so sanctioned, it acquires effectual force.

Greeting and claim may be held at a provincial chair that is not under the auspices of the Gorsedd of the paramount monarchy of the British Island; for instance, those progressive steps may take place in the chair of Glamorgan, Venediotia, or of any other locality; but efficiency can only be imparted by the Gorsedd of the monarchy of Britain.

There are four chairs of song and bardism in Cambria; viz:–

1  The chair of Morganwg, Gwent, Erging, Euas, and Ystradyw: and its motto is, – 'God and all goodness.'
2  The chair of Deheubarth, Dyved, and Ceredigion: the motto of which is, – 'Heart to Heart.'
3  The chair of Powys, and Gwynedd east of Conway: its motto being, – 'Who slays shall be slain.'
4  The chair of Gwynedd, Mona, and the Isle of Man: the motto of which is, – 'Jesus,' – or 'O! Jesus, repress injustice,' according to an old traditional record.

These four chairs may be held anywhere in Britain, as occasion may require; but the most regular course is to hold each distinctive chair within its own province, when a year and a day's previous notice will not be necessary; but if held elsewhere, such notice must indispensably be given.

A Gorsedd of the bards of Britain may be held in any accustomed and continued place of resort for that purpose; that is, in any situation duly appropriated for the occasion, by a year and a day's notice, progressively, through all the preparatory stages to that of efficiency. But places not so circumstanced must, if requisite, be qualified for conventional purposes, by the preliminary observance of prescribed forms, according to ancient rights and usages; viz., due notice, greeting, claim, and efficiency; – and a dormant chair may be resuscitated by similar proceedings, when, and wherever, requisite.

A chair that has not been held within the memory of any living person, is called a dormant one, with respect to its own province; but it is still entitled to the privileges of continued activity in every other chair or Gorsedd of regularly held conventions; so that the chair of London, of Cornwall, of Devon, or of any other district, may be held in that of Glamorgan, or of Gwynedd, (if not in disuse;) but all chairs are always deemed active in the Gorsedd of the bards of the British Island.

A chair and Gorsedd of the bards of the island of Britain, or of any included province, should, according to ancient privileges and usages, be held on any of the following high holidays of the year, which are the four solar quarters, viz:–

1   Alban Arthan, (Winter Solstice,) which falls on the tenth day of December, being the shortest day; and the first both of the winter and the year, according to the traditions and usages of the ancient Cimbric bards.
2   Alban Eilir, (Vernal Equinox,) which occurs on the tenth day of March; being the first day of the spring.
3   Alban Hevin, (Summer Solstice,) which takes place on the tenth of June, that being the first and longest day of summer.
4   Alban Elved, (Autumnal Equinox,) which occurs on the tenth of September, and is the first and longest day of autumn, when the autumnal equinox returns: – and it was on those days, together with the preceding and following ones, severally, that the bards held their chairs and supreme conventions, and transacted their principal business and general concerns.

The day previous to any Alban is called its vigil, and the day after it, the festival; each of them being, equally with the Alban, free and open for any pending observances; so that each Alban consists, virtually, of three days, on which any case requiring the sanction of a chair or Gorsedd may be determined, without having previously given the usual notice.

The times appropriated for holding any minor chair, or subordinate Gorsedd, are the four quarter days of the moon, – namely,

1   The day of its change, called – the first of the moon.
2   The day of its half increase, called – the renewing quarter day.
3   The day of full moon, called – the fulfilling.
4   The re-waning quarter day, called – the half decrease day.

It is on these quarter days that any subordinate Gorsedd, or minor chair or convocation for worship, should be held, for the information of kindred and country, and for the instruction of disciples and privileged novices in those things which they ought to learn, to know, and to practice. – But, nothing, at any such minor chair or subordinate Gorsedd, can be submitted for consideration, under proclamation and notice, nor can the progressive steps of greeting, claim, and efficiency, take place there; the course allowable on such occasions being, exclusively, that of preparatory knowledge, under the protection, but not the judicial adoption, of the bards of the island of Britain, for the latter could neither be consistently nor legally given but on the four principal holy-days.

Bards are graduated, according to the rights of Gorsedd, as follows:–

A chief bard positive, or poet, called, also, 'bard of rights,' and 'full graduate of rights,' is admitted to degrees, under primitive usage, by progression; that is, – by entering as a poetic aspirant under a tutor, or matured graduate of Gorsedd, and advancing progressively, until thoroughly-instructed in the art of vocal song and poetical criticism; – proficiently conversant in the Cimbric language, and capable of passing correct judgments on any compositions in it; – profoundly acquainted with the secrets, rights, and usages of the bards of Britain; – informed in their three vehicles of tradition, namely, the memorials of song, of the voice of efficiency, and of usage; – taught in their three credibilities, which are, national voice, wooden record, and the conservations of reason; – and until, also, so well versed in the cardinal maxims of divinity, legislation, and wisdom, as to be announced proficient and stable in them by the judgment, protection, and retention of a Gorsedd of efficiency. Being erudite in these qualifications, having substantiated them, before a Gorsedd, through the stages of greeting and claim, and attained the privileges of judicial ratification, he will be proclaimed a bard of efficiency, raised to institutional superiority, and have a chair given to him; whence he will become a bard of Gorsedd, and continue so, under the privileges of that chair. Having in this manner obtained three distinct chairs, the degree of bard of Gorsedd, according to the rights and usages of the bards of the island of Britain, will be conferred on him.

A second mode of graduating a poet, (the candidate not having previously undergone progression,) is to propose him for such distinction, under a year and a day's notice; thus presenting to all persons an ample opportunity of showing why such aspirant either ought not, or could not be admitted into the bardic order; – but if no such objection can be urged, the candidate may, under the sanction of Gorsedd, pass through the stages of greeting and claim, and attain that of efficiency; after which he may, under the privileges of chairs, be admitted a bard according to the rights and usages of the order in Britain, and take his seat of efficiency in Gorsedd.

A third way of conferring the degree of primitive bard on a poet, when three conventional bards of efficiency cannot be found in Gorsedd, is, to get a poetic aspirant of no progression, and subject him to the verdict of three hundred men, upon the testimony either of twelve true men of the country and aristocracy, – upon the word of a magistrate, or that of a minister of religion, who shall attest on conscience that such aspirant has the qualities and attainments requisite for a bard; and if he be adjudged a bard by a verdict so obtained, he shall become entitled to a chair in Gorsedd, according to the rights of reason, necessity, and national suffrage; – so that, thus, a bardic Gorsedd may be rightfully constituted: for, according to the rights and usages of the bards of Britain, neither a chair nor Gorsedd can consist of less than three primitive bards of efficiency, that is – of convention; for a majority of voices cannot be ascertained except three, at least, be present; and no judgment of Gorsedd can be given otherwise than by a majority.

Where but one bard of efficiency can be found, according to the rights and judgment of Gorsedd, that one may, under the justification of reason, circumstance, and necessity, legitimately confer degrees and chairs on two poetic aspirants, when he can certify on his word and conscience, that they possess the qualifications requisite for bardic poets; for, except by such means, the instruction of British bards could not be perpetuated; and, according to law and usage, necessity is paramount strength; and hence it is, that the bards and bardism of Britain may be preserved from dormancy and ultimate extinction; which can be effected only while primitive bards of the class of poets remain; for bardism originally emanated from poets, and nothing can in anywise exist but by virtue of its generic principle. The law of necessity enjoins that the number of bards indispensably requisite should be completed in the most available manner, when the best institutional course cannot be adopted; thus conforming to necessity, where no better alternative offered; hence this law cannot become operative, except under the immediate influence of reason and circumstance; still it is justifiable to act according to it, when judgment cannot be obtained from the verdict of a majority of voices: – but necessity being superseded in the manner described, it would not be defensible to graduate a bard otherwise than constitutionally; – that is, either by the verdict and judgment of Gorsedd, or by national suffrage, after a year and a day's notice, and then proceeding by greeting and claim, until conventional efficiency be attained.

A person is deemed a supporter of kindred and country who has recourse to the law of necessity to effectuate beneficial purposes, under the influence of reason and circumstance, when urgency might not properly allow sufficient time for ascertaining the sense of the nation, or the verdict of a Gorsedd, determined by the major number: but whosoever shall reject prescribed usage form motives of ambition or presumption, will be stigmatized as an enemy to kindred and country, when, at the same time, a just national verdict, by the choice and suffrage of a majority, might have been obtained, and, consequently, ought to have been adopted; – or, when the judgment of Gorsedd could have been sought, according to the rights and usages of efficiency in the primary manner; that is, according to a law originating in national suffrage; which law of reason and judgment constitutes the ruling principle of the bards of Britain, and can neither be contravened not dispensed with.

When no bard of the order of conventional poets can be found extant, bardism, and the rights and usages of the bards of Britain, become dormant, and cannot be legally resuscitated, but by national suffrage at the expiration of a year and a day's notice, and repeated in that manner for three consecutive years; and then advancing progressively by greeting and claim, until efficiency be obtained, according to the mode already described, as adopted in the time of Prydain, the son of Aedd the Great.

The bards of the island of Britain are divided into three kindred orders, according to the rights of primitive bards; and every member of those three distinctive classes is called a primitive bard, being so by common origin, according to the ordinance, usage, and rights of the primordial Gorsedd of the bards of Britain in the time of Prydain, the son of Aedd the Great. The first order is that of poets, or primitive bards positive, called also – Primitive bards according to the original institution; a distinction which no one can attain but a poet of innate and scientific genius, and of progression; and the duties incumbent on this class are – to compose poetry, to perpetuate the traditions of rights and usages, and to rescue bardism from corruption and oblivion. The second order is that of Ovates, who are not expected to have undergone progressive discipline, but depend on prospective graduation at Gorsedd: for an ovate is simply a person of innate genius, application, and chance; and his duties are – to improve and enlarge knowledge, and to submit his performance to the judgment of Gorsedd, until declared efficient in authority. The third order is that of Druids, which must be appointed either from the class of poets or that of ovates, by the verdict and judgment of Gorsedd. A druid acts in accordance with reason, circumstance, and necessity, and his duties are – to instruct, hold subordinate chairs and conventions, and keep up divine worship at the quarterly lunar holy-days. It is incumbent on him, also, to initiate persons into the secrets of bardism, and to inculcate godliness, wisdom, and good morals. The rights and appellation of primitive bard appertain to every member of each of the said three orders; the whole of them being coequal in privileges and dignity.

The course pursued in graduating an ovate is – first, to place him under the examination of a chief of song, that is, of a primitive conventional bard, who shall testify, upon his word and conscience, that he possesses the qualities requisite for a bard; he, then, must seek the verdict and judgment of Gorsedd, and if pronounced efficient, will thereby attain the rights of a primordial bard, and be qualified to exercise in Gorsedd the functions of a progressively instituted primitive bard of that order.

A primordial bard may assume the grade and rights of an ovate, by virtue of the extent of knowledge and poetic genius requisite for a primitive ovate which he may display before a Gorsedd, with no other protective ceremony than that of greeting; and those qualifications imply the improvement and extension of learning.

A primitive bard is entitled to an ovate's degree, who shall, upon his word and conscience, recommend any one as a person duly qualified to be a bard, *if* the person so recommended obtain, in consequence, the affirming judgment and protection of a Gorsedd; for it is considered, that whoever shall form a just estimate of the poetic genius and science of any person, and have that opinion conventionally confirmed, must fully understand such attainments, and know to what extent they are calculated, to qualify their possessor for graduation and privileges: hence we see that there are two classes of ovates, namely, the primitive ovate, and the ovate by privilege, that is, a primitive bard either of the order of poets or of druids, who may have obtained an ovate's degree in Gorsedd, by virtue of his exertions in favour of an aspirant, who had, thereupon, been legally constituted a primitive ovate in Gorsedd.

A primitive ovate is entitled to exercise in Gorsedd the functions of a primitive bard of the original order, if no poet either by progression, or by the claim and the privileges of efficiency, be present there.

When a bard of the order of primitive ovates becomes a primitive bard, he is designated a primitive bard by privilege, and not a primitive bard of the original order; but to obtain the latter grade, it will only be requisite for him to submit his own composition to the judgment of a Gorsedd of vocal song, so as to ascertain whether it be deemed worthy of conventional sanction or not; if adopted thereby, he will be pronounced a poet, and be entitled to the privileges and office of a primitive bard.

When a bard of the original ovate order takes a chair in Gorsedd, in the absence of a primitive bard of the original order, and exercises the functions and privileges of that grade, if his proceedings on that occasion be sanctioned by another Gorsedd, according to rights and privileges, and finally confirmed in efficiency, he shall be entitled to claim and exercise the functions of a primitive bard or poet: – and some say, that none but persons of this particular class are justly entitled to the appellation of graduates by privilege, and that they should not be denominated graduates of the original order, – a designation that appertains solely to primitive bards of the order of poets by progression.

A druid is graduated by conventional suffrage and judgment; but, if previously a primitive bard of the original order, an election by ballot only will be requisite to substantiate his efficiency; for every conventional transaction effected either by, or on account of, a chair-bard in Gorsedd, shall be deemed efficient, without the preparatory steps of greeting and claim; such bard being already a person by claim, and acting under the protection of that privilege.

A primitive ovate may be made a druid by conventional suffrage, – a proceeding that would establish his efficiency. Some have asserted, that a disciple by progression in poetry may be graduated a druid, and that, thence, he would become one of the primitive order of that grade; but it is an erroneous opinion, for a disciple, by progression, in poetry must, to be so, possess the genius of vocal song; and, consequently, be a poet, according to the protection and claim of the Bards of Britain; therefore, he cannot, in accordance with inherent distinction and usage, receive any other degree than that of poet, or primitive bard of the original order: for when any person of progressive discipline in vocal song obtains a degree by the verdict and judgment of Gorsedd, the distinction so conferred must be that of primitive bard of the original order, notwithstanding any thing that may possibly be said, conceived, or urged to the contrary: but it is also very certain, that the person so graduated may, immediately after, and, as it were by the same breath, be also constituted a druid.

Of what grade soever a druid may be, – or (if by progression) were he but an endowed disciple by protection, – if he assume, in chair or Gorsedd, the office or functions of any other grade, provided that such proceedings be sanctioned by a subsequent Gorsedd or chair, he shall, under the conventional rights of claim, acknowledgement, and protection, be considered a graduate of the dignity which he assumed, upon the very same principle that a person may become a primitive bard by attesting such truths in Gorsedd, upon his word and conscience, as shall obtain conventional graduation for an ovate; – for he will be considered, in adopting such a course, as merely submitting to reason and circumstance, under the law of necessity and conviction, that made it imperative on him to exercise the functions of a druid; – for nothing can be efficiently carried into effect, that is not well understood; and such a thorough comprehension will be inferred, if the extraordinary transaction, arising from the causes stated, obtain the protection and affirming judgment of another Gorsedd. Such are the reasons that entitle a person to a degree, by privilege, in the order that he assumed and explained so well, without any progressive step, beyond that of proclamation and notice in Gorsedd. An ovate, exercising the functions of a bard, will be entitled to similar privileges, if his proceedings be likewise affirmed by a subsequent Gorsedd. By the functions of a bard, are meant – the composition of poetry, and the perpetuation of oral tradition. But if an ovate exercise assumed functions, under the control of reason, circumstance, and necessity, and obtain conventional protection for such a course, he will thereupon become a druid, and be consequently entitled, by privilege, to perform religious duties, and to hold inferior chairs and subordinate conventions, at the usual and legally prescribed periods.

It is not necessary that a poet, of the original grade of primitive bards, should await the general course of conventional graduation, to be qualified for the office of a druid, and to exercise its functions, further than that previous announcement to that effect must be audibly made, by proclamation in Gorsedd or chair; for a person of his order is known to be already a graduate of all efficient knowledge, according to the privileges of bardism and poetry; for upon him devolve the duties of sustaining oral tradition, and publicly transmitting information relating to bardism, which he could not effect unless he had previously attained a true and thorough knowledge of that science; and that, too, under the affirmation of a Gorsedd; wherefore every person possessed of such ratified knowledge in poetry and bardism, whatever be his grade, is at liberty to exercise the office, the knowledge, or the science for, or in which he may be considered qualified by the attestation of Gorsedd, without any further conventional sanction; so that the grade of druid will, at once, be conferred on him in stability and efficiency; except that discretion would, in conformity to usage, suggest the propriety of audibly announcing all such transactions by proclamation in Gorsedd, to obviate disorder or any deviation from usage.

There are two classes of aspirants in poetry, namely, progressors under protection, and progressors by privilege. A progressor under protection, is one whom a chief of song, of the order of conventional poets, shall take under his tuition to initiate, and render perfect, in the art of poetry, the secrets of bardism, and the oral traditions appertaining to the rights and usages of the bards of the Island of Britain; and who shall remain under such tutelage until he acquire all that knowledge. He then must greet a Gorsedd for his degree; and, if received under its protection, he will be designated a progressor by privilege, or, in other terms, an endowed disciple under protection; for he will be entitled to a poet's endowment under the protection of Gorsedd, – that is, to the portion of an alien's son, together with the immunities, by courtesy, of a native Cambrian; and so he shall remain, until he become a conventional graduate, that is, a poet by the verdict and judgment of a Gorsedd of efficiency; or, in other words, a poet of Gorsedd or primitive bard of the original order.

There are two sorts of protection; the first of which is termed – the protection of the Bards of the Island of Britain, within the pale of which every primitive Cambrian is included, who, if versed in bardic learning and bardism, is entitled to rank among loyal patriots; for all others are stigmatized as persons of devastation and anarchy: the second sort is – conventional protection, which results from greeting a Gorsedd, and obtaining thereby its sanction; – for such protection simply signifies the verdict and judgment of Gorsedd in support of the application, so far as to assert that it may properly be granted. It is by a similar course that a progressor under protection proceeds to greet a Gorsedd, obtains its affirmation of his competency for the order of poets, and becomes, thereupon, a progressor by privilege. The expression – 'protection of Gorsedd,' implies the privileges conferred by the aforesaid judicial affirmation; and all national and territorial lords are entitled to those privileges, as well as all authorities by national suffrage, all magistrates, teachers, and ministers of religion, – all sons of aliens acting under the appointment of their lords and the nation, – all residents, by domestic and foreign permission, – all functionaries of peace and justice, – and all persons who may make improvements and discover superior modes of circulating knowledge in arts and sciences, tending to benefit vital existence. The protection extended to a bard already graduated in Gorsedd, implies a permission to proceed, from greeting to sanction, for a higher degree; – by which proceeding he will be established in efficiency. The protection of an endowed disciple, or progressor by privilege, is, that he continue in his right of conventional greeting, until he attain a chair; in which position he must remain, by conventional claim, for a year; and then, if protected by another Gorsedd, another chair will be conferred on him; and, at the end of another year, he will appear in Gorsedd by avouchment, until he obtain its protection also, when a chair will be again awarded to him, and, thereupon, he will acquire efficiency in Gorsedd, according to the rights and usages of the bards of the Island of Britain.

If a poet, of the class of endowed disciples by protection, obtain a chair in each of three different provinces, within the same year, and that such distinctions be exhibited at a Gorsedd of the bards of Britain, at his earliest convenience, he shall be pronounced a conventional bard of the primitive order, as originally instituted.

The endowments of a conventional bard are as follows: – Independent of his right to five acres in free tenure, as a Cambrian of primitive descent, he is entitled to other five acres, in free tenure, or their equivalent, to be proportionately levied on ploughs by national and professional suffrage. He will likewise be entitled to an allowance for his poem, according as it may be estimated either at a Gorsedd of province and lords, or by the suffrage of the district. A bard of learning and holy duties has also a claim to similar emoluments. A poet is entitled to a perquisite from every royal nuptials, and from every wedding of persons genteelly descended, – that is, of every Cambrian pair of aboriginal genealogy, as a remuneration for keeping their family traditions and pedigrees, so as to protect their native rights. An allowance is also due for every poem and tradition in commemoration of any praiseworthy action. If the laudable deed was performed by an individual, the poet's perquisite is confirmed by strong usage; but if it was the achievement of country and kindred, he will be allowed a professional circuit for remuneration for such patriotic poem and traditional preservation. He will also be entitled to bounties by courtesy; but, where no such custom exists, his perquisites will be, a penny from every plough. All such traditional poems must, however, in the first place, be submitted to the adjudication of a Gorsedd, so as duly to ascertain their veritable and scientific character, before they entitle their authors to the privilege of professional circuits. – Bards and progressors by privilege are likewise entitled, triennially, to professional circuits; and they may also receive gifts by courtesy, but neither law nor custom prescribes such bounties, beyond the usage of affection, respect, and liberality.

Every thing in accordance with reason may be included within the pale of custom; and every thing in accordance with reason and inherence is subject to custom and privilege; but where reason, inherence, and necessity concur, they constitute law. By necessity is meant an emergency that calls for extraordinary powers to effect a greater extent of good than could be otherwise attainable. It was under the combined rights of reason, inherence, and necessity, that the primitive privileges and customs of the British bards were at first instituted; consequently, it is adjudged that every poet, who is a primitive bard of the original order, must, also, be a primordial druid. In the earlier ages, privileges and customs could not be conferred on the bards of Britain, unless they possessed poetic genius, energy, and incident, and had also been graduated by progression; and it is on this principle that the privileges and requisites of an ovate are established; therefore, possessing those qualifications, he becomes a primitive bard according to the original order; for no other course could have been adopted at the commencement; – and that which emanated from reason, inherency, and necessity will continue so, coexistent with life and being. – It was the person who possessed the best and most correct information in oral tradition, and had the highest powers of retention, that first taught such knowledge and science in the primitive Gorsedd of the bards of the Island of Britain; consequently, a poet by progressive discipline is the person most firmly established in those requisites, and hence, he must be the most competent person, according to right reason and inherence, to hold the office, exercise the privileges, and fulfil the obligation of perpetuating, by oral tradition and retention, the mysteries, science, and knowledge of the bards of Britain. From what has been already shown, it cannot be now determined which of the three kindred orders of primitive bards was the original one, or which of them was the best and most beneficial; hence they are all considered as coequal in dignity; and all their members, after graduation in a Gorsedd of efficiency, continue in reciprocal coequality with regard to dignity, influence, and reverence; and they are accounted as chiefs and bridges, above all others.

They are chiefs over all, because their testimony is considered in law as paramount to that of every person who is not a bard; for it is neither consistent with nature nor reason, that the evidence of a bard should not be superior in veracity, knowledge, and stability, to that of any person who is not a bard: and the reason that they should become bridges to all, is – the obligation they are under to teach all good and true men of the nation, and mankind generally, by conducting them over the bogs of ignorance, and so become in effect paths and bridges to them.

Nothing can acquire the character of substantiated truth that has not been admitted into privilege by the voice conventional of the bards of Britain, which should be made the medium of announcement for all knowledge advanced in Gorsedd, until confirmed in efficiency; for no testimony, nor usage, can in anywise contravene its effect. By voice conventional is meant – the recitations given in Gorsedd of the oral traditions retained by the bards of the Island of Britain, relative to circumstances and sciences that had been conventionally verified, and ultimately established in efficiency; for nothing can be admitted as substantiated in truth, but that which has been progressively submitted to the national Gorsedd of bards, until ratified thereby, and which has, consequently, been publicly inculcated by conventional promulgation, and by efficient vocal song.

No privileges can be conferred on any poem, speech, or usage in Gorsedd, if such be untrue, unpacific, or illegal; for falsehood, discord, and illegality cannot be permitted in any poem, oration, tradition, or conduct, by the bards of Britain;

their attribute being – to support and strengthen veracity, peace, and law, and to resist every thing that may in anywise tend to contravene those moral principles.

Every candidate for privileges by vocal song and bardism, according to the rights of the bards of Britain, should apply to a bardic teacher of conventional graduation, for instruction in the judicial decisions, oral traditions, and promulgating voice of Gorsedd. The teacher shall, then, introduce such candidate to convention, as a disciple in poetry, or progressor by protection, under the auspices of the bards of Britain; after which he shall take him under his tuition, and impart general knowledge to him: it will then be his duty to present him to a chair or Gorsedd at least once a year; and to a minor chair, or subordinate Gorsedd, at least three times a year, that he may thus become conversant in rights and usages, and in the oral traditions retained by bards and voice conventional. The teacher should, also, present to a chair or Gorsedd, at least once a year, a song, or recitative poem, composed by his progressing disciple, and solicit the opinion of any conventional judge who may be disposed to give it according to reason and understanding. When the progressing disciple shall, in this manner, have acquired requisite knowledge in the art of vocal song, and shall know the three memorials of tradition, the rights, usages, and mysteries of bardism, the cardinal points of wisdom, and be capable of composing a vocal song that shall be pronounced faultless in the estimation of a chief of song, – that is, of a conventional bard, – let him greet a Gorsedd, and go on progressively, until he shall have advanced to the full extent of his capacity, according to the institutional course of proceeding already described.

Now follows an account of things that appertain to institutional ceremonies, and that accord with the reason and inherence observable in the reminiscence and customs of the bards of the Island of Britain; but which, nevertheless, are not considered as indispensably requisite parts of the system; because every truth and knowledge, – every recollection and retention, – as well as every art and science, may be acquired without them: – still they corroborate and illustrate reminiscences and primary regulations; for which reason, it is deemed laudable to perpetuate them in memory and usage; especially as they comprise the ancient forms transmitted, in continuity, by the retentive memory of Gorsedd.

It is an institutional usage to form a conventional circle of stones, on the summit of some conspicuous ground; so as to enclose any requisite area of greensward: the stones being so placed so to allow sufficient space for a man to stand between each two of them; except that the two stones of the circle which most directly confront the eastern Sun, should be sufficiently apart to allow at least ample space for three men between them; thus affording an easy ingress to the circle. This larger space is called the entrance or portal; in front of which, at the distance either of three fathoms, or of three times three fathoms, a stone, called station stone, should be so placed as to indicate the eastern cardinal point; to the north of which, another stone should be placed, so as to face the eye of the rising sun, at the longest summer's day; and, to the south of it, an additional one, pointing to the position of the rising sun, at the shortest winter's day. These three are called station stones: but, in the centre of the circle, a stone, larger than the others, should be so placed, that diverging lines, drawn from its middle to the three station stones, may point severally, and directly, to the three particular positions of the rising sun, which they indicate.

The stones of the circle are called sacred stones, and stones of testimony; – and the centre stone, is variously called the stone of presidency, the altar of Gorsedd, the stone of compact, and the perfection stone. The whole circle, formed as described, is called the greensward-enclosing circle, the circle of presidency, and the circle of sacred refuge; but it is called *trwn* (circle) in some countries. The bards assemble in convention within this circle; and it accords neither with usage nor decency for any other person to enter it, unless desired to do so by a bard.

It is enjoined by primitive usage, that one of the presidential bards should bear a sheathed sword, – holding it by the point; a bard not being permitted to hold it by the hilt: for when taken by the point, whether naked or sheathed, it is not supposed to be either held, borne, or bared against a human being, or any other object, whether animate or inanimate, throughout the world. When the sword, thus held, is carried to the conventional circle, it must be pressed out, by hand, in a contrary direction to its point, until quite unsheathed; then, being taken by the point, it must be laid on the altar-stone of the Gorsedd, and the super-proclamation shall ensue; but when the voice shall come to the part which says, 'where no naked weapon will be presented against them,' every bard must move onward to the altar-stone, and lay his hand on either the sword or its sheath, while the presiding bard shall take its point and put it just within the sheath; upon which it shall be driven quite in by all the assistant bards, with concurrent hand and purpose. This usage is observed, to testify that the bards of the Island of Britain are men of peace and heavenly tranquillity; and that, consequently, they bear no naked weapon against any one. At the termination of this proclamation, the objects of the convention must be successively effected; for which purpose it will be necessary to recite and explain the three ancient vehicles and voices of Gorsedd; to recite an ancient poem; to produce new poems presented for judgment, and to repeat them audibly to the meeting; to announce applications by greeting, claim; and efficiency: to confer degrees on deserving merit; and to hear, do, and speak all requisite things, according to rights and usages, and consistent with reason, inherence, and necessity. The business of the chair or Gorsedd being thus accomplished, the terminating proclamation shall be made, the Gorsedd closed, and every one return to his home.

Usage enjoins that every bard shall stand uncovered, head and feet, in Gorsedd, to evince his reverence and submission to God.

The ceremony of conventional asseveration prescribes, that the witness shall stand in Gorsedd, hold in his hand a poet's staff, look in the face of the sun, and the eye of light, and, in this position, give evidence upon his word and conscience: – or, according to another form, he must put his hand in that of the presiding bard, that is, the chief of song, or chair-bard, and give evidence upon his word and conscience, looking, the while, in the face of the sun and the eye of light.

A bard's robe must be of one uniform colour; but every chief bard, to whichsoever of the three grades he may belong, has a proper and distinctive colour, suitable to his own order.

A poet, if also a primitive chief bard, wears a robe of that sky-blue colour which is perceptible in serene summer weather, as an emblematic indication of peace and heavenly tranquillity; and signifying, likewise, that light, and all other visible things, are best seen through the medium of that colour. This robe, being of uniformly light blue colour, presents, also, a symbol of truth, which is uni-coloured throughout, and all over, whether considered in its analytical aggregate, or varied position, and presents no change whatever, from any possible circum-stance.

A druid's robe is entirely and uniformly white, to indicate purity of conduct, learning, and piety; for white is both the colour and emblem of light. A druid's robe is uniformly white, in emblem, also, of truth.

An ovate's robe shall be green, to signify, in emblem, the growth and increase of learning and science: it is, also, uniformly green, to present a symbol of truth.

Every conventional bard, of whatever order he may be, shall hold in his hand, at Gorsedd, a stick or altar-staff, a fathom in length, and coloured uniformly with his robe; but progressors shall severally bear a staff of the three bardic colours intermixed, to indicate progression. They shall also wear a bandlet of the same colours around the right arm. If, however, the poetic aspirant be merely under pro-tection, the length of his staff shall be only half a fathom; but if an endowed dis-ciple by right, it shall be a fathom long.

Conventional bards, when not in full robes, having no occasion for them, must each wear a bandlet about his right arm, and suitable, in colour, to his own particular class or grade; an usage that has mostly prevailed among the bards since they lost their endowments.

# 19

# THE BOOK
# OF BARDISM

## from *Barddas* by
## IOLO MORGANNWG

HERE IS THE BOOK OF BARDISM, that is to say, the Druidism of the Bards of the Isle of Britain, which I, Llywelyn Sion of Llangewydd, extracted from old Books, namely, the books of Einion the Priest,[1] Taliesin, the Chief of Bards,[2] Davydd Ddu of Hiraddug,[3] Cwtta Cyvarwydd,[4] Jonas of Menevia,[5] Edeyrn the Golden-tongued,[6] Sion Cent,[7] Rhys Goch,[8] and others, in the Library of Rhaglan, by permission of the lord William Herbert, earl of Pembroke,[9] to whom God grant that I may prove thankful as long as I live. The first is a Treatise in the form of Question and Answer, by a Bard and his Disciple – the work of Sion Cent, which contains many of the principal subjects of the primitive wisdom, as it existed among the Bards of the Isle of Britain from the age of ages. In this Dialogue, the Disciple first puts the question, and the Bard, his Teacher, answers, and imparts to him information and knowledge. In the second place the Bard examines, and the Disciple answers.

### The Second Examination
Q. Prithee, who art thou? and tell me thy history.
A. I am a man in virtue of God's will, and the necessary consequence that follows, for 'what God wills must be.'
Q. Whence didst thou proceed? and what is thy beginning?
A. I came from the Great World,[10] having my beginning in Annwn.[11]
Q. Where art thou now? and how camest thou to where thou art?
A. I am in the Little World,[10] whither I came, having traversed the circle of Abred, and now I am a man at its termination and extreme limits.
Q. What wert thou before thou didst become a man in the circle of Abred?
A. I was in Annwn the least possible that was capable of life, and the nearest possible to absolute death, and I came in every form, and through every form capable of a body and life, to the state of man along the circle of Abred,

where my condition was severe and grievous during the age of ages, ever since I was parted in Annwn from the dead, by the gift of God, and His great generosity, and His unlimited and endless love.

Q. Through how many forms didst thou come? and what happened unto thee?

A. Through every form capable of life, in water, in earth, and in air. And there happened unto me every severity, every hardship, every evil, and every suffering, and but little was the goodness and gwynfyd before I became a man.

Q. Thou hast said, that it was in virtue of God's love thou camest through all these, and didst see and experience all these; tell me how can this take place through the love of God? And how many were the signs of the want of love during thy migration in Abred?

A. Gwynvyd cannot be obtained without seeing and knowing every thing, but it is not possible to see and to know every thing without suffering every thing. And there can be no full and perfect love that does not produce those things which are necessary to lead to the knowledge that causes Gwynvyd, for there can be no Gwynvyd without the complete knowledge of every form of existence, and of every evil and good, and of every operation and power and condition of evil and good. And this knowledge cannot be obtained without experience in every form of life, in every incident, in every suffering, in every evil and in every good, so that they may be respectively known one from the other. All this is necessary before there can be Gwynvyd, and there is need of them all before there can be perfect love of God, and there must be perfect love of God before there can be Gwynvyd.

Q. Why are the things, which thou hast mentioned, necessary before there can be Gwynvyd?

A. Because there can be no Gwynvyd without prevailing over evil and death, and every opposition and Cythraul, and they cannot be prevailed over without knowing their species, nature, power, operations, place, and time, and every form and kind of existence which they have, so that all about them may be known, and that they may be avoided, and that, wherever they are they may be opposed,[12] counteracted,[13] and overcome, and that we may be cured of them, and be restored from under their effect. And where there is this perfect knowledge, there is perfect liberty, and evil and death cannot be renounced and overcome but where there is perfect liberty; and there can be no Gwynvyd but with God in perfect liberty, and it is in perfect liberty that the circle of Gwynvyd exists.

Q. Why may not perfect knowledge be obtained, without passing through every form of life in Abred?

A. On this account, because there are no two forms alike, and every form has a use, a suffering, a knowledge, an intelligence, a gwynvyd, a quality, an operation, and an impulse, the like and complete uniformity of which can not be had in any other form of existence. And as there is a special knowledge in each form of existence, which cannot be had in another, it is necessary that we should go through every form of existence, before we can acquire every form and species of knowledge and understanding, and consequently renounce all evil, and attach ourselves to every gwynvyd.

Q. How many forms of existence are there? and what is the use of them!

A.   As many as God saw necessary towards the investigation and knowledge of every species and quality in good and evil, that there might be nothing, capable of being known and conceived by God, without being experienced, and consequently known. And in whatsoever thing there may be a knowledge of good and evil, and of the nature of life and death, there is a form of existence which corresponds with the attainment of the knowledge required. Therefore, the number of the kinds and modes of forms of existence is the sum that could conceive and understand with a view to perfect goodness, knowledge, and gwynvyd. And God caused that every living and animate being should pass through every form and species of existence endued with life, so that in the end every living and animate being might have perfect knowledge, life, and gwynvyd; and all this from the perfect love of God, which in virtue of His Divine nature He could not but exhibit towards man and every living being.

Q.   Art thou of opinion that every living being shall attain to the circle of Gwynvyd at last?

A.   That is my opinion, for less could not have happened from the infinite love of God, God being able to cause, knowing the manner how to cause, and continually willing every thing to exist that can be conceived and sought in His own love, and in the desire of every animation whilst opposed to evil and death.

Q.   When will this condition happen to every living being, and in what manner will occur the end of the life of Abred?

A.   Every living and animate being shall traverse the circle of Abred from the depth of Annwn, that is, the extreme limits of what is low in every existence endued with life; and they shall ascend higher and higher in the order and gradation of life, until they become man, and then there can be an end to the life of Abred by union with goodness. And in death they shall pass to the circle of Gwynvyd, and the Abred of necessity will end for ever. And there will be no migrating through every form of existence after that, except in right of liberty and choice united with Gwynvyd, with a view to re-experience, and re-seek knowledge. And this will remain for ever, as a variation and novation of Gwynvyd, so that no one can fall into Ceugant, and thence into Abred; for God alone can endure and traverse the circle of Ceugant. By this it is seen that there is no Gwynvyd without mutual communication, and the renewal of proof, experience, and knowledge, for it is in knowledge that life and Gwynvyd consist.

Q.   Shall every man, when he dies, go to the circle of Gwynvyd?

A.   No one shall at death go to Gwynvyd, except he who shall attach himself in life, whilst a man, to goodness and godliness, and to every act of wisdom, justice, and love. And when these qualities preponderate over their opposites, namely, folly, injustice, and uncharitableness, and all evil and ungodliness, the man, when he dies, shall go to Gwynvyd, that is heaven, from whence he will no more fall, because good is stronger than evil of every kind, and life subdues death, prevailing over it for ever. And he shall ascend nearer and nearer to perfect Gwynvyd, until he is at its extreme limits, where he will abide for ever and eternally. But the man who does not thus attach himself to godliness, shall fall in Abred to a corresponding form and species of existence of the same nature as himself, whence he shall return to the state of man as before. And then, according as his attachment may be to either godliness or ungodliness, shall he ascend to Gwynfyd, or fall in Abred, when he dies. And thus shall he fall for ever, until he seeks godliness, and attaches himself to it, when there will be an end to the Abred of necessity, and to every necessary suffering of evil and death.

### Sentences of Bardism

Here are the Sentences of Bardism, from the *Book of Ieuan*, the son of Hywel Swrdwal.[14]

1   That does not but exist, from which a greater amount of good than of evil can be produced; since it cannot be otherwise in virtue of God's power, wisdom, and love.

2   The existence of that, which does good to some, and does no harm to others, is safe; since there is more utility from it, than if it had not existed; and God will not permit possible good to be lost.

3   Of that which is neither good nor bad, neither the existence nor non-existence is safe for man, for nothing in reason is known of it. Others say, that it is the material of every thing. However, there is only God that knows its good and evil, its utility and inutility, and whether the good or evil be the greater.

4   Where a great good to all, without harm to any one, can be comprehended, it cannot be but that it is in existence, since otherwise the three principal attributes of God, namely, knowledge, wisdom, and mercy, would not stand without being opposed by distress and necessity: therefore Bardism is true.

5   Truth cannot be had from that in which every truth cannot consist, and which will not consist in every truth, for truth cannot be had from what will contradict or withstand that which is true.

6   It is true that, according to justice, there should be the best of all things.

7   It is true that, according to love, there should be the best of all things.

8   It is true that, according to power, there should be the best of all things.

9   It is true that, according to wisdom and knowledge, there should be the best of all things.

10   It is true that there cannot be in God other than all knowledge, all wisdom, all power, all love, and all justice, without restraint, without measure, without cessation, without end. Therefore, in respect of the power of God, it cannot but be that the best of all things are in existence; and it cannot be otherwise in respect of His knowledge; and it cannot but be, in respect of His love, justice, and wisdom, that the best of all things are in existence.

11   It is true that God can accomplish the best of all things; on that account, it cannot but be that the best of all things are in existence.

12   According to justice, there should be ability in justice; therefore, in respect of justice, there cannot but be that ability belongs to justice.

13   In respect of knowledge, there ought to be power in knowledge, and in knowing what is best; therefore there is power in knowing what is best.

14   According to love, there should be what is most merciful; therefore, by the love of God, what is most merciful is in existence in every essence.

15 God, in respect of His power, wisdom, knowledge, and love, can produce the best of all things, the most just of all things, and the most kind of all things; therefore, it cannot but be that the best of all things are in existence.

16 It cannot but be that the extreme limits of goodness, and of what is good, are in God; on that account, there cannot but be that the extreme of all goodness, and all that is good, is, and may be found, from God, and by God, through His infinite grace and love.

17 There cannot be a God, that does not possess all power, all love, all wisdom, all knowledge, all justice, and all goodness. And it cannot but be that whatever those, who possess these things, do, is found to be without distress, without necessity.

And thus it ends.

## The Ten Commandments[15] of the Bards
### (From the *Blue Book*)

1 God is one, and there is only Himself who is God. Love thy God with all thy soul, with all thy heart, with all thy strength, with all thy endeavour, with all thy understanding, and with all thy affections. For it is He, and no other being, living or existing, that made thee, and doth maintain thee, with all His might, and with all His mercy.

2 Do not love or seek an image instead of God, whether of wood or stone, of gold or silver, or of any other material, and whether it be represented in colour or in effigy; for thou hast never seen God; and who has seen Him? Do not take this world, or any other world, however glorious it may appear to thee, in the place of God; because they are not God, but the work of God, for thy great good, and for that of others, millions of times beyond the extreme limits of thy understanding and comprehension. Do not take riches or possession of any kind, or the regard and greatness of the proud and sinful world, in the place of God. Take not either relation or friend, male or female, for a God. Do not place thy aim, thy heart, thy intention, thy affections, or thy confidence, upon one or other of these things, or upon anything that will cause thee to trust less to God, because of the claim and possession thou hast in them. Always remembering and bewaring, do not seek or retain or love any one of these things, in such a way as will make thee cleave less to thy God than if thou wert without them. If thou doest so, God will turn His face from thee, and will leave thee to stand on thy own footing, and on the rotten foundation of the things which thou worshippest.

3 Swear not to the Name of God, and do not mention His name disrespectfully and lightly, nor deem it of no consequence to listen to such language from the lips of another without reproving and counselling him charitably, kindly, and in a friendly manner, at the same time fearlessly and boldly. If this does not avail, then dwell no longer where thou art compelled to hear the Name of thy God disparaged, and do not, without necessity and cause of importance, mention the Name of thy God at any time.

4 Remember to rest on Sunday, that thy family, thy man servant, and thy maid servant, thy labouring man and labouring woman, may rest, and cast off their fatigue, – that thy ox, thy horse, and every other beast of toil, may

enjoy rest, as they require. Remember that both man and beast have a claim to the time of rest; – there is no health without it. Remember that there is need of a time for thee to reflect, to consider, and to learn thy duty towards God and man. Without this there cannot be that rotation, which ought to be, and which pleases God, in respect of man or property, of world or existence, of animation or life. God, in His six working days, made the worlds and all that are in them, consisting of heaven and celestials, of earth and terrestrials, of worlds, beings, and existences, of all essence and essentials. God rested on His seventh day, that He might consider His work; and on beholding it, He knew that all was good. Do thou, also, on thy seventh day, consider the work of thy six days, and review sharply, sincerely, and vigorously every particle of it, whether it be the work of thy hands, or the work of thy mind, or the work of thy affection, or the work of thy intellect; and then let thy conscience speak, according to its judgment, the language of God in its own undeceitful language, and it will be well for thee, and very well, if it can say that such work was good. Consider the work of thy next six days, with full purpose, and full resolution to do it better than thou didst that of the preceding. Try to bring every thing, whether it be the work of the body, or the work of the mind, or the work of the affection, or the work of the intellect, onward and onward, from better to better, as long as thy life continues, and at the end of it, thou shalt rest from all thy labour in a world and existence, where thou shalt see, and canst truly say of every thing, that 'it is very good.'

5    Remember to love and honour thy father and mother, as thou wouldest that thy son and daughter should honour thee. They have seen and heard more than thou; give credence to them with respect and obedience. They have nourished and cherished thee with love and care; do thou, also, cherish them in their need, feebleness, and old age. They love thee sincerely, they love thee indeed more than any other persons do; therefore it is from their own mouths only that thou wilt obtain truth; though they should deceive all others, they will not deceive thee, because of the love they have for thee. Believe what they say, and act accordingly. Bear in mind the loss of losing the only ones that tell thee the truth. Bear in mind the love of the only ones that have suffered in truth for thee. Repay them; render love for love; render care for care; do unto them, as they have done unto thee. Run obediently at their bidding, as they have ran carefully, lovingly, and quickly at thy cries, when thou wert a feeble child. Thou wert not suffered to complain long; do not suffer them to complain long in their feebleness. By loving and reverencing thy father and mother, thou wilt love and reverence thy God, Who on that account will bestow upon thee His blessing. Thou shalt prosper in thy life and means; thou shalt increase in wealth and understanding; thou shalt have ease in thy conscience, and consequently ease in every thing else; and from this ease of mind, thou shalt have long health, and consequently long life. And these things God promises to add to thee immeasurably beyond what may be given to thee by any thing else, or through any other means hitherto endued with existence, other than what is in God Himself, and His infinite power, knowledge, and love. He says the word; He will do it.

6 Kill not, and do no murder upon any account whatsoever. Do not take away the life of either man or beast, except to prevent thyself from being killed, as when thou killest the enemy that would kill thee, when thou canst not escape, and leave him his life; or when thou killest an animal to obviate hunger, when thou canst not have food otherwise that will keep thee from dying. He that slays shall be slain;[16] and though the body may not be slain, the soul shall be slain. If he escape in this world, he shall suffer grievously in the next world. Blood must be rendered for blood; God hath sworn it.

7 Commit no theft; take not from any man, or from any living or existing being, his own property, by forcible violence, whether it be done publicly or privately. Take not from any living being his property, by treachery, or cunning, or extortion, or oppression. Take not, in any of these ways, his goods, or understanding, or time, or opportunity, or memory, or art, or anything that belongs to one or other of these particulars.

8 Abstain from fornication, and do not commit adultery and concubinage. It is not lawful for any one to nourish the children of others. It is not lawful for any one to divert affianced affection from her whose due it is. Do unto the wife of another, as thou wouldest that another should do unto thy wife. Do unto the daughter of another, as thou wouldest that another should do unto thy own daughter and sister: and remember!

9 Tell no falsehood of any kind, nor on any account whatsoever. Be not a perjurer, or a traitor, or an unjust witness against thy neighbour, or any other man whatsoever. Bear no calumny against any man, or reproach, or satire. Do not love falsehood in another. Conceal not the truth, when it is required of thee, on any occasion whatsoever. Conceal not the truth by word, or deed, or behaviour, or appearance; because the lie that comes from these things is not less than that which comes from the tongue and speech. Though it may be against thy father or mother, against thy brother or sister, against thy son or daughter, against the wife of thy bosom, against thy own life, yet tell the truth. For the falsehood, of whatever kind it may be, will be against thy own soul – it will be told, exhibited, and performed against God and His truth.

10 Be not covetous of any thing, lest any one should give to thee what ought to be given to one who is poorer than thou – lest thou shouldest impoverish another by having what thou covetest – lest, from coveting any thing whatsoever, thou shouldest commit injustice with the view of obtaining it – lest, by setting thy mind upon what thou covetest, thou shouldest forget thy God and His laws – lest thou shouldest omit from memory what is of greater worth, for the sake of what thou covetest. Covet not thy goods, or possessions, or any of thy own property, which can be dispensed with agreeably to the laws of God, lest thou shouldest refuse to the poor and needy what, out of charity and justice, ought to be given or done to them. But love thy neighbour as thou lovest thyself; this, however, thou canst not do, whilst there is covetousness in thy heart. Thou canst not love God above all, or love His laws more than the goods of the world, or love thy neighbour more than mortal and terrestrial things. Covet not the house or farm of thy neighbour, or his wife or daughter, or his man servant or maid servant, or his ox or

horse, or any thing else that belongs to him, lest thou shouldest think of obtaining, or taking, or willing them, in a way that is not consistent with the will and laws of God. But seek of God what thou wantest, and thou shalt obtain it, if thou askest it by faith and sincere belief, and if the occasion be just, and thy necessity unavoidable, and if its acquisition be not injurious to thee. Believe in thy God, and trust in Him with hope and faith, and thou shalt have from Him what, in His sight, is sufficient and useful for thee. He knows thy wants, and what may be for thy advantage, better than thou knowest thyself, and assuredly He will not fail to give thee anything but what may be disadvantageous and injurious to thee.

By keeping these laws incessantly, thou shalt obtain from God love and peace, in the world which now is, and in the world which is to come; and from man thou shalt obtain respect, advantage, good will, and abundance, without there being need in thy house, or an enemy to thy conscience – long life in the world which now is, and eternal life, and endless felicity, in the world to come.

The end.

### Triads of Bardism and Usages[17]

1   The three foundations of Bardism: peace; utility; and justice. Others say: peace; love; and justice.

2   The three supports of poetry and Bardism, that is to say: privilege in right of usage, for there ought to be nothing that is not according to usage; usage in right of privilege, for there ought to be no usage that is not privileged, nor any usage without privilege; and privilege and usage according to reason, nature, and obligation, for there ought to be nothing that is not so – the same resting on the three foundations, namely: truth; love; and justice. Others say: truth; peace; and just utility.

3   Three incidental conditions happen to song and poetry: corruption; improvement; and restoration from corruption and loss. And under each of the three contingencies, in order to obviate non usage, they ought to be submitted to the verdict of country, and the judgment of Gorsedd. That is to say, when they are corrupted, they ought to be submitted so, that they may be improved; and when they are lost, or when they become dormant, they ought to be submitted so, that they may be resuscitated, restored, and brought to memory, as they were formerly. Then they ought to conform to the three supports, namely: usage in right of privilege; and privilege in right of usage; that is to say, nothing should be done, in right of any thing, except what is customary, nor as usage, except what is according to reason, nature, and obligation, with a view to truth, peace, love, and just utility.

4   The three principal qualities of vitality: thought; power; and will; and they cannot be complete and entire except in God.

5   The three excellences of Bardism: to be fond of meditation; to extend learning; and to popularize manners and customs.

6   From three things does truth obtain credence: from believing every thing; from disbelieving every thing; and from believing it matters not what.
Three godly qualities in man: to consider; to love; and to suffer. (St Paul.)

7   For three reasons ought a man to hazard his life, and to lose it, if there be

occasion: in seeking after truth; in clinging to justice; and in performing mercy. (St Paul.)

8 There are three principal kinds of animations: aqueous; aerial; and celestial; that is to say, the aqueous were the primordials of life, being the first that existed, namely, in the seas, before there was dry land; the aerials then came into being, and they live on dry land, deriving breath from the air; and the celestials are those which attained the circle of Gwynvyd, being the highest of all that are not subject to death.

9 The three conditions of animations: the being in Abred; in liberty; and in Gwynvyd.

10 Three things which are impossible: that God should be evil and unmerciful; that there should be evil, which will do no good; and that there should be good, which will not prevail in the end.

11 The three burstings of the Lake of Llion:[18] the first, when the world and all living beings were drowned, except Dwyvan and Dwyvach, their children, and grandchildren, from whom the world was again peopled – and it was from that bursting that seas were formed; the second was, when the sea went amidst the lands, without either wind or tide; the third was, when the earth burst asunder by means of the powerful agitation, so that the water spouted forth even to the vault of the sky, and all of the nation of the Cymry were drowned, except seventy persons, and the Isle of Britain was parted from Ireland, and from the land of Gaul and Armorica.

12 The three administrations of knowledge, which the nation of the Cymry obtained: the first was the instruction of Hu the Mighty, before they came into the island of Britain, who first taught the cultivation of the earth,[19] and the art of metallurgy; the second was the system of Bards, and Bardism, being instruction by means of the memorials and voice of Gorsedd; and the third was the faith in Christ, which was the best of all, and blessed be it for ever.

13 For three reasons may living beings be deprived of life, namely: when one kills a man intentionally and purposely; when one kills a man accidentally, or indirectly, as when it destroys fruit and vegetables, which are for the food and sustenance of the life of man; and when it will be better for the one that is slain that it should be slain than otherwise, with the view of releasing it from extreme pain, or of bettering its condition in Abred, as in the case of a man, who gives himself[20] an eneidvaddeu for some punishable evil, where he cannot render any other satisfaction and payment for what he has done, than by submitting voluntarily, at the demand of justice, to the punishment due.[21]

14 In three ways a man happens to become eneidvaddeu: one is punishment due, by the verdict of country and law, for an injurious evil – an injurious evil being killing and burning, murder and waylaying, and the betraying of country and nation. That is to say, he who commits those evils ought to be executed; and every execution takes place either by the judgment of a court of law, or in war by the verdict of country and nation. The second is the man, who surrenders himself, at the demand of justice which he feels in his conscience, to execution, for an injurious and punishable evil, which he confesses to have committed, and where he cannot render compensation and satisfaction for the injury he has done, otherwise than by submitting voluntarily

to the punishment due for what he has done. The third is the man, who undergoes the danger and chance of execution in behalf of truth and justice, at the call of peace and mercy, and is slain. Such a man is adjudged to be slain for the good, which he has done; and on that account he ascends to the circle of Gwynvyd. In any other than these three ways, a man cannot be adjudged as eneidvaddeu by man, for it is God alone who knows how to judge what is otherwise. The first of them will remain in Abred, in the state and nature of man, without falling lower; and the other two will ascend to the circle of Gwynvyd.

15  The three accelerations of the end of Abred: diseases; fighting; and becoming eneidvaddeu, justly, reasonably, and necessarily, from doing good; for without them there would be no release from Abred, but at a much later period. Herein is seen that it was for the benefit of, and mercy to, living beings, God ordained the mutual fighting and mutual slaughter, which take place among them.

16  The three states of animations: the state of Annwn and Abred, where evil predominates over the good, and hence there is essential evil – and in Annwn are every beginning and progression towards what is better in Abred; the state of humanity, where evil and good equiponderate, hence ensues liberty, and in liberty is power to choose, and consequently improvement; the state of Gwynvyd, where good predominates over evil, and there is success in love, since nothing is loved there of necessity but the good, though it be also loved of choice, and hence there is every completion of goodness, and an end to every evil.

17  The three necessities of the occupants of Abred: the predominance of opposition and Cythraul over prosperity and amendment; necessary lawlessness; and death, ensuing from the mastery of Cythraul, and from the system of deliverance, which is according to the love and mercy of God.

18  The three necessities of mankind: liberty, for there is no necessary good or evil, inasmuch as both equiponderate, and hence either may be chosen according to judgment and consideration; power, for free choice may be made; and judgment, because there is understanding derived from power, and because what is capable of being otherwise ought to be judged.

19  The three necessities of the state of Gwynvyd: the predominance of good over evil, and hence love; memory reaching from Annwn, and hence perfect judgment and understanding, without the possibility of doubting or differing, and hence, the necessary choice of goodness; and superiority over death, consisting in power derived from knowing the whole of its cause, and the means of escaping it – the same being unopposed and unrestrained – and hence everlasting life.

20  There are three common feasts, according to the order and regulation of the Bards of the Isle of Britain: the first, the feasts of the four albans;[22] the second, the feasts of worship, at the quarters of the moon; the third, the feasts of country and nation, consequent upon a triumph and deliverance, and held under the proclamation and notice of forty days. Others say: There are three feasts of endowment, under the sanction of the Bards of the Isle of Britain, at which every one presents his gift, made up of the three tributes, namely,

honey, flour, and milk. That is to say: the feasts of contribution, under the proclamation of forty days; the feasts of alban; and the feasts of worship; and it is the privilege of Bards to preside at them, and to receive gifts of the three tributes of endowment, which are, corn, milk, and honey.

21 There are three other feasts, in which Bards preside by courtesy, namely: the feast of the head of kindred; a marriage feast; and the feast of a fire back, which takes place when five fire back stones have been raised, so as to constitute a dwelling station. At them are contributed the gifts of the comot and nation to the ninth generation; and the endowments of those feasts are of tilth, fold, and wood covert, as will be easiest to obtain and give them; the Bard having things by courtesy.

22 Three things unprivileged to a Bard, for they are not proper for him, that is to say: metallurgy, with which he has nothing to do, except to improve it by means of his learning, knowledge, and doctrine; the second is warfare, for there ought to be no naked weapon of offence in his hand, since he is a man of peace and tranquillity; the third is commerce, for he is a man of primary law and justice, and his office is to teach country and nation. And because of these things, it is adjudged that a Bard ought to follow no trade other than his office and art of song and Bardism, lest what ought to belong to a Bard and Bardism should become corrupted, deteriorated, and lost.

23 Three pursuits are free to a Bard, and to every other native of country and nation, namely: hunting; agriculture; and pastoral cares; for it is by means of these that all men obtain sustenance, and they ought not to be forbidden to any one who may wish them. Others say: ploughing; pastoral cares; and medicine; for these are pursuits of amendment, under the sanction of peace and natural law.

24 The three principal endeavours of a Bard: one is to learn and collect sciences; the second is to teach; and the third is to make peace, and to put an end to all injury; for to do contrary to these things is not usual or becoming to a Bard.[23]

### Triads of Bardism
#### The Elements

1 The three materials of every being and existence: calas, and hence every motionless body and solidity, and every hardness and concretion; fluidity, and hence every cessation, migration, and return; and nwyvre,[24] hence every animation and life, and every strength, understanding, and knowledge, and the same is God, without Whom there can be no life and vitality.

Others say:–

There are three materials of every thing, namely: calas, and hence every corporeity; fluidity, and hence every colour and form, and every course and return; and nwyvre, and hence every life, being God, from Whom proceed every soul, animation, strength, and understanding, for where He is not, neither one nor another of these things can exist.

Others say:–

There are three primary elements: calas, hence every hardness and solidity, and it is dead; fluidity, and hence every progress and mutation, and every alteration, colour, and form, and every discrimination, and every concurrence, and it is dead; and nwyvre, which is God, from Whom proceed every life, strength, and intellect, and every perception and sense.

Thus, according to other wise men and teachers, as may be seen in the old account:–

There are five elements: earth; water; air; fire; and nyv;[25] and the nyv is God, from Whom are all life and orderly motion.

Others say:–

Calas, or earth, water, breath, uvel,[26] and nwyvre, and every one of them is dead, except the nwyvre, which is God, from Whom comes all life.

According to another mode, as other teachers say from an old account:

Earth, water, firmament, fire, and nyv; and the nyv is God, and life, and intellect. From the first four are all death and mortality; and from the fifth are all life and animation, all power, knowledge, and motion.

2   The three constituents of life: motion; knowledge; and awen.

3   The three constituents of knowledge: original awen; facile reason; and inevitable necessity.

4   The three constituents of art: instruction from a master, who knows it; innate understanding that will comprehend it; and the exercise of congenial awen.

5   Three principles: innate understanding; vigorous affection; and the rises of natural temperament.

6   The three concurrences of life: body; soul; and privilege.

7   The three constituents of awen: knowledge, or understanding; vigorous affection; and devotion.

8   The three concurrences of art: correct system; firm justice; and discreet skill in practising it.

9   The three elevations of art: information from him who knows it; genial understanding to comprehend it; and needful occasion to practise it.

10   Three privileges which ought to be conferred upon him who teaches and demonstrates any good art that was not previously known: the privilege of innate nobility as a Cymro; the privilege of honorary art; and the protection of the Bards of the Isle of Britain, namely, that he should not, except of his free will, bear weapons of offence, or engage in war and battle.

11   The three principal adornments of every thing: time; place; and quality. Others say: The three principal elements.

12   The three principal elements of knowledge: Awen from God; the exercise of the understanding; and the demonstration of a master.

13   The three principal elements of Awen from God: innate justice; habitual kindness; and natural understanding.

14   Three things that will confirm and honour Awen from God: energetic industry; correct meditation; and courteous affection.

15   Three things[27]

### Mutual Reasoning Between a Disciple and his Teacher

Disciple   Pray, my noble and very knowing Teacher, since you are a Teacher, and a primitive Bard, according to the privilege and usage of the Bards of the Isle of Britain, out of your usual kindness to me, exhibit your art, and tell me the nature and tendency of the voice of the Gorsedd of the Bards of the Isle of Britain, that I may know its purpose and meaning, and become myself a regular Bard of primary merit, even as you are.

Teacher    My brother in the faith and companion, Cadwgan, since thou art an institutional awenydd, under the auspices of the Bards of the Isle of Britain, I will tell thee, and will exhibit to thee the secret, with the request, and on condition, that thou listen diligently, ardently, and vigorously, to what I shall lay before thee, and not divulge what I say. It is thus, namely:–

The voice of the Gorsedd of the Bards of the Isle of Britain, is the old memorial, which has been preserved from the age of ages, and from the beginning, in respect to the art and sciences of the primitive Bards of the Isle of Britain, namely, the sciences concerning God and His goodness and dispensations, and the usages of the Bards of the Isle of Britain, and their privileges, and art of vocal song, and the arrangement of letters, and the arrangement and preservation of the Cymraeg, and the memorial of the wisdom of the nation of the Cymry, and the memorial of the privileges and usages of the nation of the Cymry, their genealogies, nobility, inheritances, and the privileges of worthy marriages, and all other privileges and usages, which ought to be worthily remembered.

D    God bless you for your kindness and amiability, for they are very familiar to me; therefore, I shall ask points of you – point upon point, until I receive your judgment and instruction.

T    Ask, and a hundred welcomes to you, and I will answer in the best way I can.

D    Why does the water rise from the bottom of the earth to the surface, where it issues out, and also falls from the sky to the earth?

T    I will shew thee the reason; – every thing tends towards life and light; in the light is life, and in the sky above the face of the earth are the light and heat; the water in the centre of the earth, and beneath the surface of the earth, being in the dark, tends towards the light, with a view to life, for in every thing it is a primary law of God that there should be a tendency and an aim towards life and light. Again, water in the firmament runs against its will along the apertures of the aerial parts, and seeks resting places, but there are none such for it in any part of the world, except on the face of the earth, and thither it tends, and that place it eagerly seeks. And, because of these two primary laws from God which exist in every thing, every thing eagerly seeks its rest, where it can get it. This lesson is a lesson taught by wise men.

D    Why is the water in the sea briny?

T    I will shew thee the reason; – the centre of the earth is a rock of stone, and a branch of that rock runs along the bottom of the sea, and melts in the water, and hence it becomes briny. And where the top of that rock approaches the surface of the earth, springs of water are found to be saline in those localities, and salt is obtained from the water in those places.[28]

## The Stars

There are three kinds of stars: fixed stars, which keep their places, and are also called stationary stars; erratic stars, which are called planets, and are fifteen in number, seven[29] being always visible, and eight invisible, except very seldom, because they revolve within and beyond the Galaxy; and the third are irregular stars, which are called comets, and nothing is known of their place, number, and time, nor are they themselves known, except on occasions of chance, and in the course of ages.

*From Bardism – Fragments about the months and other things.*

## Astronomy

There are seven visible planets, and eight are invisible, except in a long cycle of times, and vast ages.

The constellations on the stars are the following:–

1. The Circle of Arianrod;[30]
2. The White Throne;
3. Arthur's Harp;[31]
4. The Circle of Gwydion;[32]
5. The Great Plough-tail;[33]
6. The Small Plough-tail;
7. The Great Ship;
8. The Bald Ship;
9. The Yard;[34]
10. Theodosius' Group;[35]
11. The Triangle;
12. The Palace of Don;[36]
13. The Grove of Blodeuwedd;
14. The Chair of Teyrnon;[37]
15. The Circle of Eiddionydd;
16. The Circle of Sidi;[38]
17. The Conjunction of a Hundred Circles;
18. The Camp of Elmur;[39]
19. The Soldier's Bow;
20. The Hill of Dinan;
21. The Hen Eagle's Nest;
22. Bleiddyd's[40] Lever;
23. The Wind's Wing;
24. The Trefoil;
25. The Cauldron of Ceridwen;[41]
26. Teivi's Bend;
27. The Great Limb;
28. The Small Limb;
29. The Large-horned Oxen;[42]
30. The Great Plain;
31. The White Fork;
32. The Woodland Boar;
33. The Muscle;
34. The Hawk;
35. The Horse of Llyr;[43]
36. Elffin's[44] Chair;
37. Olwen's[45] Hall.

## Chronology

Prydain, the son of Aedd Mawr, was born on the morning of Alban Eilir, that is, the ninth day of March, according to the computation of the Romans; therefore the beginning of the year was fixed on his day, as a day of feast and institution, as it is still to this day. In old times it was called the first day of Cyntevin,[46] the end of Cyntevin being the feast of Alban Hevin.[47] From thence to Alban Elved[48] it was called Summer, and also Harvest; from Alban Elved to Alban Arthan[49] it was called Autumn; and from thence to Alban Eilir,[50] Winter.

According to the computation of the Church and the Courts of Law, Alban Eilir was said to be the tenth of March, but in the chronology of the Cymry and the Romans it was said to be the ninth of March.

Before the time of Prydain, the son of Aedd the Great, the beginning of the year was fixed upon the day of Alban Arthan, which was the ninth of the month of December, according to the chronology of the Cymry. (See John Jones' Almanack, 1752.)

## Chronology

Before the coming of Christ in the flesh, the Bards solemnized times according to the years of memorial and computation, namely, from the time of Prydain, the son of Aedd the Great, who was famous five hundred and sixty-six years before the birth of Christ in the flesh; and from that time it is usual with the Bards to celebrate the memorial and computation of time in accordance with the years of Christ. Prydain, the son of Aedd the Great, as far as memorial and knowledge go, lived the time mentioned before the birth of Christ, and, according to the conjecture of wise men, and well informed herald-bards, six hundred and fifty years subsequently to the first arrival of the Cymry in the island of Britain. It was thus, one thousand two hundred and sixteen years before the birth of Christ that the nation of the Cymry first came into the island of Britain, and this was called *Brut time*, because the years of memory and computation were in old times conjecturally reckoned from the time of Brut,[51] which was about a thousand years after the demolition of the tower of Nimrod the Giant, and about two thousand and eight hundred years after the expulsion of Adam and Eve from the garden of Paradise, which occurred five[52] hundred years after God had made this world.

## The Cycle of Time

The cycle of complete time is a year and a day, four weeks being in each month, and thirteen months in the year.

## The Months

1   *January*
The dead month;
The dead month;
The white water;[53]
The white stream;[54]
The white surface of water;[55]
The black month;
The white flood;[56]
The white rime.[57]

2   *February*
The month of purity;[58]
The month of lambs;
The severe time;
The season of purification.[58]

3   *March*
The agriculturist's month;
The month of violets;
The rising of the sap;[59]
The Lily of the valley;
The thunderer.[60]

4   *April*
The month of the swallow;
The month of the cuckoo;
The beginning of summer;
The beginning of ripenness;[61]
The season of the young;[62]
The spring of the young;[63]
The time of vegetation;
The pear orchard;[64]
The green grass.

5   *May*
The month of the cuckoo;
Freshness;
Opening;[65]
The beginning of summer;
The season of flies;
Superior verdancy;
Prime vegetation;
Various vegetation;
The cuckoo's song.[66]

6   *June*
The month of flowers;
The presence of summer.

7   *July*
The month of hay;
The close of summer;

The extremity of summer;
The extremity of ripenness;
The height of summer.[67]

8 *August*
The wheat month;
The season of whiteness;
Blanched stalks;
White stalks;
White beards of corn;
The month of corn;
Extreme sunniness;[68]
The bright season;
The white appearance;
The white summer.

9 *September*
The fruit month;
Reaping;
The white stalks;
The white stalk.

10 *October*
The honey month;
The wine month;[69]
The month of the honey
    gatherer;
The month of deer rutting.

11 *November*
The month of mist;
The dusky month;
The month of honey-comb;
The fall of the leaves;
Receding appearance.

12 *December*
The black month;
The dark month;
Fore-shortening;
The ventilator.[70]

### Another Mode of Designating the Months

1 The white fluid. The beginning of Alban Arthan.
2 The severe month.
3 Regeneration.
4 The beginning of summer. The commencement of Alban Eilir.
5 The summer month. The month of June.
6 The month of the excess of summer, beginning on Alban Hevin.
7 The reaping month.
8 The month of white stalks.
9 Deer rutting, beginning on Alban Elved.
10 The month of receding appearance.
11 The month of fore-shortening.
12 The dead month. The black month.

In other Books it is as follows – beginning on the morrow of Alban Arthan:–
1 The white fluid.
2 The severe month.
3 Reanimation.
4 The springing rows.
5 The beginning of summer.
6 The open summer.
7 The height of summer. The excess of summer.
8 Reaping.
9 White stalks. Bright Stalks.
10 Deer rutting.
11 Receding appearance.
12 Fore-shortening. Black month.

### The Beginning of the Year
The Ancient Cymry began the year on the morrow of the shortest day of the winter, that is, on the turn of the sun.

### The Three Circles of the Sun
The circle of the summer aban;[71] of the summer ablan;[71] and of the winter alban.

### The Four Quarters of the Year
1. Winter. 2. Spring. 3. Summer. 4. Autumn.
    Or thus:–
1. Winter. 2. Spring. 3. Summer. – White grasses.
    And the four points of the sun are thus:–
1. The point of roughness. 2. The point of regeneration. 3. The point of summer. 4. The point of reaping time.[72]
    Also vulgarly, thus:–
1. Summer. 2. Winter. 3. Spring.

### The Albans
They are as follows in the Book of *Sion Howel Gwyn* – the *Book of Tre'rbryn*:–
    Alban Elved is the calend of October;
    Alban Arthan is the calend of January;
    Alban Eilir is the calend of spring;
    Alban Hevin is the calend of summer.

### The Divisions of the Year (from the same Book)
The three divisions of the year:–
    The time of summer from Cyntevin to the calend of October;
    Winter from the calend of October to the calend of February;
    Spring from the calend of February to Cyntevin.

### The Divisions of the Year
Spring from Alban to Arthan to Alban Eilir, and thence to Alban Hovin; and from thence Summer to Alban Elved; and from thence Winter to Alban Arthan. After that: Spring; Summer; Autumn; and Winter.

*Llywelyn Sion*

### The Divisions of the Year
Some of the ancient Bards divide the year as follows: – Harvest; Winter; Spring; and the beginning of Summer.[73]

### The Divisions of the Year
The four divisions of the year: Spring; Summer; Autumn; and Winter. According to others: Summer; Winter; and Spring.

### The Divisions of the Year
The four divisions of the year: Spring; Summer; Autumn; and Winter.

*Harry the Tall*

The Spring begins in March, when the sun and its opposite are alike, that is, when the day and night are of equal length.

*Ibid.*

### The Divisions of the Day
There are eight parts of the day: 1. morning;  2. dawn;  3. vapourlessness;  4. noon;  5. evening;  6. twilight, &c.
    Or thus:–
1. Dawn;  2. morning;  3. vapourlessness;  4. noon;  5. rest;  6. twilight; 7. disappearance;  8. midnight.[74]

### The Divisions of the Day
1. Midnight ;  2. dawn;  3. morning;  4. vapourlessness;  5. noon;  6. rest; 7. evening;[75]  8. overcast.

### The Divisions of the Day
1    Midnight.
2    Dawn.
3    Morning.
4    Vapourlessness.
5    Noon; the end of day; mid-day.
6    Rest; evening; commencement of night.[76]
7    Evening; after rest;[77] evening; commencement of night.
8    Overcast.
It was in this way that they formerly computed time and the divisions of day; that is, they enumerated eight parts of the day, giving three hours to each, thus, the first hour of vapourlessness, the second, &c., and so for others, midnight, dawn, &c.

### The Divisions of the Day
It was in this way that they formerly computed time, and the divisions of day: they enumerated eight parts of the day, and three hours in each part, and reckoned thus, namely, the first hour, or the second, or the third hour of midnight, dawn, vapourlessness, &c., and so in respect of every one of the eight divisions.

### The Divisions of the Day
The four parts of the day: morning, that is, the first six hours; vapourlessness, the second six hours; noon, the third six hours; and the fourth, evanescence, reaching till the morning.

### Years of the Sun and Moon
    Twenty-nine years of the sun are thirty years of the moon.
    The days of the lunar year are 354.
    The days of the solar year are 366.
    The days of the year of memorial and computation, 365.
    Others say, 364.
It is called memorial and computation, information and computation, since the Cymry have come into the Isle of Britain.

## Years of the Sun and Moon

The years of the sun and moon are as follows:–

The year of the sun, 366 days.

The year of the moon, 354 days.

The year of memorial and computation, 364 days.

Twenty-nine years of the sun are thirty years of the moon.

In another place, thus:–

Thirty-one years of the moon make thirty years of the sun.

*From the* Book of Brith y Coed

## Years of the Sun and Moon

There are two calculations of years: one is the year of the sun, consisting of 365 days; the other is the year of the moon, having 354 days. The days which are over and above the number of the lunar year are called days of days, and they are thus distributed among the Albans, that is to say; – two days of days to Alban Arthan, three to Alban Eilir, three to Alban Hevin, and three to Alban Elved. They are free days, and let any one come from any place he may, he will be free, and exposed to no weapons weapon or stroke, since there can be no court and law of country on those days.[78]

*Bardism; fragments of the Months and other things*

## Days of Days

Days of days are the days that are over and above the lunar year, and are thus distributed according to their number; two days of days are given to Alban Arthan, three to Eilir, three to Hevin, and three to Elved. They are free days, and let any one come from where he may, he will be free, without a weapon against him, since there can be no court and law of country on those days.

---

## Notes

1    Einion Offeiriad, or the Priest, was the father of Thomas ap Einion, author or compiler of the 'Greal,' the tale of 'Pwyll Pendaran Dyved,' and the 'History of Taliesin.' He lived in the fourteenth century.

2    Taliesin flourished from A.D. 520 to 570. He is ranked in the Triads, with Merddin Emrys and Merddin ab Madog Morvryn, as the three 'privardd bedydd,' or baptismal Bards of the Isle of Britain. Many of his compositions are still extant, which, with some of later date, wrongly attributed to him, are printed in the first volume of the *Myvyrian Archaiology*. Several Bardic allusions may be discovered in his Poems.

3    Alternative 'of Euas.' His proper name was Davydd ab Roderic ab Madog, which is still to be seen on his effigies in Dymeirchion Church, of which he was Vicar, and where he lies buried. He flourished about 1340. He was an eminent and learned Poet, and had a great share in regulating Welsh prosody. There is a sacred poem by him 'Am ddiwedd dyn a'i gorph,' and a very poetical translation of the 'Officium B. Mariae,' from Latin into Welsh, which fills thirty columns of the first volume of the *Myvyrian Archaiology*.

4    He was Meurig or Maurice, treasurer of Llandaf, who died in 1290. He obtained the name of 'Cwtta Cyvarwydd' from a Book of his, so called, which contains a compendium of the History of Glamorgan, with other articles, a list of which is given by Edward Llwyd in the *Archaiologia Britannica*, page 257. He also wrote the *History of the Whole Isle of Britain*; a *Book of Proverbs*; the *Rules of Poetry*; and *Welsh Theology*. He also

translated the Gospel of St John from the Latin into Welsh, with commentaries. 'These Books,' says Iago ab Dewi, (about 1700), 'were at Abermarlas about fifty years ago.'

5 Iohannes Menevensis, a divine and poet, who flourished towards the close of the tenth century. Some compositions, attributed to him, are printed in the first volume of the *Myvyrian Archaiology.*

6 A poet and grammarian, who flourished in the thirteenth century. The *Grammar*, which he undertook at the command of the Princes of Wales, about 1270, has recently been published under the auspices of the Welsh MSS. Society.

7 Sion Cent, or Dr John Kent, a very eminent poet, and learned divine, who flourished from about 1380 to 1420. He wrote various Treatises in Latin on theological subjects, thirty-nine of which may be enumerated, and many poems in his native language, which were highly esteemed. Every manuscript volume of Welsh poetry of early date generally contains some of his productions. Three of them, one of which enumerates the Bardic Names of God, are printed in the Iolo MSS.

8 Rhys Goch Eryri, or Rhys ab Davydd, was a very eminent poet, who flourished from A.D. 1330 to 1420. About thirty of his poems on various subjects are preserved, among them one entitled 'Cywydd Cyfrinach,' which is printed in the Iolo MSS, page 307, and is full of allusions to the mysteries of Bardism.

9 A distinguished patron of Welsh literature. He was the author of a set of *Theological Triads*, which appear from the style and language as if they were of Bardic origin.

10 There are two poems printed in the *Myv. Arch.*, vol. i., and attributed to Taliesin, entitled respectively, 'Canu y Byd mawr,' and 'Canu y Byd bychan,' or the 'Great World', and the 'Little World'. The former, referring to the creation, and the latter, to the maintenance of the world, seem, both of them, to be founded on the doctrine of the text. Iorwerth Vynglwyd (1460–1500) bears his testimony to the fact that man was described in the creed of the Bards as a little world, thus;–

Saith the revered Bardism,
A little world is man in his vigour, under the light.

11 It was this doctrine relative to the commencement of life from Annwn, that was, no doubt, at the bottom of the opinion, which Julius Cæsar attributes to the Gauls. 'Galli se omnes ab Dite patre prognatos prædicant, idque a Druidibus proditum dicunt.' (*De Bel. Gal.*, I, vi, c, 18.)

12 'Ei gwrthryw,' i.e., their species may be opposed by a contrary species.

13 'Au gwrthrym,' i.e., their force be opposed by a contrary force.

14 Ieuan ab Hywel Swrdwal was an eminent poet, who flourished from about 1450 to 1480.

15 Literally, 'the ten words of the law,' which phraseology has been, also, retained in the *Welsh Prayer Book*, though it is not now popularly used. When the Cymry embraced Christianity, they manifested a special veneration for the Ten Commandments, as is evidenced by the fact that 'the ten words of the law, the Gospel of John, and the blessed cross,' constitute a Triad of the instruments of swearing, which succeeded the more ancient forms which had been used by the Bards, and which shall be hereafter described.

When Taliesin took the Bardic vow 'on the Altar of St Teilo at Llandaf,' among other things he is made to say,–

From *the ten words of the law* may God judge me,
If my lips divulge where it is. – MS.

16 This is the motto of the Chair of Powys, and is supposed to be co-eval with its foundation in the sixth century. It is quoted by Davydd ab Gwilym, –

*He who slays* another with bright steel
To prevent delay, *shall be slain.*

17 Copied by Iolo Morgannwg, October 1797.

18 'Llion' means an aggregate of floods. The bursting of the Lake of Llion is thus chronicled in the Triads: – 'The three awful events of the Isle of Britain: first, the bursting of the Lake of Llion, and the overwhelming of the face of all lands; so that all mankind were drowned, excepting Dwyvan and Dwyvach, who escaped in a naked vessel, and of them the island of Britain was re-peopled.' (13, Third Series.) In another Triad (97) it is stated that 'the ship of Nevydd Nav Neivion carried a male and female of all living beings, when the Lake of Llion burst.'

It is alluded to by Iorwerth Vynglwyd;–

The store for wine, like the moon on the increase,

Ever full, like the *Lake of Llion*, will it be.

In the British Chronicles Arthur is introduced, as saying thus; – 'There is a lake near the Severn, called the *Lake of Llion*, which swallows all the water that flows into it at the tide of flood, without any visible increase; but at the tide of ebb, it swells up like a mountain, and pours its waters over its banks, so that whoever stands near it at this time, must run the risk of being overwhelmed.' – *Myv. Arch.*, v, ii, page 311.

19　'The three benefactors of the Isle of Britain: the first, Hu the Mighty, who first shewed the nation of the Cymry the method of cultivating the ground, when they were in the Summer Country, namely, where Constantinople now stands, before they came into the Isle of Britain.' (Tr. 56.)

The benefit which he thus conferred on his countrymen is frequently alluded to by the Bards; for instance, Iolo the Red, or Iolo Goch, the bard of Owain Glyndwr, observes of him;–

After the deluge, he held

The strong-beamed plough, active and excellent.

(See Dr Pughe's *Dict.*, v, Hu.)

20　Alternative, 'his life.'

21　The doctrine of *eneidvaddeu* is recognized in the Laws of Dyvnwal Moelmud. Thus, in Triads 19, 20, we read: – 'There are three strong punishments: *eneidvaddeu*; cutting off a limb; and banishment from the country, by the cry and pursuit of men and dogs; and it is for the king to direct which he willeth to be inflicted.' 'There are three *eneidvaddeu* punishments: beheading; hanging; and burning; and it is for the king or lord of the territory to order which he willeth to be inflicted.' On the supposition that these laws were really enacted by, or under the authority of Dyvnwal Moelmud, it follows, that the doctrine which the above Triads involve, is as old at least as 430 before Christ. It seems as if a misapprehension of its real nature gave rise to the opinion which Julius Caesar entertained, that the Britons offered human sacrifices.

22　These are the equinoxes and solstices of the year.

23　In Iolo's manuscript the five last Triads follow immediately after Tr. 19; but they are crossed, as if they were not of the same series.

24　Dr Pughe gives the following meanings to this word, – 'the ethereal sphere; the firmament, the atmosphere,' and in support thereof quotes from Taliesin and Llywarch Hen: –

Glorious is the sun moving in the firmament. – Tal.

Clamorous are the birds, the strand is wet,

Clear is the *welkin*, ample the wave;

The heart is palsied with longing. – Ll. Hen.

It is compounded of *nwyf* and *rhe*, *nwyf* signifying 'a subtil pervading element; a fine ethereal fluid;' and *rhe*, 'a swift motion.'

25　'Nyf' seems to be but another form of *nwyf*, and *nwf*, and has the same signification.

26　'Ufel,' according to Dr Pughe, is 'elementary fire; a spark of fire.'

27　The rest are wanting.

28　It is to be regretted that L. Morris should have omitted from a poem, which is inserted in the *Myv. Arch.*, v, i, page 47, a portion 'containing an odd sort of philosophy about the origin of salt water, rain, and springs,' as it might, notwithstanding its oddity, have been of service in ascertaining the amount and species of knowledge possessed by our Bardic ancestors on these matters.

29　Seven of the Planets are mentioned in a poem of Taliesin, called 'Canu y Byd Mawr,' or the 'Song of the Great World'. *Myv. Arch.*, v, i, page 25.

30　The daughter of Don, and styled in the Triads (*Myv. Arch.*, ii, 73) one of 'the three beautiful ladies of the Isle of Britain.' This constellation is the same with the Corona Borealis. Mentioned in 'Hanes Taliesin,' Ap. *Myv. Arch.*, i, 19.

31　The Lyre.

32　The son of Don; one of 'the three sublime astronomers of the Isle of Britain.' Tr. 89, third Series. The Galaxy.

33　The Great Bear.

34 The Orion.

35 The Pleiades. Mentioned in 'Hanes Taliesin,' Ap. *Myv. Arch.*, i, 19.

36 Cassiopeia.

37 The title of one of Taliesin's poems. *Myv. Arch.*, i, 65.

38 The zodiac, or ecliptic. Mentioned in 'Hanes Taliesin.'

39 Styled in the Triads as one of 'the three monarch bulls.' Tr. 73; third Series.

40 There was a king of Britain of this name, who flourished from 859 to 839B.C. He founded Bath.

41 Mentioned in 'Hanes Taliesin.'

42 The Twins.

43 The son of Bleiddyd – the celebrated king Lear of Shakespeare.

44 Elffin is said to have first discovered Taliesin, in a leathern bag, fastened to one of the poles of a weir. He is frequently mentioned by the Bard.

45 A distinguished character in Welsh Romance.

46 Cyntefin, (cynt-hefin,) the commencement of summer.
> The calends of winter, rough is the weather,
> Unlike *the beginning of summer*. – Ll. Hen.

47 The summer solstice.

48 The autumnal equinox.

49 The winter solstice.

50 The vernal equinox.

51 Brut – Brutus, supposed to be the same with Prydain.

52 Alternative, 'nine.'

53 Gwyn-mer; in reference to either frost or snow.

54 Gwyn-hy-mer.

55 Gwyn-wy-bar; ice. Gwenhwyvar is also used as a proper name, three of Arthur's wives being so called.

56 Gwyn-myr; *myr* being the aggregate plural of *mor*, a sea.

57 Gwyn-hy-bar, or gwyn-y-bar. From *bar* comes *barug*, the term in popular use for hoar-frost.

58 Probably in reference to the penitential season of Lent.

59 Cyn-nodd-awr.

60 Daronwy is one of the epithets of the Deity. It was also the name of a person who is considered as one of the three molestations of the isle of Anglesey. (Tr. 81; first Series.) There is a historical poem by Taliesin, preserved in the 1st vol. of the *Myv. Arch*, entitled 'Cerdd Daronwy,' or 'Daronwy's Song'. Probably this name is given to the month of March, not from any idea that thunder happens in it oftener than in other months, but because it is a powerful month – the lord of months, as regards the severity of the weather, even as it is called Mawrth, March = Mars, the god of war.

61 'Cynhewin,' from *cyn*, and *haw*, ripe. It may, however, be but another form of Cyntefin.

62 'Canowin,' from cenaw, an offspring; a graft. It may refer to the sprouts of trees, as well as to the young of animals. We say *cenawon cyll*, the catkins of hazel, and *cenawon llewod*, lion whelps.

63 Cenaw-tardd.

64 Probably because the pear trees now begin to blossom.

65 Also 'May;' and is the name still in use.

66 'Cogerddan,' (cog-cerdd.) It may signify also the departure of the cuckoo.

67 'Gwerthefin' is likewise an epithet for the Deity, and signifies what is supreme, from *gwarthaf*, the upper part, or summit. We have above derived it from *gwarth* and *hefin*.

68 Gorhïan, i.e., gor-huan.

69 This clearly indicates that vineyards were formerly cultivated in Britain.

70 'Gwynollydd,' or 'gwynyllydd,' probably from *gwyntyll*. Many of the above names are, however, now so obsolete, and their roots so obscure, that we do not vouch for accuracy of translation in every case.

71 *Sic* in MS.; but we are inclined to regard them as clerical mistakes for *alban*, a primary oint. It seems also as if 'gwanwyn,' spring, should have been written for the former summer.

72    Or, – The winter solstice; the vernal equinox; the summer solstice; and the autumnal equinox.

73    The calends of winter, rough is the weather,
Unlike to the *beginning of summer.* – Ll. Hen.

74    Literally, 'separation.'

75    Alternative, 'after rest.'

76    The terms in the third column are jumbled together, with no particular assignment, and may be thus translated: evening, the end of day, commencement of night, twilight, ditto, evening.

77    Alternative, 'twilight.'

78    'Days of days are those on which it is not proper to prosecute a suit.' *Welsh Laws.*
Dr Pughe renders 'dyddiau dyddon,' by *blank days;* –

    Hoedl Dafydd megis *dydd dyddon.*
    (The life of Davydd is like a *blank day.* – D. Benvras.)

# 20

# THE OLD POETIC GUILD IN IRELAND

## CHARLES DE KAY

RIEND AND FOE of the Irish agree to allow them preëminence in two matters – poetry and music. Welsh history states that music came to Wales from Ireland, and nowhere do we find records of a poetic guild so abundant and minute as in the literature of Ireland, gradually being brought to the notice of the world. A sketch of this caste is all that can be given at present.

The guild of poets has been as elaborately subdivided in Ireland as in Wales, where the common term is 'bard', while in Ireland that word is either not at home or at some period sunk in the social scale, 'filé' being the proper word. But without doubt the arrangement of the profession conformed to the political fashion of the day. We hear of Ollaves or Doctors of Poetry, with an Ard-Ollave at their head; of Anruiths or Masters, who formed the next rank; of Clis, and so on. The corporation was called the Filidecht, and seems to have reached importance between the fall of Druidism and the time when Columbkille, the saint of royal Irish blood, established thoroughly the supremacy of the Church as St Patrick understood it, by eloquence, by mortification of the flesh, by political moves, and even by the sword. Before his time the guild was a great nuisance to chiefs and people, owing to the religious or superstitious awe with which the poets were regarded. Outwardly Christian, filés were merely Druids deprived of some of the terrors which pertained to them. The old histories refer to several occasions when the exactions of the poets caused their banishment; but only with the age of St Columbkille do we get anything that affords a firm basis. In A.D. 574 the saint came back from the island of I to Drom-Ceata, not far from Derry, at the invitation of Aedh, son of Ainmiré, who wished to drive all the troublesome singing and piping gentry out of Ireland. 'I do not wish to continue to maintain the Filedha,' answered Aedh when the saint begged him not to expel the poets, 'so extreme is their insolence, and so great are their numbers; for the ollave has an attendant train of thirty followers, and the anruith has a train of fifteen; so of the other

members of that order downwards, each person has his special number of attendants allotted to him according to his rank, so that now almost one-third of the
men of Ireland are members of the order.'

In reward for conforming at least outwardly to Christianity the filés were so
well defended by Columbkille that the chief king retained his chief ollave, subordinate kings their particular ollaves, and filés were allowed to chieftains. We find
in the Highlands of Scotland the piper attached to the person of each chief of note.
It is probable that the custom there represents a very primitive and simple form of
entertainment common to all parts of Europe, not excluding Rome, in which the
performer was a bagpiper, a flute player, or a harper. Wherever instruments were
introduced which do not require the breath, the voice of the performers became
important. Yet the name originally signifying the instrument would come to mean
the person. Filé may be considered equivalent to piper in its origin, but in Ireland
it was of such old standing to signify a person of higher rank than a performer on
flute or bagpipe, that its first meaning was entirely unknown to the Irish speakers
of Gaelic.[1]

The difference between the Welsh bard and the Irish filé appears to be merely in name, and springs from the difference in the instrument used at different
epochs. Welsh history records that music was revived in Wales from Irish examples not long before the Norman Conquest; with that revival we may consider that
the term of 'bard' came in. But the word bard refers to the 'burden' (French *bour-
don*), the humming sound of a stringed instrument; while 'filé' arose from the
shrill sound of the flute or pipes – earlier and more primitive instruments than the
harp. We may consider, then, that the revival of music in Wales in the Middle Ages
by Irish minstrels brought back the harp to Britain; but in Caledonia the early
colonists from Ireland introduced the bagpipes, if not already the favorite instrument there. In the twelfth century Giraldus de Barry draws these distinctions
between the three countries: 'Ireland only uses and delights in two instruments,
the harp and the tabor. Scotland has three, the harp, the tabor, and the crowth, or
crowd; and Wales the harp, the pipes, and the crowd.' So that we find the bagpipes even in Wales according to this Welsh authority, but may well doubt whether
the remote parts of Ireland, into which he never penetrated, could have lacked the
bagpipes, and can be quite sure that he omitted them in error from the musical
instruments of Scotland.

That Ireland and Caledonia had the tabor, or small drum, we may well
believe, for that is the special instrument for summoning spirits; but as such the
tabor was disliked by Christians, since its monotonous noise was used while the
Druid or poet went into a trance. The process by which a poet threw himself into
an ecstasy is very similar to that found by Castrèn among the Lapps and Samoyeds
of Siberia, even to the eating of dog's flesh as a preliminary. A curious story of the
pursuit of the Fomori by the Dagdé, or 'good god,' has an invocation of a captured harp, in which the Dagdé cries: 'Come summer, come winter, from the
mouths of harps and bags and pipes!' And a later legend, containing in verse an
adventure of Fion, says:

The household harp was one of three strings,
Methinks it was a pleasant jewel:

A string of iron, a string of noble bronze,
And a string of entire silver.

The initial shows a bagpipe common to the British Isles. Minstrels of Finland still employ a harp when singing the long runes of the *Kalewala*; the latter resembles a large zither. A harp like this must have existed in Ireland down to the Middle Ages, when the small upright harp as it appears on the coins of Ireland and on the flag became the fashion. The harp in Dublin Museum called the harp of Brian of the Tribute, but probably an instrument of the fourteenth or the fifteenth century, not the eleventh, is the modern type. The harp of Tom Moore is given in order to show the most modern form of this harp. It belongs to a revival of harpistry at the close of the last century, when very fine harps were made for some years in Dublin.

The poetic guild suffered during the later Middle Ages from the bad character of many of its members, who became degraded into strolling adventurers ready to commit depredations; they became bad 'fellows' in England and *filous* in France. The Bulgarians called certain fairies or elemental spirits *vilas*. In Ireland they had bad and good characteristics very sharply expressed long before the Middle Ages. The laureate, or official poet, of Ireland, who had shown himself the possessor of a wonderful memory, was distinguished by a seat at banquets and public ceremonies, a certain arrangement of his hair, and a special cloak decorated with the feathers of song birds. In the last point, and in the superstition that his satires could produce disfigurement or blemishes on persons satirized, the Irish filé again recalls to the wizards of the mediaeval Finns and modern Samoyeds. Another very ancient musical instrument was a stand of crotals, or small bronze bells, now used only on animals. The cut shows these adapted for young girls, children, and pets.

The dread of satire is yet alive in Ireland. Within the last decade a local bard of Limerick is said to have procured for himself an office by satirizing in verse the town council. Aenghus O'Daly, one of a famous family of bards, who is supposed to have lived about A.D. 1600, has left a most venomous satire on the Irish septs of his day, which has been published by John O'Donovan under the title of 'The Tribes of Ireland'. Edmund Spenser was concerned at the number of 'carooghs, bardes, jesters, and such like' who straggled up and down Ireland, or 'miche in corners amongest theyr frendes idlye'. Yet the great poet, while reproving their tendency to laud the greatest robbers of the country, remarked of their songs: 'I have caused diverse of them to be translated unto me that I might understand them; and surely they savoured of sweete witt and good invention, but skilled not of the goodly ornamentes of Poetrye; yet were they sprinckled with some prety flowers of theyr owne naturall devise which gave good grace and comeliness unto them.' Had Spenser been able to read Gaelic; had he learned the language and made himself one with the people whom he helped to oppress, – and who destroyed his castle at Kilcolman after all, – what a difference there would have been in the estimate placed by English grammarians, poets, politicians on matters relating to the Gaels! Spenser would have brought to light not only the histories, legends, and poems we now have, but many others which have disappeared under the persecutions from which the Gaelic-speaking and Catholic natives have suffered, not to mention the loss of manuscripts through sheer ignorance that they possessed any value whatever.

That vileness which was the dark side of the Druid, and which reflects itself in words allied to the same root in many languages, was also in some degree part of the early filé. Indeed, we have notice of the period when it was found necessary to define the duties of a poet, who among other things was at one time very much the same as an advocate at law, while his magical verses made him a physician, or caused him to be feared like a Druid. At the foundation of the tripartite rule, or rule in succession, of three kings at the Navan, near Armagh, the compact was witnessed by Druids, poets, and champions – 'the seven Druids to crush them by their incantations, the seven filés to lacerate them by their satires, and the seven young champions to slay and burn them, should the proper man not receive the sovereignty at the end of each seventh year.' We have also an amusing instance of the obscurity of phrases used by two great poets in a contest of words. This reached such a pitch that the court revolted and the guild of poets was deprived of some of its privileges. The Druidic side is shown in the famous circuit made by Aithirné the Importunate, a poet whose virulence was such that no one dared say him nay, and whose greed and luxury finally brought many chiefs to death. His purpose was to stir up strife and give a chance for champions to collect human heads and acquire fame. Secure in his privilege, he asked whatever the chiefs most objected to part with, not excluding their wives, of whom he collected a troop and marched them off into slavery. The prophetic powers of a poet are shown on this circuit. A clod of earth containing a big brooch having fallen into the lap of a king, flung there from the hoof-stroke of a horse, Aithirné not only explained what was in the clod, but told exactly who had buried the brooch. On the hill of Howth, near Dublin, are the remains of an earthwork which is said to be the fort into which Aithirné fled when his insolence finally overcame the fears and hospitality of the men of Leinster. There he warded off their attacks under circumstances in which he showed barbarity to his own men of Ulster who were defending him.

The extortions of the poets were conducted with a good deal of system. They were at times supported by the people; but it was difficult for them to collect tithes from the folk, or to get pay from chiefs whom they eulogized and whose genealogy and tributes they knew by heart. Often they went in bands, attended as fully as they could afford, and carried with them a large pot, or caldron, called 'The Pot of Avarice.' This was presumably the sign of an intention on their part to claim food from the chief they visited, though in the legend it was meant for the gold and silver they expected as perquisites. Caldrons of ancient make are found in the Dublin Museum, 'The Pot of Avarice' was swung from the points of nine spears by nine chains, and was said to be made of silver. When they approached a house the leader of one of these parties, at one end of the line of minstrels, would begin with a verse. The second verse would be recited by the poet at the other end, and the third by the one next the leader. Thus the song jumped from one end of the line to the other. We have inferred that at one time the filé was no other than a piper and that the poet became also the singer, after a change of instrument left his mouth free for vocal music. But the separation of *Filé* from *Cruitiné*, or harper, must have been very ancient, for the Psalter of Cashel makes a distinction between northern and southern Ireland on this very point, giving the finest music to the south, the greatest poetry to the north.

The sweetness of string music, blandness, valor,
In the south, in the south of Erinn are found,
It so shall be to the end of time
With the illustrious race of Eimher.
There fell to the share of the northern man
The professor of poetry with his noble gifts.
It is a matter of boast with the north that with them has remained
Excellence in poetry and its chief abode.

The native brought up to speak Gaelic rarely obtained sufficient ease and mastery of the English language to achieve greatness as a poet. If he devoted himself to the tongue through which he might hope for some of the prizes offered by the wealthier nation and the English-speaking settlers in Ireland, he lost his hold on his own fine language. Talents of the highest order have been stifled in Ireland owing to this unlucky situation, for the land was too impoverished by bad government to allow of a modern literature in Gaelic.

The filés who wrote and sung their ballads in Irish, how shall they be estimated fairly? It is a task that cannot be undertaken with any hope of useful conclusions until far more of the old ballads and legends shall be translated and their age, their historical elements, and their allusions explained. Almost everything is still to be done before the old literature of Ireland is sifted and annotated to the point where it can be compared with that of other lands. A beginning has been made by Professor Arbois de Jubainville of the Collège de France, for whose 'Essai d'un Catalogue de la Littérature Épique de l'Irelande' and his two volumes of 'Cours de Littérature Celtique' all Irishmen, and all who hope to learn something of primitive Europe through the remains of Irish literature, must be profoundly grateful. Very thorough studies of the music and musical instruments are found in Eugene O'Curry's *Manners and Customs of the Ancient Irish*, with an introductory volume by W.K. Sullivan.

The apparently complete independence of Irish literature of the early writings by Britons is a constant surprise, and the professors of poetry among the Irish have no parallels in England. One must go to the Gaelic Highlands, to the bards from whom Macpherson obtained very late variants on many of the old stories and legends common to both countries, before a correspondence is discovered. In Iceland, on the other hand, we get figures among the scalds which are practically identical, and some of them bear Irish names. But we must give up the idea long cherished by students of Norse that the Icelandic literature antedates the Irish. Everything points the other way. The Icelanders appear to have had political as well as commercial reasons for knowing more about Ireland than about Norway, for their natural neighbours were the Faroe, Shetland, and other islanders who are connected by blood as well as by language with the Kelts. Their scalds found it easier and more profitable to study in Ireland and Great Britain than in the countries about the Baltic. Viollet-le-Duc says that in the Middle Ages the best harpers came from Brittany and Ireland.

In the later centuries there is apparent among the filés a tendency to be lavish of adjectives, florid in narration, given to the grotesque and absurd. In the more ancient lays there are grotesque and far-fetched things, but these appear to come from some root of cosmology, mythology, legend; not from that striving after novelty which destroys literature in the eyes of judges. The effect of the Norman Conquest is very clear in many of the later stories. This could hardly fail to be the case if, as we may be pretty sure, the fashion of writing down and reading off pieces, instead of reciting them from memory, only began to be general after the Normans arrived. Yet the wildest, most turgid Irish poem can hardly be said to contain comparisons so far-fetched as a large number of the Icelandic sagas, though written down about the same time, say from the twelfth to the fourteenth centuries. Alliteration, which is the chief artifice in the *Kalewala* of the Finns, and only less popular with the Saxon poets of England and Norse poets of Iceland, is used with the utmost discretion, so that even in those poems where it is the rule it does not force itself on the ear. The ordinary or end rhyme is common to Irish verse and has been thought to have driven alliteration out of English. The memorized tariff of tributes preserved in the *Book of Rights* has a good deal of rude rhyme; but so far as the present writer has observed, rhyme never became in Irish so fixed and artificial as it now appears in English and French poetry.

A mediaeval version of the battle of Magh Rath (Moyrà), which retains the metrical parts of an older version scattered through a prose account, after a fashion usual with Irish bards, shows slight traces of alliteration except in the lists of names of heroes, and hardly any of rhyme proper – at the most one may say of assonant rhyme. The battle was fought A.D. 637, between Domnall, the chief king of Ireland, and Congall Claen, a fugitive prince of Ulster, assisted by a large army composed of Highlanders, Picts, and Saxons.

Congall had exiled himself because he took it as an insult at the banquet of the king that poor food was set before him. The king sends a band of monks after him. When Congall sees them he is so fierce that they run away, but do not fail to curse him with bell and book. Then the king sends the poets of Erin after him, when Congall exclaims: 'The munificent character of Ulster is tarnished forever, for we gave the poets no presents at the banqueting house, and they are following us to upbraid us.' So that the man who is depicted as crazily fierce and violent, a ruthless, insufferable tyrant, receives the poets well and gives them presents according to custom.

On reaching Scotland in his flight, Congall is met by the four sons of the king of Scotland with a demand from each that he shall make his stay with him. But each wants a certain caldron belonging to his father which has very convenient traits. 'Why was it called Caire Ainsicen?' asks the writer. 'It is not difficult. It was the *caire*, or caldron, which was used to return his own proper share to each, and no party ever went away from it unsatisfied; for whatever quantity was put into it, there was never boiled of it but what was sufficient for the company according to their grade and rank.' From a caldron like the one in the illustration, king, poet, and hero obtained their porridge, their boiled beef and mutton, and their venison. They ate flesh without forks, using their short skeans and their fingers to tear the meat. Their drink was ale or milk, kept in large receptacles like vats and served in wooden *methers*, or mead-cups. The wooden mether was of course copied in metals or overlaid with thin shells of metal, but the great bulk of the people used those of wood. They are found from time to time in the bogs where they were concealed and forgotten, sometimes full of a curious substance which is supposed to be petrified butter.

'The Battle of Moyrà' is a very curious and beautiful medieval poem, containing later as well as ancient traits, some primitive pagan, others old Keltic, and not a few Norman. The night before the battle Domnall did not sleep, though some, remarks the poet, may have slept soundly to the 'thrilling, agreeable, and symphonious musical strings,' and to the 'low, mournful, soft strains of minstrels.' When addressing his army Domnall compares himself to the sledge that drives the nail home, and his five sons to sparks driven from an anvil.

> My own five sons of ruddy aspects –
>    Fergus, Aengus of troops,
> Ailel and Colgu not penurious,
>    And the fifth Conall.

> These are the sparks of my body,
>    The safety of all lies in their attack,
> Ready in each road, furious their action
>    When coming against foreigners.

The Druid of the exile's camp, going out to view this king and his army, returns and, to the great fury of Congall Claen, makes a magniloquent report of their appearance. As to Domnall himself:

> Oh the size of the expert blue sword
>    Which is in his valiant right hand!
> And the size of his great shield beside it!
>    The size of his broad green spear!

> There are three clouds over his head –
>    A blue cloud, a black cloud, a white cloud;
> The blue cloud of fine bright valor
>    And the white cloud of truth.

Families in Ireland, as in Scotland, maintained their harpers to celebrate the deeds of ancestors and of the living, and we have most tragical instances of their devotion to such patrons, like the story of Loyal Ronins in Japan. But all is not tragic with them.

Craftiné the harpist was an early prototype of the crowders and blind harpers now vanished from Ireland, but still found in Finland, and in other countries even less popular with the tourist. Of him the pleasing tale is told how he outwitted the parents of a princess who fell in love with his young master. Cobhtach, by a crime the king of the greater part of Ireland, – for he had killed his elder brother and poisoned his nephew, the chief of Leinster, – sought at first to keep his grand-nephew Maen an idiot, since Maen was dumb from his birth and could not be chosen king. But Maen destroyed these hopes by suddenly developing the power of speech in an altercation with a schoolmate on the play-ground. As this made him eligible to the throne, Cobhtach banished him and his tutor Craftiné on the first good excuse; whereupon they took refuge with a powerful chief near Bantry Bay, Kerry. Here Maen fell desperately in love with the daughter of his host, but without the aid of his harper would have failed, as all previous lovers had, because a watch was kept on the girl by night and day, her parents themselves taking turns.

Craftiné chose the hour of banquet as the time when people were least on their guard; he called for his harp and played with such expression and skill that all eyes were fixed on him. The lovers stole away from the hall, and then Craftiné began a measure which lulled the court into a slumber or state of trance, during

which the prince and princess had time to exchange pledges of eternal affection. As soon as they returned to their seats the harper changed from the Suantraighe, or sweet measure, to the Geantraighe, or lively measure, the effects of which were not only to awaken people from their trance, but to throw them into the happiest mood. Perhaps he changed again to a third measure generally mentioned in turn – the Goltraighe, or lament. At any rate the mother of the lovely Moriath heard the sound of sighs, which the maiden was too artless to suppress, and managed to extract from her the unwelcome news that she had pledged her troth to the exile. As the princess was inflexible, Maen obtained Moriath for his wife.

The poets of Ireland have been the men who collected the legends of Finno-Ugrian and Kelt and fused them into early songs out of which a later generation composed the literary treasures extant. They took the cosmological ideas common to each of these two races, made them more human, brought the gods from their sublime or malicious positions into flesh and blood, and made history serve as a framework on which to hang the curious, stirring, sometimes beautiful thoughts of the past races. The poets recorded the actual warfare between the fierce pagan Finns still lingering on the islands off Ireland and Scotland, and the mixed Keltic-Ugrian tribes of Erin and Caledonia. But to make it interesting they identified the Finns with the autumn or winter, and with night, calling them *Fomoraigh* (Fowri), and attributing to them complexions unnaturally dark, and magical powers of great virulence, as noted in 'Early Heroes of Ireland' in the *June Century*. The Finns treat the Lapps in the same way.

Whether as giants or as magicians who turn into seals, these men are still remembered on the north coast. To coast-dwellers the Giant's Causeway is nothing but the remains of a line of stepping-stones joining Britain with Ireland, once used by the Fomoraigh. The basaltic columnar groups of rock are called *clochan nabh Fomoraigh*, and the sea-caves thereabouts are thought to be haunted. Everything related is on a scale suited to giants, so that it is plain that the historical element in the tradition is faint compared with the mythological. The poet, as well as the tale-teller who does not compose in verse but uses prose, has preserved all these ideas after a fashion, so that one may still hear how Fion mac Cumhal met a giant who came across the sea by this causey, and how he fought or did not dare to fight him. The old myths, developed by the more learned poets into tragedies and comedies fitted for the listeners of their age, have retained in some places their early bigness and vagueness, and are merely nursery tales. In the grounds at Blarney Castle is a small flight of steps under a rock which has been seized by the imaginative in the same way, though apparently quite modern, and dubbed the 'Witch's Staircase.' But the great number of past filés has given to all the landmarks of Ireland a wealth of legend which can hardly be exhausted for many years, let ever so many volumes be published. Nearly every lake has its story of a city overwhelmed for the sins of its inhabitants, or its dragon slain by Fion mac Cumhal, St Patrick, or some other favourite of the people.

The long training of the people in verse-composing and verse-reciting predisposes them to the composition of poetry of some degree of excellence. Irishmen and Irishwomen as a rule have a knack at writing if they receive any education at all, and are natural journalists and writers at an early age. The last remarkable poet of the filé kind known in Ireland was Carolan, the blind bard of the last century, whose portrait, and some of whose verses, translated and in the original, were published by James Hardiman. He was as peripatetic as Homer is said to have been, blind also, and certainly a fine if not a great poet. Though the race is not extinct, little except the most ordinary verse is published in Irish to-day, the audience being too small to tempt the most ardent patriot. With all its inherited shortcomings, and with the evils that befell it owing to circumstances, the poetic guild of ancient Ireland did the world a great service in keeping from destruction historical and national data lost from other parts of Europe. It also added not a little to the world's stock of tragic, of noble, and of comic fiction.

## Note

1    Through Keltic *F*, for Finno-Ugrian *P*, this word is traced in Finnish and Esthonian *pilli*, Esthonian *wile*, a pipe, a bagpipe, a flute. Proscription of minstrelsy brought the filés so low that *filou* was degraded in French to the meaning of thief, and *gwilliad* in Welsh to that of stroller, vagabond.

# 21

# THE DRUID PATH

## MARAH ELLIS RYAN

PHADRAIG, SON OF NIHIL of the Ua Dinan, held silent his white hound on the hill of Cromm Cru, and looked down the far valley of blue mists where the sea of the west rolled in.

Back beyond the sweet-smelling reaches of the heather he could hear the bay of the hounds of his uncle Kieran, Tiern over North Tormound. He could no longer hear the clink of their silver bridles, nor the laughter of their ladies, nor the scream of hawk on dove.

But the hill of the ancient god was a sweet place in the silence, and he rested there, and made him a pillow of fern – and listened to the soft breath of the wind in the rowan tree. Its sigh of love for the green earth was a sweet song, and he slept there to that music, while the sun rushed beyond the wide seas of the west, and soft-footed dusk crept after, filling all the hollows with the gray web in which the night is held.

A curious dream of white birds came to him there; the dream had come to him before, yet not with clearness – and in the dream was a dusk path in an ancient wood, and a well there – a well rising and sinking with the tide, and a vision of a maid moving before him into the shadows – a vision swathed in a white cloud, with hidden face but a voice in which was held all the music of beauty of life in all the world. His soul was as a harp on which that music played, and his body was but as a shell left behind while the wings of harmony lifted him – lifted until he was borne as a cloud far from the touch of the earth – and he heard a word over and over in his ear, until he strove with might to echo it, and then, in the striving, the smell of the heater was again in his nostrils, and the forefeet of the white hound were on his breast, and above him a shar stone in the soft rose of the sky.

He lay entranced, thrilled by the ecstasy of the perfect dream, and somewhere from the very earth came a song to his ear and an earth echo of the word he had striven for and missed. And this was the song he heard:–

Make strong your charms against Danaan,
    Danaan of the snowy breast,
Who lured the souls of the Gods of Old,
    To the land of the mystic west.

The voices were those of two boys, and with them was an old shepherd who bore fire in a strange bowl of thin carven stone, and in the arms of the boys were dry heather and branches of yew. And in fear they let fall the yew at sight of Phadraig, and at sight of his white hound beside him.

'Peace to you,' spake Phadraig, 'And who be you to sing here a song of charms? And who is Danaan?'

'A blessing of all saints on you from Jerusalem to Innis Gluiar,' spake the ancient who bore the fire. 'We bear here boughs for the puring fires of Beltain, and the mothers of these boys bade them make a prayer and sing the song ere they crossed the three magic circles of the Tor of Cromm Cru.'

'And is this that hill?' asked Phadraig. 'As a childling they tell me I was nursed in sight of it, but never before have I stood on it, and who made the song of the charm?'

'One of the anointed of the saints who loved every plain and black crag and forest dell between us and the sea. It was no other than Nihil of the Deep Wood.'

'Strange, that is,' said Phadraig, the son of Nihil, 'other songs of that singer I have been taught, but never this one until I hear it as in a dream in this strange place; and look, there are white sea birds against the stars – and they also were of the dream.'

'On the night of Beltain strange power is abroad – and strange dreams! And what is the name of you who venture to sleep on the hill of the ancient gods in the dusk of this day?'

And when Phadraig told him, the old herdsman would have knelt, but Phadraig took his hand and spoke to him in kindness, yet could not get from him no other word as to the song of Danaan.

'Go to Roiseen of the Glen, the wise woman down by the sea,' he said. 'She was nurse to you and knows all your father Nihil would have had you know of the names of the ancient gods of the land.'

'But Danaan was the name of a people – the old, old people, soul brothers to the fairies!'

'Ay – it may be. And may not a people have a spirit, as has a person? Have we not our own this day in Erinn, our Mother of the land? Ask me no more, O Lord of the Ua Dinan, but go you down to Roiseen of the Glen, and peace go with you.'

And with his white hound at his heels and one of the shepherd boys as guide, Phadraig took trail to the sea glen and would have gone through a deep wood in the valley, but the boy drew back.

'Not there, my lord,' said he.

'Yet it is a shorter way.'

'No way is shorter if you never come out alive, O Lord of the Ua Dinan.'

'What abides within the wood?'

'No living thing, my lord, but the water in the Druid's well, and it pulses there as if it might be the heartbeat of the ocean beyond, yet the water is not salt.'

'This is a land of strange riddles I am coming back to this day,' said Phadraig, 'but do you not hear music in the wood – or is it the wind through the new buds?'

'The priest tells us it is the winds, or the waves, or the night birds in their shelter, and that is the thing we must say,' said the boy, and neither of them spoke of the white birds above them against the sky.

To Phadraig it was as if he had walked into a new life from the hour he slept on the western hill of Crommu Cry. And all the path of it held music to make the heart glad of life – yet sad with inarticulate yearnings. The life of the halls of Kieran was left behind, and he trod the heath as an exile returned.

In the cost of Roissen of the Glen there was a rabbit stewing on the hearth, and Roissen herself spinning the silver flax at the open door in the starlight.

'Oh, it is yourself come back on your own feet to greet me this day?' she said, and wept with very gladness, and kissed the young hand of him. But he kissed her brown cheek instead, and they talked long after the shepherd boy was asleep in the forest leaves in the byre.

But it was that night of Beltain that Phadraig asked of the unknown things, for he had noted the salt sprinkled on the threshold to bar out influences of the old gods; so that night they talked of Nihil, dead ere he had seen his son, and Kreda, his wife, dead at the birthing, and all the grandeurs of the house of the Ua Dinan where Phadraig had lived his life of training for the work of a chief. Yet out of it all he had come back with the heart of a boy, and sat on a three-legged stool at the door of Roiseen, and fashioned a flute of alder-wood, and piped on it in the sunshine of the morning.

Then, when the milk was put away, and Roiseen settled with the distaff and the whirling strands, he spoke the name singing in his heart.

'Mother Roiseen, it is to you I am coming with a thing to ask: who is Danaan of the birds of white?'

'That you should ask it, and you with the name of a saint on you! Get you to your hawking or hunting the deer! And see that you pluck primroses to scatter at your door this night that the Ancient People send you no call of Danaan – the men who follow the call wander far.'

'To the land of the mystic west do they wander?'

'Ay, that they do; far over the green meadows of the waters where the horses of Lir have their pastures. From the cliff below you can see them running in races endlessly to the shore.'

'I see the waves run in,' said Phadraig, but she was not to be fooled.

'Ay, and more than the waves to you, as to your father! But you are idling in thought, Phadraig, son of Nihil.'

'What other task when there is peace in Tormond? And the Ua Dinan, as you mayhaps have heard, cannot abide the sight of me near his ailing son, and Kethlen his wife, bitter as gall because she has borne me a weakling.'

'True that is. You stand in their eyes as a threat at the crowns they wear.'

'To me a pipe on the hills instead, and the songs of my father to sing! Roiseen, why has the song of Danaan never been given me?'

'That name has been through the ages a hated word to the women of your house and in each generation they try to smother it out.'

'And why is that?'

'It gave a youth the seeking eye and the wandering foot, and it was said to keep young the heart of a man when all his mates went tottering under the sod. No – the women could not abide the thought of that, and they smother it out. Ay, that is the way with the woman-heart.'

'Mother Roissen, there is a deer for you in the forest. Shall Snard and I bring it in tomorrow's morn?'

And the white hound, hearing his name spoken, flailed the floor with his tail and rose up and waited.

'To what would you bribe me, Phadraig, my heart?'

'To peace and content while I tell you I heard the song of Danaan on the hill of Cromm Cru in the dusk of Beltain – and I felt the music that all the songs of Nihil, my father, could not give voice to, and in my dream I looked in that Druid well of the wood, and saw the heart of the ocean beat there under the stars! All this came to me by chance in the place of fire to Beltain, so mine is the right to ask what I ask.'

And Roiseen, the wise woman, looked on him and made the sign and plucked primroses for her door.

'Yours is the right,' she said, 'come you away from the house and out under the hawthorn tree and what I can say with no hurt to the saints and their faith, that I will. It is said that while many a family trace in pride their fathers to the ancient barbarians, few trace their descent from yon Wise Ones who took themselves into the air with their own enchantment sooner than be conquered. This I heard when I was a girl in the home of the king, your father's father. But Nihil of the songs learned much from a master of tricks, an aged man who said he had lived on the earth in other days when the sea covered all this valley, and that this was the last edge of the land where the Danaan lived on the earth as people, and ate the honey of bees, and drank the water of the Druid well in the wood beyond.'

'Ay,' said Phadraig, and he looked over the green velvet of the valley running down to meet the white foam of the sea, white as the hawthorn bloom above them, and from the dark hills he looked to the islands beyond, and it was all a sweet picture of summer under the blue sky. 'Ay, Mother Roiseen, of all places in the whole world where would they find another spot so fair? In truth, I believe your word that it is the last corner of the land they could let go to the hard people of the iron pikes.'

'So it was, the last place they let go of – and they lingered long after the stranger-people swept over the land to the east. And to your father, Nihil, came a "sending" of sight through fasting, and enchantments of music, until he spoke aloud the word no other dared ever to speak for them.'

'And what was the word, Mother of the Glen?'

'It was of a bond of birth and blood between the Ua Dinan and the Tuathe de Danaan, but the legend of it is against all Christian teachings – and we are Christian now in Erinn.'

Phadraig looked up to the mount of the Druid god where fires of propitiation had burned but a night agone.

'Ay, so we say,' he agreed, 'but tell me more of Nihil and his song of Danaan.'

'He all but had the ban of the Bishop of Clare put on him – and it was backed by some of his own blood whose names I will not speak, for it is evil to speak against the dead! They were mortal shamed to be thought of the blood or the spirit of enchanters, the while Nihil was so proud of it that church itself was called to the question. That was a time of trial! For there was your mother, the Lady Kreda of Kilfernora, not yet either wife or mother, but loving him and holding him to church, and there was the bishop with his power to bless or ban, and there was Nihil stout in rebellion against all but the sweet Lady Kreda. For his word was this: that if all the mothers for a thousand years could not stamp out the call of Danaan in the heart of a man, was it not proof that it was a bond of the spirit, and was for good and not for evil?'

'And then?'

'He was banished to a forest cell for a year and a day for expiation, and that was the time the Lady Kreda chose to ride beside him and do penance beside him. And, at the last, to pleasure her, he made the song of warning against Danaan, and he went into the forest away from the sea, but he was never the same man after! A true singer sings only the sings in his heart, and that was the song made at the word of another, for he, Nihil, had walked the Druid Path to the well over back of beyond, and the white sea birds of Danaan had come to him there, and he heard music of sweetness in the closed hills where the Ancient People are waiting to this day and holding secret the sacred things shut in for the people of the future who will see as your father Nihil saw. That was his word of it many a day as he walked above your cliff, or up to the hill of Cromm Cru. And the priests beyond could do naught with him, though your mother hated the thoughts he spoke, as did all the women of your race of the Ua Dinan.'

'Mayhaps they were but jealous of a knowledge not for them.'

'Mayhaps, for true it is the Lady Kreda loved well his songs when he was wooing under her window there in Kilfernora but turned away her head when the songs were of things not of her ken.'

'I have had few years, yet I have lived to see that with other lives,' said Phadraig. 'What power may a man gain for the world if he only sing songs of love to a mistress who only smiles from a window?'

'You are older than your years, Phadraig, my heart, else it would be myself sitting here under the hawthorn telling you the ancient things that the priests tell us are false things.'

'I do not think in my heart they are false,' said Phadraig, son of Nihil. 'Into the forest I am going now for your deer, Mother of the Glen, and then, till the next day of Samhain, I will live in the open to give proof to my own heart that Nihil, my father, saw true, and spoke true.'

And thus did he, though his kinsmen raged and their women told the priests, and the Ua Dinan tore down the stone of Cromm Cru from the moment and broke it into pieces with iron chisels – for it is well known that spirits of the Tuathe de Danaan hate the touch of the iron brought into the land by the barbarians.

But Phadraig with his pipe of alder was somewhere in the deep wood with only the white hound and his dreams and his calls to the tamed sea birds on the cliff, and never a sight could kindred get of him unless it was in a boat, dancing on the far waves toward Inis Mor – or high on the hill where the forest veiled him if any tried to follow.

And a wail went up from the shepherds that year, for the murrain got the sheep despite of all, and some wells went dry, and the herders gave sullen looks to the virtuous lords and ladies who had done the pious work in tearing down Cromm Cru of the Tor.

And one day there came to Roiseen of the Glen a lady riding on a white horse with golden trapping. Her eyes were dark with desire and her braided her had the gold of the sun glinting its brown shadows. With her came a priest of the south whose looks were down and ill.

'I am Yva of Kilfernoa,' said the maid, with a blush sweeping her face. 'Have you, O woman, speech with Phadraig of the Wilds?'

'That was the place his mother came from,' said Roiseen of the Glen, 'and I have seen no sign of him this seven days, barring the white sea birds hovering over the forest of the Druid well.'

'Woman,' said the priest, 'what would drive sea birds to the forest on days like this?'

'Ay, it is a big question, your holiness, and a thousand years have not given us the answer.'

'Do you mean the blasphemy of enchantment too strong for church to conquer?'

'I would not dare, your holiness; mayhaps it is that the church has not striven. Sea birds are a small thing to take note of after all.'

'O woman,' said Yva the brown-eyed, 'will you tell him I have ridden the horse he loved to these wilds he loves, that he may know the message is a true message, and that I watch from my window ever to these hills of the north?'

'That he may find the way to that window, O Lady?'

'Ay, that he may find the way. The Ua Dinan and the head of my clan have clasped hands and emptied bowls of mead on the pact, and I bring my own message to his hills.'

'How great is your patience, Yva of Kilfernora?' asked old Roiseen of the Glen, and the priest frowned at the forwardness of the peasant, but Yva of the dark tresses leaned forward in the saddle.

'What mean you?' she asked, her lips red and parted over white teeth.

'Would you take him as Nihil, his father, was taken, with his quest not finished, nor his heart content?'

'Nihil, the Singer died,' said Yva, her eyes staring.

'Ay, he died! With love beside him – earthly love keeping step, yet not understanding, he died! Would you fain have Phadraig, son of Nihil, dead by your side or alive and free to choose after he has made the circle that was broken for Nihil?'

'Woman – are you taking on yourself the weighing of a soul?' demanded the priest in anger. 'What blasphemy is that of lives in circles and like enchantments? Is it evil craft if Druid witcheries by which the young lord of the Ua Dinan is held here in the wilds?'

'I have not dared to ask him that myself,' said Roiseen of the Glen. 'But I am an old woman, and I know the men of the Ua Dinan and their women, too! By bell and book and candle their women have driven out or smothered a wild Something in the blood of the Ua Dinan of the west land, until the clan is weak this day because of it! They have not dared dream their own dreams lest they range beyond the church rules and the women they wive; and what man does any great thing without the Dream – or woman, either? O Lady of Kilfernora, you are beautiful as the wild rose on the heath, and there are many chiefs to break a lance at your nod; better to give your glove to any one of them, then enchain an Ua Dinan before he has followed the Dream till it makes the circle.'

The priest was prone to chide such speech, as was his duty, but Yva of Kilfernora put out her ringed hand.

'She speaks truly, and I see it,' she said. 'No one has ever spoken thus to me before today. Think back, reverend father, over the years: Nihil dead with his songs half written; the king, his brother, a man of gloom with a crippled child; the old king, his father, tired of rule and in a monastery ere his time; yet, all these men were strong in youth and to the fore in wild beauty. Not until now has anyone dared read me that riddle of the Ua Dinan. Woman, you are wise and you have Yva of Kilfernoras for your friend. I ride back and dream my own dream, and leave him all the freedom of his. Fare you well!'

'Now indeed may a great day come again to the children of the Ua Dinan,' said Roiseen of the Glen. She went back to the spinning of her flax, with a great jewel hidden in her bosom, let fall there by Yva of the dark hair and the burning eyes.

And in the green-gray dusk of the twilight there was the flash of white wings against streaks of yellow sky, and the white hound came down the glen by the sheep path, and Phadraig the wanderer, with a hare of the hills ready for the twigs over the roasting fire.

'Art tired of the quest, Phadraig?'

'Nay, not that, Mother of the Glen. I am no longer alone, though I cannot tell you what walks beside me.'

'None of us can, and for lack of faith few can feel them,' agreed Roiseen.

'But Nihil, my father, spoke the truth, we do belong,' said Phadraig. 'Once I saw the shadow of her in the Druid well in the moon's light, but the face was still veiled for me, but the music is piercing sweet, and I would I had my father's gift to catch and hold it.'

He would eat not any of the hare, but drank fresh milk from the cow and stood at the door looking tired and white in the starlight.

'May I let stay Snard, the hound, with you?' he asked. 'He is weary of my trail; and will not walk in my paths; only today did I learn I was cruel to him; and tomorrow is the feast of Samhain, and where I go I cannot say, but I think it is not for Snard to follow me.'

'Phadraig, my heart, do you ever think of someone there in the south, who –'

'Ay, Roiseen. I thought of them all today when a storm cloud swept in from the sea with a clammy cloud in it. For it was not so cold as the welcome in my kinsman's home lest the day come when I claim rule there.'

'Ay,' said Roiseen of the Glen. 'That is a picture we all see some days in life, but Time is a good story-teller, Phadraig aroon, and I'll wait the other day when the sun shines for you and the human call comes.'

'You are the only human thing, Roiseen,' he said, and touched her hair. 'You understand.'

'How did you tame the sea birds of Danaan, Phadraig, my heart?' she asked, but he shook his head.

'I only spoke to them as I would to Snard – some souls have the gift of taming – that is all.'

'Ay, your father had it before you,' she said. Then, as he turned into the darkness, she spoke again as she held back the white hound. 'Do you look to come back to me here, Phadraig, son of Nihil?'

'I do, Mother of the Glen, though I cannot see clearly the path I may come – or when.'

'I thought as much,' she said, 'but Phadraig, take this from me ere you go; for all ills of youth and life there grows somewhere an herb; find it, Phadraig aroon; search till you find!'

But he went across through the night to the hill of Cromm Cru, singing the song of his father –

> O white Danaan of the sea birds,
>> Danaan of the snowy breast!
> O sweet the song on the Druid Path
>> To lead me to her nest!
> She takes my hand at the sea marge,
>> She whispers low on the wind,
> She sets her sail for Tir-nan-Ogue

'Ay,' said Roiseen, twirling the spindle.

> And leaves dear Life behind!

Then, as a muttering of thunder came on the wind from the sea and a flash of fame cut the gray of the sky, she took the hound within, closing the door on the night, and chanted the song of Nihil, as a prayer, in the dim light of the peat blaze.

> Make strong your charms against Dannan,
>> Danaan of the snowy breast,
> Who lured the souls of the Gods of Old
>> To the land of the mystic west.

The feast of Samhain in that year was a time of wonder, for the yew branches on the old altar place of Cromm Cru were struck afire by the lightning, or so it was said. All the people, fearful of the crashing thunder, yet clasped hands in a circle below the mount, while the man with fire made his way to the top and bent to place it when the stroke came. The blaze from the sky flashed down, and flamed upward again, and the stunned man fell downward among his mates and was borne in fear across the valley, and all knew that night that the vengeance of Cromm Cru of the Tor could be a thing to put the fear of death on any man. Let the churchman say their say 'neath every bell in Erinn, it would not change any man's mind. And all had known it as a sign of evil to come when the altar of the Ancient People had been defaced.

And there were those, fleeing under the lightning flashes, who vowed they passed Phadraig, son of Nihil, running before the wind with eager gladness in his face, and looking neither to the right nor left, and chanting the song of his father as he went down to the sea.

> O white Danaan of the sea birds,
>     Danaan of the snowy breast,

And the white birds were screaming and circling above him in the storm as he sang –

> She takes my hand at the sea marge,
>     She whispers low on the wind,
> She sets her sail for Tir-nan-Ogue –

And then a great wave caught the currach he launched and tossed it out on the night, and the white foam made the curtain and hid him from all of life.

Ages on the bosom of the ocean seemed to pass over him after that storm. There was light, and then again there was darkness, but he knew it only through closed eyes in a trance-like dream. He was conscious ever of the whir of wings sweeping over his face and knew the sea birds were there, and then he heard voices, and the laughter of a woman, high and sweet and mocking.

The movement of the boat ceased as it grated on sand. There was a sudden silence, and the sound of running feet.

'But what use to try?' said a sweet, tired voice. 'All white things go to Danaan, and look: every bird is white!'

'Danaan comes not out of the forest, and the youth is fair. He is treasure of the sea on our shore; if for her, the birds should have borne him into the lake of the pulsing heart. My hand shall give him to drink.'

Then a cup was held to his lips, a drink of sweet-smelling fruits was offered him. He did not drink. He was no longer in a boat but in a lady's bower where bloom was on every bough, and the air heavy with the sweetness of orchards.

'Where am I?' he asked, and out from a shadowy doorway of stone a tall and wondrous woman smiled on him.

'You are in the Summer Land of the Long Day,' she said. 'The birds of the sea brought you, and what thing do you seek? For your wishing must be great to win your way here.'

'I do not know the thing I seek,' said Phadraig, whose mind was veiled from the things that had been lived. 'I only feel that I shall know again when I find it.'

'Then we will wander, a-seeking,' said the woman of beauty, and took his hand.

Whereupon, without seeming to take a step, he passed through and was a part of a wonderful people. Their slightest cup was of gold, and many wore crowns at will, and held court and ordered games at which all played merrily, and then the crowns were tossed aside as a part of the game no longer amusing. He moved with his mistress, whose name was Una, along the seashore where pleasure boats were held without rope, and he found himself sitting there alone, wonder-

351

ing how the boats were held together, for there was no iron in them, and that word 'iron' was the first word his mind had as a link with the old life and changing skies.

For the skies never changed in the Summer Land of the Long Day, and all the people laughed and played games as if to pass the time while waiting. No one told him for what, and when he asked, Una the beautiful would laugh her sweet mocking laugh and bid him to her bower.

'Other earth lovers have come our way, but none like you,' she whispered. 'Do you never know you are fairer than blossom on the bough – or golden fruit of living trees?'

'Whence came your orchards where no one labours?' he asked, and she laughed again.

'They are the fair memory of the sunken world to the south – as is the castle of stone by the water's edge, for what need is there here now for walls of stone?'

'Whose hands made it thus strong here by the sea marge?' he asked, and she took his hand and held it.

'Weary would fare in this our land if I gave you all the words of that building, for it is ancient as the very earth of which you came. There was no sea at the walls in that day, and the Great White Land of the South was in the midst of waters, and ruled the world. Then the lands broke away and the waters covered it, and only little lands of it kept above the waters or kept the old gods. Your Inis Erinn to the sun side of the world was one, and another one far on the sun-path beyond the waters is one, but the links between have been forgot by the people of Earth. It all lives here because we are the People of Memory. We went out from your Earth Land proudly, letting the body and the soul go that we might hold memory alone, and in that memory we hold only Day and only Summer.'

'Ay,' said Phadraig, and he sat a long time in the tower looking across the moat where the tides of the sea swirled in, 'but in all your games and pleasuring, is it not that memory holds you instead, and makes you as endless slaves to the Great Past? Would it not be rest to forget?'

Upon which she drew away from him and screamed at him to begone, for his earth thoughts were cruel as is the iron of the stranger-people in the heart.

He wandered away from the place, and into a wood – and her cries came after him calling him back, but he could find no gate to the moat and he could not go back.

Gay companions danced about him, and made jeweled crowns for him in the games they played, but he looked at the white birds circling above him, and looked at the sea, and wondered whence they had led him, and at times he could close his eyes and see them circling above the black cliffs of Erin though he had no memory of that place.

And the day was heavy in the Summer Land for the reason that a quest was in his heart, but the mind kept no record.

But white deer came to a lake in the wood to drink, and after them gay fays with shepherds' staves; and they danced and sang their songs of the woodland things, and that touched his heart more than the games of crowns and castles.

'Make me a shepherd, too,' he said, 'for you herd the white things, and the things of white are dear to me.'

'Why is that?' asked a maid of the wood.

But he did not know, and as they laughed, all suddenly Una, gorgeous and jeweled, flashed in their midst and caught at his hand.

'Not yet have you seen her?' she asked. 'Then come with me,' I weary for your voice.'

'I am a shepherd of the wood, and herd the deer.'

'The deer need no shepherds; it is only a game to play. Come! I will sing my music and dance you a dance in the woods alone, see! Is the dance not a fair dance?'

'Ay, but I would you could give me the word of why I wander here where this lake wells with the tides of the sea.'

'Come! We will hunt in a forest far away. This lake in the wood is a place we never seek.'

'Yet the white birds come – and the white deer.'

'It is a place where earth life is remembered, and the dread enchantment of night may fall.'

'And the stars?' he asked, for all suddenly he thought of the night as a thing dearly beloved and to be desired more than the Ever Day of the changeless sun. The night stars had been dear to him.

'Ay, and the moon and their mistress. Come out of the dusk of the wood.'

'But I hear music of sweetness here!'

'Come, and I will sing beyond sweetness of woman!'

'I listen.'

'By this lake of Danaan, I may not sing.'

'And that is best,' said Phadraig, for out of the rock-wall by the lake, or up from the water, there came the music of dreams on the hill of Cromm Cru, and to an altar of stone by the lake-side came a figure of a maid, and before her and after her swept the white birds of the sea. Her face was veiled as by a cloud circling her to her white feet – and it was the white cloud maid he had visioned in the well where the heart of the sea throbbed here in the lake of the wood.

'Come with me now for pleasure,' said Una of the gold crown and jewel eyes.

And he looked deep into her wondrous eyes and read there the shadow things of some forgotten past.

'Somewhere, in some life, your music of Life has held me, and I followed after. Was I lost in some forest through that following, O Woman of the Memory? And do the white birds of the sea lead me at last out from the shadows of that? This pulse of the lake beats more close to me than the pulse of your heart, O Una, most beautiful! And – I follow my dream!'

And at that the white cloud fell away from the maid, and he saw the white hands of her make new fire in the ancient way on the stone of the altar place, and maids and men in green clasped hands and circled her, and chanted a song he had sometime known of.

Samhain! Samhain! Samhain!
Take the new fire! Send the rain!
Banish care and banish pain!
Speed the ghosts who ban the sheep,

Light the path to spirit sleep!
This our fire to light the way
This eve:
    Samhain!

And as he heard them he saw again the hill of Cromm Cru and the circled bands there, but never on Cromm Cru or in all the world had he seen such a priest at an altar, for she was all of white and silver and in her hair of gold was a fillet of silver with a crescent moon. And he broke through the circle to kneel by her.

'O new moon of the world!' said Phadraig as he unclasped the strong hand of Una.

'I hear your voice but may not look on you until the prayer is worked. The Lords of Flame send thus the strength of altars to the sun! 'Tis Summer Days' farewell!'

'The day is endless here – and no farewell!' came the whispered music-sweet voice of Una. ''Tis witchery of Earth, her mother's earth! I beg you to come with me!'

But he made no answer, so thrilled was he by the enchantment of the music of the white maid who gave fire to her men and maids, and bade them to the four ways.

Then she turned and smiled upon him, and in her smile was the glory of dawn.

'You have followed the quest, O King Phadraig, soul of Nihil?' she said.

'Not king, O Wonder Maid! You have given back the name I had lost, but no king am I. I am the son of Nihil, and am your shepherd of the white deer, or knight of yours if fighting men are called.'

'Danaan calls no more battles these many thousand days.'

And with the name came the strange witchery by which he had been held in thrall since the night of Beltain on the heights.

'Danaan – Danaan!' he whispered. 'I have followed the quest. Your white birds led the way, O snowy-breasted maid! I am in bond to you these many days!'

'We are all bound by links forged by the gods. What quest was yours?'

'I never knew till now. I thought it but the music of the past – I sought to find it through your magic name – and now –'

'Ay! Wishful human hearts,' she said, and rested her hand on his hair where he knelt beside her. 'Come you, and tell me of your life on other shores.'

'I have forgotten all,' he said, and in truth he had; only flashes of vision came to him as she spoke, but they went again.

She laid her hand on his. 'Now look again,' she said.

And he looked. And there was the great cliff and the glen by the sea and the sheep on the far moors. And at the door of the cot sat Roiseen spinning the flax, and the white hound at her feet looking out to sea. It was as if he was looking into the eyes of Phadraig, and seeing him, yet taking no note, and Phadraig felt a longing for the shore. He had loved well Roiseen and the hound. And Danaan beside him laughed, and clapped her hands as a child would do.

'I saw it, too!' she said. 'And that is the shore my mother loved! Once she made me to see her honey-sweet hills. She died with the sickness of longing for them, but never could I see it alone. Oh, lend me your eyes, and look for the deep well in the wood in the valley below the altar – it was there he, my father, found her, and drew her from her people. And she trod with him the Druid Path and came from the pulsing well here to the pulsing lake. Did you know that each is a mirror for all that reflects in the other? It is the path of dreams – and the guide is the living sea. It has led you as it led my mother from the land of Inis Erinn.'

'And when was this?' asked Phadraig, after he had looked with her into the pulsing well and over the cliffs, and in all the places she had been told of and longed to see.

'I only know it is so long ago that the sea is changed there. For the water ran in where you showed me the sheep in the valley. Ay, always I wanted to see that earth life again, and I wished it till you came to me.'

'And I wished for the voice of Danaan out of all the world till my wish met yours somewhere between the shores, and only the sea birds knew!'

She looked at him long, and sighed.

'My mother came for such a wish – and for love, but she could not stay alive with us, and her spirit went out on the wings of the wind to find her way back to the primrose dawns and purple dusks. How will you go out, O Phadraig the king, when the time comes?'

'Why am I here but to do your will?' he asked. 'And since you name me king, then a king's way must I go out when the time comes; but bear you with me I will, Danaan, my soul.'

'Ay, if that might be,' she said, and played with the girdle of sea pearls about her. 'My mother left with me the earth longings else I never had wished you here' – and then she put her hand on his once more and had him look back to the land, and softly she crooned over to herself the charms it held for her through the sick longings of the mother. And when he thought of the night there, and the stars circling above and shining in the still water of the well, she arose and paced the grove.

'Look you,' she said, 'the others who abide with me gave up Earth and Spirit in an ancient day that they might live ever in the strong memory of joys that were. My heritage is different – as my spirit is. They never weary for the dusks of the night; I do, because of the bond with earth in me. Thus I make my own world, and do the moon prayers my mother knew, and make the Festivals of the Age of Youth, and here for love of it I have my night all alone where it gives dread to Una lest I plunge them all in shadow – they are in fear of earth enchantings. You are stronger than I, O Phadraig, for you have the soul of the Danaan and the strong earth body. You have fared forth on the quest of Nihil, though you know it not! But Nihil was not a king and the gods decide, Phadraig, that you are to be that. Wearily one more life must you serve ere you win the right to return.'

'Will you, O Danaan?'

'If you will it so, for you are stronger than I, Phadraig.'

'What pledge may I keep?'

She gave him the sharp flint spear from the altar.

'Cut there in the wall of the rock something sacred to you and to the land of my mother.'

He did so, and cut the central star of the north, and the wheel of the wings of it at the four seasons.

'It is the most steadfast sign in our skies,' he said, 'and every circling dance of prayer to the gods, old or new, is built on it.'

Then Danaan, holding his hand, stood beside him at the edge of the lake of the tide, and with her finger drew a circle around the symbol there.

'The forest will wither, and the heart of the lake will be still, ere the bond of that circle dies for you and for me,' she said. 'If ever in doubt, O Phadraig the king, fare you forth again from your own shores of Inis Erinn and look on the wall and my pledge here. But never look back to it but once in your lifetime, and noe – come away!'

He followed where she led, and in a grotto by the sea they sat with clasped hands and she told him what she might of the People of Memory. Yet often she seemed to tell him without words. The music of a wondrous life swept over him in great floods of light unspeakable, and again he could hear an undercurrent of a lament ever dying away, and coming again, and he felt what that meant, too.

'We will not be parting,' he said as he held her. 'I say it!'

'That is as may be,' she answered. 'I am free of the wood and rule there, yet I belong to the Tuathe de Danaan, and there are bonds of this life.'

'I broke them to find you,' he said.

'So you did. But you have the wonderful earth body, and the doubled strength of Nihil and the others who have longed through the ages to prove the bond they felt. I will be alone. There will be no one to help me.'

'I will help,' he said.

'You have your will, and you see no content till you try,' she said. 'But this is the time of trial, and I will not see you linger till your soul goes out on the restless winds crying for the blue of the heather on the hill and the primrose dawns after the sweet nights! It may be a long farewell you are to give me here, Phadraig, O King!'

But he lifted her in his arms as if she had but been an armful of the fragrant blossoms above them, and he strode down to the shore with the white sea birds screaming.

She uttered no word as he placed her in the currach and set it on the waves, and from the castle walls no face looked out. It was as if all the land there, and her heart as well, had been made quiet by the strength of his will to bear her away.

But only the whispered lament of the music was heard, and the world was very still. The birds had ceased whirling above but swept steadily onward as if drifting on the wind, and it was a world of green water and green sky they went into.

But the cold came down, and the birds flew low. He touched the hand of Danaan; it was very cold, and his heart was sick with fear for her. He lifted her to his breast that his body might give her warmth. But it did not, and his very soul seemed frozen with unearthly cold as he lay beside her and held her close.

And then she smiled, the most wonderful smile in the world, into his eyes, and whispered, 'I did not know how it would be coming, Phadraig, O King. But it is the farewell – and it is sweet as honey on the hills in your land of love.'

But he could not speak; he could only look on her face until his own eyes closed, and the currach went steadily on through icy air. There was no longer any thought left in him as to where they were borne, for he felt the sleep of death was over them both.

❧

And on the day of Samhain, as the sun went into the western mists and left a path of glory behind, the white hound at the feet of old Roiseen of the Glen stood up looking out to the sea, and the whine of him was like a chained soul in travail. Roiseen looked the way he looked, and in the path of the sun on the water a currach came in to the shore, and over it a white cloud hovered. Yet when it came nearer, the cloud was only white birds flying low on the sea.

'The strength of the saints to us – and Saint Brighde to the fore!' she prayed, for no mortal currach ever came in like that against the tide. And to shepherds bearing yew to the mount of Cromm Cru, she made a call.

'Come you who bear cheer to the ghosts who walk on the night of Samhain,' she said, 'come you down to the sea where the ghost of Phadraig, son of Nihil, is waiting on the waves!'

In fear they came, and, led by the white hound, they went down to the sea, and there was Phadraig in the white sleep. But the hound crept near to him and gave tongue in joy, and Roiseen of the Glen lifted his head to her.

'The luck is on him that he yet holds breath,' she said. 'Men, take him up. Fiann, make you the fire. Eard, go you the priest in the cave of the hills, for he is a holy man. Ay! Achone! Phadraig, that you should come back to us with the ice in your blood like this!'

And only the bravest of the men would bear Phadraig, for the others stayed on their knees in fear of the white birds whirling wearily over.

And the night fires of Samhain were sending their flames to the sky when he spoke.

'Danaan, Danaan, it is again I have lost you.'

'He dreams,' said the holy man of the cave where Saint Colman had lived his seven blessed years, and ever after that time the monk lived there in retreat.

'Nay, father, call it not a dream, for it is a part of the life of his people – and he has been bold to go forth to find.'

And that was the time she told, under confession, the legend of the race of Ua Dinan.

He was very aged, and had seen many things on earth, and in hearts, and he did not chide.

'What is the blaze on the night sky?' asked Phadraig. 'Do they burn today the yew wet by the rain last night of Samhain?'

The monk looked at the woman.

'Ay, Phadraig, my heart,' she said. 'It is the feast fire of Samhain.' But she did not tell him he had gone out with the ghosts of Samhain a year gone, and came back with them!

Then there was sound of horses' feet, and voices of men of degree, and a chief of Tormond entered the cot and bent the knee to Phadraig, and beyond the door stood many chiefs.

'We have guarded your claim till you came, Phadraig, son of Nihil, son of Ua

Dinan,' he said, and the chiefs lifted their lances, and one by one entered the cot and spoke fealty and passed out.

And thus he learned that Danaan spoke true in Tir-nan-Ogue of the Long Day, for Kieran the king had fallen in a raid of the south, and his frail cousin had gone out like a rushlight in the wind.

'Come another day, and I will hearken to you,' he said, 'other cares await me this night.'

They went away at that, and Phadraig asked again for Danaan, and was told that the currach was empty but for himself, and was so old that it fell to pieces as the men drew it ashore, and that not lately could it have ever borne the burden of two bodies.

This he knew was not true, and he said it, and the fever of him ran hot, and he talked of the trees of magic where white flower and fruit of gold grew on the same branch, and where music was achingly sweet, and spoke without words! Back there to Tir-nan-Ogue would he go for Danaan, despite all, and he bade them as their king that they bring him a boat for the journey!

And so prayerful were the eyes of Roiseen that the holy man of the cave bade him sleep in peace, for with the rising of the sun the boat would be ready.

'Achone! Ay, father! But what shall we do if he wakens alive and holds you to that?' asked Roiseen, making the sign.

'What is there to do with god or man but to keep the faith?' said the priest. 'He is not to be bound or held to life for the cares of this land except he be rowed to some island in the sea, and have the dream blown away on the wind.'

And it was so.

The chiefs waited on his word while he walked the hills with the priest and listened to the music unheard by all but him, and called on Danaan to come alive to him.

Strange tales went abroad that the king walked with angels, and the chiefs were patient, but to the holy man they said he must wear the crown or forfeit it, also that he must wet with a maid of degree, else no chief could bring wife or daughter to the halls of Ua Dinan, as was the custom in Tormond.

Phadraig, the king, listened and laughed with bitter thoughts.

'How may I wed a warm maid of the clans when my arms are yet chilled with the icy bosom of Danaan?' he asked. 'The heart of me craves only a boat, and strength to fare forth to the shores where I held her.'

'And if we find a shore and no waiting maids, will you then take up the work waiting here to your hand?'

'That, if I cannot find her,' said Phadraig.

'And will you wed the lady who waits in the south, and hold court as of old for the good of your race?'

'Rather with her than another,' said Phadraig. 'She is a fair and honest lady, and sweetly kind.'

And the holy man kept his word. He bore sacred symbols and a church bell and sailed away with Phadraig to the west, and the chiefs on the shore were told it was a vow, and waited as they might and made prayers. The bells were rung from every tower that day to pray that Phadraig, the king, come again in health and safety.

No one ever knew what island in the sea they came to, but come to an island they did, and it was far away.

The wood grew down to the shore, and there were mighty trees cast down as by a great wind, and the desolation of it was so great that no living thing moved or fluttered a wing, and out beyond the shore rested the white birds of Phadraig, the king, and they rocked on the waves there, and by no effort could be made follow.

'This is the farthest unknown land,' said the holy man. 'By faith and prayer have we found it, and by the grace of God only shall we ever fare safely home or see again the faces of your clans. Look about you, Phadraig of the Dream, where are the ever-blossoming boughs and the castle of stone with the many towers?'

'Hear you not the music?'

'I hear only the sea wind moaning through the branches of dead trees.'

'Smell you not the fragrance of orchards?'

'I smell only the twists of seaweed cast up on the shore,' and the priest pushed aside a branch of wild thorns with green leaves reaching out from a gnarled and ancient bole.

But Phadraig caught the thorn branch, and under the scant green leaves was one tiny blossom, white and thick-petaled and with the fragrance of all sweetness of all the orchards in the world.

'See! Of this I told you, and it is alive here!'

'Then it is the sole live thing on the shore, for there is not even fish in this sea.'

But Phadraig led him over stones of great size piled high. Broken stone was there covered by sands – and other stone not broken, but squared on the four sides and grown over with lichens and wild vines.

'This is like the place of the tower where the sea tide swept into the moat,' he said.

And the holy man went over the stone, and stood on a broken wall. And beyond was a great place of sand piled high where the walls of a moat once stood.

'Come away,' he said, and crossed himself in fear. 'This is no place of living things. No life has been here for a thousand years.'

But Phadraig held the blossom and heard the music of Danaan and would not.

'Come out first, as by your vow, to the forest,' he said, 'for it was there I found her. Once only in my lifetime I was to come back if I had doubt. I have no doubt, yet I am here with you. Come you in.'

It was a wilderness beyond words, and the twisted thorn trees were gray and dead there, with neither green leaf nor white bloom.

'I am sorrowful to bring you through them,' said Phadraig, the king, for the priest was old and the way hard. 'But over beyond the hill is the great forest – and there by the blue lake the pulse of the sea is –'

But the forest was a jungle with no path, and the lake was not there; only a bog stretched from the gray wood to a cliff of gray rock, and Phadraig could say no word but sat there on a crumbling stone and covered his eyes with his hands.

'Now, O Phadraig, will you come back to the warm blood of your own clans?' asked the priest. 'For here is the end of the dream.'

But Phadraig, the lover, stood up and walked to the wall of the gray rock at the edge of the bog.

'Not yet – O holy father,' he said. 'Once only I was to come for proof in one lifetime, and here am I! Come you and look.'

He tore away from the rock wall the gray and green lichen and placed his fingers into the carving made there for the star of the north, and its circling seven, which makes both cross and wheel in the night sky.

'See! I drilled them deep as the flint knife would burrow the stone,' he said, 'and the storm has beaten away the face of the rock until only the traces are here. But Danaan took one finger of her white hand and drew a circle as her bond, and it has eaten deep into the rock as if carved with tools of iron this day. Father, what should that tell to me?

And the holy man looked in the face of Phadraig, the king, and made a prayer against enchantments, and rang the sacred bell of church there in the gray wood before he would speak.

'Since written bond it is, O Phadraig, rest your soul with the thought that it was a bond with a forbear of yours a thousand summers agone! You have only dreamed the dream that was born in your blood of that bond. You have kept the tryst for your ancestors, and risked your life and soul in the keeping. No more of duty for your race will be required of you in this life – naught but to wear the crown and rule in the ways of the clans.'

So Phadraig knelt there by the written bond of union, to the harmony of the circling stars, and he touched the circle of Danaan while he made his prayer, and then they went out again from the wilderness to the sea, and the white birds flew silently ahead of them on the sun-path to the home land of Erinn.

'Look not behind you,' said the priest, 'but follow the birds and pray for all lost souls.'

For well he knew what would come of the church bell, and the Christian prayer in the gray wood. And come it did, for when he looked back the ancient island of enchantment was no more to be seen. And no living man has seen it to this day except its shadow every seven years far across the gold haze of the sunset path, and then the gray wood is glorified and young again – but there are those who can still hear the music of Danaan across the water in dusks and dawns.

And Roiseen of the Glen went to the great hill of Phadraig, the Ua Dinan, and nursed his children there, and gave comfort to Yva of Kilfernora, who was wife to him, and counseled her never to hedge in a child of the Una Dinan from the open life and the old faiths; for in strange and dangerous ways they would cross the barriers, and it was safest to let them range free till they made the circle and came back to bide at the hearthstone and under the bell of the church.

The holy man of the cave of Saint Colman was given merit by the bishop for saving the soul of Phadraig, the king, who was known to have won a strange power through some holy source.

His hair whitened but his eyes were ever young, and his strength and wisdom grew, and his children's children could not keep pace with him on the moors. He trained his eldest son to rule, and when the times were safe, he gave up the crown and wore the monk's robe of white, and crossed over to Dun Aengus of the Isles of Arran. The singers of three centuries sang the songs of Nihil, his father, and the poets wrote of Phadraig, the king, as of a holy man by whom the white birds were tamed. Also he loved the stars and learned wisdom of them in the night, and in the blessed Isle of Arran he was always out under the sky when the wind blew from the west – and the music he heard then made him walk in beauty with the glad eyes of a lover who is beloved.

And when the Time came, he laid him down in the white robe and bade all doors be open, and all windows, that the west wind come over him! And the white birds came on the wind and circled the room and hovered there. While the brother monks lit candles and chanted the words for the dying, he smiled in content and whispered the music of the song of Nihil –

> She takes my hand at the sea marge,
>     She whispers low on the wind,
> She sets her sail for Tir-nan-Ogue
>     And leaves worn Life behind!

No pain was with him, and no sickness, but he went out on the wind as the birds went, and the monks who knelt by him, waiting some vision of his patron saint, heard him say at the last:

'Danaan, the star stands steady these thousand years and the circle closes. I come back on the breath of the gods!'

There was much learned discussion over this saying of his. Some thought he spoke of Daniel of the Hebrews, who was never a saint but was once a strong prophet. Others thought it was David, the king, of whom he spoke, for David was once a shepherd – and such were ever wise in the ways of the stars of night.

As to the 'breath of the gods' – they could by no means make out the meaning of that, which would have been blasphemy had it been said by anyone, high or low, and in their charity the monks united to disbelieve their own ears and content their souls with the miracle of the white birds – which was a beautiful miracle indeed – and, of course, a holy one.

So Phadraig, the king, was buried in consecrated ground, and only two souls had lived in his day to read the riddle of his life. One was the Wise Woman of the Glen and the other a holy man of the cave of Saint Colman in the hills.

But each had passed on, long years before, and made their choice between heaven and Tir-nan-Ogue.

# 22

# POEMS BY FIONA MACLEOD

## (WILLIAM SHARP)

**The Cup**

*Chuir Muiril mirr ann,*
*Chuir Uiril mil ann,*
*Chuir Muirinn fion ann,*
*'S chuir Michal ann buadh.*

*'Muriel placed myrrh in it:*
*Uriel placed honey in it:*
*Murien placed wine in it:*
*And Michael strength.'*

The Cup of bitter-sweet I know
That with old wine of love doth glow:
The dew of tears to it doth go,
And wisdom is its hidden woe.

Where I but young again to throw
This cup where the wild thistles grow,
Or where, oblivious, ceaseless, slow,
The grey tumultuous waters flow!

**The Love-chant of Cormac Conlingas**

Oimé, Oimé, woman of the white breasts, Eilidh![1]
Woman of the golden hair, and lips of the red, red rowan!
　　Oimé, O-rì, Oimé!

Where is the swan that is whiter, with breast more smooth,
Or the wave on the sea that moves as thou movest, Eilidh –
　　Oimé, a-rò; Oimé, a-rò!

It is the marrow in my bones that is aching, aching, Eilidh:
It is the blood in my body that is a bitter wild tide, Oimé!
    O-rì, Ohion, O-rì, aròne!

Is it the heart of thee calling that I am hearing, Eilidh,
Or the wind in the wood, or the beating of the sea, Eilidh,
    Or the beating of the sea?

## The Death-dirge for Cathal

Out of the wild hills I am hearing a voice, O Cathal!
And I am thinking it is the voice of a bleeding sword.
Whose is that sword? I know it well: it is the sword of the Slayer –
Him that is called Death, and the song that it sings I know: –
O where is Cathal mac Art, the white cup for the thirst of my lips?

Out of the cold greyness of the sea I am hearing, O Cathal,
I am hearing a wave-muffled voice, as of one who drowns in the depths:
Whose is that voice? I know it well: it is the voice of the Shadow –
Her that is called the Grave, and the song that she sings I know: –
O where is Cathal mac Art, that has warmth for the chill that I have?

Out of the hot greenness of the wood I am hearing, O Cathal,
I am hearing a rustling step, as of one stumbling blind.
Whose is that rustling step? I know it well: the rustling walk of the
    Blind One –
Her that is called Silence, and the song that she sings I know: –
O where is Cathal mac Art, that has tears to water my stillness?

## The Crimson Moon

Behind the legions of the Sun, the Star Battalions of the night,
The reddening of the West I see, from morn till dusk, from dusk till light.
A day must surely come at last, and that day soon,
When the Hidden People shall march out beneath the Crimson Moon.

Our palaces shall crumble then, our towers shall fall away,
And on the plains our burning towns shall flaunt a desolate day:
The cities of our pride shall wear tiaras of red flame,
And all our phantom glory be an idle wind-blown name.

What shall our vaunt be on that day, or who thereon shall hear
The laughter of our laughing lips become the wail of fear?
Our vaunt shall be the windy dust in eddies far and wide,
The hearing, theirs who follow us with swift and dreadful stride.

A cry of lamentation, then, shall sweep from land to land:
A myriad waving hands shall shake above a myriad strand:
The Day shall swoon before a Shade of vast ancestral Night,
Till a more dreadful Morn awake to flood and spume of light.

This is the prophecy of old, before the roaming tribes of Man
Spread Multitude athwart the heirdom of an earlier Clan –
Before the gods drank Silence, and hid their way with cloud,
And Man uprose and claimed the Earth and all the starry crowd.

So Man conceived and made his dream, till at the last he smiled to see
Its radiant skirts brush back the stars from Immortality:
He crowned himself with the Infinite, and gave his Soul a Home,
And then the quiet gods awoke and blew his life to foam.

This is the Dream I see anew, when all the West is red with light,
Behind the Legions of the Sun, the Star Battalions of the night.
Verily the day may come at last, and that day soon,
When the Hidden People shall march out beneath the Crimson Moon.


### The Tryst of Queen Hynde

Queen Hynde was in the rowan-wood with scarlet fruit aflame,
Her face was as the berries were, one sun-hot wave of shame.

With scythes of fire the August sun mowed down vast swathes of shade:
With blazing eyes the waiting queen stared on her steel-blue blade.

'What, thirsty hound,' she muttered low, 'with thirst you flash and gleam:
Bide, bide a wee, my bonnie hound, I'll show ye soon a stream!'

The sun had tossed against the West his broken scythes of fire
When Lord Gillanders bowed before his Queen and Sweet Desire.

She did not give him smile or kiss; her hand she did not give:
'But are ye come for death,' she said, 'or are ye come to live?'

Gillanders reined and looked at her: 'Hynde, Queen and Love,' he said,
'I wooed in love, I come in love, to this the tryst we made:

'Why are your eyes so fierce and wild? why is your face so white?
I love you with all my love,' he said, 'by day and by night.'

'What o' the word that's come to me, of how my lord's to wed
The lilywhite maid o' one that has a gold crown on his head?

'What o' the word that yesternight ye wantoned with my name,
And on a windy scorn let loose the blown leaf o' my shame?'

The Lord Gillanders looked at her, and never a word said he,
But sprang from off his great black horse and sank upon his knee.

'This is my love,' said white Queen Hynde, 'and this, and this, and this' –
Four times she stabbed him to the heart while she his lips did kiss.

She left him in the darkling wood: and as she rode she sang
(The little notes swirled in and out amid the horsehoof clang)

*My love was sweet, was sweet, was sweet but not so sweet as now!*
*A deep long sleep my sweet love has beneath the rowan-bough.*

They let her in, they lifted swords, his head each one did bare:
Slowly she bowed, slowly she passed, slowly she clomb the stair:

Her little son she lifted up, and whispered 'neath his cries –
'The old king's son, they say; mayhap; he has Gillander's eyes.'


## The Love-kiss of Dermid and Grainne

When by the twilit sea these twain were come
Dermid spake no one word, Grainne was dumb,
And in the hearts of both deep silence was.
'Sorrow upon me, love,' whispered the grass;
'Sorrow upon me, love,' the sea-bird cried;
'Sorrow upon me, love,' the lapsed wave sighed.

'For what the King has willed, that thing must be,
O Dermid! As two waves upon this sea
Wind-swept we are, – the wind of his dark mind,
With fierce inevitable tides behind.'
'What would you have, O Grainne: he is King.'
'I would we were the birds that come with Spring,
The purple-feathered birds that have no home,
The birds that love, then fly across the foam.'
'Give me thy mouth, O Dermid,' Grainne said
Thereafter, and whispering thus she leaned her head –
Ah, supple, subtle snake she glided there
Till, on his breast, a kiss-deep was her hair
That twisted serpent-wise in gold red pain
From where his lips held high their proud disdain.
'Here, here,' she whispered low, 'here on my mouth
The swallow, Love, hath found his haunted South.'

Then Dermid stooped and passionlessly kissed.
But therewith Grainne won what she had missed,
And that night was to her, and all sweet nights
Thereafter, as Love's flaming swallow-flights
Of passionate passion beyond speech to tell.
But Dermid knew how vain was any spell
Against the wrath of Finn: and Grainne's breath

To him was ever chill with Grainne's death;
Full well he knew that in a soundless place
His own wraith stood and with a moon-white face
Watched its own shadow laugh and shake its spear
Far in a phantom dell against a phantom deer.

### The Sorrow of the House of Lir

Happy our father Lir afar,
With mead, and songs of love and war:
The salt brine, and the white foam,
With these his children have their home.

In the sweet days of long ago
Soft-clad we wandered to and fro:
But now cold winds of dawn and night
Pierce deep our feathers thin and light.

The hazel mead in cups of gold
We feasted from in days of old:
The sea-weed now our food, our wine
The salt, keen, bitter, barren brine.

On soft warm couches once we pressed:
White harpers lulled us to our rest:
Our beds are now where the sea raves,
Our lullaby the clash of waves.

Alas! the fair sweet days are gone
When love was ours from dawn to dawn:
Our sole companion now is pain,
Through frost and snow, through storm and rain.

Beneath my wings my brothers lie
When the fierce ice-winds hurtle by:
On either side and 'neath my breast
Lir's sons have known no other rest.

Ah, kisses we shall no more know,
Ah, love so dear exchanged for woe,
All that is sweet for us is o'er,
Homeless we are from shore to shore.

---

### Note

1   Eilidh is pronounced Eily.

# 23

# TALIESIN SINGS OF HIS KNOWLEDGE

## JOHN MATTHEWS

Once I knew
everything there was to know;
in a moment of burning ecstasy
I became transformed,
knew every rock, tree, bird,
animal and fish;
and, in that moment,
perceived every meaning to be one.

Then, just as swiftly,
from lightning to returning dark,
I forgot all I had learned;
it was as though, where I beheld
only unites, now I perceived
only fragmented moieties
which once were whole.

Since then, long years of seeking,
of striving,
to recover the lost fragments
which might, somehow,
put back the broken littoral
into that same whole –
which is eternal
and which does not change.

But instead, I gave changed, become
somehow frozen.
Now I look back
at the past and push
the fragments into new patterns,
eternally hoping to find
their true relationship –
that the fire of creation
might be re-kindled in my bones.

# 24

# BARDIC POEMS

## CAITLÍN MATTHEWS

**The Song of Making**

I will sing you one-o
What is your one-o?
One it is the sacred head that sings the mystery over

I will sing you two-o
What is your two-o?
Two are the hands upon the loom that weave the fated threads-o
One it is, etc.

I will sing you three-o
What is your three-o?
Three is the web of the worlds so wide that wraps the mantle round us.

I will sing you four-o
What is your four-o?
Four are the seasons of the song, that root and seed do sing-o.

I will sing you five-o
What is your five-o?
Five are the virtues on the shield, that keep the weapon bright-o.

I will sing you six-o
What is your six-o?
Six are the coursers of the car that race the golden track-o.

I will sing you seven-o
What is your seven-o?
Seven are the crystal caers of night, the stars within the earth-o.

I will sing you eight-o
What is your eight-o?
Eight are the pathways on the wheel, the wheel that turns the year-o.

I will sing you nine-o
What is your nine-o?
Nine are the nuts within the stream that keep the awen bright-o.

I will sing you ten-o
What is your ten-o?
Ten are the patterns of the dance, that spin the sacred song-o.

I will sing you eleven-o
What is your eleven-o?
Eleven they are red-eared hounds that cleanse the world of pain-o.

I will sing you twelve-o
What is your twelve-o?
Twelve they are the watchful ones who sing the world awake-o.

Eleven they are red-eared hounds that cleanse the world of pain-o.
Ten are the patterns of the dance, that spin the sacred song-o.
Nine are the nuts within the stream that keep the awen bright-o.
Eight are the pathways on the wheel, the wheel that turns the year-o.
Seven are the crystal caers of night, the stars within the earth-o.
Six are the coursers of the car that race the golden track-o.
Five are the virtues on the shield, that keep the weapon bright-o.
Four are the seasons of the song, that root and seed do sing-o.
Three is the web of the worlds so wide that wraps the mantle round us.
Two are the hands upon the loom that weave the fated threads-o
One it is the sacred head that sings the mystery over

With dance and song, with dark and light
We weave the web aright-o.


## The Woman of Beare[1]

(i) *Christian*

An unnatural thing: hurrying east of west.
The yeast of me scurrying widdershins.

All things speed deosil: caught each wing,
Beached each fin: fraught with sin.

Ploughs point north – seed toil in stars.
Uncoiled, each ragged weed dies haggard.

369

My grianan's south, where suns uncover
A nun's despair – youth's disrepair.

I'll make no journey east! Bright my hopes once:
This sky lends distance to my sight, my self-reproach.

I'll coax the western wind, scull his tides on each approach
To my islanded west and a homely coast.

(ii) *Pagan*

I who am Anu, Buí and Brighid
Sit anchored to a fireside.
Despite the cleric's ire,
I am one who sinned well.

The four winds in my bag:
Each tower they'll topple down to hell.
Unleashed, my curses fluently
Will quell each cloistered hag.

And saints now chaste and virgin
I'll corrupt; each pilgrim sell
His relics to embrace a nun.
The culdee slakes his fast on sturgeon.

All kinds of sexual sport and harmless fun
I will let loose. No innocents
May plead exemption: at every airt
I'll make them seem degenerates.

They'll lip no creed. In every part
The quiet clip of thigh and heart –
The *paters* and the *aves* die
In homage to my faithful craft.

## A Plea to the Daughters of Invention

Wield the whetstone, smooth the iron to sharpness,
Scythe the years sheer of their time-wrought locks,
Sever the piercing compass of Urizen from our horizon.

The manacles of techno-minded man jangle the synapse:
Swift and sweet, the reek of corruption wafts from our wounding.
Corrosive shards of base metals tinsel our blood.

Handle the flint now: shivering edge, hard-wrought and fragile:
Tactile antiquity of first labour, sliver of moon's crest,
Blade of faery regions, scion of deer-haunted topographies.

With the stone's shaping and remaking, the human hominid's emergent
Perspicacity: urgent to cut and carve the spiralled whorling
Of the soul upon the dragonfly stillness of the lapid skin.

Cradle the pliant, purring keyboard, motivate the motionless mouse;
With incandescent artistry of light, kindle the alembic monitor;
With kiss of quartz, chip the swift-etched hieroglyphs of fire.

Let sing the saviour words along satellited song-lines,
Fibrilate the fibre-optic nerve-ways, repair the techno-wasteland
Of Urizen's vast, unceasing shade of lightless gloom.

Celebrate the marriage of invention and the opposable thumb
That, thrust under the bite of necessity, imagines and creates
From sliverèd flint-flake to the soundless flow of quantum quartz.

Alchemize the techno-faction, turn first matter into gold.
Crown the patient Daughter of Invention with honest stone
Whose corner needs no whetstone, whose green no blade can burn.

---

## Note

1     The Cailleach Beare is the ancient mountain goddess of south-west Ireland. A ninth-century poem speaks of giving up everything to become a nun and regretting her youth. This poem also tells the other half of her story, as the inciter to passionate love. Her image remains over many church doors in the shape of the Sheila na Gig statues – grotesque and naked, she points to her own vulva as the true door by which we enter and leave life.

# 25
# POEMS BY
# MARTIN LUDGATE

**The March of the Trees**

In a season and no season
When the trees were standing still
And the summerfolk were sleeping
Under hedge and holt and hill,
    When the squirrels ceased to prattle,
    Came the summoning to battle,
        And it stirred the restive trees.

In a season and no season
When the trees grew green again
And their leaves produced a clamour
In the turmoil of the rain,
    Up the hill of murder marching
    With their angry branches arching
        Came the armies of the trees.

In a season and no season
When the trees were shedding seed
In a foison which outnumbers
All that human loins could breed,
    Over earth with wild elation,
    Smashing home and habitation,
        Unrelenting, tramped the trees.

In a season and no season
When the trees trod through the sea
In a torrent of true promise
Like a vengeful victory,
    With a surge of fury rising,
    With no hint of compromising
        Strode the regiments of trees.

In a season and no season
When the trees climbed o'er the hill,
Hanging stars upon their branches
And defying winter's chill,
    With unlettered imprecations,
    Under unknown constellations
        Came the unrepentant trees.

In a season and no season
Armoured only with the air,
Guerdoned only with their passion,
All the trees came leafless, bare –
    Naked, filled with stubborn folly,
    Malice, pride and melancholy,
        Came the hosts of wilful trees.

In a season and no season
Ere the battle was begun,
When the fevered moon was bleeding
Like the dying of the sun,
    In a dawn bereft of daylight
    To a doom bereft of reason,
    Mirthless, all the trees came marching
        In a season and no season.


**Kenning the Name**

I dreamed a fine net so my vision could claim
    The breath of his being, the wealth of his name.

In long hours I wove it from midnight to day,
    As the weft of the air directed my way.

With stealth I proceeded, with guile my wit travelled
    Until all dark knots I had wholly unravelled.

Freed threads fell like down through the warp of the breeze
    While the Alder in safety was taking his ease –

Unwarded, unwitnessed, drowsing alone,
   Like a trout set for tickling beneath a dead stone.

Caught napping at noontide, unkeyed was his keeping:
   He unlocked his lips and spoke naked while sleeping –
Stripped as a sacrifice, naked as flame,
   Naked as hatred, I heard his true name –

A name to slice silence or sever strong rock,
   An unuttered tonguing, a hush like a shock.

Few list'ners could bide the brute stroke of that sign;
   Knowing was vict'ry –
                  And knowing was mine!

# FURTHER READING

THE FOLLOWING IS ONLY a selection from the huge literature on the bardic traditions as they relate to Celtic literature. These titles were useful in the compilation of this collection, and are especially valuable for a study of the heritage of bardism. Details of the sources for the works contained in this collection will be found in the footnotes to each chapter.

Adamnan, *Life of St Columba* (ed. W. Reeves), Llanerch Enterprises, Llanerch, 1988

Aneurin, *Y Gododdin: Britain's Oldest Heroic Poem* (ed. and trans. A.O.H. Jarman), The Welsh Classics, Dyfed, 1988

Anwyl, E., 'Prolegomena to the Study of Old Welsh Poetry', *Transactions of the Honourable Society of Cymmrodorian*, volume 4, 1903, pages 59–84

Bergin, Osborn, 'Irish Bardic Poetry', a lecture delivered before the National Literary Society, Dublin, 15 April 1912, *Journal of the Ivernian Society*, v, 1912–13, pages 153–66, 203–19 (reprinted Dolmen Press, 1970)

Bloomfield, M.W. and Dunn, C.W., *The Role of the Poet in Early Societies*, D.S. Brewer, Cambridge, 1989

Bonwick, J., *Irish Druids and Irish Religions*, Dorset Press, Marlborough, 1986

Bromwich, Rachel (ed. and trans.), *Triodd Ynys Prydein* ('The Welsh Triads'), University of Wales Press, Cardiff, 1961 (2nd edition, 1978)

Caesar, Julius, *De Bello Gallico* (trans. by S.A. Handford), Penguin Books, Harmondsworth, 1951

Caldecott, M., *Taliesin and Avagddu*, Bran's Head, Frome, 1983

Caldecott, M., *Women in Celtic Myth*, Arrow Books, London, 1988

Carmichael, Alexander (trans.), *Carmina Gadelica* (5 volumes), Scottish Academic Press, Edinburgh, 1928–72; Floris Books, Edinburgh, 1992 (English text only)

Carney, James, *Medieval Irish Lyrics* with *The Irish Bardic Poet*, Dolmen Press, Portlaoise, 1985

Chadwick, H.M. and N.K., *The Growth of Literature* (3 volumes), Cambridge University Press, Cambridge, 1932–40

Clarke, B. (ed. and trans.), *Life of Merlin by Geoffrey of Monmouth*, University of Wales Press, Cardiff, 1973

Connelan, Owen (ed. and trans.), *The Proceedings of the Great Bardic Institution*, John O'Daly, Dublin, 1860

Corkery, Daniel, *The Hidden Ireland*, T. Cahill & Co. Ltd, Cork, 1924; Gill & MacMillan, Dublin, 1967

Cross, T.P. and Slover, C.H., *Ancient Irish Tales*, Figgis, Dublin, 1936; Harrap, London, 1937

Curtin, Jeremiah, *Myths and Folk Tales of Ireland*, Dover Publications, New York, 1975

Davidson, H.E. (ed.), *The Seer in Celtic and Other Traditions*, John Donald, Edinburgh, 1989

de Jubainville, Henri d'Arbois, *The Irish Mythological Cycle* (trans. by Richard Irvine), O'Donoghue & Co., Dublin, 1903; (trans. by R.I. Best) Hodges & Figgis, Dublin, 1903

de Kay, Charles, 'The Old Poetic Guild in Ireland' in *Century Magazine*, 39, 1891

Dillon, Myles, *The Cycles of the Kings*, Oxford University Press, Oxford, 1946

Ellis, P.B., *A Dictionary of Irish Mythology*, Constable, London, 1987

Evans, J.G., *Poems from the Book of Taliesin*, Llanbedrog Wales, Tremvan, 1915

Evans, William, *The Bards of the Isle of Britain* (edited by Graham Elwell), privately printed, Pen-y-Bont, Anglesey, n.d.

Flower, R., *The Irish Tradition*, Clarendon Press, Oxford, 1953

Forbes, A.R., *Gaelic Names of Beasts, Birds, Fishes, Insects and Reptiles*, Oliver & Boyd, Edinburgh, 1905

Ford, Patrick K., 'The Well of Nechtan and "La Gloire Luminesse"', *Myth in Indo-European Antiquity* (ed. G.J. Larson), University of California Press, Berkeley, CA, 1974, pages 67–74

Ford, Patrick K., 'The Poet as Cyfarwydd in Early Welsh Literature', *Studia Celtica*, X/XI, 1975–6, pages 152–62

Gantz, Jeffrey, *Early Irish Myths and Sagas*, Penguin Books, Harmondsworth, 1981

Ford, Patrick K. (ed. and trans.), *The Mabinogion and Other Medieval Welsh Tales*, University of California Press, Berkeley, CA, 1977

Giraldus Cambrensis (Gerald of Wales), *The Journey Through Wales/The Description of Wales* (trans. by L. Thorpe), Penguin Books, Harmondsworth, 1978

Gose Jr, E.B., *The World of the Irish Wonder Tale*, University of Toronto Press, Toronto, 1985

Graves, R., *The White Goddess*, Faber & Faber, London, 1952

Green, Miranda, *The Gods of the Celts*, Alan Sutton, Gloucester, 1986

Greene, D. and O'Connor, F. (ed. and trans.), *A Golden Treasure of Irish Poetry*, MacMillan, London, 1967

Guest, Lady Charlotte (ed. and trans.) *The Mabinogion*, J.M. Dent, London, 1906; David Nutt, London, 1910; Ballantyne Press, London, 1910

Gwynn, Edward (ed. and trans.), *The Metrical Dindsenchas* (Parts 1–5), Hodges, Figgis & Co., Dublin, 1903–35

Harrison, A., *The Irish Trickster*, Sheffield Academic Press, Sheffield, 1989

Henderson, G., *Survivals in Belief among the Celts*, J. Maclehose, Glasgow, 1911

Henry, P.L., *The Early English and Celtic Lyric*, George Allen & Unwin, London, 1966

Hull, E., *The Poem-Book of the Gael*, Chatto & Windus, London, 1912

Humphreys, E., *The Taliesin Tradition*, Black Raven Press, 1983

Hyde, Douglas (trans.), 'The Cooking of the Great Queen' (Fulacht na Mórrigna), originally published in *The Celtic Review*, x, 1916, pages 335–50

'Idrison', 'The Mabinogi of Taliesin' originally published in *The Cambrian and Caledonian Quarterly*, 1833

Jackson, Kenneth Hurstone, *A Celtic Miscellany*, Routledge & Kegan Paul, London, 1951

Jones, Edward, *An Historical Account of the Welsh Bards and their Music and Poetry*, privately printed, London, 1784

Jones, G. and Jones, T. (trans.), *The Mabinogion*, J.M. Dent, London, 1974

Jones, O., Williams, Edward and Pughe, William Owen (eds), *The Myvyrian Archaiology of Wales*, Thomas Gere, Denbigh, 1870

Jones, T.G., *Welsh Folk-Lore and Folk-Custom*, Methuen, London, 1930

Joyce, P.W., *A Social History of Ancient Ireland* (2 volumes), Longmans, Green & Co., London, 1903

Kinsella, Thomas (trans.), *The Tain* ('The Cattle Raid of Cooley'), Dolmen Press, Dublin, 1970; Oxford University Press, Oxford, 1970

Knott, E. and Murphy, G., *Early Irish Literature*, Routledge & Kegan Paul, London, 1966

Lloyd, John Edward, *A History of Wales* (2 volumes), Longmans, Green & Co., London, 1911

Lofmark, C., *Bards and Heroes*, Llanerch Enterprises, Llanerch, 1989.

Loomis, R.S., *Wales and the Arthurian Legend*, University of Wales Press, Cardiff, 1956

Ludgate, Martin, *Gwydion: Words for Nine Voices*, privately printed, London, 1997

Macalister, R.A. Stewart, *The Secret Languages of Ireland*, Amorica Books Co., St Helier, 1976

Mckenna, L., 'Historical Poems of Gofraidh Fionn O Dalaigh', *Irish Monthly*, xlvii, 1919

Mackenzie, Donald A., *Scottish Folk-Lore and Folk Life*, Blackie & Son, Glasgow, 1935

Macleod, Fiona (William Sharp), *Poems and Dramas*, William Heinemann, London, 1929

MacNeill, E., *Duanaire Finn*, Irish Texts Society, Dublin, 1908

McNeill, F.M., *The Silver Bough* (volume 1), Canongate, Edinburgh, 1989

Mallory, J.P., *In Search of the Indo-Europeans*, Thames & Hudson, London, 1989

Matthews, C., *Mabon and the Mysteries of Britain*, Arkana, Harmondsworth, 1986

Matthews, C., *Arthur and the Sovereignty of Britain*, Arkana, Harmondsworth, 1989

Matthews, C., *Elements of the Celtic Tradition*, Element Books, Shaftesbury, Dorset, 1989

Matthews, C., *The Celtic Book of the Dead*, Thorsons, Wellingborough, 1991

Matthews, C., *The Celtic Book of Days*, Godsfield Press, Alresford, 1995

Matthews, C., *A Celtic Devotional*, Godsfield Press, Alresford, 1996

Matthews, J., *Fionn MacCumhail*, Firebird Books, Poole, Dorset, 1988

Matthews, J., *A Celtic Reader*, Aquarian Press, Wellingborough, 1991

Matthews, J., *Song of Taliesin: Stories and Poems from the Books of Broceliande*, Aquarian Press, Wellingborough, 1991

Matthews, J., *Taliesin: Shamanism and the Bardic Mysteries in Britain and Ireland*, Mandala, 1991

Matthews, J. (ed.), *The Druid Source Book*, Blandford Press, London, 1996

Matthews, J. and C., *The Aquarian Guide to British & Irish Mythology*, Aquarian Press, Wellingborough, 1988

Matthews, J. and C., *An Encyclopedia of Celtic Wisdom*, Element Books, Shaftesbury, Dorset, 1993

Matthews, J. and C., *The Little Book of Celtic Wisdom,* Elements Books, Shaftesbury, Dorset, 1993

Meyer, Kuno, *The Voyage of Bran, Son of Febal* (2 volumes) David Nutt, 1895

Meyer, Kuno, *Fianaigecht*, Hodges & Figgis, Dublin, 1910

Miles, D., *The Royal National Eisteddfod of Wales*, Christopher Davies, Swansea, 1977

Minahane, John, *The Christian Druids*, Sanas Press, Dublin, 1993

Morgan, P., *Iolo Morgannwg*, University of Wales Press, Cardiff, 1975

Morgannwg, Iolo, *The Iolo Manuscripts: A Selection of Ancient Welsh Manuscripts* (ed. and trans. Taliesin Williams (ab Iolo)), Welsh Manuscript Society, Llandovery, 1848

Morgannwg, Iolo, *Barddas*, volume 1, Llandovery: D.J. Roderic (translated by J. Williams ab Ithel), Longman & Co., London, 186?

Morgannwg, Iolo, *The Triads of Britain*, Wildwood House, 1977

Morris, J., *The Matter of Wales*, Oxford University Press, Oxford, 1984

Murphy, Gerard, *Early Irish Lyrics*, Oxford University Press, Oxford, 1956

O'Beirne Crowe, P. (ed. and trans.), *The Amra Chohium Chilli or Dallan Forgail*, McGlashan & Gill, Dublin; Williams & Norgate, London, 1871

O'Curry, Eugene, *Manners and Customs of the Ancient Irish* (3 volumes), Williams & Norgate, 1873.

O'Driscoll, Robert (ed.), *The Celtic Consciousness*, Canongate Publishing, Edinburgh, 1982; Dolmen Press, Portaloise, 1982

O'Grady, S. (ed. and trans.), *Silva Gadelica* (2 volumes), Williams & Norgate, 1892

O'hOgain, Daithi, *The Hero in Irish Folk History*, Gill & Macmillan, Dublin, 1985

O'hOgain, Daithi, *Fionn mac Cumhail: Images of the Gaelic Hero*, Gill & Macmillan, Dublin, 1988

O'Rahilly, Thomas F., *Early Irish History and Mythology*, The Dublin Institute for Advanced Studies, Dublin, 1946

O'Suillebhain, M., *The Bodhran: A Practical Introduction*, Walton's Musical Instrument Galleries, Dublin, 1984

Parry, T., *A History of Welsh Literature*, Oxford University Press, Oxford, 1955

Pennar, M., *The Black Book of Carmarthen*, Llanerch Enterprises, Llanerch, 1989

Pennar, M. (trans.), *Taliesin Poems*, Llanerch Enterprises, Llanerch, 1989

Piggott, Stuart, *Ancient Britons and the Antiquarian Imagination*, Thames & Hudson, London, 1989

Rees, Alwyn and Brinley, *Celtic Heritage*, Thames & Hudson, London, 1961

Rhys, Grace, *A Celtic Anthology*, George Harrap & Co., London, 1948

Rhys, John, *Lectures on the Origin and Growth of Religion as Illustrated by Celtic Heathendom*, Williams & Norgate, London, 1888

Rhys, John, *Celtic Folklore*, Welsh and Manx (2 volumes), Wildwood House, London, 1980

Roberts, B.F. (ed.), *Early Welsh Poetry: Studies in the Book of Aneurin*, National Library of Wales, Aberystwyth, 1988

Robinson, Fred Norris, 'Satirists and Enchanters in Early Irish Literature', *Studies in the History of Religion*, presented to C.H. Toy, edited by D.G. Lyon and G.F. Moor. Macmillan, London, 1912

Ross, Anne, *Pagan Celtic Britain*, Cardinal, London, 1974

Rowland, J., *Early Welsh Saga Poetry*, D.S. Brewer, Cambridge, 1990

Rowlands, R.F., 'Bardic Lore and Education', *Bulletin of the Board of Celtic Studies*, 32, 1985, pages 143–55

Ryan, Marah Ellis, *The Druid Path and Other Stories*, Talbot Press, Dublin, 1917

Schofield, W.H., *Mythic Bards*, Harvard University Press, Cambridge, Mass., 1920

Sjoestedt, M.L., *Gods and Heroes of the Celts*, Turtle Island Foundation, Berkeley, CA, 1982

Skene, W.F. (ed. and trans.), *The Four Ancient Books of Wales* (2 volumes), Edmonston & Douglas, Edinburgh, 1869; AMS Press, New York, 1984–5

Stephens, M. (ed.), *The Oxford Companion to the Literature of Wales*, Oxford University Press, Oxford, 1986; Irish Academic Press, 1986

Stephens, Thomas, 'The Poems of Taliesin', *Archaeologica Cambrensis*, n.s. 2, 1841, pages 149–55, 204–59, 261–74

Stewart, R.J., *Celtic Gods, Celtic Goddesses*, Blandford Press, London, 1990

Stewart, R.J. and Williamson, R., *Celtic Bards, Celtic Druids*, Blandford Press, London, 1996

Veitch, John, 'Merlin and the Merlinian Poems', *The Journal of the British Archaeological Association*, 45, 2 and 3, 1889, pages 123–30, 207–14

Wentz, W.Y. Evans, *The Fairy Faith in Celtic Countries*, Lemma Publishing Co., New York, 1973; Colin Smythe, Gerrards Cross, 1977

Williams, G., *An Introduction to Welsh Poetry*, Faber & Faber, London, 1953

Williams, I., *Lectures on Early Welsh Poetry*, Institute for Advanced Studies, Dublin, 1970

Williams, I., *The Beginnings of Welsh Poetry* (ed. Rachel Bromwich), University of Wales Press, Cardiff, 1980

Williamson, Robin, *The Craneskin Bag: Celtic Stories and Poems*, Canongate, Edinburgh, 1979

# INDEX